MW00966741

AND RIGHTLY SO

SELECTED LETTERS AND ARTICLES OF NEIL MCCAFFREY

EDITED BY PETER A. KWASNIEWSKI

ROMAN CATHOLIC BOOKS

Printed in the U.S.A.

978-1-934888-56-8

ROMAN CATHOLIC BOOKS
PO Box 2286
Fort Collins, Colorado 80522
BooksForCatholics.com

Table of Contents

1964, for the Conservative Book Club announcement

Publisher's Preface

This is one of two planned volumes of correspondence by Neil McCaffrey. A successful entrepreneur who launched three companies that were central to his public identity and reputation, Neil was the proverbial self-made man. But, despite the pride in these accomplishments implicit in some letters and memoranda, his greatest skills lay elsewhere and are on display in this book's religious and political letters.

Neil, for example, "transformed my interest in Newman into his own love for the great Cardinal," wrote the prolific Catholic author, Michael Davies. "My appreciation of the faith we shared was made far more profound by learning from the wisdom and following the advice of this great Catholic gentleman."

He was an editorial mentor to the younger Davies, two of whose books he introduced to the U.S. market via Arlington House Publishers. He was also, at least for a good while, a trusted confidant of William F. Buckley Jr. and Pulitzer Prize-winning author Garry Wills (before the latter flipped to the Left). Neil was an astute observer of human motivation and politics who knew Church life and history and quietly interacted with a swath of intellectuals, political strategists and writers on the political and religious right.

***

Neil's interest in the America of the 1920s–1950s, and his founding of the Nostalgia Book Club in 1968, and indeed his early employment at Doubleday and Macmillan, sometimes earned him lifelong friends of a more liberal persuasion. Richard Sudhalter, *New York Times* reporter (and Arlington House biographer of Bix Beiderbecke), was one of many.

My father described himself, not with any self-deprecation, as "semi-educated"—true in the sense that he lacked a doctorate or even facility in foreign languages. Not true, in the larger sense. He was broadly read in contemporary politics and religion and easily held his own with some of the leading intellectuals of the day. His mastery of the works of John Henry Newman illustrates this point.

He read ravenously, long into the night, despite a punishing business schedule. And, by the by, wrote some of the most literate advertising pieces ever penned.

1

Far more valuable, though, is a cache of thousands of letters and memos to friends and to staff at Arlington House Publishers, Conservative Book Club, and Nostalgia Book Club—his companies—and now, with the indispensable assistance of this volume's editor, Peter Kwasniewski, a large sampling of that correspondence is at last here. Our primary goal is to share Neil's views with fellow Catholics—especially now that he has been vindicated by the course of events in the Church and in the West since the Council he deplored.

The takeover of the Church by a variety of ignorant careerists, opaque liberals, radicals particularly in the religious orders, and a large quantity of sex-addled and perverted half-men, shook him to the core long before its severity hit the rest of us. By the time he died, on the Feast of the Immaculate Conception in 1994, he was expecting "far worse to come" in Church life. This was not idle prediction, but the product of his massive reading of both Catholic periodicals and Catholic literature of the 19th and 20th centuries, certainly including those on the Left, principally Commonweal, America, and the National Catholic Reporter.

It was the implications of the loss of faith among Church leaders that concerned him while others sought refuge in optimism and pope-worship, mainly in the form of adulation of John Paul II—who largely stood by, or promoted prime offenders to the highest positions, as the Church collapsed.

John Paul II—who declared Vatican II a great success on its 25th anniversary—to be sure had to grapple with the mess he inherited from Popes Paul VI and John XXIII, who set the Church's modern course. But, he was part of an enthusiastic troika of mainstream liberal popes (by the standards of their predecessor, Pius XII) and their conservative enablers. Combined, Neil asserted, they were fatal to the institutional Church as we knew it. The practiced deceit and neglect on the part of many conservative Catholics in authority incensed my father.

Neil spared no one in his analysis. His pique at Msgr. Eugene Clark must be seen in this light. Clark he found increasingly glib, and worse. He had a doctorate in history from Notre Dame but scarcely practiced his craft, preferring, he often said in genuine jest, his "apostolate to the rich"—whom he knew by the score due to his positions in the chancery directly under Cardinals Francis Spellman and Terrence Cooke.

Both Clark and Neil were formed by New York Catholic schools—including the minor seminary, Cathedral Prep—in their heyday. Neil decided the priesthood was not for him and enlisted in the Coast Guard. He served in the Aleutians for two alternately boring and harrowing years during World War II—his base camp at one point wiped out by a tsunami—then studied journalism at Fordham University and, best of all, lucked into marrying Joan Melervey, a New Yorker herself, in 1952, "and she has exercised her proprietary rights over [my heart] ever since." She became his closest collaborator and supporter, in season and out.

Six children (myself included) and a healthy career later, he died of lung cancer. Happily, Joan survives him, and she has participated carefully in the composition of this book.

The briefest professional history is required. Neil was a junior executive at Doubleday Publishing and then ran the marketing department at Macmillan while serving as director of advertising for its parent, Crowell Collier Publishers. Tiring of the leftwing bias at these Houses, which forbade any serious line of conservative books, he launched Arlington House Publishers and its related Conservative Book Club, and then Nostalgia Book Club, which reflected his passion for classical jazz and American culture of the first half of the 20th century.

Just as he had assisted Bill Buckley in the explosive growth of National Review in the late 1950s, so did Bill play a key role in helping Neil launch his companies by lending his enthusiastic support and connections, and his friendship when the chips were down, in 1965-66. Buckley and Neil were close friends and co-warriors for more than a decade, but the friendship was later strained by what Neil regarded as betrayals in two business dealings, and by Bill's wholesale cooperation, as chairman of the board of Starr Broadcasting, in the cultural revolution, chiefly by the foul counter-cultural music Starr radio stations featured, for profit. But Neil also saw Bill's anti-populist utterings as a way for Buckley to sneer at his more unwashed followers—the people who in part made him a success. Still, they shared many cordial exchanges in later years despite the bitter disappointments Neil had experienced. Bill, too, was there at the Requiem Mass.

Neil's copywriting flair was the distinctive feature of his companies. Nostalgia Book Club was launched by his own fabulously successful full-page ad in *The New York Times* with the headline, KIDS UNDER 35: THIS AD IS NOT FOR YOU.

A few words to set the context for some of the controversies that follow in these exchanges. Vatican II seriously damaged Neil's friendship with two priests, now deceased—friends so close that my brother Gene and I are their namesakes: Monsignors Eugene V. Clark and Donald "Roger" Pryor. Both men were political conservatives. Pryor, later archdiocesan superintendent of schools, was a theological moderate for his day, and Clark, was forced by Cardinal Edward Egan to resign as rector of St. Patrick's Cathedral after a scandalous accusation about him and his secretary hit the newspapers, attempted to juggle his orthodox theology and ambitions. Clark adamantly and bitterly denied that he had betrayed his vows, and it's my impression that friends indeed accepted the denial, but remained puzzled or troubled.

Both Clark and Pryor, in short, came quickly to terms with the revolution wrought in Catholic life and the Mass by the Council. Pryor later had second thoughts about the liturgy changes, which Clark, despite his defense of the New Mass herein, never really embraced.

Neil on the other hand would have none of it from the get-go, and called out his friends, who he said were in denial at the very least, and risked complicity with the revolution. Clark, who as noted worked at the top of the New York chancery as aide de camp to Cardinal Terrence Cooke—whom they knew as teens at Cathedral Prep—ceased conversing after the exchange of letters published herein. Customary dinners among them, one of which I recall as a verbal slugfest, ceased by the early 1980s. Clark visited Neil at the end of his life, reminiscing about the old days when they were of one mind, and appeared in the sanctuary of Neil's Requiem Mass, which was offered by Pryor—who told me he was happy to say the Old Mass but did not want to wear black vestments, "because I would feel as if I were in a costume." (So he wore purple—a compromise, by the way, Neil would have approved, throwing up his hands.)

Regarding the Clark correspondence, Clark—aided, I feel certain, by the historian F.D. Cohalan, a monsignor who mentored all three men at Cathedral Prep and was a Clark confidant—relentlessly defended the new order of things. His case for the New Mass particularly frustrated Neil, who in response made points (to a Clark who sidestepped them artfully with a faux earnestness that his old friend detested) that were later made by none other than Pope Benedict XVI in Summorum Pontificum and its attendant letter to the world's bishops.

Crucially, for example—and contradicting defenders of the liturgical revolution—Benedict XVI flatly declared that the old Latin Mass "was never abrogated." In so saying, the pope erased a central argument of Clark and the "papolaters" Neil so scorned.

Roger McCaffrey
October, 2019

Left to right: Natalie & Garry Wills, Frank & Elsie Meyer, Joan & Neil McCaffrey. Comrades and friends, 1961 National Review *Gala at the Waldorf Astoria in New York.*

This book's title recalls Neil's signature-column in the Conservative Book Club Bulletin, "And Rightly So."

Tribute to An Old Friend

Remarks by Msgr. Donald "Roger" Pryor at the Memorial for Neil McCaffrey, May 1995.

Joan asked me to say a prayer in the form of a benediction at the conclusion of this evening; but she also said, "Why don't you say some words about Neil?" I demurred, knowing the quality of his friends and that I would be so outclassed that it would be better to sit down quickly. But I thought later: I'm one of the few people who knew him when he was an adolescent; and since you all love him so much perhaps it would be of interest to you to know something of Neil as an adolescent.

Mary McCaffrey is probably the only one in the room who knew him longer than I did. I got to know him in 1939, when we started high school together. He was about six weeks past his fourteenth birthday and I was a few months before mine. Actually we had met the Spring before, at the entrance examination for this high school. For some odd reason he and I and Wally Grant, who was an excellent friend of his from Pelham (they went to elementary school together), wound up sitting close together and got to chatting after the exam. And then I ran into him again when we started school in September. As Vic Gold said, and Marvin [Nagourney] said, we kind of fell in together right away, had a meeting of minds, and enjoyed one another's company very much.

We went to an extraordinary school, extraordinary partly because it was located on 51st Street at Madison Avenue. It had been an orphanage, but I guess the orphans needed something better so it was given to us as a high school. It was called Cathedral College [the "minor seminary" for the Archdiocese of New York] because there were six years: four years of high school and two years of college. Such schools are connected with the students traditionally, because they are meant to be for young students who were thinking of becoming priests, as Neil very seriously considered becoming a priest.

The great part about going to school at 51st Street and Madison Avenue was that we'd gulp down a sandwich very quickly and have the rest of an hour's lunch time to wander around the city. Part of Neil's great love for the city came from those years. New York City—I don't want to down it now, but it was such a marvelous place in 1939 and 1940. It was vibrant; it was lovely; the people were great. It was such an interesting place, and such a marvelously friendly

7

and open place. I guess Neil would have to be described as an urban person. To try to think of him embracing a tree or visiting haunts of coot and fern.... . Although as an adult he only came to New York City, as I understand it, for pleasure, to go to a night club or to listen to music, he was really an urban person. Part of his love for the city came from those four years at 51st Street and Madison Avenue.

You know, he was defined as a person—later on he would be defined as a family man—but then, as a fourteen-year-old, he was defined by two qualities. One was his faith, which was obvious then. Neil didn't have faith; he was faith in a sense. And he spent so much of his time in reading and trying to develop his understanding of the Faith—fides querens intellectum—just to become more familiar with it, to understand it, to be able to defend it and to explain it to other people. And he was also defined by his intellect, even at the age of fourteen. I would think a good caricature would be to picture him as an intellect floating out in space, but it wouldn't be fair to him because he was also a very earthy person.

The two qualities I remember that I would like to share with you are his sense of humor, which was a delight at that age, and his love for music.

Neil laughed all the time. Everything was funny. He saw humor in places other people didn't see it and he shared it with us. It was a ball to be with him and to go to school with him and to enjoy so many things. Of course having that sense of humor in a minor seminary led us to some difficulties. We were the wild crowds, if you'd believe that, because we didn't put up with cant or flamboyance or pretension too much. Neil would make that known in class by what he thought was a whisper. One of the skills he never mastered was the ability to whisper. The teacher would say something and Neil would put his hand up and say something to us in a loud voice and we'd all collapse in laughter. We pushed it to the limit. None of us were thrown out, although I'm sure it was seriously considered many times.

Neil was a lot of fun to be with, particularly at the age of fourteen, when there were so many things we were coming to know for the first time.

Of course I have to talk about his love for music because we fell into that together. I was always amazed that at the age of fourteen or fifteen he knew so much about music. He was a real student of it even then. I shared some of that learning experience with him because—Terry, you can eat your heart out—we used to go to the Paramount to listen to Tommy Dorsey, when Frank Sinatra was the vocalist, and put up with those screaming hordes of teenaged girls just to listen. We had an odd schedule. We didn't go to school on Thursdays. We went to school on Saturdays. And many Thursday mornings we spent at the Apollo on 125th Street, where all of the great black bands and all of the great black dancers and comedians appeared. We were there for the eleven o'clock show in the morning. I think it cost us fifteen cents—if Neil were here I'd turn to him and he'd say, "No, no, it was—" whatever. He would have it exactly. We met a few months ago with another friend, in from California. We were talking about high school days and going to delicatessens to have a sandwich and I said, "Remember? It used to cost—" and he said, "No, no, that's not right." I would never cross him on a thing like that because he was always right on facts and figures. Stan mentioned his mastery of figures in business; well, that was part of him: he was a master of that kind of thing.

In New York City in 1940, '41, you would never consider that there was any problem with going to the Apollo Theater; it was just a given, just one of the things that we did.

You know, we had four years of Latin and three years of Greek, a modern language and all the rest of it. I think that curriculum formed and disciplined Neil's mind, and helped him to focus his mind. We had an extraordinary faculty of diocesan priests. Most of you who know Neil also know, at least by name, Monsignor Florence Cohalan, who was our history teacher in our third year of high school. The course was the French Revolution. That's all we did: sixteen-year-olds, we studied the French Revolution for a year.

I think of other people like Father Dave Rea, who had such a great love for reading. He was such a great fellow. He was an ordained priest but he had that great ability to get along with kids—and also to imbue us with a love of reading, which Neil picked up from him.

Father John Monaghan, whom we never had in class, but who was on the faculty, had organized the Catholic Workers in the middle '30s into the Association of Catholic Trade Unionists because the Communists, who were very few in number, had dominated union meetings through their master of Roberts' Rules of Order and parliamentary procedure. John Monaghan organized these workers to teach them how to defend themselves at these meetings. A great thing he did for simple working men so they couldn't be pushed around by Communists.

Just one final thing, to mention Roger's field of baseball. Neil was a good athlete. He loved to play ball. One morning—I think it was a holy day of obligation because there were no other students there—he and I went up to Mount St. Michael, which was a high school located between where he lived and where I lived. Our team was playing

Mount St. Michael and it was missing two players. Mount St. Michael was coached by Howie Smith, who had been a lineman for Notre Dame. He was built like a fireplug, but most linemen in the 1930s were built that way: very small and very wide. He was a ferocious coach and a demanding coach, and he had terrific teams. Mount St. Michael dominated high school sports at that time. So now Cathedral College is playing Mount St. Michael and they're two players short. We're sitting in the stands. So we're pressed into service. I always remember this. Neil was always smarter than I was; but he was also quicker, because the two spots on the team that were open were right field and second base. He came on the field and said, "I'll play right field." He spent an hour and a half out in the sun and I was on second base with these huge kids coming in with spikes up to here trying to crush me.

A lot of good memories. A lot of wonderful memories. When Neil met Joan Melervey, I was still in the seminary. Gene Clark was very much a part of all this. We were invited with Wally Grant to meet Joan. We used to go swimming over at Travers Island at night. Joan was trotted out not so much for our approval, you know, as kind of saying, "Can you believe I'm this lucky?" And we agreed that he was very lucky, which has certainly been proven over the years.

So in conclusion I will finally get to the prayer that Joan has asked for. This is a prayer that was written by one of Neil's intellectual heroes, John Henry Cardinal Newman. With Neil he shared a great love for God, a great devotion to the Church, a great interest in history and a great skill at writing.

"May Our Lord support us all the day long, 'till the shades lengthen and the evening comes, and the busy world is hushed and the fever of life is over and our work is done. Then in His mercy may He give us a safe lodging and a holy rest and peace at the last. Amen."

Editor's Preface

Neil McCaffrey (1925–1994), born in Rye, NY and a lifetime resident of Pelham, was the founder of Conservative Book Club and Arlington House Publishers, which he ran for decades, and a respected behind-the-scenes political organizer.[1] He worked from 1955–1961 at Doubleday-Image Books under its founder, John Delaney, and in the mail order division as editor of the "Know Your Bible" program. He was an executive at Macmillan Publishing Company from 1961–1964. While there he shepherded a handful of national bestsellers into prominence. A graduate of Fordham University's journalism program in 1950, he was a product of the Archdiocese of New York's educational system, possibly the best in North America at the time. Neil was a knowledgeable enthusiast of old films and the music of the 1920s, 30s, and 40s, an enthusiasm reflected in his founding of the Nostalgia Book Club in 1968 and his leading of the Movie Entertainment Book Club from 1978. He and his wife Joan had six children.

It has been an honor for me, in truth a delight, to edit this collection of letters, memoranda, articles, and occasional essays by Neil McCaffrey at the request of his son Roger. Many months spent studying the thousands of documents in the archives have taught me that Neil McCaffrey was an exceptional observer and wordsmith—clear-eyed, unsentimental, urbane, eloquent, realistic, passionate but almost always relentlessly logical. He was, above all, a man of deep personal integrity determined to be intelligently Catholic in an age marked by an increasing flight from both faith and reason. He exposes errors without apologizing for hurting feelings, and yet one senses a friendly glint in the eye, because his motivation is not to score points but to tell the truth for the other's benefit. I almost have the sense that many things he wrote were written as if to restore a sort of cosmic balance: if one could soundly object to nonsense and vanity, one had made the world a better place for the moment. And he could speak with breathtaking bluntness.

There is so very much in these documents, even from decades ago, that will strike the reader as uncannily pertinent to our battles today, whether we are political conservatives or Catholic tradition-

---

1 See Patrick Buchanan, *The Greatest Comeback: How Richard Nixon Rose from Defeat to Create the New Majority* (New York: Crown Forum/Penguin Random House, 2014).

alists (or both). This ongoing relevance has a number of causes. First, many of the issues McCaffrey dealt with are fundamental and thus unavoidable, and the stakes have only gotten higher as the cultural divide between a worldview rooted in natural and divine law and a worldview of radical individualism gapes ever wider. Second, in a way few could have predicted, the relatively stable pontificates of John Paul II and Benedict XVI have given way to the chaotic circus of the pontificate of Pope Francis, who seems a Paul VI *redivivus,* only worse. The great confusion, anxiety, and scandal through which McCaffrey and faithful Catholics of his generation had to pass is now being repeated in a penitential *déjà vu* for us who are alive today, and when we read what he wrote in the 1960s and 1970s, we recognize ourselves, our church, our pope and bishops, in his vivid (and, at times, withering) critiques.

Certain readers may be surprised by the warm sympathy Neil exudes for Archbishop Lefebvre, matched only by his scorn for Paul VI. Those who read extensively will discover, however, that Neil was not an uncritical admirer of Lefebvre or his followers (among whom he never counted himself), nor was he ever unwilling to give his due loyalty to the Church's hierarchy. He *did* know the Church inside-out; he knew something of Catholic history and politics, the limits of the charism of papal infallibility, and the precise duties of Catholics, about which he writes compellingly in these pages.

A sketch of key turning points in Neil's career in business and politics will assist the reader in navigating the various allusions and personalities who come up again and again in the letters.

Bill Buckley and Neil McCaffrey met briefly in 1955. Neil began to promote *National Review* in 1957 and it went stratospheric, but he did it in secret because Doubleday and later Macmillan (his two key employers) would have gone berserk if they had known about it. The Conservative Book Club starts in 1964, with Bill and Mike Bernstein, who worked for Goldwater on the Hill, playing assisting roles. Arlington House was launched soon thereafter, and Nostalgia Book Club in 1967–1968 with Arlington House funding. Randy Richardson of Vicks fortune, and Gerald Gidwitz of Helene Curtis fortune, who with Neil co-owned the original company after putting up launch money, tried to take over the CBC. After a battle, Neil won. In 1968–69 Computer Applications Inc. bought into the companies with Bill Buckley's involvement and with a promise of stock windfall, but that company failed and Bill helped to engineer the purchase of all three companies by Starr Broadcasting, which Bill served as chairman.

Neil straddled two worlds. Unlike his friends on the right who were the writers and intellectuals, he was a businessman as well as a penetrating thinker. When friends like Bill came by, they did not talk business. It was ideas and it was intelligent politics—nothing like the moronic political analysis that is dumped on us all today. Neil wrote thousands of mail order ads, one of his many talents, which, for obvious reasons, are not included in this collection. These he would write in a few hours, polishing things that would in many cases bring dead books to life and result in thousands of books sold. This was the backbone of his successful companies. It is estimated that he brought in $25+ million in net profits over about 30 years for a small publishing company, with salaries generated in the many millions on top of that—a highly successful performance envied by many on the Right. While he avoided most of these people, he was considered a key player anyway by 1968. For example, Buchanan mentions his presence at a key meeting with candidate Nixon.

In the early 1960s, his then good friend Garry Wills published a book which was in part stimulated by *Mater et Magistra*. Neil provided much of the material for the book. Regnery published it in 1964 under the title *Politics and Catholic Freedom*. Author Wills acknowledged that Neil McCaffrey should be considered co-author. Neil nearly always kept his name off the mastheads of all the organizations, like *National Review*, to whom he provided support or with whom he cooperated. The reason was simple: he knew that if Doubleday and later Macmillan knew the extent of his professional involvement with what they considered the extreme right, his career would be harmed—and he had eight mouths to feed.

He strove to keep his name out of the spotlight but was identified in 1966–68 as one of the Manhattan Twelve, and Buchanan refers to him in his book on Nixon in that regard.[2] Eventually Neil resigned from that group too, even though by then he was running his own companies, having left Macmillan in 1964 to start CBC and then Arlington House. As President of CBC, etc., he also wished to keep his name out of things, on the grounds that customers might get offended if he were identified with the wrong *group* of conservatives. At that time there were no anarchists, but there were various stripes of libertarian and plenty of Ayn Rand disciples, some of whom were genuine friends of his, like Murray Rothbard, with whom Neil exchanged serious letters over a period of many years.

It is true that, in an ideal world, correspondence would be published with all of the letters sent on both sides. In selecting the

---

2 See also John B. Judis, *William F. Buckley, Jr.: Patron Saint of the Conservatives* (New York: Simon & Schuster, 1988), ch. 19, "The Manhattan Twelve."

content for this volume, certain letters sent to Neil were chosen for the sake of providing context for Neil's own reply. However, many other letters were passed over, lest this book become a multi-volume project. My aim has been to publish letters that can "speak for themselves," without the need for a lot of commentary or context.

When editing correspondence, there is "excess material" one can cut for the sake of publication, such as the repetition of mailing addresses, and certain obscure personal references that mean nothing to the contemporary reader. In the letters I have felt free to omit addresses and postscripts but have always indicated other edits with ellipses [...]. I have also inserted the last names of addressees rather than including their name and address at the end of the letter, as McCaffrey did, in accordance with the epistolary conventions of the day. Unless otherwise noted, "Bill" is William F. Buckley, Jr.

With his gritty New Yorker's knowledge of human nature and his many-sided catholicity, McCaffrey still has much to say to us today. This collection, reaching from the late 1950s to the mid-1990s, is a historical, cultural, and intellectual treasure, and reminds us of what a Catholic "man of parts" looks like—a man of broad interests, serious commitments, and versatile mind.

This project could not have been done without the persistent labors of two assistants of mine, Samantha Stancliffe and Mary Frances Johnson, who scanned all the documents given to me by Roger McCaffrey and, once I had made a selection, converted the chosen documents into Word files and cleaned up the text for their inclusion in this volume. The project would simply have been impossible without their help, and Roger and I are most grateful for it.

Peter Kwasniewski
October, 2019

1

Politics and Economics

April 14, 1957

Mr. William F. Buckley, Jr.
National Review
211 East 37th Street
New York 16

Dear Mr. Buckley,
This is a personal note, not for publication, on four diverse matters. First, a profound and long overdue bow for NR. Literate, eloquent, civilized, witty, Christian, it is incomparably the best journal in the land—and has been from the first issue. American conservatives can never thank you enough.

Second, I would like to offer you my services in promoting NR. No, I'm not job-hunting; I'd like to do this free, as a modest contribution to the cause. I write direct mail copy at Doubleday and know the trade; and I can communicate intellectually to the kind of reader NR is aimed at.

I got this idea when I read your plea-for-subscriptions Letter last year, and it was confirmed when I received my subscription renewal letter a few months ago. I write as a lesser writer to my betters when I say: nobody on your staff can *sell* by mail. To be sure, [indecipherable], and does, to anyone who is even one-third alive. But we conservatives know all about original sin: most people have to be *sold* on anything higher than the animal functions.

And please—when I say "sell" I don't mean that NR should be sold like a used car. You can sell "hard" and be smooth about it.

Perhaps you would like to test my effectiveness, or perhaps just talk about this a bit more. I'll be glad to do a trial letter or circular for you, and I also have some thoughts on possible sources of new readers for NR. Would you like to chat about it over lunch some day, or meet in Grand Central for a drink some evening before we catch our trains?

Third, my wife and I were intrigued at your reference to the recent Mike Wallace show (a superlative performance you put on, by the way) to the school your father is founding; doubly so when we read another reference to it in a recent classified ad in the London *Tablet*. How can we learn more about this school? We've been planning to send ours to parochial school, where they will fare better than most children. But we are conscious of the disadvantages: crowded classrooms, and the fact that the nuns—fine women—are a little light on erudition and on some reactionary principles. Your projected school sounds like—the kind we would start if we inherited an extra $50,000 or so! And fourth, would you like an occasional book review on Catholic subjects? I work on them at Doubleday and do much of my leisure reading in this field. Do you want a few paragraphs— or columns—on Philip Hughes' new book, *A Popular History of the Reformation*? I promoted it and helped with the editing, but of course I wouldn't give you a "house" review; and I'd naturally enter it under a pseudonym. I think it is a valuable book, but it has faults.

One way or another, I hope I can help NR.

Sincerely yours,
Neil McCaffrey

಄

Peldean Court
Pelham, New York

July 31, 1959

Editor
The Freeman
Irvington-on-Hudson, New York

Dear Sir:
Mr. Dean Russell forgets that our income-tax exemption applies to all dependants closely related, not only to children. It is therefore something more than a baby bonus: as an admission that at least some claims on our income take priority over the state's, it has a significance more than financial. Let those of us who prize personal rights be grateful for small favors.

Mr. Russell seems to suggest that *any* interest the state takes in its citizens is bound to be paternalistic or worse. Granted the danger, and that it is usually realized; but is it *necessarily* sinister for the state, in the interests of preserving and protecting family life, to foster a climate that helps it to thrive? It seems that we are in the twilight zone of state activity in this matter. The state is obliged, at the very least, to protect its members; and who can deny that we need protecting against the tax collector?

Extreme, irresponsible individualism is not the answer to collectivism, but merely a prelude to anarchy.

Sincerely,
Neil McCaffrey

CS

April, 1960

Dear Neil,

Fast work on the Protestant check. I was surprised to see it. Thank you very much. Received the Bernanos; I had read, long ago, *The Song of the Scaffold*, and find it hard to work through this version. Movie scenarios are a frustrating thing to read, I think. (Rob't Phelps likes to read them— filming the movie in his mind, I suppose).

No further opportunity for theft, yet. I haven't been to Yale all this last week. I've been resting with deliberate fervor to get rid of a bad cold, but the more I pamper it, the lustier it gets with the attention. Natalie curses me because I can't pick up the baby when he cries, now.

I got a very nice letter from Michael Mason, thanking me for the review and telling me Maisie [Ward] is impressed with the book and will almost certainly do it. I wish she'd let *me* know that. I wrote Phil Scharper about a conference in New York some time ago; but he didn't reply.

Michael Mason told me about his most recent plays (he does Catholic plays for children on the BBC's Sunday service; and, strange fellow, *likes* to. He also writes plays for his children to act out or do toy-theatre style). If you are looking for someone to do a pamphlet for you, I feel sure he could do an excellent one; and, since he works for S & W [Sheed and Ward], he could use the money. I'll send his address if you're interested in sounding him out on it.

Too bad about Bob Morris. By the way, how would you evaluate these reasons for voting for Nixon?

1. On the hypothesis that Kennedy were the Democratic candidate, to avoid the unpleasant consequences of having a Catholic president.

2. On the hypothesis that The Kennedy-Humphrey position on bomb-banning forced Nixon to take a stand for strict tests as the condition of further suspension. Would this issue be drastic enough to take precedence over your calculated risk for a reunified Republican party?

How's Joan? John Christopher thrives amid the cold germs.

Sincerely,
Garry [Wills]

CS

19

And Rightly So

April 27, 1960

Dear Garry [Wills]:

Father Anselm, his wrath assuaged, wrote in his last letter that both he and the censor thought your treatment of poetry in the Bible "really first class", and George Weiss, who doesn't like *anything*, also thought it very good. As, needless to add, do I.

I have nothing at the moment to give Michael Mason, but will keep him in mind. Could you give me his address some time?

You raise pointed questions on the election. As to the undesirability of a Catholic president, I think we must be careful not to beg this question. Certainly, it would have mixed effects. It is probably true that Catholics as a body would get less from a Catholic president; but they get so little now that it hardly matters. I presume, though, that you are referring to the antagonisms that would arise, and also to the equation of the church with the man. To take the latter first, I think Catholics as a body would rise up to challenge the equation, and in the long run this would be all to the good: it would be emancipating, and would serve further to distinguish the Church proper from her temporal adventures.

As to the antagonism, I rejoice at the prospect. It would put us on our mettle. We should be a scandal to the world. This is a real danger in togetherness, that we get so involved with being the nice guys.

I don't mean, of course, that I oppose responsible dialogues and civilized intercourse; but none of this, by definition, would be in the least affected by a Catholic president. We have nothing to fear from those who know better. The antagonisms, which are really widespread and so deep as to be pathological, would not be *produced* by a Catholic president, but merely brought to the surface. This would be healthy. The mindless majority of our fellow Catholics would get their backs up; this would make them even more unlovely than the Liberals—and thus less likely to be seduced by them. Remember, we are playing for time. The ghetto is a useful device to delay the complete conquest of the Catholic Liberals. Responsible Catholic conservatism must be nurtured before it can flower; but meanwhile the Liberals must be kept from scattering the bad seed *all* through the garden. If external antagonism delays their conquest, it may well be providential.

The whole question of test banning is a fraud, since there can be no adequate checks and since we cannot deal with an adversary who is certainly not in good faith. Thus I would be inclined to dismiss as spurious the issue *as you pose it*. On the other hand, the defense of the West is so transcendent a problem in the political order that I think we should support *anyone* who stands for firm-ness—no matter what his views on other issues. A case in point might be someone like Senator Dodd. He is thoroughly sound in his anti-Communism, even on the domestic front; yet in every other respect he is the complete New Dealer.

Farrar, Strauss turned down the book. They said nice things but thought—or said they thought—that it wouldn't sell. I should hear from Holt in a week.

All's well. Let me know when you are coming in to meet Scharper.

Best to Natalie and Jack the Ripper.

Sincerely,
Neil

ශ

May 6, 1960

Dear Garry:

I quite agree with your general reading of the situation in the event of a Catholic president, but I don't think that situation will lead to the consequences you predict. There will certainly be no immediate sloughing off of Liberalism, but the ghetto will be fortified; and I still see this as a useful holding action. The ghetto tends to preclude Liberalism—and therefore makes the ghetto Catholics receptive to the ideas of anti-Liberals. (You don't think Bill is their hero because he wore the Yale blue, do you?)

Of course I agree with you—and Newman, and Johnson, and Burke, and every other responsible conservative—that the forms of civilization are essential to preserve. My point is, on the one hand, that we *really* don't observe these forms; and on the other, that I do not look for overt persecution, which it would be literally rash to court. I say only that the animosity is a stark fact, both among Liber-als and Protestants; and it might not be a bad thing to strip away the pretense and hold it up for what it is. Decent people would be repelled—to our advantage; and the anti-Liberal Catholics would be fortified. Then, to look at it another and not necessarily contradic-tory way, the nation is likely to learn that life goes on, even with a Catholic in the White House.

I must add that Father Cohalan and Gene take your position, so that I offer mine somewhat diffidently against this weight of sober judgement. Let's pursue this.

I am working with Brent on the Goldwater book, and would love to get into it deeper than my knees.

Joan felt the first twinges last night, so we may have some news

And Rightly So

for you before long. Thank you a thousand times for your prayers.
Sincerely,
Neil

ଔ

May 18, 1960
MEMO TO: Fathers Clark, Cohalan, Pryor, Miss Burton
             [Natalie Burton, editor at Doubleday, British
             convert], Messrs. Bozell, Buckley, Meyer,
             Molnar, Wills
FROM: Neil McCaffrey

A few random thoughts on the low-level missile launched from Rome and reported on page one of today's *Times* and *Tribune*. ["Vatican Paper Proclaiming Right of Church to Role in Politics", NYT, May 18, 1960. Front page.] (McBurn's account in the *Tribune* is fuller, more balanced, and therefore less shocking.)

To describe a Church document as semi-official is rather like calling a girl semi-virginal: of course it has no real force. Yet it can't help but have a profound influence on Catholic opinion.

I think that when the Church makes authoritative pronouncements—not to mention doctrinal definitions—we show bad faith when we indulge in hair-splitting emasculations after the manner of the Jansenists. But we *must* make careful distinctions in this gray area where the full magisterium is not exercised—or, more accurately, where the magisterium is not really exercised at all. Otherwise we allow the magisterium itself to be fatally compromised by involving it in the (very numerous) abuses in which it has indulged and will continue to indulge.

The statement is aimed primarily at Italy yet clearly has worldwide implications. Was it phrased in this way to give the appearance of taking the Italians off the hook? Or is it another instance of the curial indifference to, or even contempt for Catholics in other countries? The principle of running to the bishop for every answer is becoming increasingly irrelevant, even in the so-called Catholic countries; and of course it effectively would eliminate Catholics from any serious political action in mixed societies.

Paul and Augustine went that-a-way. Whatever happened to the "freedom of the Christian man"; "love and do what you will"; etc? How can they seriously expect to have a mature laity, yet not trust the laity to make a moral decision? It is really an affront to personal dignity.

We hear a lot of prating these days about a theology of the Church; how desperately we need a theology of authority!

I almost feel sorry for Kennedy—I said *almost*. This statement

22

will be grist for the bigots' mill; much more seriously, it will stagger those non-Catholics who are making an honest effort to overcome their atavistic fears.

Bill, you might draw a useful debating point from this statement for next Wednesday's bloodletting with William Clancy. I don't mean to suggest, of course, that you should deign to notice it in your formal presentation. But some sort of related issue is certain to come up in the question period, Catholic audiences being what they are these days. You might then use the statement to inquire whether the editors of *Commonweal* have cleared their ADA [Americans for Democratic Action, a leftist group] affiliations or sympathies with their bishop (since the ADA is clearly dominated by the kind of men with whom political collaboration is forbidden in the statement).

This statement makes the Catholic conservative book even more urgent, since the book will explore the question of the limits of authority on both the theoretical and practical levels. But by the same token, it may have applied the *coup de grâce* to the book's publication, at least for a time. Would any member of the hierarchy dare to sponsor it, or even give it an *Imprimatur* after this? Would we not all be treated as heretics? I wonder if it would be prudential to go ahead. We expected that our enlightened critics would have imputed heresy anyway; Bill knows all about *that*. How much more so now? Isn't it important that all of us preserve our "orthodox" image in order to keep our audience among Catholics and bide our time for a better day? I'd appreciate your comments on this.

As an afterthought to the paragraph above alluding to the need for preserving the *real* rights of authority of the Church, it is ironic to reflect how little the "conservative" Ottaviani has of the historical sense. How we suffer from phony conservatives.

℀

September 24, 1960

Dear Neil:
A little while back Bill sent me your comments on the *Information* article about him. I have been meaning to write you ever since to tell you what an exquisite job I thought it was. Your rebuttal, in terms of logic, was absolutely devastating, as I would have expected. But I was not prepared for a writing job that was quite so brilliant and polished, and I wonder if you are not missing your vocation.
Best regards,
L. Brent Bozell

℀

And Rightly So

September 30, 1960

Dear Brent [Bozell]:
I am really quite overwhelmed at your gracious note, which just arrived. What can I say but to thank you most warmly?

I'll take this opportunity to beg you, as I have just begged Frank, to write something suitably devastating on our flight from national responsibility in foreign policy. If there was room for doubt before, the events of the past few weeks have proved beyond peradventure that we no longer see ourselves as *having* national interests distinguishable from the policies of the UN. I found last week's *Bulletin* editorial frightfully inadequate in terms of the debacle.

Again I ask, could we get together next time you are in town?
Sincerely,
Neil

ᘓ

October 17, 1960

Dear Bill [Rusher],
As promised, here is that portion of my Catholic file on the UN that was ready at hand. As you will observe, the Catholic debates on the subject are a dreary business, and I dearly hope that the question period can be kept on a higher level than is traditional at Catholic gatherings; but I am not sanguine. Hence, forewarned . . .

I am also enclosing an article I wrote in answer to *Information's* attack on Bill. (In characteristic Liberal fashion, they found reasons, not very good, for rejecting it, and I am now trying to get it placed in some more sympathetic journal, of which there are not many.) While the article does not treat expressly of your subject, parts of it, especially at the end, might suggest useful lines of argument before a Catholic audience, if the questions they fire at you take the form I think they will. You can make a good *debating* point with the quotes from *Mirari Vos* on the last page: this is an *encyclical*, and therefore a more authoritative document than the semi-formal, semi-private talks in which Pius XII and John XXIII have given their carefully qualified endorsements of the UN. Would your heckler subscribe to the strictures in *Mirari Vos* and in the *Syllabus of Errors* (excerpts from which can be found in *The Catholic Church in the Modern World*, which I think Bill may have lying around the office somewhere)?

Another point you might stress if the argument degenerates to these illegitimate invocations of the Popes, one that is lost on all but the most sophisticated Catholics, is that Rome's abiding policy is to

24

play ball with any government or temporal agency with which it can achieve any kind of *modus vivendi*. The pallid endorsements of the UN must be seen in this context: the UN is a fact of life and, prescinding from any ultimate endorsement of it (which it is not properly the Church's place to give), the Church wants to influence it.

The real argument, which unfortunately you can't say in so many words, is that the Popes can err and often have erred in their existential judgments on concrete temporal situations, which have nothing to do with papal infallibility. One of the alarming developments in the modern Church is the tendency to deify the Popes, and no group is more guilty of this than American Catholics. Needless to say, to adopt such an attitude a Catholic must be sturdily fortified against some towering truths of theology and facts of history.

This is a terribly large and complex question; if I can be of any use, we can chat about it on or before the 25th.

I would like to get the clippings back eventually, but the article is yours if it is of any use to you.

Best,
Neil

೮೩

October 20, 1960

Dear Bill [Buckley]:
On the assumption that Kennedy wins (I think it could be a landslide), here is what I hope you will agree is a roaring idea for a post-election feature: an exclusive interview in depth with Goldwater, covering his views on the elections, his analysis of the task before us under the new administration—and, of course, his first blast for the 1964 campaign.

This should take the form of an interview with Brent rather than an article: it's more lively that way. It should be lengthy. It should be heralded, all by itself, on the front cover. We should load up every newsstand we can, and give them a poster. We should include a special offer subscription in these issues. And we should send out press releases on a grand scale.

If we don't do this, rest assured *U.S. News* or *Human Events* will.

Why shouldn't we be the ones to pilot the Goldwater bandwagon—for his sake as well as ours?
Sincerely,
Neil

೮೩

25

And Rightly So

January 3, 1961

Dear Bill,

I couldn't reach you over the weekend to chat about the Goldwater interview, which rocked me. I wasn't prepared for such a remorseless succession of banalities. On top of these, he actually contradicted previous statements he had made, as on his willingness to accept the '64 nomination. Is he essentially frivolous? Can he be force-fed? It may be that your instinct was right, that he is not heavy enough to bear the mantle of Mr. Conservative.

The question remains, can he be led, and trusted? Will he listen? Will he behave?

Best regards,
Neil

ଓ

January 23, 1961

Dear Bill,

I found your reply to Corrigan *et al* very effective—given the rigid taboos that so limit Catholic debate on papal pronouncements. This is our salvation as regards these non-doctrinal pronouncements—and *their* weakness; they have something for everybody, but are generally so vague and ambiguous that they go nowhere. But I'm glad that we are starting to quote Scripture, and not leaving it all to the devil.

My ambition is someday to write an article and suggest, in my usual gentle fashion, that the Popes might have done well to learn some economics. Alas, I think this manifesto will have to wait until a) I am not making my living in Catholic publishing and advertising, and b) the kids have all graduated from Catholic schools!

You may be challenged on the article, but you are on strong ground on the level on which you chose to debate. The worst that can happen is that Monsignor Higgins will quote Father Massa, who will quote Father Smith, who will quote Father Cronin, *ad nauseam*. The article is very shrewdly done, both rhetorically and in terms of Catholic public relations.

Until we can arrange to dispose of the other Neil [there was another Neil McCaffrey from Larchmont who would call Bill Buckley and be put through], just remember that if you call the PElham exchange, you can only get either my father or me; we are the only McCaffreys in PElham. By the way, it's PElham 8-3749.

Another solution: have the oil company send the other Neil to

Saudi Arabia. After all, he *is* enterprising.
Best,
Neil

ᘓ

January 27, 1961

Dear Garry:
A quick note to congratulate you, most warmly, on the review of Frank's book. It is simply stunning, one of the finest reviews I have ever read, by anyone. I wish I could say the same for Niemeyer's. Terribly disappointing, don't you think? He spent half of his space criticizing Frank for not writing another kind of book, and managed to miss many of the nuances of the book under review, so bemused was he by the idea of the book he wanted Frank to have written.

I saw the *Wall Street Journal's* write-up on the [Barry Goldwater] Manifesto, as well as the *U.S. News*. I can't say that the thing upsets me. Granted the omissions (perhaps to be corrected in subsequent installments), errors and clumsy phrasing in spots, where else can you find a politician talking such broadly good sense? The "Forgotten American" theme is, by the way, an example of *good* public relations (or whatever you choose to call it)— good because it a) is true and b) projects an idea that can capture the imagination of the dolts he must inspire if he is serious about getting anywhere. These dolts are not moved by principles; they need concrete images. I regard it as a surpassingly healthy sign that Frank's instant reaction was, "Madison Avenue!" Like most intellectuals, he does not distinguish between the good and bad uses of what is really just old-fashioned salesmanship or, more basically, human relations. No matter how he inveighs against the notion of a philosopher-king, this is really all he would ever be satisfied with. I think you take a more hardheaded view of the limits of the political order and the possibilities to be realized therein, and I therefore think you should read the complete text (which I will send you as soon as I get an extra copy) with that in mind.

I thought that Barry floundered last night on TV, and that is the unanimous view of four others to whom I have spoken. But he did finish strongly. I don't think debating is his medium; he is neither mentally agile nor articulate enough to be equal to its demands. I think McCarthy demagogically effective, and historically and philosophically scandalous.

Scharper [Phil Scharper, editor at Sheed and Ward] wants to go ahead, and now it only remains for him to clear the arrangements with headquarters.

Love to Natalie and John.

Best,
Neil

ೞ

September 27, 1961

Dear Victor [Lasky],

Enclosed: The Documentation [regarding President Kennedy's purported marriage to Durie Malcolm; see glossary].

To recap later developments, the *[New York Daily] News* cub reporter to whom my friend gave this lead kept calling Mrs. Smith (who helped with the book; she is Blauvelt's daughter) and getting the run around. Finally, he nailed her one day. Cornered, she told him he'd never get the letter that was supposed to "explain all."

"Wouldn't it look suspicious if I ended my story on this note?" he countered. "Wouldn't it look like you had something to hide?"

"We're counting on it that your story will never get printed," she replied, and hung up.

Meanwhile, back at the Buckley's, they have a friend who has known the girl for years. The friend confirms the affair, but thinks there was no marriage.

Maybe not; but then, why all the mystery? The book is certainly explicit and people don't usually confuse steady dating, or an affair, with a marriage.

If the marriage took place, it would almost certainly have been a civil ceremony, and so would not be, in the eyes of the Church, an impediment to Jack's later marriage, since the marriage *of a Catholic* must be in the Catholic Church, or is not recognized by the Church. On the other hand, the Church also wants to know, for purposes of *civil* legality, whether a person to be married is "free to marry", i.e., not already married. Now, Catholics always must sign such statements, under oath, before the Church will marry them; but the form of the statement will vary from diocese to diocese. One diocese may simply ask if the person is "free to marry" and let it go at that, in which case a Catholic who has contracted a civil marriage could reason that this was not, in the Church's eyes, a real marriage, and simply answer Yes. But if the diocese asks whether the Catholic has "attempted marriage" (ecclesiastical jargon for going through a ceremony when one is already married, or in the case of a Catholic, marrying outside the Church), then the respondent must either 'fess up or commit perjury (not *legal* perjury, to be sure, but perjury in the eyes of the Church).

I am launching into this short course in theology because it could have an interesting bearing on this case. If Jack and Durie did marry, and if the diocese of Providence (Jack and Jackie were married in Newport) requires the specific information I mentioned above, then the record (now in the vault of the church where they were married) either acknowledges this, or, more likely, bears witness to an act of perjury.

Neither the putative first marriage, nor the possible perjury would bother non-Catholics, I don't think, since it is an internal Catholic matter, though even non-Catholics might feel it was a bit shady of him to hide this. But I need not emphasize what this will do to his image among Catholics. I doubt that he could be reelected.

Please call me if I can throw any further light on all this.

My best to Pat. Perhaps Joan and I will see you both Friday?

Best regards,
Neil

℘

Dear Dr. [Stephen] Tonsor,

As you may have heard from Frank Meyer, your brilliant "Politics and Papacy" passed from him to Bill Buckley to me, who am editing a supplement NR plans on the encyclical controversy. We'd like to include your article in the supplement, at NR's regular rates.

It is, I think, the best short statement of the essential position that has appeared in our time. We have corrected certain typographical errors, and would like to raise a few questions that might serve to strengthen the article. I have keyed them by letter in the enclosed manuscript:

A) The simple statement that the Church "identified itself with aristocracy and the feudal order" could leave you open to challenge. Certainly, the Church worked within the feudal order, as she will try to work *within* any political and/or social order: she also fought a bitter struggle to keep from becoming submerged by these temporal forces. Moreover, your phraseology (unintentionally) suggests a kind of class struggle which implies that the Church was remote from or even allied against the common people—which of course was not the case.

B) It is a question whether the Church emerged from Vienna "more powerful than it had been at any time since the mid-seventeenth century." It was now totally dependent on Austria and/or France; though I may be quibbling over low-water marks.

And Rightly So

C) Who was the Catholic writer who called the Papal states a "benevolent theocracy"? Hales, perhaps?

D) I enjoy your ironic use of the phrase "deposit of faith", but because of its solemn associations, I fear that Catholics on our side may find it jarring, and the Liberals may find it a useful weapon. I feel that your piece is strong enough, and then some, without it.

E) Here you throw away your most telling point in a subordinate clause. You should enlarge upon and *specify* "the dangers that would devolve upon the Church". It seems obvious enough to us, yet virtually all Catholics are innocent of the notion that extending the doctrine of Papal Infallibility beyond its careful limits renders it *untenable*: and there goes the *Church's* infallibility. We make a critical point—and, incidentally, score heavily in this debate—when we stress that those who would 'defend' papal prerogatives actually undermine them, and the Church, by exaggerating them.

I'll be eager to hear from you. Should any of this require discussion, please call me any evening at 914 PE 8-3749; and please reverse the charges.

Sincerely,
Neil McCaffrey

ɔ8

December 7, 1961

Dear Bill:
I just heard from Fritz [Wilhelmsen], who was pleased about the supplement and would like to expand his article a little.

I know the encyclicals recommended by Fr. Denis. They have many good sections on egalitarianism, unrestricted democracy and secular liberalism, but are not really germane to this controversy. Certainly, they condemn ideas that Catholic Liberals espouse at least implicitly, but it would take exhaustive analysis to prepare an airtight case. The two by Leo, *Libertas* and *Humanum Genus*, also expound the traditional views of religious toleration and the separation of Church and State which we find confining and which have been undergoing reevaluation since the time of Pius XII. *Pascendi* instituted a system of ecclesiastical spying which was too harsh a response to the actual threat.

I applaud Fr. Lester's campaign against *America*, and certainly hope it has some effect. I must say, though, that his request for documentation on *America's* Liberal slant leaves me amazed. It is as

30

if he asked the same information about the *Times*: one could refer
him to any issue.
Best,
Neil

ↄઝ

January 17, 1962

Dear Bill [Rusher]:
I feel constrained to reiterate the thesis I advanced at lunch—even
though, admittedly, it doesn't blaze with originality. The Liberals
first found that they couldn't ignore us; then they tried smearing,
without measurable success. Now their tactic is subtler and more
serious: divide the right, and thus reduce it to impotence. It is a
tactic conservatives are peculiarly vulnerable to (especially conservatives who have been long out of power). The disagreements on
the right are for the most part not substantive. Even where they are,
nobody but a fanatic should expect to have it all his own way. Most
important, our disagreements are dwarfed by agreement over the
common enemies.
    Squabbles on the right should, as a matter of fixed policy, be
settled quietly and tactfully. Better still, they can very largely be
subsumed under the imperatives of a common cause—and especially a common leader. The Communists understand this; the Jesuits understand it; even an individualistic nation like Britain understands it. If we want power—and we would be derelict not to—we
must recognize that some sophistication in these matters is the *sine
qua non.*
    I go on like this because the matter is so critical. Needless to add,
my views are not confidential.
    We're looking forward to seeing you on the twenty-seventh.
Best,
Neil

ↄઝ

February 1, 1962

Dear Ken [Templeton]:
Sorry you couldn't make the party. It seems to have been a pretty
good one. Let's be sure to get together next time you are in town.
    Do you recall that Catholic Conservative book that we talked
about last year and for which you said the Fund would make a grant
of $1,500 upon my signing a contract? Well, the book idea has now

31

taken on a slightly different coloration. At the instigation of Bill Buckley, I'm putting together a "white paper" on the Liberal Catholic campaign against *National Review* and other conservative Catholics. This will take the form of a rundown of early attacks, the meat of the current controversy on the encyclical, *Mater et Magistra,* and finally a series of essays giving the conservative Catholic position—which really amounts to a declaration of independence of the hierarchy in political and economic affairs, except where they bear *directly* on *manifest* moral issues. In short, the *truly* liberal position.

Thus, the theme is essentially the same, but now tied to a specific controversy. In light of this, do you think the grant would still apply? I am well into the project now, and with any luck should have it wrapped up in another two or three months. Meanwhile, Devin-Adair has expressed interest, and I honestly don't think it will be hard to get a contract from Devin. It's the sort of theme that appeals to him.

Did you hear that George Koether had some kind of heart scare about a month ago? He still doesn't know what it was, but seems to be quite all right now.

Best regards, and let's get together soon.
Sincerely,
Neil

ᥫ

February 16, 1962

Dear Dr. Bouscaren,
Bill Buckley referred your timely article on "The Encyclicals, Social Justice and Communism" to me since I am putting together a kind of "white paper" on this very controversy, and the role of *National Review* in it.

I've thought long and hard whether to include your article in this collection, and I've come to the conclusion that it would be better not to—but for a reason entirely extrinsic to the very real merit of the article.

As you know, Catholic conservatives have tended to take two different approaches to *Mater et Magistra.* The *Tablet* and the *Wanderer,* on the one hand, have taken the position that the encyclical confirms their conservative stance; but *National Review* and a good many of its Catholic writers and readers have taken the position that the encyclical is not above criticism. To include your article in this collection of opinion would be to introduce a subtle inconsistency, and leave us open to the charge that we don't quite know our own

32

minds, and want to have it both ways.

At the same time, I was delighted to see your article in the *Tablet*, and I hope you can also get the *Wanderer* to reprint it. The *National Review* position is strong meat for many Catholic conservatives: they are simply not equipped to entertain *any* kind of criticism of the Pope. Yet they know in their bones that the Liberals are wrong. Your article should ease their consciences and enable them to get on with the serious business of our time. You have performed a real service.

Sincerely,
Neil McCaffrey

ભ

February 23, 1962

Dear Ken [Templeton]:

Thanks very much for your note. I am enclosing an outline of the book as it now shapes up, but I would like to elaborate on it a bit.

I don't know how closely you have followed the controversy in *National Review* about last July's papal encyclical, *Mater et Magistra*. At any rate, to begin with the background, the Catholic Left has been after Bill Buckley since 1951, when he published *God and Man at Yale* and dared to defend free enterprise. Other Catholics, such as Father Coogan (who is contributing to this book) and Father Edmund Keller of Notre Dame, both of whom have taken positions on right-to-work laws, have been subjected to comparable abuse and ostracism. The attacks mounted, and when *National Review*—needless to say, not a Catholic journal—commented unfavorably on the encyclical, an unprecedented campaign of abuse was mounted in most of the Catholic press.

The encyclical, in case you spared yourself the dreary task of wading through that depressing document, went much further than earlier ones in advocating state intervention in the economy and social life. More, it actually offered very specific recommendations for such intervention, such as farm subsidies, and even paused to praise the work of particular, mischievous bodies such as the ILO. Now, there is nothing in Peter's mandate that made him or his successors economists; yet, *National Review* and its sympathizers, Catholic and non-Catholic alike, were the only ones who challenged these statist papal nostrums. Ironically, only less than a year before that Catholic Liberals were busy assuring the nation that a Catholic in the White House would have complete political freedom; and they were right. But when Catholics who disagreed with their views took them at their word, their disingenuousness lay exposed.

Thus the controversy put in sharp focus two urgent questions, both for Catholics and for the nation as a whole. First, may Catholics really behave in the political and economic and social order as free men, or is their behavior to be subject to hierarchical veto? The Catholic Liberals refuse to face this issue; but this book will force them to face it and I have no doubt that, when the question is posed in these stark terms, the typical American Catholic will opt for freedom. If not, then the nation at large will have to ask itself, Is the nation's largest religious minority really to be trusted to play the American political game according to the rules?

These questions cry out to be aired. This is the only book on the horizon that will air them in a concrete situation. When the questions are raised by convinced Catholics (not, as in the last election, by non-Catholics whose good will was often questioned), the impact on Catholic and non-Catholic alike must be tremendous. The contributors will state their case urbanely, but with no attempt to mask the real issues. The book is bound to get major national publicity; we will state the case in a fashion that will embarrass the inhabitants of the New Frontier; and, I am convinced, the book will become a landmark in the coming-of-age of American Catholics.

Meanwhile, I can use the grant. I am running into the usual expenses of putting together a book—not the least of which is a sharp curtailment on my other free-lance writing (which for the past few years has formed a significant part of my income). I have had research expenses, travel expenses, phone expenses; these will grow, and I will also have to get the manuscript typed.

Please let me know if you need any further information. Meanwhile, I hope we can get together next time you are in town.

Sincerely,
Neil

છ

March 2, 1962

Dear Bill:
Probably you will have heard of the disastrous item enclosed by the time this reaches you. I don't know the story behind it, but I'll let you know if I learn anything. It seems to be the same report that Fr. Cronin submitted to Archbishop Cousins at the last bishops' meeting—the one that was leaked to the *Times* but was not adopted as part of the bishops' annual report. The fact that it is published by the Paulist Press suggests some enterprise on the part of the Paulists or the Social Action Department of NCWC: Normally, NCWC reports

are printed by NCWC or not at all, and they get much less extensive distribution than do pamphlets issued by the Paulist Press. The statement that the report was issued under the aegis of the bishops cannot of course be taken at face value. The analogy here to a trial balloon launched in some speech by a State Department official is, I think, apt.

Meanwhile, it is a bitter pill for Catholic conservatives—and, ultimately, a grave blow to the Church in America. Clericalism + Liberalism = something very close to totalitarianism. The Liberals seem determined to isolate, discredit and drive conservatives outside the mainstream of American Catholic life. It is depressing, especially since we have no Catholic journal that can make an adequate response. I will let you know the reactions of the *Wanderer* and the *Tablet*: those of the Liberals are predictable.

It is now Monday, and I enclose the editorial from yesterday's *Times*. Fr. Clark and I had a pow wow and suggest that NR question the launching of this as an "official" Catholic statement. Having taken on the Pope, we should not be frightened by Fr. Cronin. If we quote J. Edgar Hoover on internal Communism, along with those splendid paragraphs by Spellman and Cushing that the magazine ran two months ago, we can give the lie to Cronin's whole thesis.

Mundelein [not the Seminary] is the largest girls' college in the country. It is in Chicago. Tom Miller (who is at ABC TV in Chicago) tells me that they have sold so many tickets that they have moved the debate to Loyola.

Volker is a stronghold of arch-libertarianism, and therein must lie the seed of their suspicion of NR. Further, and this is sheer speculation—there is an evangelical Protestant element there that may gag when it gets a whiff, in NR, of "the whore of Babylon".

I'd be very grateful if you would check with your host on Bob Galvin [Motorola CEO; conservative]. Any information will prove useful, perhaps indispensable.

Best,
Neil

ଔ

March 12, 1962

Editor [of the *Wanderer*]:
If Father John F. Cronin had simply issued another of his anti-anti-Communist tracts, most of us would have merely yawned and gone about our business. But the circumstances under which he launched his latest tirade pose urgent questions for the American

Catholic community.

At the time of the annual Bishops' Meeting last November, Father Cronin's report to Archbishop Cousins was loaned to *The New York Times* and presented to the American public as "official". The report itself was not adopted, and the inference drawn from it by the Liberals, Catholic or non-Catholic, prompted the Archbishop to set the record straight in blistering language—a correction that was ignored in some Liberal Catholic journals.

Now Father Cronin's latest essay in anti-anti-communism is issued in much the same fashion. The secular prose treats it as the "official" attitude of the American Catholic hierarchy, and Father Cronin encourages this interpretation.

Surely, something is amiss here. It is unthinkable that the bishops would issue a formal statement of policy through the medium of a minor functionary; official statements are far too serious to be treated in this casual fashion. This being so, one wonders whether there might not be grounds for an investigation by the hierarchy of Father Cronin and his superior in the Social Action Department of CWC, Msgr. George Higgins. Are they abusing their position by presuming to speak for the hierarchy? If so, they would be guilty of the gravest malfeasance and presumption, and would be manifesting a callous disregard for the consciences of the Catholic laity.

Furthermore, how can Father Cronin be so disingenuous as to suggest that his views on the internal Communist menace represent those of "95 to 99 percent of the American bishops", when the staunchly anti-Communist (and anti-Cronin) views of Cardinal Spellman, Cardinal Cushing, and Cardinal McIntyre are matter of public record, reiterated time and again over the years? Only last December, Cardinal Spellman said, "I beg all Americans courageously to continue and to intensify their anti-Communist programs." On July 15, 1961, Cardinal Cushing wrote: "We cannot afford to be apathetic or indifferent. Within our own America, the Communists are carrying forward a clever infiltration of many organizations."
Neil McCaffrey

ᦉ

April 11, 1962

Dear Bill:
Did you see the current *America*? Specifically, Davis' column, up front, and the lead editorial? I think we have now entered Phase Two, as presaged by Fathers Cohalan and Clark: the open attempt to invoke ecclesiastical sanctions.

Politics and Economics

I see no cause for alarm—to equate you (and all of us) with the New Orleans racists is too shabby. But we see what he is capable of—even more in his attempt to conjure up the bogey of anti-clericalism. I find it hard to take this seriously intellectually; and for him to offer it seriously is a terrible indictment of his grasp of history. (Properly, anti-clericalism is a euphemism for the bitter anti-Catholicism among atheists and agnostics in the Latin countries, principally. And what an exercise in arrogance, for him to liken someone's opposition to the political views of him and his allies to the total attack on the Church that "anti-clericalism" really represents? Actually, he uses the term in the crude *clericalist* sense of daring to disagree with Father.)

Davis may feel threatened; he remembers the fate of Hartnett [anti-communist, see glossary]. I doubt that the Society wants anyone too controversial in his slot. He would be "vindicated" if he could turn the hierarchy against you.

His case is feeble, but we shouldn't simply dismiss him. A malevolent man with an obsession, and a temper, can work damage. This is not a call to paranoia, and I think you've been handling the matter with an increasingly sure touch.

I intend to make these and other points in the book. How vulnerable he is, and how short-sighted.

Best,
Neil

☙

Human Events, Vol. XIX, No. 18, Section IV (May 5, 1962)

How to Answer Six Attacks Conservatives Will Face This Election Year
by Neil McCaffrey

Conservative Criticisms of the Administration are beginning to draw blood. The Administration chose to ignore them for a time, hoping they might go away. *New Frontiersmen* reasoned that, with all the publicity resources at their command, the President could rise above these "petty" voices of discontent.

But conservative criticisms have proved too telling to be shrugged off—especially after a full year of Kennedy disasters. Accordingly, the Administration has counterattacked. The main lines of the new maneuver are spelled out in the columns of liberal commentators, in the editorials of Left-leaning publications, and in recent tirades by Senator J. William Fulbright, State Department spokesmen Harlan Cleveland, Carl T. Rowan and G. Mennen (Soapy) Williams, Vice President Johnson and President Kennedy.

The six main lines of assault are now clear, and all six have two striking characteristics in common:
1. *Not one of them deals with any issue. Quite the contrary: All six are smokescreens, cleverly designed to distract the electorate from the real issues.*
2. *All six are personal attacks on conservatives. The strategy, in short, is to make conservatives the issue and thus to enable a fatally incompetent Administration to escape the day of reckoning on November 6.*

The Administration strategy is itself a confession of the inherent weakness of its position—since it dares not debate the issues. *But this is no guarantee the strategy will not succeed.* The same strategy has worked time and again over the past 30 years, and conservatives will have to be up early every morning to see that it does not succeed again.

It behooves us, then, to isolate these six attacks, the better to see them for what they are.

1. Conservatives are divisive.
Indeed they are. They are bent on 'dividing' the nation from the busy ideologies who work to remold us in the ADA pattern.

We should not overlook the supreme irony of this liberal smear. Political theorists agree that a republic cannot function without a high degree of agreement among its members *on essentials*—on the nature of that republic and its institutions. Given this underlying consensus, political parties may and should disagree—*on details.*

Before 1933, we had this kind of broad consensus. Then we saw what proved to be, not merely a change of Administrations, but a revolution. The Constitution was traduced; class and racial hatreds were fomented for political gain. New Deal votaries applauded this revolution, conservatives deplored it; but revolution it was.

Now this revolution has become, to an alarming extent, institutionalized. A vast bureaucracy has been installed to administer it.

And, suddenly, those who respect the nation's institutions, those who work to preserve them, are called "divisive"—by the very revolutionaries who divided the nation in the first place!

Conservatives should ask those who call them divisive: Is it the function of a political opposition to serve as rubber stamps? Communist Poland tolerates "opposition" parties—but heaven help them if they really *oppose!*

We should remind Mr. Kennedy, gently, that America has not yet gone behind the Iron Curtain.

2. Conservatives are very rich.
The Liberals have gotten good mileage from this Marxist argu-

ment for years, and they continue to use it in the clinches.

In point of fact, the conservative revival is in good part a grass-roots, middle-class movement: a *democratic* movement, however this disturbs the ideological preconceptions of the Left. (Interestingly, the liberal *intelligentsia* is not above exploiting this fact with thinly-veiled appeals to snobbery. In *The New York Times* and other organs of the liberal line, repeated references to "know-nothings" always provoke the anticipated Pavlovian response from the pseudo-intellectuals of the Establishment.)

Some conservatives are rich, yes: but all too few, if we examine the balance sheets of virtually any conservative enterprise. Maybe what conservatives need are a few Kennedys, Harrimans, Lehmans and Roosevelts.

3. Conservatives are frustrated.
True enough. They see a Ukrainian butcher [Khruschev] insult us with impunity *on our own soil,* and it rankles.

• They see a Red demagogue 90 miles from our shore make us the laughing stock of the world, and it annoys.

• They see their government proclaim as "'victory" the plan to take Communists into the government of Laos, and they wonder how long before the lessons of China and Poland and Spain penetrate the fog of liberalism.

• They see our money financing the slaughter of citizens of one of our few African allies, Katanga, and they ask where blindness ends and madness begins.

• They see the reports of spy rings radiating out of Soviet embassies and "cultural exchange" groups, and speculate whether our liberal leaders are not possessed by some suicidal mania.

• They see all this, and much more, and wonder whether the liberals are still *capable* of mature concern, or righteous anger.

4. Conservatives are addicted to "simple" solutions for complex problems.
This is a tricky one, and serves a double purpose. On the one hand, it appeals unblushingly to intellectual snobbery, enabling the liberal to strike a pose as the thinking man who sees life in all its complexity. On the other hand, it serves as an admirable excuse for liberal confusion, fuzziness and double-talk—since our problems are allegedly too "complex" to admit of straightforward solutions.

The liberals, of course, want it both ways. They aspire to be the intellectual guardians of our society, yet they refuse to be held responsible for providing the solutions which their superior wisdom should presumably yield. There are no solutions, we are told, in this "long twilight of the cold war"; still we must leave to the liberals the management... of...problems... that... have... no... solution. They never explain why.

In truth, the conservative approach is a sensible blend of simple principles and a judicious application of these principles to the complexities of a given situation. The conservative is a *realist*.

The conservative believes that our government's first duty is to protect its citizens from internal and external threat—not to establish parliamentary democracy or trade unionism in Afghanistan, for example.

The conservative recognizes Communism as by all odds the gravest threat the nation faces, and therefore scrutinizes every policy in light of the one supremely urgent question: Does it aid communism or help defeat it?

The conservative is devoted deeply to freedom and justice—and tempers these enthusiasms to the circumstances of time and place, realizing that human material reacts stubbornly to abstract theories, and that a perfect world will never be achieved by imperfect men.

By contrast, it is the *liberal* who is really wedded to simplistic solutions. This, in fact, is what makes him a liberal. For all his protestations about "complexities"—protestations which, as we have seen, serve merely to cover up his failure to *deliver*—the liberal approaches each new problem with a 12-year-old's simplicity.

Trouble in Afghanistan? Send them another $100 million! *(Never mind that the first $100 million caused the trouble!)*

Unrest in the Congo? Call in the UN! *(Never mind that the UN provoked the unrest.)*

Interracial strife in a housing project? Page the government! *(Never mind that the government created the conditions that bred the strife!)*

Thus it is the liberals who are the authentic reactionaries. Decades of failure, scores of discredited policies—yet they never learn from their failures, never correct their policies.

Nothing fails like failure. If Americans are indeed a practical people, next November they will judge the liberals by their *results*. The Bible says "By their fruits you shall know them."

The conservative task must be to hammer home the facts about this unparalleled record of disaster—the legacy of liberalism.

5. Conservatives ignore the external threat of communism and conjure up an imaginary internal threat.

This is the most obviously phony charge but it serves to point up some fundamental flaws in the liberal approach to communism.

Communism is a world-wide conspiracy. Its heart is Moscow, but its arteries extend into every nation.

So much is obvious, even to the liberals.

What is not so obvious to liberals is that this conspiracy *means business.* Communists are not primarily interested in capturing this or that country by democratic means. They have only won one country by the ballot; their literature does not suggest that they seriously expect to win many more.

The liberals like to think of living with them—against all evidence. They like to scoff at the 10,000 known members of the American Communist party—ignoring the crypto-Communists, the fellow travelers and the dupes (both willing and innocent). They like to ignore the mountain of data on Communist infiltration—meanwhile crippling every effort to smoke out the subversives that are operating right now.

Conservatives take a more balanced view. They see external and internal Communism as two aspects of the same threat. *Moreover, they know external Communism would be much less of a threat had not internal communism influenced our policies and betrayed our secrets at key moments over the last 25 years.*

Without the help of American Communists (often working through those pushovers, the liberals), Russia would not today control Eastern Europe or China; would not possess nearly the atomic arsenal it now has; and very probably would not exercise anything like its present influence in the "neutral" nations.

This is the conservative thesis. Compelling arguments support it. If it is true—and certainly it deserves the most searching and sober analysis—then obviously our entire foreign and much of our domestic policy cries out for overhauling.

Since America belongs to liberals as well as conservatives, and since survival is both a liberal and a conservative concern, it would seem on innocent examination that the liberals would make it a matter of first priority to discover what has caused the debacle.

But no. The liberal reaction, when these questions are even raised, is *sheer hysteria.*

The question arises, *Why?* What are the liberals hiding? Why should the truth terrify them so, *even when their own survival is at stake?*

Conservatives might add, when this canard is voiced, that they care deeply about *both* external and internal communism.

Conservatives were not the architects of Yalta and Teheran and Potsdam. Conservatives did not sell out China. Conservatives never urged us to turn our backs on the Hungarian and Polish and East German freedom fighters—or to turn our planes over to Tito.

41

Between now and November 6, let's take a hard look at the record—on communism.

6. Conservatives dwell at the lunatic fringe.
The tactic here is the familiar Hitlerian-Communist technique of the big lie: Never mind how untrue it is, just keep repeating it.

To buttress the charge, liberal hatchet men will quote an ill-considered sentence or two from this or that conservative—and then proceed to indict the whole movement.

To fight this tactic use the readiest and most congenial of weapons: *truth*.

Thus the arguments—or, more properly, the smears—that conservatives will hear in crescendo for the next year. Old-time conservatives will recognize familiar patterns; young conservatives may be shocked at the level of political "discussion" on the *New Frontier*. But we owe it to our country to ponder these smears; to learn to recognize them, in whatever guise; and above all, to *answer them convincingly*.

Most Americans are simply not equipped to counter this slick 'professional' character assassination. Conservatives, as the elite of the patriotic revival, must show their fellow citizens how.

ങ

May 29, 1962

Dear Murray [Rothbard]:
Joan and I are most grateful, and honored, for the inscribed set of your new opus. We hope and believe that it will come to be regarded as a classic. We also hope that it does not become an unread classic—especially in the McCaffrey household, where we have the damnedest time just keeping up with our friends' books. I am deep in one of my own at the moment, and so everything else has suffered.

I am going to take a brief vacation later this week, but I'd like to call you for lunch early next month.

Best to Joey.
Sincerely,
Neil

ങ

Politics and Economics

An Open Letter to Catholic Journals of Opinion
L. Brent Bozell
El Escorial, Spain
(1962)

On March 31 the Jesuit magazine *America*, which calls itself "The National Catholic Weekly Review," featured a four-page article by the distinguished Fordham philosopher, Norris Clarke, S.J., strongly disapproving the thesis I advanced (but hardly invented) some time ago in *National Review* that the West, given the theology of the Incarnation, ought to be defended as "God's civilization." It was the second time *America* had taken out after me on this subject, the earlier instance having been an inconsequent philippic by a Minneapolis priest who fancied himself adept at satire. Deeming Fr. Clarke's carefully-hewn arguments an effort to keep the discussion process functioning, and more—an attempt to elevate the dialogue between conservative and Liberal Catholics to a level where their respective philosophical and theological assumptions could be examined—I prepared a reply and sent it along to *America*. And I sent a copy to Fr. Clarke. The return mail brought a pleasant letter from Thurston Davis, S.J., *America's* editor, advising that the piece was under consideration. A week or so later a second Davis letter arrived, purporting to "summarize the opinions of our staff and . . . to explain my decision not to publish . . ."

The summary included several captious observations that, in charity, I shall not relate, since Fr. Davis agreeably dismissed them as "not substantive [or] determining considerations." The real explanation, he said, is this: We chose *America* as the medium for Fr. Clarke's reply to your NR article, and did not request its publication in *National Review*. By choosing not to offer it to *National Review*, we hoped to make clear by implication that this was all the attention and all the space we could presently devote to the question. [In other words: By publishing Fr. Clarke itself, *America* was trying to get across the idea that it did *not* want to devote further space to the problem; whereas if it had referred Fr. Clarke to *National Review*, that would have implied *America* did want to go on with the discussion. Get it?] Hence, since I am sure you can publish elsewhere . . . I am returning your manuscript."

I have no appetite for public diagnosis of Fr. Davis' 'explanation' beyond admiring its strategy: an unintelligible position is, of course, always harder to come to grips with than an intelligible one. I write to remark on a problem of more general interest, namely: How do conservative Catholics and Liberal Catholics, at a certain level of

43

discourse, go about talking to each other? Should I have submitted my article in the first instance to *National Review?* That surely would have been improper. The discussion in question, at least my part in it, is distinctively Catholic at many points, and would thus have been an imposition on a majority of *National Review's* readers. To *The Wanderer* then, a sturdy champion of the Catholic Right? But what confirmed Liberal reads *The Wanderer?* There are several other small Catholic journals with a conservative orientation, but let us face it: because such journals are not normally geared to polemics and because, anyway, the reading habits of most Liberals are quite different from those of my conservative friends who regularly follow *America* and *Commonweal*, these publications are not able to sustain an inter-camp dialogue.

Under the circumstances, I think it appropriate to question the operating assumption of those Liberal journals— "The National Catholic Weekly Review" and a few others—that now constitute a clear oligarchy in the Catholic journal of opinion field. Are their obligations exhausted when they have finished hammering the nails into the coffins of their political opponents, and have prettily decorated the deed with an ad from the Sisters of Mercy? Or have they a residual responsibility: to their own professed belief in the dignity and utility of the discussion process? Are their exclusionist policies compatible with their commitment to catholicity?

Philip II [16th century King of Spain —Brent was in his Royalist phase] and I have tired of Liberal summonses to open-mindedness. After reading Fr. Davis' letter, we decided not to peddle our reply to Fr. Clarke: we would just drop it in the mail to our agents at 150 East 35th in case anyone was interested. We have our pride, and besides, the saving in stamps from not sending the thing around will give us a start toward a new journal of opinion we are founding and which we will have to call of course (for we would not want our purposes to be misunderstood) *La Inquisición*.

CB

June 15, 1962

Dear Brent [Bozell]:
An excellent reply to Davis. I only wish you had quoted *in extenso* from his letter. Would it be proper to use the entire correspondence in the book? Even if not, could you satisfy my sadistic urges by letting me see his letters? I'll return them promptly.

The Catholic journal of opinion is of course long overdue. It faces one problem in terms of audience: the division in Catholic conservative ranks between the sophisticated and the naive. The naive keep telling themselves that the Pope is really on their side, politically. I doubt that they have the maturity to entertain the notion of disagreeing with him on temporal issues.

Best,
Neil

∞

December 10, 1962

St. Anthony Messenger
1615 Republic Street
Cincinnati 10, Ohio

Editor:
To draw an analogy between the men who crucified Christ and political conservatives is not merely a travesty of history: it borders on blasphemous to interpret our Lord's Crucifixion in political terms ("An Apostolate of Right Thinking", December, 1962). It takes a special kind of arrogance to enroll the Savior of mankind as a Deserving Democrat.

No doubt Miss Tansey's two-dimensional view of world problems is not important in itself. But she reflects a spirit abroad in Catholic circles—the error of immanentism—that has victimized more sophisticated thinkers. It is one thing to "bring Christ into the marketplace," quite another to make him huckster for one's own political nostrum.

"Render unto Caesar . . ." Our Lord was content to leave the details of temporal affairs to our considered judgment. His kingdom lay elsewhere; and He wasn't speaking of the UN.

Neil McCaffrey

∞

February 25, 1963

Metropolitan Daily
614 East 14th Street
New York 9, New York

Editor:
Hearty thanks for bringing us Victor Lasky's hard-hitting column. I especially enjoyed today's article showing how JFK has manipulated

the Cuban crisis for his own political purposes. It's rare to find a columnist who speaks out as candidly. Can't we have Lasky more than one day a week?

Neil McCaffrey

ᬍ

April 12, 1963

Dear Bill:

I heard about the Editorial That Wasn't—and thank God it wasn't. At the least it would have seriously compromised you and the Magazine, at worst it would have been disastrous.

I read the encyclical [John XXIII, *Pacem in Terris*, promulgated April 11, 1963] with something like relief. I had been primed for the worst; and yesterday, before I had gone through it, Frank [Meyer] called to read (and misread) a dozen or so of the more outrageous passages. The old agitator left me quivering. It was thus a pleasant surprise to confront the document itself.

Don't misunderstand. It's a bad encyclical—unrealistic, utopian, flawed in most of its emphases, suffocated with abstractions. But it is these very abstractions that render it comparatively innocuous. Most of them are surrounded with qualifying phrases, and there are even a few good passages. It is not the document to send us all to the rack. I find it less objectionable than M and M [John XXIII's 1961 encyclical *Mater et Magistra*], because it is less specific, more objectionable only in that it deals maladroitly with more urgent issues.

Certainly, it is not worth mounting the barricades over. I'm inclined to think that if we pretty much ignore it it will soon sink without a trace: only if we inflate it will it be remembered beyond the week after next. I think the tactic of having Herberg and Frank write on it is sound. If Catholic Liberals indulge in extravagances, you can dispose of them easily enough.

It's a shame you can't make it on May 6th. I suggested May 9th, but that will be impossible for Frank. Since it's really his party, I think we should stick to the 6th. If Washington is demolished before then, do come.

You graciously asked me to let you know when we would be in Bermuda. The boat is due in on Monday morning, May 13th, and will leave on Wednesday night, May 15th. It would be great fun to meet someone congenial, but I beg of you, please be sure nobody puts himself out or feels obligated in any way. It is most kind of you to think of us.

This will reach you too late, but anyway, a very happy Easter to you and Pat.

Best,
Neil

P.S. I miss Pius XI. I even miss Alexander VI (*NOT for publication!*)

ⓒ

May 7, 1963

Dear Mike [Bernstein]:
You write the warmest and most heartening letters. And this one comes at a good time: no word from the Admiral [Lewis Strauss regarding becoming a sponsor of the Conservative Book Club], and things have exploded so at Macmillan that I've had to take on two jobs here and been forced to cancel our Bermuda trip.

I'm going to write to Roger Milliken [conservative industrialist] immediately—as you suggest, essentially the same letter as the one to the Admiral. And to say that I'd be grateful if you should take up the idea with B.G. [Barry Goldwater] would be understatement bordering on affectation.

Even on the commercial level, it is daily brought home to me how acute the need is. I see it with the Lasky book [*JFK: The Man and the Myth*]. People here expect it to sell well—but they haven't the dimmest idea of the book's real potential. And at the root of their relative coolness is nothing more sinister than simple Liberal provincialism. In a small way this points up the growing schism in our country.

I get the strong impression that the money boys have decided upon Romney [George], after Rocky's political suicide [Nelson Rockefeller's divorce]. Unless the grass-roots sentiment for B.G. is overpowering, it would seem to make our efforts for him quixotic; which is not to say that we shouldn't make them anyway. At the least, they should push Romney further to the right and perhaps get us a Tower for Vice President.

Conservatives I talk to seem almost unanimously hostile to Romney. He is another Wilkie, another Rocky, another Attila the Hun. While I would never be tempted to mistake him for an ideological virgin, I think he has saving qualities that may in the long run make him tolerable. I take his disavowal of the Party as an electioneering device; I recall him walking in all alone to address a caterwauling union meeting; I remember him grabbing the TV mic from one of Reuther's boys who was apparently hitting below the belt and giving it back to him with both barrels for twenty uninterrupted minutes; and John Chamberlain tells me that he learned his economics from a good man (whose name eludes me). Above all, he is his own man. I can't picture his knees shaking in the presence of Khrushchev.

Or am I grasping at straws? Do you hold out any hope for him?

We yearn for the fleshpots of Washington; but I hope something unexpected brings you up here before July.

Please say hello to Helen and Ted [Lit].

Best,
Neil

℃

May 15, 1963
MEMO TO: Bill Rusher and Cliff White
FROM: Neil McCaffrey

As I sit home and brood about The Campaign, I keep getting that old 1952 feeling. Our prospects *could* be bright—since we're in one of these situations where *nobody* can win. But we face one massive obstacle, endemic to conservatives.

The pros shrink from "extremes". You know the type: the one thing they don't need is problems. Nothing in their background equips them to tilt with windmills—or cope with *new* situations.

It therefore behooves us to begin the mating dance with the so-called "moderates" in the Party. The Nixon crowd, for example, is looking for someone, and Dick's price never comes high. Secretary of State would do it. The same tidbits would lure other hungry young middle-of-the-roaders like Gerald Ford, Morton [Senator Thruston Morton, Republican of KY.], Scott [Senator Hugh Scott, Republican of PA.] and such.

Let's not be stuffy about this. And let's not be weak in the stomach. And let's rise above vendettas. The prize is worth the game. If we don't do some prospecting in this region, our chances for the nomination, much less the election, are indeed forlorn. And anyway, we could not hope to staff a Goldwater administration solely with donors to *National Review*.

There is so little realism and professionalism among us professed realists, the conservatives. I appeal to two of the few I know.

℃

June 21, 1963
MEMO TO: Bill Buckley and Frank Meyer
FROM: Neil McCaffrey

When I called Msgr. Cohalan to deplore the astounding [papal] election, he told me that he had a few days before run into Fr. McNaspy of the *America* staff while waiting for a bus. (The Cathedral faculty and the *America* staff live within a block of one another, both near the corner of 108th Street and Riverside Drive.) They greeted and introduced each other. McNaspy recognized Flo's name from his review in *NR*. He marveled that Flo had "infiltrated" *NR* and had been able to hoodwink you—because the review had suggested that the British government and the wealthy landowners had done less than they should to combat the famine! Flo was amused, and I am amazed: these Liberals invest their straw men with flesh and blood.

I glean one crumb of comfort from the disaster in Rome. Montini is being heralded all around as a Liberal. Thus labeled, people may think of him as a partisan figure. This in turn will tend to lessen his influence.

He and Spellman have disliked each other for decades. The clash is more personal than political.

ᙍ

August 22, 1963

National Review
150 East 35th Street
New York 16, New York

Editor:
Run up the flag. Roll out the artillery. Fire all twenty-one guns, to salute Russell Kirk for his remarkably acute profile of Senator Goldwater. Show this article to most men of good instincts; assure them that Dr. Kirk has got it right; and they might just say: There is a man. There is a *President*.
Neil McCaffrey

ᙍ

And Rightly So

November 19, 1963

Voice of the People
New York Daily News

Editor:
With Jackie now being photographed so often with Jack—even at Mass, no less—you just know an election year is right around the corner.
Neil McCaffrey
Pelham Manor, New York

⍥

June 9, 1964

Dear Cliff [White]:
I have an idea that should take much of the curse off of inaccurate reporting of the Senator's remarks, perhaps even turn this to our advantage. The Senator should make it a point of prefacing his every speech—especially on TV—with something like this:

> "First, I'd like to ask you to pay particular attention to what I say here tonight. Then check your newspapers and your television tomorrow and see whether I am being quoted accurately. As you know, 80% of the Washington reporters are Democrats. Some of them are honest reporters, but many of them have been careless—or worse—with their facts. I think every American, regardless of Party, believes that each candidate should get a fair shake. We want to know what *each* candidate says, so we can make up our own minds. We don't want reporters trying to make up our minds for us. So I urge you to check your radio and television and newspaper tomorrow and see if they are reporting me fairly."

This tactic will have obvious advantages: 1) It makes Goldwater the wronged underdog, and so wins him sympathy. 2) It raises doubts in the listener's mind about the veracity of all the anti-Goldwater material he's read or heard. 3) It almost forces the media to play fair. It puts *them* on the defensive. 4) It is an attention getter and almost forces the listener to follow the Senator's words closely and sympathetically.

It's a marvelous tactic in its own right; and, looked at negatively, if the Senator doesn't use something like this *in advance*, they will continue to give him the business.
Best regards,
Neil

50

⊂⊃

November 20, 1964

Dear Dan [Mahoney]:
For future campaigns, why don't you work up a "Twenty Questions for the Candidates" ploy? Ask the hard questions that most candidates avoid. E.g., how do you stand on the right of a property owner to rent or sell to whomever he pleases? On neighborhood schools? On stiffening the penalties for crime? On cutting welfare expenditures? On prayer in the schools? On loyalty oaths?
This would smoke them out. If they refuse to answer or if they hedge, you gain. If they answer the wrong way, many a Republican or Democrat will discover he is really a conservative. If you make these questions more or less statewide, and focus on them, you could break through the curtain of silence the Liberals drape over the hard issues.
Best regards,
Neil

⊂⊃

February 23, 1965

Dear Willmoore [Kendall]:
I'm indebted to you for taking me into your confidence on these projects. To take them one at a time:
The Stephen [Tonsor] sounds fascinating. I don't know it. We'd like to take a look at it. I can order a copy through the secondhand book-sellers, but it might save time if you would be kind enough to lend us yours.
Assuming it to be within the ken of our members, I think you would do better publishing it with us as a hardbound book. You make far more money that way and get more review attention. There can always be a paperback later. Besides which, if it came out first in paperback we would be most unlikely to use it in the Club.
On the other hand, I think both Montesquieu books would be better published as paperback originals. There I think you might well stay with Henry [Regnery] or a line comparable to Gateway. People have lost the habit of buying classics or near classics in any but paperback editions; and besides, that is the only way now to get this sort of book used in the colleges.
I know you can cite collections here and there that have made

51

their way as books. So can I. But the general pattern is that they don't. While my mind isn't closed on the subject, I must own that a wall has grown up around it.

We have no plan to become a textbook house. You can go into that field with as much money as Harriman and all the expertise of McGraw-Hill and Prentice-Hall, and still take a bath. Not that we have either. It just happens that the market there has become the special preserve of a few publishers who have labored long in the vineyard and have learned how to keep the NEA smiling.

Your other two books sound like they should be brought out by a good university press.

Should I infer from your letter that your major efforts for the next several years will be directed toward the academy? If so, I can't quarrel with your decision, but personally I am a little sorry. It cuts you off from the intelligent non-professional, the market we exist to serve. You are one of the very few writers who can talk with equal authority and eloquence to both audiences. When you are pouring in your high hard one for the NR reader (who is also our reader), I can't think of anyone who can stand up to you.

Which brings me to my point. We have in mind a book to be called *How They Made Our Constitution*. It would not be simply a theoretical discussion of the issues, but also the little human dramas and personality clashes that got played out before, during, and after the Convention. It would be an unabashedly popular book that would make many serious points: history without tears. Would you be interested, now or in the foreseeable future? If you say yes, we'll do right by you. E.G., we'll pay you a decent advance. We'll do the kind of selling job we did on the enclosed book by Dr. Kubek. We'll commit ourselves to an *initial* advertising campaign of $10,000. What say?

Best regards,
Neil

ભ

June 7, 1965

The Daily Times
126 Elm Street
Mamaroneck
New York

Editor:
Latest landmark in Congressman Ogden Reid's mad rush to the Left is his bill to outlaw the non-Communist loyalty oath, which is still

administered to students getting federal funds for studies in science and education.

Mr. Reid apparently regards it as an imposition to ask these sensitive young men and women to swear loyalty to their country—though these same young people are not too sensitive to accept a government handout.

The effect of the Reid bill will be to encourage still more campus Leftists, peaceniks and beatniks to climb aboard the government gravy train and get themselves "educated"—with your tax dollars. If you object to paying taxes to support people who can't bring themselves to pledge allegiance to our country, remember that Congressman Reid comes up for re-election next year. Surely the Conservative Party will offer us a choice more congenial to patriots.

Sincerely,
Neil McCaffrey

ભ

July 19, 1965

Dear Bill:
We are meditating a project, but honestly aren't sure about it. I wonder if you would have any ideas.

The book might be called *Conservatives Speak Out*. It would consist of taped interviews with about a dozen leading conservatives who would cover the spectrum from Nixon to Rousselot and Courtney and Ayn Rand. Among the others whom we might interview are you, Burnham, Meyer, Kirk, Goldwater, Clif White, Bernstein, Leonard Read, Moley (if Nixon says no, as is likely), Bauman and Milione. We would ask tough questions, though our motive would not be to put anyone on the griddle. The tapes would not be edited except for grammatical errors or something egregious. We would give the person interviewed a general idea of our questions before we met with him.

The idea would be for conservatives to search their souls. What about the possibility of collaboration with Liberals on specific objectives? Can the hard right collaborate with the sane right? Is the conservative movement short of talent? Why? Are conservatives relatively unsophisticated? If so, what can be done to broaden them?

You get the idea. Would the book do more harm than good? Is our linen too dirty to air in public?

Best,
Neil

ભ

July 26, 1965

Dear Willmoore:
I've read half the Stephen [Tonsor] and must regretfully report it's not for us. I found it prolix, think it gives the State too much (it's 1965; Leviathan is here), and miss in it that precision of thought, and sense of the nice distinction that a writer must carry with him when he tries to navigate the rapids of liberty. Sure, he gives Mill a good going over, but not, I think, from a position that will be useful or meaningful to a conservative today. The sophisticated among us won't find enough in Stephen to justify the effort, and the unsophisticated will be asleep before page 9.

I'm sorry. We haven't had much luck so far in getting together on a project. But I've not lost hope.

Where shall I send the book?

Can we still hope to see you before you embark?

Best regards,
Neil

ﾂ

September 3, 1965
MEMO TO: Mike Bernstein, Bill Buckley, Vic Gold
FROM: Neil McCaffrey

The last session of the YAF Convention, just in case you haven't heard about it, will have repercussions. The new chairman, Tom Huston, devoted the bulk of his address to a specific attack on the Birchers, on two counts: a) they don't tell the truth, and b) they pick secondary issues to waste their energies on. He had about three-quarters of the audience with him; the other quarter sat in stunned or confused or angry silence. The only murmurs I heard came from a few tables when he dismissed the Liberty Amendment.

His attacks on the Liberals were less harsh. The last part of his address was given over to dismissing most of the conventional conservative arguments as ineffective with the electorate. Fair enough; but his alternative? The free economy is necessary to the free society. Over and out. Like air escaping from a paper bag.

I don't want to suggest that Huston is a menace. Far from it. He is a canny, likeable Hoosier. 110% politician. He will never get YAF into trouble. But neither will he save the West. I suspect his objective is more modest: a congressional seat from Indiana.

He is in every way an appropriate leader for YAF. They are a mannerly, likeable, respectable crowd, intelligent but hardly intellectual, and quite without style. They are the sons and daughters of the decent middle-class citizens who nominated Goldwater. They show every sign of growing political maturity and sophistication— *but maturity and sophistication within the presently acceptable limits of American politics.* I mean to say, they have learned the old lessons well but show no signs of the kind of creative and imaginative ideas that will lift us out of minority status. Not that they can be blamed for this: their elders are giving them no example.

I guess I am simply saying that they are predictable....Did anyone betray the smallest awareness that crime is the only issue we have that will stir the masses today? I saw no sign of it. To conventional polls, the issue is much too ticklish, too hot to handle. We have to show them how to handle it, how to avoid both racism and hypocrisy. (This is why Bill's campaign is so important.)

The funniest moment at the convention: Joan was talking to some kid from Iowa who asked her, earnestly, "Is it true that Bill Buckley used to be a card-carrying Communist?"

CB

September 15, 1965

Dear Willmoore:
I have just finished the lectures and, as was to be expected, I found them deft and provocative. Before you publish them, however (or at any rate, before we try to get in on the publishing), I'd like to register a few questions:

1. You have made what seems to me a solid case against the myth of American concern for individual rights before the Bill of Rights. But how far does this take us? The Bill of Rights has long since become part of the American myth. I don't think we can, you should pardon the expression, turn back the clock now. And I'm not sure we would want to; it's an ill wind that blows no good: what else protects beleaguered conservatives in this day and age against the omnicompetent State except the ritualistic, if you will, concern for the Bill of Rights. I get nervous when you leave me to the mercies of a "virtuous people" no longer very virtuous, and/or a Congress that now appears mostly in the role of a ratifying Reichstag.

2. Which brings up the second objection. We conservatives have been hammering away at the theme that Congress has declined. Burnham's book does it best. I would not like to support the opposing view.

3. I think you must grapple with the two objections above and make your alternatives much more specific if you want this read by the lay reader, the sort of reader who makes up most of our Club.

4. You must explain the special sense in which you use the word "myth" lest they think you are scoffing at Genesis.

5. Would it be useful to print the complete text of the four pre-declaration documents in an appendix?

I noticed what seems to me a slip. It is not at all odd that those Connecticut and Massachusetts Roundheads should have omitted any reference to the king in 1639 and 1641. By that time they looked on poor Charles I as anti-Christ.

Enjoy Paris.

Best,
Neil

ᘯ

September 27, 1965

Dear Willmoore:

I appreciate your candor, the more so because it brings home to me that we are talking at cross purposes. I decline the mantle of censor that you seem to be conferring on me. I am only a poor business man. It's no part of my role to tell people what to read; it is part of my role to try to guess what they will read. My best guess is that your recent writings are too tough for them, and also not what they want to hear. If I guess wrong, so much the worse for me; but that is how I read it.

The question of integrity and inclination plays a part, of course. This doesn't mean I have to put my private seal of approval on everything we publish. We could always bring out something with a here-it-is—we-don't necessarily agree attitude. And I can see us doing that, with a book that looks as if it can sell with that sort of treatment. I just don't think your recent writings answer that description. The alternative would be to oversell them to try to make them into something they are not—or, at least, something I don't think they are. Ethics apart, I think that bad business.

Remember, our people are tough. If they don't like what we offer, we hear about it. Now, I don't mind defending something I have said about a book if I mean it; but I get all flustered if I am asked to justify some advertising claims I don't believe in. You have chosen a lonely way, maybe the prophet's way. But having done so—please forgive me for being as frank with you as you were with me—I think you should go all the way. You can't really expect to offer unwelcome ideas in a tough style and also find popular acceptance. Can you have it both ways? Can anyone?

Best regards,
Neil

P. S. Let there be debate and dialogue. The place for it *par excellence*, especially at this time, is *National Review*.

September 29, 1965

Dear Bill:
I hate to say this, but it feels like last fall all over again. *Mutatis mutandis*, I am afraid you are making the same mistakes Barry made. You are talking the "in" language of the initiate. You are not getting specific. Above all, you are acting too detached.
Spell out what you mean by residency requirement. Give us word pictures. They can be at once compassionate and get people steamed up. You can make it clear that you want to take care of the really desperate, but you are not about to subsidize junkies, sluts who make a career out of childbearing, etc.
Take a few such issues—on which your opponents are so notoriously weak—and keep hammering at them: crime, welfare, the police review board.
I am not, believe me, suggesting that you change your style. At its best, your style is alive with imagery. But you are no different from anyone else: generalizations and abstractions take the life out of your style too.
On Barry Gray and on CBS, you were at your best when exposing the vapidities of the other two. But that is not quite enough; you must come across as caring, as someone who has sense-making alternatives.
You haven't done badly. It's just that you could be doing so much better.
Best,
Neil

December 14, 1965

Dear Garry [Wills]:
I think you erred in signing the Berrigan statement [Daniel Berrigan, S.J.]. Granted Spellman handled it wrong, is the issue clearer? Here is a priest counseling, on civil rights, what borders on lawbreaking and anarchy; on Vietnam, what borders on lawbreaking and treason—and maybe crosses the border on both?
A further consideration: we are at war.
Again: does a priest have the same freedom in these matters—an

Order priest at that, one vowed to obedience—as a layman? There is no easy answer.

Again, the conservatives are the stupid party. Spellman could have accomplished this and less heavy-handedly, and with greater effect.

Looked at from some distance, his sins of omission stand out sharply. What has he done to counter the Liberal *Zeitgeist*? To choose the right bishops and priests for diocesan schools and seminaries? To arrest the Liberal trend in his own diocesan paper?

Had he given better leadership, Berrigan's superiors would never have allowed such a situation to develop. Indeed, had he given better leadership, the Catholic community itself would have inhibited the rise, or at least the prominence of Berrigan types. Spellman need never have intervened, need never have lowered himself, could have given the example of a real conservative's liberality and a good shepherd's magnanimity.

But how do you make a vulgar little egotist into a gentleman?

Best,
Neil

&

December 1965

A letter from Garry Wills to Bill Buckly, with Neil copied

Dear Bill:

I have not talked to a single person who was not overwhelmed by your talk. [Secretary of State Dean] Rusk was denounced as a dirty fascist, but you are praised on all sides! You give me renewed hope for our peer campus.

Natalie says your bouquet is the most beautiful she has ever seen.

I enclose my book choices for Commonweal after reading NR's paragraph on Rex Stout. It looks almost as if I "cleared" my place with the magazine, so united is our front.

Speaking of united fronts: I wish we had been able at mere leisure to boil down our disagreements on the Berrigan statement. I think they could be considerably narrowed, if not removed. Let me at least try to state what they are (as I piece it together from the conversation), since I cannot imagine our standing very far apart on this if we understand each other. I have gone over the problem since I talked to you (there being, still, time to withdraw), and here is what occurs to me:

1. You objected to the term 'silencing' as too strong, in the face of the Jesuit refusal to admit anything and the statement's profession

that it is not using inside information. But, from the public accounts we know there was a) eleventh-hour withdrawal from commitments the Order would normally insist that they meet, and b) a statement from the three priests, when reached by phone, that they could not speak on the subject. These are the normal public signals of a silencing, and if the substance were not there behind these signs, the Order would go out of the way to reveal the disparity between appearance and reality. (Actually, there has been public confirmation from the Jesuit superior of Fr. Kilfeyle).

2. You insisted that the Order had the right and the subject the duty, to practice the command/obedience discipline for the good of the Church and the Order, and that good as conceived by the superior. Admittedly. Nothing in the statement questions this, it seems to me. The question is whether the community has the right to express disappointment with the wisdom of that decision, and claims upon members of a religious order who engage in public life. More on this later, since it is the key point. But at least I hope you will agree with me that the right obedience is not questioned.

3. You objected to the rhetoric as typically liberal— "great Vatican Council" and "conventional wisdom" are the phrases I think you drew especial attention to. I don't think either really carries a creed along with it, though I admit each carries an atmosphere. If a liberal must be entirely fumigated of his rhetorical atmosphere before one can join with him in a worthwhile protest, then this would damn the whole statement. But I find it hard to get that excited about a phrase or two—as I would think it unbalanced of a liberal to draw back from joining in a protest at, e.g., *America's* [the Jesuit magazine] treatment of you four years back because, in writing a statement of protest, someone on our side used one of the "signature phrases" of conservatism (e.g., "Communist sympathizer"). I think more liberals should, at that time, have expressed their horror (as Hoyt did) at the imposition of Catholic politics. I think we should express horror when the same thing happens to the liberal who protests on such a prudential matter as when and how to make war.

It seems to me that 1 and 3 are not very important. But 2 is. And here is where I wish I had been more reflective in getting at your mind on the matter while you were here: I don't understand your objection to the parallel I suggested, that a priest who is only a representative of his Order's line should not be treated more seriously than a Communist. You said, if I understand you, that a political group has no right to criticize a priest or his superiors if the priest is withdrawn at any time after making certain commitments. If, at the margin, a priest can be withdrawn without being subject to

59

any criticism of the decision to withdraw him, how are we to know if any position the priest takes is not taken solely to prevent that marginal crisis? In other words, he can be expected to act always out of a set of hidden motives—to prevent suppression, to stay in his Order's good graces, etc. Are we unable to criticize *these* moves made for the good of the Order?

Admittedly, everyone has private motives at work when he says anything in public—his status in his work, his political future, his family's good, etc. But we criticize his statement, not on the presumed grounds for reticence etc. deriving from his private life but on the merits of the public statement itself. You, for instance, do not refrain from criticizing *America* because it operates with a set of inhibitions derived from the religious responsibilities of the priests involved. If they advance an argument in public life, it should be treated on its own terms. Priests have no right to expect that they will be excepted from this procedure—unless, like Communists, they try to make us accept puppets as real agents in discussion.

Even if we agreed on what the preceding paragraphs touched— (and it is here that we disagree, I suppose)—there would be no reason to sign the Berrigan statement if you do not think the silencing tactic a profoundly stupid and self-crippling one. I do. I think it, more than anything else, has soured a whole generation of priests on the ecclesiastical conservatives and made them patsies for anything liberal. If it can be done to Murray, it can be done to anyone—and it does not particularly matter who the victim is in this one case; the whole tactic should be discredited. I wish conservatives would make it clear that they have as much reason to want the tactic defeated as anyone; after all, there is no doubt you would have been silenced long ago if you had been under a religious superior's jurisdiction.
—*Garry [Wills]*

൦ൠ

January 5, 1966

The Editor
The New York Herald Tribune
230 West 41st Street
New York, New York

Dear Sir:
Your long obituary on Marguerite Higgins was properly admiring, but I notice that you omitted any mention of her new book, *Our Vietnam Nightmare*. To be sure, this book is less than enthusiastic about

the performances of many of your newspaper's political heroes. Even so, the book is in its third printing in less than two months, and is the February selection of the Conservative Book Club. For that matter, when an American correspondent calls for victory in Vietnam, surely that is news.

Sincerely,
Neil McCaffrey

ભ

January 11, 1966

To The Editors
National Catholic Reporter
P.O. Box 281
Kansas City, Missouri 64141

The "peacefulness" of the demonstrations by the National Liberation Front in South Vietnam has been disposed of by the late Marguerite Higgins, who went there ten times and tells all about them in a book Miss Ann Thureson will surely avoid, *Our Vietnam Nightmare.*

But what is more interesting about Miss Thureson's letter is her casual use of my straightforward language. I asked, of course, when you last read of a peaceful demonstration in *Hanoi*, not Vietnam: a distinction Miss Thureson was careful to overlook. On such flights from accuracy are the peaceniks carried away. Or is misquoting a canon of the new higher morality?

Neil McCaffrey, President
Conservative Book Club
New Rochelle, New York

ભ

April 18, 1966

The Editor
Newsweek
444 Madison Avenue
New York, New York 10022

Your enthusiasm for the growing "cooperation" between big businesses and big Lyndon is understandable. As Liberals, you would logically applaud centralization. But don't pretend it's new. The same sort of "cooperation" was achieved back in the Thirties—in Germany.
Neil McCaffrey

And Rightly So

CB

April 19, 1966
MEMO TO: Bill Buckley, Bill Rusher, Jim McFadden
FROM: Neil McCaffrey

NR, I hope we are all agreed, has been floundering. May we have an agonizing reappraisal?

1. The conservative movement is quiescent. This is at once a cause and an effect of *NR's* quiescence. Into the vacuum pour the Birchers on the one hand, the tired conservatives who now want to play ball with the Nixons and the Romneys—on *their* terms—on the other. The abdication of Clif White's team, and the disgraceful performance of the ACU, are sufficient testimony to *NR's* failure on the political level.

2. *NR* has no business on the political level? Let's not kid ourselves. *NR* performed superbly on the political level from 1960 through 1964. *NR* is and should be many things; but if it is not first and foremost a political magazine, we have to expect a decline in circulation, not growth. Our market is first and last political. *NR* wants to give its readers more than mere politics. But to do so, it must give them plenty of politics first.

3. As Jim pointed out at our last promotion luncheon, *NR* is no longer sore at anyone. It is therefore losing its main thrust. We have always reached new plateaus on wings of indignation. But lately the magazine has been suffering from creeping moderation—this at a time when indignation was never more appropriate. The history of *NR* has proved that it is possible to be indignant yet responsible. It is also good business.

4. I can't help thinking that part of this has been, willy-nilly, the result of Bill's column. When the column started to circulate widely, Bill properly aimed it at the uncommitted and softened his tone. But the columns came to be used in the magazine, and a subtle change of direction is making itself felt.

5. What with the campaign and the book and the trial, *NR* has suffered from absentee editorship. Lord, but it shows.

6. The front of the book is diffuse, aimless and arch. Above all, arch. Humor is fine. Nothing is so embarrassing as humor that shows itself straining, humor that doesn't make it. And cuteness for its own sake went out with Shirley Temple.

7. The magazine's stance on Vietnam has been entirely too judicious. It's all very well to give Lyndon points where he deserves them, but for balance you should go after him even harder for temporiz-

ing. For the first time, the indecision and malaise of the Republican leaders seem to be affecting NR as well.
8. The back of the book gets ever duller.
9. The decision to attack the Birchers should not have been taken without at the same time making vigorous new attacks on the Liberals. Unless the magazine does both, it risks its leadership position in the conservative movement. Or rather, it threatens to become a leader without followers.
10. We need campaigns, special issues, planned articles, *crusades*. Are we suffering from middle-age fatigue?
The larger strategy, I know, is to replace the conservatives of yesteryear with a new breed. Nothing wrong with that—if you can. But you need excitement. And can you ever replace their drive and dedication? Isn't it better to reclaim them?

ෆ

December 6, 1966

To the Editor
Time Magazine
Time and Life Building
Rockefeller Center
New York, New York 10020

Sir:
Time describes Rockefeller as "a big upset winner." He polled 45%. Would *Time* describe 51% as unanimous?
Time goes on to write of Nellie's efforts "to erase the aura of narrow exclusivity that [the G.O.P.] acquired during Barry Goldwater's 1964 campaign." Yet *The New York Times*—but not *Time*— quotes Rockefeller as excluding Goldwater conservatism from the Republican Party.
Neil McCaffrey

ෆ

December 14, 1966
MEMO TO: Bill Buckley, Bill Rusher, Jim McFadden
FROM: Neil McCaffrey

It is a tough assignment to forswear mentioning candidates and yet to come up with a question that potential subscribers would feel compelled to answer. How does this strike you? The prospective subscriber would be asked to check the statement he most agrees with:

☐ I expect to vote for any Presidential candidate the Republican party is likely to nominate in 1968, on the theory that any Republican will be better than anyone the Democrats are likely to name.

☐ I will vote for the Republican candidate in 1968 only if he is conservative.

☐ I will vote for the Republican candidate in 1968 if he is a conservative or at least a middle-of-the-roader, but not if he is a Liberal.

☐ If the Republicans nominate a Liberal in 1968, I will vote for a third-party candidate or write in a conservative candidate.

☐ If the Republicans nominate a Liberal in 1968, I will vote for Johnson.

☐ If the Republicans nominate a Liberal in 1968, I will not vote for a Presidential candidate.

I'm not sure that this poll will work. Certainly, it won't work as well as a poll of potential candidates.

You have mentioned that our Club poll has interesting questions (a copy is attached). But you will notice that two of the questions mentioned possible candidates, and another question asks the member to name his favorite conservative. There's no beating names. From a promotional standpoint, doing a poll without naming names is like giving a course on nutrition without mentioning food.

ᑕᔆ

January 17, 1967

Dear Marvin [Liebman]:
The 50th Anniversary of the Glorious Soviet Revolution is next November—the 7th, I think. They are already starting to exploit the great event in *Pravda*. Gene Lyons is writing a book to assess the fifty dreadful years and hopes to have it published on or about November 7th.

When Gene told me about this, it immediately occurred to me that you might want to run a rally in the Garden that week. November 7th would not be the right day: it is Election Day. But some day that week.

Would it be good public relations for *National Review* to sponsor the Rally? Or is it better if one of your *ad hoc* committees did it? In case the former appeals to WFB and WAR, I am sending them a copy of this letter.

And who knows, you might maximize the impact and make some money if you put the whole affair on videotape and then cut it back to one hour and packaged it as a TV special, or a film you could sell to conservative groups. I doubt that anyone gets rich from this sort of TV special, but you might come out with something. Tom Miller (who, as you have no doubt heard, has just felt the Richardson-Gidwitz axe) could probably give you a good idea of your prospects in that area.

Anyway, this is an election off-year, and we should have something to bring out the troops.

Best regards,
Neil

ɔ

July 26, 1967

Dear Bill:

I think you missed by a mile on the Moynihan column. Though professedly an attempt to rise above ideology, you finally came down on the Liberal side with the threadbare old lament that if only we'd done enough . . .The problem goes far deeper. It gets down into the dark regions best explored by Nietzsche; and it's time responsible conservatives got over being afraid of the dark.

A few thoughts on the crisis.

1. When all the cops in the city are on riot duty, don't the other crooks have fun?

2. Likewise our national troops (whom we will be using more and more). With the armed services spread paper-thin now, we might well have to pull some back from Vietnam. And God help us if another crisis erupts in another country.

3. Johnson played politics by stressing the failure of Romney to keep order. A case of the bathtub calling the sink white.

4. Mike Bernstein made an interesting observation a couple of years ago. Speculating on who would be the political beneficiary of the inevitable backlash, he suggested it might well be somebody with an unexceptional "civil rights" record, who finally got fed up. Fino? Well, somebody like that.

5. The Birchers will make hay out of this, most especially because NR, at least until now, has provided them their vacuum.

6. But the Birchers aren't the main worry. In this national convulsion, we could wind up with someone who will make

65

George Wallace look like the moderate he probably really is. Dust off your historical sense. The people who gave Hitler his plurality were not most of them Nazis. They were scared and angry citizens looking for a lifeline. Yet whatever Germany's problems in the early Thirties, they were trifling beside the nihilistic frenzies we are witnessing now. When everything you take for granted in life is threatened, including life itself, you reach for anything. It *can* happen here.

7. Never has it been more amply demonstrated that the Establishment sets the terms of a discussion. Let's quit playing by their rules. All men are *not* created equal, in most senses. Order comes ahead of opportunity, indeed is the condition of opportunity. There may well be genetic differences between races and even between ethnic groups. American Negroes are better off than most white men in the world. Harlem, as George Schuyler points out in *Black and Conservative*, is less crowded now than when it was occupied by whites. And so forth. Conservative insights are not only useful but humane; bottle them up, and when they finally do burst forth, they may look ugly.

Best,
Neil

ℭ

December 14, 1967

Mr. Neil McCaffrey
Arlington House
81 Centre Avenue
New Rochelle, N.Y. 10801

Dear Neil:

I have delayed thanking you for that splendid $200, which meant so much to us, because I wanted to give the rest of the office a chance to ponder the letter that accompanied it. The letter, and not only because it comes from you, means even more to us.

My own reaction is generally shared here. We do not rejoice in the departures *Triumph* is making from conventional conservatism in its critique of the social order, for we too are patriots and hold the usual prejudices in favor of the fatherland. But our calling is to assert Christianity, not Americanism; and the two, especially regarding bottom questions, are not always compatible. For instance, one of the newer members of our staff, a Protestant, commented on your letter this way:

"Re Mr. McCaffrey's question: 'Must the defense of orthodoxy involve alienation from American values?'

"My answer to this question is, 'Unfortunately, yes.' If there are 'American values' that are at variance with immutable spiritual and moral principles, they are spurious. The Declaration of Independence states that governments 'derive their just powers from the consent of the governed.' Holy Scripture states, 'The Powers that be are ordained of God.' *One* of these statements is true, not both'."

To call this "Spanish Catholicism" is, I think, to take a parochial view of the Faith as you accuse us of.

There are also practical considerations involved in *Triumph* 's approach. We think that the collapse of the American Church is very closely connected with its historical attempt to be more American than Catholic; its present course does not involve a rejection of American values, but precisely an attempt to make peace with the values that have and do govern the country. We think it follows that the defense of the Church requires the distilling of the religious faith from the national faith.

Is *Triumph* competent to take this on? No. But we must try, with the kind of mixture of caution and boldness that takes account of our limitations. To whom do we look for guidance? Well, to all sorts of people, including yourself, and including also the spokesmen for what you call "pre-1960 English Catholicism." The latter means pretty much Newman, Chesterton, Belloc and Waugh; and I judge *Triumph* to be pretty close to that group, which was even less pro-American than pro-English.

We have made, will make, many mistakes. And they will be more serious than my regrettable vulgarism at St. Paul. (It is *not* always wise to allow off-the-cuff remarks to be taped.) But stay with us, and help us to grow wise. Please. And again so many thanks for the contribution.
Cordially,
Brent

ᴄʒ

December 19, 1967

Dear Brent:
Thanks so much for your nice letter.
I hope you will pass this on to your new staffer with a quick

lecture about the difference between proximate and remote causes. The notions of sovereignty advanced in Scripture and the Declaration of Independence are not mutually exclusive.

Of course, the American Church is coming apart because it is whoring after American Liberalism. Why this means we should desert *traditional* American values—the conservative values—eludes me. You are giving away much too much. You are saying that Liberalism *is* Americanism.

Don't surrender your country so easily.

My very best to you and Trish and the family for Christmas and the new year.

Best,
Neil

○ʒ

February 19, 1968

Triumph
927 15th Street N.W.
Washington, D.C. 20005

Editor:
No conservative will dispute Mr. Bozell's argument that constitutional government is running into heavy weather. But we may legitimately question whether it is time to inter the Constitution because it has been spectacularly flouted for a generation. The funeral may be premature. Mr. Bozell may be succumbing to the same "mindless historicism" he scores in his article.

Mr. Bozell reminds us that governments may not exceed the authority they derive ultimately from God. Just so. Neither may individuals. But individuals, like governments, do. What follows?

Not, I suggest, the theocracy Mr. Bozell teases us with. God gives us the privilege of freedom: perhaps Mr. Bozell would rather I said "condemns us to freedom." God declines to force us to be good (an oxymoron Mr. Bozell might not acknowledge as such). We get our clue from Scripture: the infidelities of God's people in the Old Testament, the betrayals by His friends in the New. We reenact these betrayals each time we sin. God foresees them all, and allows them. Since He allows them, I wonder how Archbishop Lefebvre or Mr. Bozell hope to improve on His plan.

Our Founding Fathers were too sensible, too modest, too straightforward to pretend they had a direct line to and from the Almighty. They realized that the only One who could claim direct communica-

tion died two thousand years ago, leaving us to muddle through our mundane affairs. We have to keep reminding the Liberals, but Mr. Bozell needs reminding too: His kingdom is not of this world.
Neil McCaffrey

ᦆ

May 13, 1968

Dear Bill:
Naturally, you went after [Leander] Perez. And naturally, the old fool deserved it. Here and there, you flashed the old wit. But more than once, you showed all the suavity of my 14-year-old. In contrast to the reverence you assume toward a [Floyd] McKissick.

Mike Bernstein used to describe this sort of thing as the ADA sneer. Now we have a variation, the Wills sneer. It came across at its sneeriest when Perez mentioned the whites who had been driven out of the Washington schools. You pretended to be incredulous. (Applause from over there where Garry and Murray [Kempton] and Norman [Podhoretz] are sitting.)

But you know better. Once you sympathized with white parents who want their kids to come home with a little learning, not with razor slashes. These white parents who rushed to get their children into Chevy Chase High School (the poor man's Portsmouth Priory) are not so different from the bigots who gave you 341,000 votes, and a couple of million dollars over the past decade. This is the first time I've ever known you to lose touch with your admirers, and show contempt for their concerns. Resign yourself: you'll never be the Senator from SNCC.

A few more of these programs, and you'll be getting raves from Jack Gould. But if your father were here, I bet he'd give you hell.
Best,
Neil

ᦆ

October 2, 1968

Dear Bill:
The intellectual Left, never mind their marriage of convenience with labor, have always despised and feared the workingman-in-the-flesh; unconsciously, to be sure. Why shouldn't they? The workingman believes in God, in his country, in morality; he harbors the conventional (rather than the fashionable) prejudices; and he keeps control of his bowels if he happens to confront the President of Yale. He is

prey, in short, to all the simple superstitions that Murray Kempton's friends have shed.

Now that these workingmen have begun to discover deeper values than the wages-and-hours law, they are turning from their mentors, breaking ranks, voting wrong. What a liberation for Murray and his friends! Now they can give themselves over to their hatreds.

And find a forum in *National Review*.

What in *hell* is happening to you? Did you *mean* to affront conservatives? Or have you so lost touch that it never crossed your mind?

And if you really feel more kinship (as distinct from friendship) with Murray than with, say, a Birmingham cab driver, then I can only borrow a piece of advice you used to give yourself and say: go and lie down for awhile. Or make a retreat.

There was once a carpenter who called the Murray Kemptons of the day a brood of vipers.

Best,

Neil

ങ

October 4, 1968
MEMO TO: Bill Buckley, Priscilla Buckley, Jim Burnham,
                      Terry Catchpole, Arlene Croche, Bob Kephart,
                      Frank Meyer, Bill Rickenbacker, Bill Rusher,
                      Allan Ryskind, Tom Winter
FROM: Neil McCaffrey

I hope you caught the debut of Curtis LeMay. Accurate but impolitic, and looking as uncomfortable as Drew Pearson taking a lie detector test, Curt said that he saw no difference between nuclear weapons and any other weapons, then hurried on to say that he saw no need for using nuclear weapons in Vietnam.

Whereupon Nixon and Humphrey promptly went before the microphones to denounce General LeMay's plan to escalate the war in Vietnam with nuclear weapons. As someone is sure to observe, there wasn't a dime's worth of difference in what they said.

As fellow members of the Council Against Demagogues (Southern), a distinguished group in spite of the unfortunate acronym, I'm sure you will spring to your typewriters and View With Alarm this base attempt of the two major candidates to court not the white or black vote but rather the yellow vote; this reviving of the bogey that could finally disarm us.

The big question now is, will Nixon or Humphrey be the first to attack the LeMay plan for defoliation? It would be useful to have an early warning, so we have time to formulate the Right Position.

ᥴᴈ

October 12, 1968

Dear Bill [Rusher]:
Thanks for giving me an advance look at your Miami piece. What a pity it could not have appeared right after the Convention, when it would have seemed more convincing. As it is, by the time it appears Nixon will have won his landslide, the Establishment will have hailed it as a victory for 'moderation', Nixon will sense that if he behaves even Herblock may do a new rendering of him, several [William] Scranton types will be appointed to key jobs, and we'll think it's 1953 all over again. Strom Thurmond will be invited to the Inaugural Ball, and be seated with the musicians.

I think your article erred not so much in what it said (although when you describe [Everett] Dirksen as an "incontestable conservative" I begin to think you fell asleep in 1954) as for what it, perforce, left unsaid. The fact is that *National Review* and *Human Events*, by favoring Nixon at the expense of Reagan, created a vacuum on the Right for which we may be paying for the rest of our lives. Nature and [George] Wallace abhor a vacuum. Then, with a club-footedness that must be unique in the history of modern conservatism, NR and HE went on to misplay an infield bobble into a four-run error. (Wallace picks his teeth; didn't Joe McCarthy used to belch? Bill Buckley says he would rather be governed by the first thousand names in the Manhattan phone book, and we all applaud the sally; Wallace says the Birmingham cab drivers have more common sense than the Harvard faculty, and he is a demagogue. Wallace the demon welfarist increased old-age pensions in Alabama; is Nixon going to abolish Social Security?) The nadir—so far, anyway—came when NR sought to make common cause with that old responsible, Hubert Humphrey, against the menace of Wallace. Even the Republican high command had sense enough to veto that one. Whereupon NR withdrew, careful not to outflank the Republicans on the Left.

The disarray of the conservative respectables in the face of the Wallace surge would make an interesting psychological study. May I speculate? It is not merely a hankering after respectability, though I don't under-estimate the force of that yearning. I think guilt, in the pristine Freudian sense, plays a big role. Here is a man who takes conservative issues and conservative concerns, scorns euphemisms, and goes right for the gut. Could it be that he is saying what

71

most conservatives think, but not saying it prettily enough? So we construct our elaborate rationalizations about proto-fascism and welfarism; but some of us know better, don't we?

What troubles me most deeply about this split in conservative ranks is the superciliousness with which the respectables view the Wallace followers and their genuine concerns; the shabby arguments; the dishonest and dangerous rhetoric. John Smith, insurance salesman, knows he is no fascist; he knows that he responds to Wallace for reasons that have nothing to do with fascism; but by God, if you call him fascist often enough, you may just turn him into one.

Somehow I think you are not immune to some of the points I raise here. If only you could evangelize some of your colleagues.

Best,
Neil

C3

October 18, 1968

Dear Bill [Buckley]:
Thanks for your note. Of course, I don't object that you publish Murray [Kempton]. I object when you publish him on *that* subject; worse, when you dignify his piece by calling it a guest editorial. It strikes me as a case of using any stick to beat Wallace with.

The Left intellectuals have always pretended to be the allies of the workingman. Under it all, they have always feared him because his view of life clashed sharply with theirs. Their alliance was purely adventitious, and anyone with a scintilla of political judgment could have foreseen, no later than five years ago, that the racial question, and all that it brings in its train, had to shatter the old Roosevelt coalition. For a variety of reasons, none of them admirable, conservative spokesmen have neglected the opportunity here, and thus created the vacuum Wallace is filling. What price respectability?

And so to my *real* point. The cab drivers and the insurance salesmen may not make the best company. They are nowhere near as interesting as Murray. They are unsophisticated, unrefined, imprecise in their formulations, terribly flawed human beings.

And they are the backbone of our country. They are, beside Murray and his friends, the salt of the earth when we get down to essentials. They work hard, try to do right by their families, generally leave their neighbors alone, want to be left alone, fumble their ways towards God.

In the crunch—even before the crunch—I am with them. Up

until recently I would have taken it for granted that you would be too. After all, you used to say you would be. But now I'm not so sure. Especially after Murray's editorial.

Best,
Neil

 C3

October 29, 1968

Dear Bill:
Yes, I inspect myself more or less regularly. What I see—which is not to say I see everything there is to see—neither elates nor shatters me. My present mood is one of unease at what seems to be tactical (though perhaps not strategic) errors made by many conservatives in the current campaign.

I don't think I have become a witch hunter; it just isn't my style. I don't even think I would ascribe tactical differences to flabbiness. I would simply put them down to just that, tactical differences; in the case of Murray's guest editorial, a serious difference.

But you have put me on warning: I am about to go on your list of cranks (if I haven't made it already). I respect the warning, and your feelings. I promise—seriously but not sulkily—not to make a nuisance of myself.

Having made that promise, may I just add one footnote? Not to prolong the thing about Murray, but I really think you have misread me. I was objecting to his views on this matter; objecting to them appearing as a guest editorial in NR; objecting so strongly that I worry lest it be a sign of a new coalition with Liberal intellectuals over against the hard Right. That I would take to be not treason but a disastrous mistake. And it would desolate me.

I have had one deep ideological difference this year, with Garry, and one not so deep, with you. I am not aware of any others. Sure, I disagree here and there with lots of people, always have and always had. But I don't see any of these differences as of major importance, and I hope nobody else does; certainly not important enough to have me read out of the club, or to even think about trying to read anyone else out. On the contrary, my error in this matter will usually be on the side of ecumenism.

Best,
Neil

C3

73

November 4, 1969

Dear Bill:
On your proposal to send only volunteers up to the front lines, have you considered that this would have the effect of decimating the best of American youth? And that it would give a much too easy out to the selfish, the cowards, the traitors? A volunteer army made good sense in 1929, made little sense in 1959, makes no sense in 1969, with a war on.

The fantasies of [John Stuart] Mill and, yes, Rousseau may seem harmless when the libertarians are just building castles in Irvington-on-Hudson. When they are made the basis of public policy they become dangerous; and move from dangerous to pernicious when our institutions are under attack. The state is not a social club, something you join or stay out of as you please. The state is *necessary*. As such, it has *rights*. In time of crisis, you might as well recommend that taxes be made voluntary.
Best,
Neil

ය

November 6, 1969

The Honorable Richard M. Nixon
The White House
Washington, D. C. 20500

Dear Mr. President:
I applaud your speech on Vietnam, and I think you made a neat point by alluding to the silent majority. This majority, or some part of it, tends to be shaken when bombarded from the Left. These people need to be fortified. and reminded regularly that their instincts are right. And only their President can remind them. So I hope you will reiterate the message of firmness regularly, and even get specific about the Leftist agitators.
Kindest regards,
Neil McCaffrey

ය

November 11, 1969

Dear Neil:
Re yours of November 4th:

1. As a matter of fact, the general fear is the contrary. It is assumed that the regular Army, which would then do the front line fighting, would consist largely of unemployed, therefore would have a heavy percentage of Negroes. There is nothing much that can be done about that, but it would not have the effect you predict. And in any case, it is not realistic to talk about decimating any part of the population at the rate of about ten thousand casualties per year.
2. Freedom itself gives special opportunities to the selfish, the cowardly, and the treasonable.
3. We had something not all that far removed from a volunteer army even during the Civil War when it was possible for $300 to purchase an exemption.
4. I do not deny that the state has the right to call on all young people to engage in a war. But I defend the notion that where a total national effort is unnecessary, a total national effort should not be made. I remind you that the peace was kept in England during the nineteenth century by a volunteer army. And remind you further that even today, and even during the Second World War, many forms of hazardous combat duty were done by volunteers.

As ever,
Bill

ca

November 14, 1969

Hon. Spiro T. Agnew
The Vice President of the United States
United States Senate
Washington, D. C. 20510

Dear Mr. Vice President:
I think your Des Moines address on the television media will rank as the most important domestic political speech of our era. You have articulated the outraged feelings of the Silent Majority.

You were right not to ask for censorship. Characteristically, the presidents of the three networks, in accusing you of that, only reinforced the very points you were making. Theirs was the reaction of knee-jerk liberals whose hands have been caught in the cookie jar.

Since the networks apparently have not accepted your suggestion to correct voluntarily their bias, I believe the next step must be legislation to extend the fairness doctrine. I think this should take the form of requiring that television news announcers and commentators and news writers be divided equally among conservatives and liberals. If the networks prove unwilling to hire on this basis, some mechanism could be set up to assure it. I think this would appeal to all fair-minded Americans.

My hunch is that this law would seldom if ever have to be invoked. The networks, stubborn though they are, are likely to get the message. And if the existing management fails to get the message, these are publicly held corporations. I am confident that the stockholders would not want to jeopardize the valuable licenses these networks hold and would therefore replace the present managements with men who are more sympathetic to the American tradition of fair play.

Although this is only the morning after your address appeared on television, I have already spoken to thirteen people who are nothing less than enthusiastic about it. It is no exaggeration to say that you have given us all a new lease on life—after twenty years of all but constant bias and abuse at the hands of this little band of liberals. But this is nothing to the abuse that you are going to be subject to because of your courage. I hope you will be sustained in the conviction that you have the prayers and good wishes of tens of millions of us.

Yours respectfully,
Neil McCaffrey

CC: Mr. Leonard Goldenson, ABC
       Mr. Julian Goodman, NBC
       Mr. John W. Kluge, Metromedia
       Dr. Frank Stanton, CBS

ᔆ

December 8, 1969

Voice of the People
New York Daily News

Editor:
The Catholic bishops of New York, in their letter on poverty, are as innocent about the feelings of their own people as they are about poverty. We do not condemn the poor; we condemn the undeserving poor. St. Paul, in a book the bishops are supposed to know something about, said the last word on the subject: "this we commanded you, that if any would not work, neither should he eat." (II Thessalonians 3:10).
Neil McCaffrey

Politics and Economics

☙

March 9, 1970

Dear Dr. Zoll[1]:

May I unburden myself of a few thoughts after reading the third round of your exchange with Frank Meyer? Over against Frank, I think you are well ahead on points. But I think your own position suffers from the same lack of concreteness that afflicts Frank's. I think you are both talking about roughly the same sort of livable society; and alas, I am afraid the chances for recovering it are slim.

You and Frank are both bending over backwards to avoid the suspicion that you are in league with the radical right, that you are advocating repression. Fair enough. Part of the game is semantics, and we should avoid giving the Left any semantical advantages. At the same time, I think you and Frank run the risk of giving half the game away. With all due regard for choosing our words carefully, what we all aim for is a society where the law is respected and enforced, and where its violation is punished. Since neither 19th century Liberalism nor Tory conservatism anticipates a society in permanent revolution, a society with a permanent class dedicated to overthrowing all the rules, somebody has got to get tough. If I am correct that neither Frank's instrument nor yours is adequate to cope with the present crisis, and since any anarchical situation will presumably provoke some sort of reaction in the direction of suppression, the only question will be how to structure the new system. I believe Frank would suggest, at least privately, maintaining the old forms but having the rulers act tough. I'm not exactly sure how you would make your plan concrete and I hope you will pursue this in future writing.

Parenthetically, I am puzzled indeed over what reservations you might have on Washington. And I was surprised to read that you had anything good to say about Bismarck. Nor do I think we get very far by comparing Washington and Metternich. It is like comparing apples and onions. Washington would be unthinkable in the context of 19th century Central Europe, but no more so than Metternich in the context of early America. Each was fine for his role.

Possibly this controversy you are embarked on will provoke some longer writing, and if you think it might ever issue in a book, we would be keenly interested in considering it for publication. But

1   Dr. Donald Atwell Zoll, Chairman, Department of Philosophy & Classics, University of Saskatchewan, Regina Campus, Saskatchewan

77

meanwhile, I hope you and Frank keep it going. The American right is intellectually constipated on this whole issue, but you and Frank have at least made a beginning in coming to grips with the great problem of our time.
Kindest regards,
Neil McCaffrey

అ

July 21, 1970

Dear Brent:
Thanks for the invitation to comment on your 'Confessional' article. You seem to be following out the logic of positions you have taken before, so I doubt that my comments will have much new to offer.

I can go with you part of the way. The American system as we have known it may be nearing bankruptcy, and certainly the old politics is dead. But I don't think this means we give it one last kick before consigning it to the scrap heap. Much can still be saved, if we can find leaders who understand that we are in a new ballgame and are willing to break out of the politics-as-usual mold. Most Americans, conservatives included, still think you can amp down a revolution with editorials. They don't know much about human nature, and they know less about history.

But I'm afraid I would make the same criticism about your position. I think you and your band are sublimating a private alienation. I take it as a given that most Americans are redeemable, and that they want to save as much as they can of a decent way of life. They are not going to follow you into the wilderness, and I don't think they should. You fasten too much on the evidences of collapse (real enough) in our society without balancing these against our still considerable moral resources. Half-truth is the father of heresy.

I also go part of the way with you on what is wrong in the Church. Everyone from the Pope on down has lost his nerve, his confidence, his zeal. The old moxie is gone. But the answer is to recover the spirit, not to proclaim ourselves outcasts or to play at being martyrs. Martyrdom is not for us children, and courting it has always been accounted rash. When the Catholics in Elizabethan England were really under the gun, they did everything possible *not* to antagonize a state that was not merely indifferent or hostile to some Christian values but actually out to *kill* Catholics. I think everyone in your band ought to read Waugh's biography of Campion or Chambers' life of More, then count his blessings.

You even look wistfully at the Church behind the Iron Curtain.

You will have no trouble getting volunteers to trade places with you.
Best,
Neil

P.S. I am enclosing a contribution for *Triumph*—not, heaven knows, because I buy its approach; but at least you aren't one of the bland and the lukewarm, whom the Lord will vomit from His mouth.

ය

ON THE RIGHT
by William F. Buckley, Jr.

FOR RELEASE SAT. OR SUN., JULY 25-26, 1970,
OR THEREAFTER

MRS. GALLETTI'S PROBLEM

Consider, if you will, this letter: "Dear Mr. Buckley: For some time many things have bothered me. The constant chipping away of our American rights. But today the straw broke my camel's back.

"1. The Supreme Court decided we don't have to defend our country.

"2. A friend, with heavy heart, told me today that his 16-year-old daughter is a mainliner, is in the hospital with hepatitis, caused by a dirty needle and has given birth to an illegitimate baby which has been given out for adoption.

"3. Sunday evening, June 14, at 7 PM, two young brothers, sons of an acquaintance, aged 15 and 17, left their home to play baseball. . . (In) Jackson Heights, a 15-year-old boy started a fight with the other 15-year-old. He put his baseball bat down to have a fair fight. One of the onlookers picked up the bat and threw it to the arguer, who started to use it. The 17-year-old brother went to defend his brother, but was . . . beaten with the baseball bat. The 15-year-old is in the hospital in fair condition. His older brother underwent brain surgery and is not expected to survive.

"All I know is, things are getting too close—before I just read about it—now it's at my front door. What can I do to stop all this nonsense? Maybe I can be the person, like Mrs. Murray, and put prayer back in the schools? What I'm trying to say is—I could be a guinea pig? Sincerely, Mary Galletti."

In Times Square, on the same day I received this letter, a young man immolated himself at midday. The passersby—and indeed the journalists—seemed strangely uncurious; as if, in this vale of tears, one never needed to ask what is the proximate cause for taking one's life. It is as if the miracle were that so few people take their lives.

I have always tended to be impatient with the professionally gloomy, and continue to cherish the advice I was given years ago by a European intellectual, to wit that in this day, in this age, one can only be objectively pessimistic, and subjectively optimistic. Things do look bad, viewed objectively; but, viewed subjectively, we do snatch our little pleasures, and are constantly being surprised by joy.

Mrs. Galletti, and millions more like her, including I guess myself, are desperately in need, I think, of evidence that something can be done. About what? It doesn't, really, matter: evidence that something can be done about *anything*. The Vietnam War is in the special sense a great villain: because it occupies the mind like a birth mark. The drug problem is a problem concerning which nobody, not one living soul, has suggested a program the results of which would guarantee a diminution of the curse, which is literally engulfing us. Anybody who has traveled the waters of Long Island Sound this summer knows that the pollution we have all read about as belonging to Lake Erie say, or the lower Hudson, is finally here: sailing across the Sound is like canoeing down the Paris sewer. One hundred million words after the reformers ousted Carmine deSapio in New York City and, in the words of Murray Kempton, promised daffodils in the street, the garbage, the refuse, the dirt, thickens.

No one can direct Mrs. Galletti to a paradise where innocent children are free of the terror of a baseball club wantonly used, or even of a society in which a young girl cannot become addicted to drugs, let alone can we suggest means of saving the Supreme Court. But I do believe that her morale, and others', would greatly improve if something—anything—were accomplished. Something everybody could see, or experience: something that would restore the sense that we can direct our destiny.

I would suggest, for New York City: traffic control. Why? Because it is so easily do-able, by a careful orchestration of toll charges at the gates of the city. Accomplish that, and great social energies would arise. For the nation, a crisp, one-sentence executive order from the White House: Henceforward, no American will be sent into combat duty in Vietnam, except volunteers.

Those two: one the trivial accomplishment of a minor bureaucracy, the other an imperial—a gallant, even—dispensation by the Commander-in-Chief, would restore the national morale. And that, Mrs. Galletti and I believe, is what we need right now. Urgently.

ॐ

July 27, 1970

Dear Bill:

I doubt that Mrs. Galletti, and her millions of friends, will take comfort from your column. It is, ah, off the point. What troubles Mrs. Galletti (I know her well, because I know myself) is that no one speaks up for Christian morality. Startling thought: you are the only major columnist who is a practicing Christian; nor is there more than a handful among the minor columnists. Which imposes on you a glorious burden, and opportunity. It could make you unfashionable—and bring you wild new popularity. And sustain Mrs. Galletti.

Granted, it is now gauche to invoke Christianity. Is there a better measure of our decline? Brent is not so wrong in his diagnosis as in his cure (see enclosed) [July 21st letter to Brent].

So let's be unfashionable. Back when Catholics and Protestants thought nothing was more important than doing away with each other (at that time, by the way, they were right, except for killing Turks, at which I'm proud to say we were better than the Protestants), they both responded as one to the Anabaptist threat, as befitted God-centered people who understood that the antinomians made religion and indeed civilization impossible.

The ACLU, had the 16th century enjoyed their presence, would have leapt to the defense of the Anabaptists. So the Christians would have put them to the sword too. Properly.

I know—times change, and all that. But I stick to my point. Toleration is dishonored in the abuse. One of the beliefs on which I have moral certitude is that God is not impressed with the arguments of Earl Warren, and means us to be unimpressed with them.

Which brings me to my other point. Could the American system have survived this awful century had we enjoyed different leadership? It makes an interesting academic discussion. What is clear now is that it hasn't survived. The Liberals put too great a strain on it.

It now behooves thoughtful men to face the realities, so that they can lead the salvage operation. Brent's answer might be right for a few holy men and scholars, tomorrow's Benedictines. The libertarians have hold of some useful insights, and would only be dangerous if there was any chance that the world would take them as seriously as they take themselves (since if you follow them relentlessly on out in today's crumbling world, it would be tantamount to putting an alcoholic to work as a bartender).

The real danger is the unimaginative, conventional people—conservatives are preeminent here—who think you can tame a lion with a flyswatter. They aren't wrong to *want* to. It's only human to prefer the familiar—who doesn't?—especially when the familiar has been kind to us. But God is not mocked, human nature takes its revenge, and now we must pay for letting things slide. The interest compounds every day.

Ultimately, we are in a crisis of belief, so we must reassert the old truths. But not apologetically; not defensively.

Proximately, and as B follows A, we are in a crisis of authority, so we must reassert the rights of authority. Dramatically. Drastically.

And so, as we wave goodbye to the world of Richard Nixon, tears dim our eyes. It was grand while it lasted, and he might have been as wonderful a President as Cal Coolidge, if only he'd been with us between 1923 and 1929.

Wallace? I sometimes think he worries you more than Bobby Seale. But anyway, relax. First, because he's just an American politician, however sweaty he looks to us effete Easterners. More important for your peace of mind, the day George becomes a plausible candidate, it won't be George, but someone much hairier; and then we'll have other things on our minds, like survival.

Which gives us a clue. Americans want someone who looks familiar. The man on horseback will have to switch to a Dodge. Augustus was careful to retain the forms of the republic.

But how do you get from here to there? It should look like— and should be—a transition, not an exotic growth. I think a few issues, important substantively as well as symbolically, can become the demarche. E. g. (in no special order):

1. *Crime*. To advocate a crime, verbally or in writing, should be the legal equivalent of committing it.

2. *School prayer*. Revive it. Make every pol stand up and be counted.

3. *Pornography*. Local option. Recommended for serious communities: mandatory death penalty for, say, the third offense.

4. *Busing*. Only by local option, and then only with parents' consent. (Good Christian doctrine, good natural law, good sociology, good education, good American law, if you believe the Civil Rights Act.)

5. *Drugs*. For anyone selling or giving a hard drug to anyone, mandatory death penalty. For anyone possessing a hard drug, a year in a labor camp (where, piquantly, everyone could be put to work on anti-pollution projects).

6. *Welfare*. State and local option. Immediate phase-out of all federal programs at the rate of 10% a year. From the $6 billion saved each year, give half back to taxpayers as mandated personal and

corporate tax cuts; use the other half for beefing up the defense budget, or for cutting the national debt, or for both.

7. *Integration.* Try freedom. Anything less is foredoomed—and a monstrous invasion of personal rights.

8. *Television.* National "Media Watch" Committee demands rough equality between conservatives and liberals on network news staffs. Alternative: boycott sponsors.

9. *Education.* Where to begin? For openers:

a) End all federal aid to education. (Exceptions: ROTC, research contracts, aid to vets, and such.)

b) Tax deductions for all expenses for higher education.

c) No tax exemptions for any school that refuses to administer a loyalty oath to all administrators and faculty. Ditto for any school that retains a non-juring teacher.

10. Subversion. New Anti-Subversive Act updates criteria, mandates investigation of all government, academic and media personnel. Schools and media to be denied licenses if they keep subversives on staff. Congress to be sole judge and last court of appeal on what and who are subversive.

11. Violence. Stiff penalties for attacking any government employee, fed or local, cop or fireman or even bureaucrat. For second offense, death. Volumes could be written on each of these eleven, as for example on the appellate jurisdiction of the courts; which ones of the eleven are likely to be productive; why these radical-sounding programs are, in the context of crisis, really counsels of moderation; why some of them in fact merely restore the practices of a more peaceful day; why all of them follow, more or less directly, from a serious commitment to one's religion and country; and the tactical value of the counteroffensive and the quantum jump. But you get the idea. Peace—and, incidentally, freedom—would begin to return. People would understand that America meant to survive. You could leave the front door open. You would no longer have to pay people for corrupting your children. And the next time you hear from Mrs. Galletti would be a nice card at Christmas.

Best,

Neil

P.S. I hope you won't reject this new vocation just because the idea for it comes from a prosaic source.

⬥

And Rightly So

Dear Brent:
Sure, feel free to run my letter.

The trouble with such letters—to you, to Bill, to anyone—on Large Questions is that they have to be elliptical. My premise with you is that we shouldn't turn away while the barbarians sack the city. My premise with Bill is that the barbarians *are* sacking the city, so it is late for speeches in the Forum.

I never expected much from politics, since I'm not a utopian, and man's important business is elsewhere. But I once thought that our political system could raise up enough barriers across the road. Like most people, I did not anticipate such a rout in the Church, and so fast; nor was I expecting a wholesale, total attack on our culture and institutions. Nor, finally, did I expect such a feeble response from conservatives. Beside the conservative leadership, the men of Weimar loom as giants.

So you begin to wonder whether we aren't whistling in the whirlwind. Sure, you can make a case, as Frank does, that the system has the resources to throw back the attackers. You can make a neat theoretical case. But nothing happens. Everyone prefers to keep talking in the context of 1962.

Hence my letter to Bill. Among other things, it was an effort to break us out of the politics-as-usual mold, to get us thinking creatively in a political context (even though I acknowledge this is only a partial answer), to suggest that we have more serious things to argue about than monopoly unionism.

But if my letter to Bill concentrated mostly on points of departure in the political order (after all, he is a political commentator), I was suggesting that they might be approached in a larger social and cultural and above all religious context. That's where the game is now.

But I hope Bill and others move beyond politics. I don't want him to move over to theocracy or anti-politics. Aha, you say, my *Christian* society! Well, not exactly.

I take it that there are three kinds of society: anti-Christian, non-Christian but tolerable, and a society presided over by people who are more or less Christian, who more or less bow to Christian principles. (Note that I didn't say a Christian society. I don't think such exists, or can. Man is a pilgrim.) America was once a blend of the second and third. Through most of our lives, it has been a mix of all three, but with the second dominating. Lately the first has gained the initiative, at the expense of the third and even the second.

The trick is to recapture the initiative. If the people in Group Three can do so, at this point they would pull along grateful members of Group Two. We have the muscle. What we lack is the leadership. History is not made by inchoate sentiments, or by little people. Though we can't command grace, at least we can smooth its path, at least we can watch and wait, work and pray. What we mustn't do is try to get off cheap. Getting off cheap is pretending that Nixon is all. Getting off cheap is also retreating to the wilderness.

I guess what I am saying is that there has to be a middle ground between the Republican Party and the reign of the saints.

Human institutions, like the Constitution, are to be cherished while they still show twitches of life. But they are all finally *instruments*, in the Ignatian sense. The temptation of the earthbound is to deify human institutions and creatures. The temptation of the enthusiast is to leave this vale of tears before the Lord has called him away. I'm in favor of using any instruments that serve, and ruthlessly discarding those that don't. I think our conservative leaders are hiding behind instruments that are being used against us. I think you are scorning instruments that still have their uses, out of a distaste for the human condition and for secondary causes.

I keep asking you: haven't you ever read Knox's *Enthusiasm*? Won't you?

Best,
Neil

P. S. I just read your lecture to the fundraisers of Thomas Aquinas College, and I confess that the last few paragraphs staggered me. I was not prepared to find you seeking salvation from the exotic East. Mother India is a cesspool of zombies. Surely the West can still do better.

ᘓ

January 6, 1971

Editor
Newsweek Magazine
444 Madison Avenue
New York, N.Y. 10022

Dear Sir:
In "What The V.P. Should Learn," Walter Lippmann engages in what he has so often denounced—deliberate quotation out of context. He writes, "The Vice President in his campaigning said . . . that the men

85

he opposed were outside the American community, were exiles, were rotten apples . . . ."

That is distortion. During the recent campaign the Vice President at no time spoke of his political opponents in such terms. He did, however, urge the moral and social ostracism of bomb throwers who commit criminal acts and deserve to be separated from society, i.e., jailed.

The Vice President repeatedly pointed out that the men he opposed in political combat were honorable and patriotic. Indeed, the record shows that many of these political opponents themselves joined the Vice President in denouncing those engaged in violence.

It is unfair and divisive for anyone to equate the terrorists whom the Vice President denounced with all "the men he opposed" in the campaign. The Vice President made this important distinction. Mr. Lippmann should be equally careful.

Sincerely,
Neil McCaffrey

ෆ

February 23, 1971

Dear Mike [Michael Lawrence]:

Your fund appeal makes me search my soul. On secular matters, *Triumph* is against America (which I notice it is beginning to spell Amerika) and against capitalism. It is against our whole system, and rejoices with every revolutionary blow against it. It is therefore against *me*; and I have no intention of fulfilling Lenin's prediction about capitalists financing their own overthrow.

Triumph has left the conservative movement. If it had only left to do the Lord's work, only the earthbound could complain. When *Triumph* announced its departure, most of us assumed that it would be a fellow traveler occupied on a more important assignment, our Father's business. Not many would have guessed that *Triumph* would wind up anticonservative, losing no opportunity to beat conservatives over the head. If it had merely contented itself with criticizing conservatives where we need it, it could provide a priceless service that nobody else is offering right now. But *Triumph* is bitter and unbalanced about conservatives, and refuses to acknowledge anything good there because it refuses to see anything good in "Amerika".

All right, you say, we disagree on secular matters. But what about the faith? That comes first, doesn't it?

It does. But I'm sorry to say that your alienation has worked itself even into the main artery. I don't see that you are much interested in the crises that face the Church today, and I think I know why. For you to become interested in preserving the old values would be tantamount to endorsing The System. Most Catholics like the way the Church was and the way America was. Not *Triumph*. At one time *Triumph* was doing good work on the liturgy. No more. It gives little attention to violence (except for muted applause), pornography, catechetics, the condition of the clergy and the schools and the seminaries and the religious life, not even much about the breakdown of morals—because then you would be forced to make common cause with all these contemptible middle-class Catholics and other Americans.

Sure, a lot of what you are saying is true. But Eliot was right: the worst treason is to be right for the wrong reasons. You criticize merely to vent your own resentments and to destroy. It makes all the difference whether you criticize from within a family or from outside, to bring it down. People who take up religion must beware of a subtle, terrible temptation, to use it as an instrument for private ends.

Even on abortion, I can't argue away my suspicion of your grand strategical motives. You are too quick to condemn a whole society and a whole system because of one heinous crime. And I would be more impressed with your concern over the sanctity of the person if you would occasionally condemn the attacks on them that take place on the streets where you live. But if criminals will bring down America you'll put up with them, won't you?

This letter makes me sadder than it makes you. Lord knows we need surgery on the system; but to cure, not kill.

Kindest regards,
Neil

☙

September 20, 1971
MEMO TO: Manhattan Twelve
FROM: Neil McCaffrey

To follow up Jeff Bell's excellent idea, a few proposals for our shopping list:

1. Increase the budget for military hardware by $20 billion.

2. Reduce the budget for health, education, welfare, and similar boondoggles by a corresponding $20 billion.

3. Begin the campaign for a constitutional amendment to outlaw involuntary school busing. No busing without the consent of the parents.

4. Double the budget for the FBI, the federal court system, the

87

federal prison system.

5. Outlaw the paroles in the federal prison system for the next five years.

6. Disbar for five years any lawyer guilty of contempt of court in the federal court system. Disbar for life any lawyer convicted of advocating any criminal act.

7. Upon conviction for a second offense for any federal felony, mandatory life imprisonment.

8. Make it a federal offense, with mandatory death penalty, for the murder of any policeman, fireman, prison official or public official.

9. Balance the budget.

10. End wage and price controls.

 C3

October 22, 1971
MEMO TO: Bill Buckley, Stan Evans, Allan Ryskind
CC: Other Manhattan Twelve Members
FROM: Neil McCaffrey

I agree with Bill that the rearmament plank is uniquely important. It so transcends the others as to differ in kind, not just degree. If Nixon gives us *real* rearmament but nothing else, I think we would be foolhardy not to support him.

But there were two domestic issues that showed up on one of the lists but were treated as minor: the "child protection" veto and the busing amendment. These are of a different order of importance from the other domestic issues.

The "child protection" bill and involuntary busing are both totalitarian—and I am not using the word in its rhetorical sense. Both invade the fundamental right of parents to arrange for the education of their children. There is no essential difference between them and the educational practice of the Nazis. Indeed, if you read the chapter on education in Grunberger's excellent new book, *The Social History of the Third Reich*, it may strike you as it struck me that our educational system has already gone farther than the Nazis had dared to go.

All of you know, in a general way, that educators today are the cutting edge of revolution, consciously setting about to overthrow in their charges the values that the parents have tried to implant. But if you had kids in the public or parochial school systems, the outrages would be brought home to you more vividly. Busing and the "child protection" bill are nails in the coffin: the educators showing the mailed fist, with more than a little help from their friends in the government.

For a change, we have two issues here that won't burden the President. He can only gain by coming out more firmly against busing (which he will have to do in any case). The public sees mostly the secondary consequences of this outrage: their children terrorized, their children torn from their own neighborhood, their children learning little in school. Whatever the reason, busing is desperately unpopular. It should be our business to suggest that Nixon will not be able to get by this time with a few speeches. Three years have revealed his hypocrisy.

Although his veto of the "child protection" bill would yield no big political dividends, neither would it do him any harm (except among fanatics who won't vote for him anyway). If we don't treat attacks on the family as uniquely grave, of a different order from ordinary political and economic issues, then I have to go back and read again what Brent Bozell said about the value system of conservatives.

December 1, 1971
MEMO TO: The Manhattan Twelve
FROM: Neil McCaffrey

As I mentioned at yesterday's meeting, I don't want to sign any activist manifestoes because I think it creates bad will for CBC and Arlington House. I think the focus for a book club or a publisher should be on its books, not on its principles. So I think it would be prudent if I dropped out of the group and out of further deliberations. If anybody notices (which I doubt), the official reason can be press of business.

I voted against the various primary and third-party alternatives yesterday on [Baltasar] Gracian's principle that it's best not to show your wounded finger. I think our nuancy little candidate, whoever he might be, will quarry in that mine of voters who are desperately seeking a middle position between St. Peter and St. Paul. On second thought, however, it might not be a bad idea if we get mussed up a little. It just could lead to that soul-searching now so long overdue.

One *sine qua non* of a good soul-searching, as the spiritual writers tell us, is the willingness to change. If we ever get to the point of agonizing, I hope we will put these two questions on the agenda: a) did the conservative movement get in Nixon the President it deserved, and b) should it really be our first priority to reestablish limited constitutional government in Sodom and Gomorrah?

89

And Rightly So

January 7, 1972

Dear Bill [Marshner]:

I found your contribution to the [Jim] Fitzpatrick controversy provocative, the only one not wholly swallowed up in the whirlpool of enthusiasm. (I exempt the Brewster piece, which I found unreadable.) Your first point is too facile to be taken seriously. There is of course a sense in which *Triumph* is not anti-American; and a sense in which it is. No point in going over that old issue again. But Fitzpatrick does give a good quick reading of Augustine, and it is *Triumph's* failure to grapple with his ideas on earthly society that tempts it into alienation, which is only a curse or two away from anti-Americanism. The trick for the Christian, of course, is to combine detachment and realism with concern. I'll let you know when I find the formula.

Your third point is right on target.

I rejoice in your observations on the two World Wars. But you let our country off too easily. Apart from the War of 1812, the issues of which I have always found obscure, I think we have fought only two just wars in our history, Korea and Vietnam. And we lacked the moral courage to see either of them through.

I find your reference to 'Countervalue' obscure.

Your remarks about the conservative movement are often acute. I hope you write more about this. The conservative movement is indeed pretty much of a bust, but I think it is wrong to take an either/or attitude. It was never realistic to believe that the movement could transform America. Its roots—spiritual, intellectual, historical, popular—don't go deep enough. But it does serve a rearguard purpose, and out of it may, though I doubt it, come something more serious.

You are on shaky ground when you accuse the movement of not being concrete enough. It takes concrete stands every week. Far more concrete, I need hardly add, than you or *Triumph*. What could be more abstract than "the social doctrine of Christ"?

The social doctrine of Christ can be summed up in two of His observations: a) My kingdom is not of this world, and b) Render unto Caesar...The best gloss on this remains Augustine, and Fitzpatrick summarizes his position fairly.

Everything else is mythology. The "social doctrine of the Church" is a dangerous misuse of language. It debases the coinage of doctrine, because Catholic doctrine says nothing about the social order. And Catholic practice, Catholic history, reinforce this indifference. The Church is interested in camping ground; her home is not here. The objective of the Church in the temporal order is to breathe, to work for not the good society but the tolerable society:

My kingdom is not of this world.

What is passed off as the social doctrine of Christ is a hodge-podge of utopian political schemes and economic nonsense. Being a fastidious thinker, you are sure to come to realize this when you think on it.

The last two paragraphs of your piece are unworthy of what went before. It is as much a travesty to make Dupanloup the father of modern American society as to make Antonelli the progenitor of Hitler. Please—some rigor. By the way, you mean Pius IX, not Leo XIII, don't you?

Incidentally, earlier in your article you are unfair when you suggest that the conservative movement has embraced abortion. Most conservatives oppose it. The fact that NR ran the Luce article is really a symptom of how little they empathize with their own rank and file, much less with the apolitical millions. At that, NR ran the definitive article on Paul VI (an act of presumption that left *Triumph* sputtering).

So I don't think the movement has failed in not being concrete. It has failed for want of vision. Ideologues more than humanists, much less Christians, most conservatives have absolutized the American system. It is their substitute for religion. No realist, no Christian, thinks that any *system* works. People make it work—more or less. Conservatives have programmed themselves to make a series of responses that no longer respond. Conservatives are not equipped to deal with proto-apocalyptic situations. All they have is a Constitution, and it's getting cold out there.

What American conservatives lack is a religious sense, more specifically a Biblical sense, most specifically an Old Testament sense. If ever a nation were under a judgment of God, in the Old Testament sense (as far as human eyes can discern), this one is. But lest I sound perfervid—lest I sound like a *Triumph* staffer—I hasten to balance off that remark by saying that the answer is not (for most of us) the wilderness, but survival. The issue is survival because a Christian humanist knows that civilization is itself good, though only a partial good, and worth saving. But a Christian humanist, who is perforce a realist, knows the odds against survival and is too sophisticated to put his faith in the shibboleths of a more innocent age, which shibboleths conservatives cling to.

I don't pretend to know whence the judgment will come (from Russia, or from the cancer within), nor much of anything, except that God is not mocked. I also know that God may stay His hand if he finds ten just men in Sodom. (Isn't it interesting that He was ready to save even Sodom? *Triumph* might ponder this, before dumping that jewel of creation, Western civilization.) So I consider the business of survival at once a work of Christian prudence, a protection against enthusiasm, an effort to give the Church and our civilization breathing space—and a sign of life.

Because the surest sign to me that we are under God's judgment is our sclerotic response not only to offenses against Him, but even against ourselves. *Triumph* has had little to say about the cancer within us (not that conservatives have had much to contribute either). Old and young bar their doors three times over when night falls; hippie barbarians spit in the faces of their betters; God is profaned in His temples; educators and churchmen give their lives to undermining parents and the family; the most intimate human acts (and the most bestial) are paraded before young and old by constitutional warrant; drug takers are now encouraged, now 'treated', now 'understood', but never punished; every organ in society where authority should reign practices the averted gaze—and *Triumph* chuckles quietly. And conservatives discuss the Republican Party.

At least *Triumph* isn't afraid to be different. What a shame its compassion is aborted at the threshold of the womb.

Kindest regards,
Neil

cs

July 17, 1972

Dear Bill [Rusher]:

Thanks for your letter. After my memo to the board, Stan [Evans] wrote me a letter covering much the same points that Larry set forth in his memo. Since their position doesn't begin to satisfy my objections, nor in some cases even wrestle with them, I resigned from the board. Nothing personal, as I explained to Stan. I quit because I don't want to be associated with an operation like that, because I'm weary of the struggle, and because it isn't good for the board to have a member who is 180 degrees opposed to the path it is charting. As Stan himself put it, neatly, the arrangement is Faustian.

As to the political situation, heads they win, tails we lose. It now appears that the dogs are to be denied even a crumb from the table in the form of a protest vote for Wallace; though from his point of view, he is smart to stay within his party. He may be the one to pick up the pieces. A Wallace-Agnew race in 1976 is not impossible. But then there will be a radical third-party candidate who may sneak in, Lindsay fashion.

Of course, I buy your views on Nixon. (You may recall that we

92

shared the same view over many a lunch in the late 50s.) It is the measure of our plight that we may need McGovern in the White House to shake us up. We need shaking. As it is, Nixon will win big because Americans want to pretend that he stands for the old values, that the system hasn't broken down, etc. Anything to keep from having to look down into the pit.

Ironically, it is Nixon who benefits from a mood of inchoate conservatism—or, more precisely, a mood of reaction.

I once thought that the so-called conservative so-called movement would be able to buy us time, maybe even start up the juices of regeneration. But I'm afraid we've run through our Christian capital faster than anyone could have predicted. So it seems that God means to strip us of our paper ramparts: conservatism, our constitutional system, even the Church. We are left naked; and not for the first time in human history.

Conservatives, of course, will be the last to know. They are still acting out the [Frank] Meyer Charade (which, thank God, he gave up on, only just in time). Even if conservatives prefer to stop short of religious revival, someone should whisper to them that the center is no longer holding. We no longer are getting any nourishment from the husk of ideological myth. Conservatives had better rediscover old-fashioned morality. A dash of righteous indignation might be unmannerly, might blow our respectability cover; but it has a warrant from on high. While America goes public with sins that cry to heaven for vengeance, NR celebrates the debut of the closet queens of Morningside Heights. I say it's rightwing Liberalism, and I say the hell with it.

If the forces of the West are ever to rally, the battle will not be fought over the right-to-work laws. And if conservatives are ever to get off the sidelines, they will have to learn something about passion, and compassion; and something about pragmatism. They will have to find somebody who not only makes the trains run on time but who catches, and punishes, the barbarians who stand beside the tracks and throw rocks through the train window.

But beyond that, we need a new Ignatius. However, I'll settle for Jeremiah. But not Jefferson.

Best,
Neil

☙

And Rightly So

April 9, 1975

Dear Vic [Victor Gold]:
The April 7th issue of *Publisher's Weekly* lists your book among Morrow's key books for the month of June. The column on our Shirl was one of the best you have done in ages. Keep *swinging*. Try to get mad at least once a week. You write better, and the reading is more exciting.

I have two thoughts on the Vietnam disaster. 1) When a nation declines to protect its women and children from violence and even murder, should anyone be surprised when it runs out on its allies? 2) We import orphans to silence our liberal consciences, to do something—*anything*—to distract ourselves from the betrayal, and above all to look busy, and thus imitate a great power.

Best,
Neil

ભ

April 23, 1975

Dear Vic [Gold]:
The America First line is seductive; I was once seduced myself. It is a mix of good sense, self-interest and rationalizing. I believe power enjoins responsibility. When God gives you power, He means you to use it well. How have we used ours? By turning over better than half the world to predators. I don't pretend to a private line to Heaven, but my hunch is that the judgment in store for us is enough to make brave men shudder. It was somehow fitting that Jerry [Ford] should be golfing while our friends were busy getting slaughtered. Symbols count.

A man has an obligation, implied if not explicit, to defend the old ladies on the block from the neighborhood mugger. He has a weightier obligation if he has promised, over the years, to defend them. If in defending them, he assures them that they don't have to lock their doors, or does other foolish things, this doesn't acquit him of the obligation of defending them. The fact that he has been doing it badly doesn't mean he no longer has to do it at all.

It's part of the liberal syndrome to do this sort of thing badly. The liberals have made a career of denying responsibility all around. Is it any wonder that they haven't expected our allies to behave responsibly? They shrink from the very concept. After all, once you open that door . . .

There is something to be said for not defending people who

don't want to defend themselves. That doesn't apply to Greeks, Israelis, Vietnamese, and many others.

Incidentally, if we won't defend them, what makes you think we will defend ourselves? Wasn't there a man who once said something about twenty years of treason? Who'll raise it to forty? (No doubt somebody will, soon. It is so much easier to cry treason than to grapple with the more complicated, more degraded vice called liberalism.)

I think you would soon write yourself out of most papers if you came on like Pegler five days a week. But one day? One day every two weeks? I disagree here with some diffidence, because I'm not in the business. But I can't believe a column dies when the sparks fly. Your editors may *think* they know what they want. But I believe success in any enterprise consists in finding something the consumer likes or needs. And only rarely do you wait until he tells you he likes it or needs it. You have to tell him.

Best,
Neil

ဃ

Society's Future: 'A *Liberal* Zoo'
By Neil McCaffrey
December 3, 1976
[Op-ed article for *The New York Times*]

NEW ROCHELLE, N. Y.—We all know about the liberals and crime. But as far as I can tell, nobody has projected the trends of the 60's and 70's off into the fearful future. Let's take a deep breath and try it.

First of all, it is obvious that under a liberal society with a liberal legal system, crime must rise, and keep rising. So, at some point, the inexorable arithmetic dictates that the criminals will outnumber the law-abiding. But, as I have actually read from some liberals, only a small percentage of the population have been crime victims, so quit worrying.

The only trouble with this thinking is that it's heartless and wrong. Other factors come into play, and they assure that the rise in crime will be not arithmetic but geometric. Even the dumbest of the punks now understand that crime pays. The system is on their side. The police also understand this; increasingly, they are coming to realize that *they* are the minority, *they* are isolated. Should we be surprised if they decline to play martyr for a populace too besotted with self-indulgence to care, or too numbed by fear to back them up? Cops aren't fools.

Even more ominous, in the late lamented elections, did you

notice that crime became the Great Unmentionable? This means that the liberal "solutions" are now seen to be bankrupt; but since a liberal society tolerates only liberal solutions, no alternatives could be offered. An unsentimental, serious approach to public order and safety (never forget: this is the first duty of government) is impossible in a liberal society. Anyone proposing it is called racist, reactionary, fascist; and our politicians don't care to stand up to that sort of abuse.

The result is that we have a tacit agreement that society is to become a zoo, with the animals in charge; but a *liberal* zoo. Better to have 80-year old women raped and mutilated than risk offending the American Civil Liberties Union and *The New York Times*.

Not that I mean to put *all* the blame on the Establishment. Our fellow citizens must come in for their share too. Crime tends to finish about fourth or fifth when pollsters ask about current problems. Which I interpret to mean that most people don't care unless they had a murder on their block last week. Or, alternatively, it means that they have given up caring, knowing that the system guarantees more killings, beatings, rapes, thefts.

If the former is the correct reading; if our fellow citizens are indeed so insensate that they are unmoved when elderly men and women are brutalized in their own homes by beasts, then we already have a peek at the World of Tomorrow—the world the liberals have bequeathed to us.

If, on the other hand, the public is indifferent to crime because it has given up hope, then we have a *different* reason for concluding that the liberal system is bankrupt. If, after all, a government cannot assure the safety of its citizens, and if the citizens recognize this, then the very basis for that government's legitimacy has collapsed.

The logic of our crime projection, we repeat, is that one day the beasts must outnumber the decent people. Then, according to the logic of liberalism, crime won't be crime. Majority rules—doesn't it?

But of course, it won't happen that way. We will be spared the nightmare of seeing liberal democracy carried to its logical conclusion. Instead, something else will intervene: the "Clockwork Orange" society, where the sadists reign unchecked. Am I saying, then, that things are hopeless? Not exactly. Things are never hopeless, and nobody who cherishes the Western tradition can hold that man's fate is simply determined. What I am saying is that things look hopeless as long as America lives by liberalism. And the liberal cancer runs deep. Does America have the internal resources to stand up to major surgery? Can it still cut out this cancer? *That* is the question. The only question.

ભ

August 5, 1977

Dear Murray [Rothbard]:
I guess our letters crossed in the mail. I'm indebted to you for that clipping on KMPX. I only get fragmentary reports about the station. Never having heard it, I don't know what they are doing wrong, if anything. Maybe my million-dollar idea is only worth $12.38. But I'm not ready to admit that yet. They may not be programming or promoting imaginatively, or they may not have the right deejays. Or again, the music may just be beyond the capacity of native Americans.

I infer from your letter that you are planning to settle out there. I think you have made the right decision. I may do the same. Although I luv people, all people, all the peoples of the world, I have never been able to handle relationships.

I am only sorry that you and Joey missed our Festival of Looting. It occurred mainly on Festival Day, July 14th. We discovered that our deprived masses were suffering from Desperation. It was a unique sort of Desperation; it surfaced 12 minutes after the lights went out. And it was accentuated when some of the looters discovered that they had captured suits that were not their size. This led naturally to a series of bombings, last Wednesday. They were meant to demonstrate for Puerto Rican Independence, the one radical cause I have always cherished. In fact, I have a program: Puerto Rican Independence next Wednesday; Puerto Rican Repatriation next Thursday; war on Puerto Rico next Friday.

Meanwhile, we are in the midst of something called our mayoralty campaign. This is a ritual popularity contest held every four years. It is meant to test the sexual prowess of male candidates and the charms of females. Accordingly, Bella Abzug is the favorite. She has been quiet since the looting, since she understands pre-revolutionary situations. Somebody is said to have asked her recently how she managed to stay married so long to one man. "Good sex," she is supposed to have replied. The story is clearly apocryphal, and I can't think how the press can be so irresponsible as to report this sort of thing.

The last winner of this popularity contest was a little man named Abe Beame. He won because we are becoming a city of old-timers, and the old-timers all voted for him. They wanted to show that a man could still be vigorous at 83. Now he is running commercials explaining how he warned us about all the problems we would have but, thank God, has already solved.

97

There is another candidate named Percy Sutton. He comes from Harlem, and explains that the looting has helped his candidacy.

Then there is somebody named Mario Cuomo, who is the candidate of the Five Families. Incidentally, the real greatness of our city emerged a couple of days ago when the Super-Don (I think his name is Carmine Giacante) announced that he was turning his boys loose to rub out the Son of Sam. He was swamped with congratulatory calls. We are finally turning our law-and-order problems over to somebody who understands them.

The conservative candidate, Barry Farber, wants to call out the National Guard. He is misguided. I happen to know that there is no National Guard, just as there is no volunteer army. I know what you are going to say: what about all those fine young men, the flower of our youth, who go marching off to defend us, to the strains of acid rock? They are part of an exchange program we have worked out with the Soviet Empire. At the present rate of exchange, we give nine Yanks for one Jew. I think that's fair, don't you?

There is no Irish candidate. The Irish have all moved to a place called Central Islip.

Neither is there any WASP candidate. The WASPs don't need a candidate, since they Control Everything.

The treatment of Lefebvre is perhaps the greatest scandal in the history of the Church. He may be a bit shaky in some of his formulations, and he may blunder tomorrow under pressure of his troubles. But these troubles are not of his making, and the injustice of these troubles is enough to make the saints weep. If I did not know that the Lord triumphs in the end, I would be shattered.

Love to Joey.

Best,
Neil

P.S. As aliens in Lotusland, both of you *must* read Waugh's *The Loved One.*

ভ

November 28, 1977
MEMO TO: Richard [Band], Karl [Pflock]
CC: Neil III, Roger [McCaffrey]
FROM: Neil

You all remember Nock's *Our Enemy, the State.* Aren't we overdue for another one, perhaps to be called *Our Enemy, Uncle Sam*?

We would have no trouble finding a libertarian to write this book. But I think the real point of the book must be that you don't have to be a libertarian to feel this way. There are the usual libertarian arguments, many of them good. But there are other arguments too: the government has failed to provide for our defense against internal enemies (in which I include criminals, though that of course does not exhaust the category) and is in a fair way toward failing to protect us from leftists all over the world. The government has all but institutionalized inflation. Even if one does not buy all the libertarian arguments, the tax burden is crushing. An exorbitant judiciary and an impossible bureaucracy are quite literally the enemies, increasingly hostile to everyone but its own allies, and the criminal underclass.

All this is made possible because we are afraid to admit that the system has failed, that it probably *can't* work.

And because we fail to acknowledge this, we continue to support the very system that is eating away at our prosperity, our freedom, our security.

I'm not sure how far we dare go along these lines in a book. But we certainly need a book that goes a good way along this path to realism.

Need I add that my views are confidential? In light of the perhaps necessary Pollyanna attitudes of most people on our side, it wouldn't do if they knew I saw things more bleakly than they do.

Another book, although similar in thrust, might be called *Is the American System Doomed?* Rather than come right out and say yes (the matter is, regardless of anyone's views, debatable), maybe we should make it a debate. Maybe we should have a lengthy essay by two different authors, pro and con. Then, each author would have a chance to read the other's contribution and refute it. We would present the responses in evenhanded fashion. But whom would we get to represent both schools? I suspect that Stan Evans would make a good spokesman for the position that the system can be salvaged. He is literate, knows lots of facts, has a good grasp of theory, and understands that the system is weakening. In other words, the person who debated him would not have to spend too much time convincing his opponent that the system is in trouble. But who would debate against him? Thomas Molnar would certainly embrace the thesis. But would he have the sort of facts, statistics and such, to buttress his theories? Would he be willing to do that sort of research? He may feel that it isn't necessary. But Americans love facts and figures. Up to a point at least, it *is* necessary.

Using Tom Molnar would give us the added advantage of using an author under contract, and perhaps using up the advance we have paid him on another book. Not only that, but Tom is familiar with the arguments of people like Stan Evans, since he often confronts them and debates them at ISI assemblies.

Incidentally, I see no reason why, when we do this book, one author can't be handled by one of you and another author handled by the other. We can mesh without too much difficulty.

Richard, want to explore this with Tom? Karl, will you explore it with Stan? I would be willing to pay a fairly respectable advance on such a book. Obviously, the two authors would have to split royalties. As a matter of policy, I would keep the advance equal for both. I wouldn't hold each author to exactly the same amount of space. That would be artificial. But we should make clear to them that it would be desirable that they hold to approximately the same space, lest the cards look stacked for either position.

You may want to talk to each other about this so that you agree before you approach your two authors.

In recent years, we haven't been as adventurous in exploring new political questions. If you go back and look at our books from the 60s, you will notice that we anticipated many an issue that has come to the fore in the 70s. We still do, up to a point. But we haven't been quite as productive in this regard.

Incidentally, apropos of my first book idea above, one possibility might be Brent Bozell. Here again, you must touch base with each other. If Karl wishes to contact Brent on the MacArthur book, probably that should take priority. But if the widow has already made a deal with Colonel Yale, then that might free Brent for the other assignment. If so, I think Richard should approach him. I understand he is living up in these parts, in or around Sharon. If so, it would be handier to have Richard work with him. But if we are getting him in on the MacArthur project, then it would be better if Karl worked with him, despite the distance. After all, the MacArthur book is one that Karl was working on, so it would be a waste to change that.

ɔ

December 27, 1977

Editor [*Human Events*]:
You do well to call attention (Dec. 24) to the scandal that makes it almost impossible to fire federal bureaucrats. But there is a solution. I believe conservatives should unite behind a plan that would mandate an annual 10% cut in every federal agency, until the number of drones is reduced to 50% of the present swollen size. Sole exceptions: the armed forces, and law enforcement officials.

We might profitably use the same formula for state and city governments. For good measure, we should forbid any pay increases (a move that might prompt a few of them to make a pass at holding down inflation). These reforms would have an immediate benign effect beyond the tax savings. It would help get the bullies off our backs. Let us be clear on the central point: the bureaucrats have long since ceased to be our servants—if they ever were. They are, most of them, our enemies. Why do we support them in luxury, to torment us and destroy our way of life?

Neil McCaffrey

ဆ

June 7, 1978
MEMO TO: Richard [Band], Karl [Pflock]
CC: Roger McC, Gail [Winson, PR], Neil III,
           Maureen M., Pat S., Marv [Nagourney]
FROM: Neil

Proposition 13 may go down in history as heralding a sea change in American life. At the least, it demonstrates that our demise will not proceed along a straight line. Come to think of it, history never does. And the importance of Proposition 13 is accented by Jeff Bell's astonishing victory, and the defeat of the school bond issue in Cleveland. Some of the sheep are plainly tired of the shearing.

This of course represents an attack on the entire liberal establishment. They will respond with their usual hysteria; already have, in fact, though we haven't seen anything yet. Which means we must be there to join in the fun. I think first of the two new Hazlitt books, not to mention the older ones. I also think of Paul Craig Roberts. Karl, pursue him relentlessly. I think of Tovey. I think of finding someone for *The Government Will Get You.*

And I also think of a note I got from Richard yesterday. Americans do prefer the upbeat. They like to see some grounds for hope. And, however corrupted they may be by liberalism, they are not so corrupted as their mentors. So I anticipate some turnaround in the fortunes of our conservative books, and especially of CBC.

Along these lines, it would still not be too late to change the title of our new book to *The Death of Christian Culture?.* In other words, we simply add a question mark to the title. That will give the book a different thrust, not so pat, and probably do something for sales. Richard, will you check out your author and make sure he has no objection? I'm sure he won't when you give him our rationale.

It may take a few months, maybe longer, for the surge of adrenalin to work itself into the conservative blood stream. But I think we will see it happen. To the benefit of all of us.

cs

August 14, 1979

Dear Mike [Bernstein]:
Like everybody, I have always assumed that the secession question was settled in 1865. Yet when I looked for it in the Amendments, I found nothing. Do you happen to know where or how it was made illegal? Or is everybody wrong and has it not been settled? I am sure that can't be the case.

What prompts this strange question is, in my judgment, something that must come, perhaps in a generation. The American system doesn't work, and therefore can't last. But what would be entailed in real decentralization? Would it simply be a change of law, or would it involve a Constitutional amendment?

The only argument in favour of not breaking up is Russia, and that argument makes less sense each year as our defenses collapse. If the Soviet Empire breaks up, as it just might, then the Free State of, say, Montana becomes an interesting idea.

I suppose you think I'm crazy.

One of these years we will get down to see you. Meanwhile, love to Helen.

Best,
Neil

cs

November 9, 1979

Dear Bill [Rusher]:
It was nice to see you last night on Channel 5, after what must be a couple of years. It was a pungent spot, stylish and strong, and I was happy to note that you have not lost your flair for irony.

The punch line could not have been better. You won't mind, I'm sure, if I stay on a few stops longer. Come to think of it, we could be taking the ride together. Because we both know how seriously to take the morning-after intentions of a drunk. He sits down, resolved to draw a hard line; but his hand keeps shaking. One more drink will put him right . . . Our situation is well described in the second half of the first chapter of Romans. And let us recall that Paul was

Politics and Economics

there addressing himself to the Jewish equivalent of the established churches, yours and mine included. (No, I don't think John Paul's major job is to become a bigger and better circus impresario.)

I hope you won't be too harsh on Carter. He deserves some credit. He is, after all, the first male impersonator to make it to the White House. His principal rivals are also men for our time: a gallant [Ted Kennedy] who leaves his girlfriend drowning in the Atlantic and his wife in Old Hickory, and a flake [Cal. Governor 'Moonbeam' Jerry Brown] who wants to spend himself protecting the earth but who retains enough of his Jesuit training to keep his paramour off camera while he instructs us on the virtues of discipline.

Best,
Neil

ఐ

April 7, 1980
MEMO TO: Alan Ryskind, Tom Winter
FROM: Neil McCaffrey

It's not too early to be thinking about people for the Reagan administration—not just for jobs, but for advisors. I'm not concerned that Reagan will repeat the performance of Nixon. He lacks that consuming ego, and he is more inclined to delegate, and to seek counsel from reliable people. For that matter, he knows in many areas who the reliable people are.

In due time, you are going to be asked for recommendations. (If you aren't asked, then we are in deep trouble.) So I would like to suggest some uncommonly talented people who might get overlooked or, almost as bad, get tapped for jobs that are beneath their abilities.

I'm not going to recommend political workers. The Reagan people know their own foot soldiers, and will undoubtedly take care of them. Nor will I suggest academics. Their names can be found in a few journals, or on the membership list of the Philadelphia Society. It is hard to see how our poor corporal's guard could get overlooked when Reagan is looking for staffers or advisors.

So my list will deal in people who might get overlooked, but shouldn't.

Richard Band.
By an accident of alphabetical order, I start with someone who would rank last in seniority and accomplishment, but only because he is no more than 27 or 28. Richard was the Arlington/CBC editor for our last few years there, and easily the best we ever had. In fact, I think it

103

is no exaggeration to describe him as the only first-class book editor ever to emerge in the conservative field. He is a careful thinker and a very good writer, living proof that Yale can somehow still turn out a superior product. Far more important even than those qualities, he is a God-fearing young man of exemplary character: hardworking, straight as an arrow, warm, and blessed with a sense of humor. He is now doing PR for a Boston bank, and I don't know how his talents might be put to best use. But they are real and rare, and no serious administration can afford to pass them up.

Mike Bernstein.
As you know, Mike is retired. But he remains a young man for his years, and that fine mind is as sharp as ever. In all his decades on the Hill, Mike suffered the fate that sometimes befalls a man of protean talents. He became indispensable in a minor job (or, at any rate, a job that required him to use only a fraction of his ability). Though he is the shrewdest political strategist I have ever encountered (and, after Vic Gold, the second best political tactician), this was unfortunately missed by Taft, and he was shunted aside shamefully (and stupidly) by Goldwater and his cronies.

How does something like this happen? I have a theory. A man like Mike is too much a gentleman, too refined, to push himself or his ideas where they are not wanted. And then when they emerge anyway, it is unfortunately a common failing among mediocre men to feel uncomfortable around someone who is clearly their superior. And make no mistake, Mike is. His whole political consciousness is informed by moral principle and keen social observation (part of the reason why he is such a master strategist). He is widely and deeply read in the classics, ancient and modern. If he were simply the paradigm of [John Henry Cardinal] Newman's educated gentleman, that would be distinction enough. But when you add in political insights that are profound and seemingly endless (for example, he thought up the whole concept of the Forgotten American—a good decade before anyone else, and thus suffered the normal fate of premature prophets), you have a man it would be madness to overlook.

Rev. Harold O.J. Brown.
Protestants are stirring. Better late than never. In this still inchoate movement, Harold is unique. Evangelical Protestants have their share of scholars; and even a decent number of competent writers. And then there are the Jerry Falwells, popularizers who have a place in a society as religiously disoriented as our own; and these people need no promoters. But Harold stands alone as scholar and good

writer *and* conservative thinker. He understands why Protestants have been diffident about the political order—and tries to do something about it, but on a serious level. But this is a delicate area whose theological roots go back beyond Luther to Augustine, and then to Peter and Paul, and even to Christ Himself. It would be all too easy for an amateur to blunder here; and crude appeal would be something of a blunder among *serious* evangelicals. Nixon and Carter both sensed this great political resource, but blew it because of their manifest weaknesses of character. Reagan should do better here; but if he means to, he would find in Harold a congenial and sophisticated advisor (and one who is very well connected in important evangelical circles; among other things, he is related by marriage to Billy Graham).

Msgr. F. D. Cohalan.
If I had to pick the single great unmined lode on our side, here he is. A professor of history for some quarter of a century at New York's minor seminary and now a pastor on Staten Island, Msgr. Cohalan probably stands alone for his knowledge of modern Church *and* European *and* American history probably because his approach to history is unfashionable. There may be men who have read as widely and deeply in all three areas of history, though I doubt it. But what sets Msgr. Cohalan apart is the way he integrates a grasp of practical affairs and human motivations that is astonishing, mind-opening. If you were to ask a member of the Reagan team to identify Antonelli and Merry del Val, could anyone help you? If you were to ask the entire federal bureaucracy, would anyone among the first half million come up with the right answer? And if anyone did, could he give you more than a sketchy paragraph on either man? If you ask Msgr. Cohalan, he will talk on either man in vivid prose for two or three or four hours, until his voice gives out; at which point, you are wide awake and eager for more. He will unfold the life of each man extemporaneously, without notes. He will show you the strengths and weaknesses of each, why the one finally failed and why the other did not go all the way to the papacy. In the course of the lecture you will get a superb overview of the Church in the 19th and early 20th centuries; its relations with Italy, Germany, France, Austria, Spain, Britain, America; wonderful portraits, rich with anecdotes, of the popes they served and the national and Church leaders they dealt with; and in truth, a fresher picture of nearly a century of modern history than you have ever enjoyed before.

Sounds fascinating, I can hear you say, but what does all this have to do with Reagan? Before I answer, let me say that it doesn't stop there. Msgr. Cohalan probably knows more about American political history than anyone in the Reagan entourage. His father was a prominent New York judge, one of the two or three closest advisors to Al Smith; and, need I add, one of the last of the conservative Democrats. (He spotted FDR for a charlatan the first time he met him, around 1911 or 1912.) It may be here at any rate that Msgr. Cohalan got some of his astounding knowledge of practical affairs, and politics at every level.

But I still haven't answered your question. I answer with a few of my own. Shouldn't an American President have one person he can call for some background on the people who make up almost a quarter of his nation? Who make up the largest Christian body among our allies and would-be allies? A man whose knowledge of *today's* Church and the men who run it, here and abroad, is as encyclopedic as his knowledge of their forebears over the last few centuries? A man, moreover, who can sympathize with and support Reagan all the way down the line?

Brutus Coste.
Brutus was head of the Assembly of Captive European Nations until the early Sixties, when the Kennedy crowd dumped him for being too tough. That in itself would be enough to make it mandatory for Reagan to use him as an advisor. That Nixon failed to is one of his less conspicuous mistakes, the blame for which Kissinger must surely share. But Brutus is much more than a displaced and knowledgeable anti-Communist. He is a man of learning, polish, urbanity: a pre-war Rumanian diplomat. But that's still not all. His knowledge of international affairs is vast, and encompasses strategy, diplomacy, economics, everything. I always think of him in the same breath with Burnham, to the discredit of neither. If Burnham has a shade more flair for strategic initiatives, Brutus has a much more detailed knowledge of dozens of individual countries. As for Kissinger, he can probably charm you a little better than Brutus, but Brutus is no slouch either. But Brutus is a man of real principle, which gives him an edge that Kissinger will never overcome—and, yes, I mean an edge in *practical* affairs. I don't mean that Brutus has the ideological rigidity of a Frank Meyer. Anything but. He manages that nice union of principle and pragmatism that is so necessary in foreign affairs, and so rare. In this area, there isn't a single person who would prove more valuable to Reagan.

Clifford Forster.
A key figure in New York's anti-Communist community since the

Thirties, Clifford knows everybody. He and his late wife ran for some thirty years the only anti-Communist salon in New York, and probably in America. There can be few people who have his contacts among anti-Communists in Europe, Latin America, and even Australia. At one time he was working in some way (probably informal) with the CIA, though that seems to have been dried up by the Kennedy-Johnson crowd. He was for years a staff attorney with the ACLU, but lost out with the other anti-Communists when the organization resolved that issue the wrong way in the middle Fifties. Since then he has been a prominent trial attorney.

Meanwhile, his contacts and his experience have been fallow for a dozen years. Gracious, civilized, generous to a fault, multilingual, widely experienced in the fight against Communism, he deserves a high place in the State Department—since we have to assume that Reagan would like to insinuate a few Americans there.

Vic Gold.
Vic is not likely to go unnoticed by the Reagan team. Who, after all, could fail to notice him? But I mention him here because he has so far suffered the same fate as Mike Bernstein, in that he was foolish enough to become expert in a comparatively minor job. Underutilized: his flair for words, and his brilliance as a political tactician. Vic is one of those writers (one out of every 477) who has a *feeling* for words. More to our point here, his ear for liberal cant is unsurpassed. It is just the sort of thing Reagan would like. I hope he gets to enjoy it, firsthand and regularly.

Even more to our point, he is easily the best tactician I have ever encountered. When a critic makes an attack on Vic's candidate, he has five answers ready, three of them funny, before the candidate and the rest of the team have brought forth one. Is brilliance suspect on our side? I'm afraid it is. Don't cite Bill Buckley, because the comparison is not apt. At this point in his life he would be incapable of the self-effacement required of an advisor. Moreover, his brilliance is self-indulgent and arch, sometimes obscure and even devious. Whereas Vic works on the staff level, behind the scenes. He can't help sparkle, but he never lets the sparkle get in the way of the problem at hand. Moreover, as a strategist I consider him second only to Mike. Between the two, they are a team that any candidate on our side should embrace (unless, as often happens, the candidate is uncomfortable in the presence of excellence).

Stan Goldstein.
An able accountant who started one of the more successful of the

And Rightly So

younger, medium-sized firms. On professional merit alone, he should be considered for the top spot at IRS. I suppose there are accountants who know taxes better; I wouldn't know about that. But Stan would bring to the post far more than mere technical excellence. I doubt that there is a prominent accountant in the country more articulate, more personable, more experienced in politics—or more conservative. Besides which, he is like everybody else I am mentioning in this memo, a man of many parts. Accountants as a breed are not conspicuous for getting their noses out of the ledgers. Stan is delightfully different. He would be an adornment to the Reagan administration, and far more sympathetic to its objectives than almost anyone they will find in his area.

Tom Miller.
Tom and Frank Shakespeare (old friends, by the way) are I believe the only unambiguous conservatives in the upper reaches of television. Frank is sure to be tapped for some sort of job. But surely we can use two such talents. Our conventional analysis of the media is all too accurate, alas. Reagan should have more than one person he can call on for advice on dealing with this awesome power center. Tom and Frank know how Paley and the others think and operate, firsthand. They also know what business problems the broadcast giants must cope with. This information can be important, perhaps decisive. Reagan would be foolish to overlook a resource like Tom; again, a man in complete sympathy with what Reagan would be doing.

Solzhenitsyn!

Rudi Strasser.
Rudi is an Austrian who has lived here for some thirty years but has kept up his contacts with the old country. His activity as a student in the Catholic party in Austria won him a few years in a Nazi jail. After the War, he was the aide to, if I recall, the first Catholic premier after the War. He later came here and worked on Wall Street, specializing in European investments; but he kept up his political writing and broadcasting, interpreting this country to the old country. His contacts are wide in both politics and finance; he is urbane and well informed; and he is wholly on Reagan's side. He is another of the sort (Brutus Coste and Clifford Forster could put you in touch with many more) who ought to be hired or at least consulted by a reformed State Department.

I haven't discussed this with any of the people mentioned here, but my guess is that most of them would not be eager to take a

108

federal job. But I could be wrong. In any case, however, I am sure they will all be eager to put their talents at the service of the Reagan administration if only as consultants. My point is, people like this *must* be used. Our ranks are thin enough, and nowhere so thin as in the areas where these men are not merely competent but *expert*. Indeed, even that word fails to do most of them justice. because most of them are quite simply the best in their specialties. Taken all in all, they are a national treasure; and it is the measure of our crisis that they are, by and large, a wasting treasure. In dark days that are sure to get darker, not to use them is a national disgrace.

ଔ

January 28, 1981

Dear Vic [Gold]:
You can be pardoned if this has escaped your notice, but the Catholic hierarchy is breathing hostility toward the new Administration. Joan suggests that I write and point out to you, in case you can ever use this in your speeches or counseling, that Reagan and Bush can safely discount all this. Catholic bishops can no longer be considered spokesmen for that portion of the Catholic electorate that retains its conservative instincts. They are now the exact parallel to the Protestant left, as represented by the National Council of Churches. The only people the bishops speak for now are the Catholic liberals, and they are so liberal that they regard the bishops as conservative. Reagan and Bush can be polite to them if they choose (more polite than they deserve), but it would be a fatal political error to be in the least intimidated by them.

I see by the tube that the yellow ribbon has become our new national symbol. Quite right, too. But it must be yellow and it must be a ribbon.
Best,
Neil

ଔ

October 14, 1981

Dear Murray [Rothbard]:
I just read your *cri de coeur* to your old comrades. I think I see a logical flaw. The libertarian creed is of course Benthamite, me-first. But you are calling them to an ideal outside themselves. There is no logical reason why they should respond, unless it happens to suit their interests at the moment; and this on your own premises.

109

Human material is unpromising enough. Human material that is encouraged to be solipsistic is hopeless.

How about Bob [Kephart]? He is the second friend in recent weeks who has retired in his forties a millionaire. What are we doing wrong?

We hope to see you soon.

Best,
Neil

cs

October 16, 1981

Dear Neil:

Uh, uh. Libertarianism is *not* Benthamite at all, much less "of course." The libertarian tradition, from the Levellers through Paine and Spencer and down to Nock in the present day is squarely natural rights and justice-centered. Benthamism is confined nowadays to the evil Friedmanites, of whom only David is in the libertarian movement. Philosophically, the current movement is Randian/Rothbardian. Bentham is consigned to the fifth circle of Hell.

No, I think the basic problem of the libertarian movement is twofold: Kochian opportunism, and through and beyond that, that most libertarians are a bunch of cretins and creeps. Philosophy, I'm afraid, has little to do with the problem.

Has Bob really retired? If so, how come he's kept the seminars— which I thought was one of the most depressed "industries" in the country, worse even than autos and housing.

Good hearing from you; hope we'll be seeing you soon.

All the best,
Murray

cs

October 26, 1981

Dear Murray:

I yield to your correction, up to a point. I wasn't attempting to use "Benthamite" in a precise philosophical sense; in fact, wouldn't know how to. I was using it in the generic sense in which it has been used by Britons for almost two centuries. In that sense, I think I was not inaccurate.

Indeed, I don't think we read the problem all that differently, though we don't phrase it in quite the same terms. I was suggesting that the nature of the appeal of all your different schools is the same: to man absolutized, not to man the contingent creature. This in my judgment ineluctably leads people to treat life in terms of stark self-interest. To ask them as you do to dedicate themselves to a dogma outside themselves and frequently clashing with their own self-interest introduces an internal contradiction at the root of your cause, and I don't see how you can ever overcome that. Opportunism is *built into* the appeal.

I suspect that Bob retained the seminars because he likes to get around. He is restless by nature and will never settle into anything for long.

When should we have another evening at the Blazer?

Best,
Neil

ॐ

March 12, 1982

Dear Joey [Mrs. Rothbard]:
Thanks for offering to read for us. I'm taking you up right away because something came in that might interest you, a short manuscript by Henri Lepage on the future of capitalism. Normally this is a book we would consider as an alternate rather than a main selection, but sometimes a book on economics has enough appeal across the board to justify naming it as a main selection. Here commercial considerations are paramount, and the choice between main and alternate has nothing to do with quality.

I suppose this book is more in the conservative than the libertarian line, but I would be interested in where it fits. If it would appeal to neither then obviously it isn't for us.

We have a chance, if we want to use the book, to get in on the publisher's run. So if you can do this fast, please do. Then you can bill us $50 instead of $30. But if it is inconvenient for you to, then take your time and don't feel guilty.

The Randians are humorless to the end. I see that [Leonard] Peikoff sent her off on her next journey (a journey that will surely surprise her) with a dollar sign for her guide—but a giant dollar sign, which only goes to prove that they don't read the papers. The new Randian dollar sign should be reduced by 90%, and moreover should be made of a material that slowly shrinks. Call Galt [character in *Atlas Shrugged*]. Get his marketing people busy.

By the way, Ayn is no longer an atheist.

Best,
Neil

111

And Rightly So

November 7, 1984

Dear Vic [Gold]:
It occurs to me that Lew Lehrman rates a place on the serious list of veep candidates. He will enable you to outflank your opponent on the Right, yet he carries none of the heavy baggage that might encumber somebody similar. He comes from a major state that nicely balances Texas.

The first Jewish veep? It couldn't hurt—especially because he would not be chosen for crass Ferraro-like reasons but for what he is.

Somebody is sure to object that he lost the only campaign he ever waged. But that argument can slice either way. He is the doer, the self-made businessman untainted by politics, etc.

Roll it around in your glass. The more you do, the better it tastes. And when you hold the glass up to the light, I doubt that you'll find any sediment.

By the way, I'm not grinding an axe. I hardly know the man.

Now that your labors are over for the nonce, why don't you treat yourself and Dale to a few days in Babylon? Remember, you can always hang your hat in Pelham Manor if you feel inclined.

Best,
Neil

൪

June 18, 1985

Dear Vic:
You have yourself a formidable task with this book, as I know you realize. The puff piece has its own iron rules, but you know that. On top of which, politicians tend to be one-dimensional.

But I think you'll rise to the challenge. You have one thing going for you. The prime market, GB's [George H. W. Bush] admirers, want to like him and the book, and *want* to find him and it interesting. There lies your opening. You might just break out into the clear.

Your average WASP isn't much given to introspection, so I suspect you can make him more interesting than he realizes he is. Besides, he *becomes* interesting because of his position. The people who read this book won't be demanding; indeed, probably won't expect to be entertained. So a little humanity will go a long way, and may just defeat the expectations of those who expect another boring campaign book. (It has to be the world's most boring genre.) Since women buy and read most of the books, be generous with your quotes from BB [Barbara Bush]. How did she and the children take the death of the daughter? All the family moves? Something about the early married years with a husband still a student would be evocative for many of us vets.

Talk some about the contrast between Connecticut and Texas. What does he like about each? What does he miss about each? Is Texas hospitable to Yalies?

Most of your readers will be interested in his years in Congress. What does he think about Congress? Can anything be done to improve it? Is that part of the system working? Let's have lots of stories about Congressmen *and their wives*. Have BB talk about the life of a Congressman's wife.

Talk about the UN, and be as snide as possible. Tell some stories about the bad guys. Remind the reader of some of the routine outrages.

Make your subject search his soul. Is there anything he regrets about his life? Anything he would do differently?

What was it like to grow up an upper-class Republican in the reign of FDR? Was entering the service a culture shock? (It was for me, the biggest in my life.) Did his family think he was marrying too young, with college still ahead of him? Did B's family want her to finish college first?

What are his hobbies?

What would he do if he had a leisurely retirement staring at him?

What role does religion play in his life?

Suggested last chapter: what *realistic* hopes does he have for the country? What does he expect it to look like in the year 2000? (Suggestion: make it hope tempered by concern. That will sound convincing and make him sound appropriately serious.)

Don't forget to throw in nice comments about as many places in the country as you can.

I'll think of more minutiae along the way. But my guiding thought is: I want to meet the man, get to know him, get to like him, feel that I could spend a comfortable evening with him. If every reader comes away from the book satisfied on those points, you will have a unique campaign book. His admirers will talk about it, give it to their friends, use it to persuade people that the country would be well off under this man.

Best,
Neil

113

P.S. A occurs to me that you already know, but that his Madison Avenue friends probably don't; so I mention it merely to second what you will tell them: GB is what he is. Don't try to make him over. He should neither flaunt nor blush about his background. Sober Americans—our people—respect it, find it fitting. A touch of dignity and distance in an egalitarian age is, I'm convinced, an asset; and moreover makes a virtue of necessity. GB would be a lousy Hubert Humphrey. (Hubert Humphrey was a lousy Hubert Humphrey.)

ᘓ

June 16, 1986

Dear Vic [Victor Lasky]:
Just in case you haven't thought of this, the media have presented you with a new *handle* for marketing the Nixon book. The title should express this. Something like:

UP FROM THE GRAVE
The Life of Richard M. Nixon

I'm sure you won't have to change much in the manuscript, just a little touch here and there, and especially something up front and at the end.
You continue to avoid us, and my rage knows no bounds. Nevertheless, as one of nature's noblemen, I stand ready to forgive, and eager to take you and Patti to dinner next time you slink into town.
Best,
Neil

ᘓ

Mr. Neil McCaffrey
Conservative Book Club
15 Oakland Avenue
Harrison, NY 10528
4 April 1989

Dear Neil,

Can you help me with some information? I don't know the first thing about economics/business/finance and I would like to. Tell me, where do I start?
I know some names—Milton Friedman and Ludwig von Mises. These strike me as philosophical from your descriptions of them over

the years. I'm very interested in the philosophy but perhaps you can suggest something more "introductory." What I need is something practical. I want to know how to be a businessman, banker, economist. And I would like to know from our perspective, the conservative perspective. If you would suggest books and schools it would be a big help.

I am very grateful for the club. I am one of the "prodigals" that you mentioned in this month's editorial. I joined in '75 then left around '77. I rejoined around '82 and have been a much appreciative member since. You mentioned enjoying hearing from your constituents. I've thought of writing often but, as with most of us I guess, it seems I never got around to it. I've shared the club bulletin and the selections that I've received from you with many friends. I'm very definitely an "evangelistic" CBC member!

I must say too, though, that I share the sentiments you shared in your editorial. I was an Army Chaplain until July of '87. While I was serving in Germany with my family I found I could no longer be silent and compliant over the atrocious immorality and "secular amorality" of the command I was serving with. When nothing was done to remedy the situation I requested release from active duty. I'm still in the reserves where I now serve as a Major but now I serve with a unit whose command has something of an appreciation for Judeo-Christian culture.

Just as there is a great deal of evangelical lingo bantered about today there is a great deal of conservative sounding sentiment and lingo bantered about. The talk in either case is not reality though. When push comes to shove those in authority back away from their conservative sounding points of view. May I be so presumptive as to criticize former President Reagan for such a stance (keeping in mind the many good things he did while in office). People like LTC North and Jim Dobson, now suffering from taking on the covert pornography lobby, wind up flapping in the breeze while those in authority apparently look the other way. That was my experience. But then I guess we must remember that this isn't heaven!

Perhaps you might also recommend schools where I could pursue a degree in business/finance/economics. I am a graduate of Colgate University (BA '70 in Fine Arts) and I have 3 graduate degrees in theology, one a doctoral degree in Marriage & Family Therapy. I also have eight children. I take very seriously my obligation to provide for them. When I left active duty I had hoped to pastor a church. This has not worked out. Though I have a small practice now in Marriage & Family Therapy I am not able to support my family with it. We have lived on a Missionary Compound for almost 2 years since my return from overseas. By the end of June we must find a new home to make room for other missionaries on furlough from overseas. Now I must find a new course to provide for my family. I am therefore turning to the world of commerce for that purpose.

In the course of my ministry I've helped many people with their finances. I've had some success in investing in things like Mutual Funds. I think I would enjoy working in a bank or a financial institution of some kind. One that operated on conservative principles though, not wide eyed, New Age, crap shoots like some of the financial institutions seem to. But I need a place to start. Therefore, can you suggest books and school? I will be relocating this summer as I mentioned so the location of the school is not critical. It would be difficult for us cost wise though to live in a major metropolitan area like NY or Chicago. I will be very appreciative of any help you can give.

Thank you for your wonderful work. You have been a blessing to me and many of my friends. My prayer is that the Lord will use your work to turn our country around from its slow movement leftward to a healthy movement rightward—Godward! However God sovereignly chooses to direct the course of our nation I pray that all of your efforts will continue to be for His glory!

Sincerely,
Dr. Robert S. Mortensen, Jr.

CB

April 17, 1989

Dear Dr. Mortensen:
After twenty-five years, your letter stands out as perhaps the most impressive I've ever received here at the Club, out of many. I couldn't agree with you more about the failure of some of our leaders to recover their wounded.

The two best introductions to sound economics are *Economics in One Lesson* by Henry Hazlitt, and the book we offered recently, *Basic Economics* by Clarence Carson. We had the former for many years but we are now out of stock. So I am sending you the Carson, with my compliments because you have to watch your pennies these days. Both of these books are excellent primers, but not too jejune for a person of your education.

I'm not too clued in on the academic world, but I have heard that there are good economics faculties at places like Grove City, Hillsdale and Claremont. One person who might be able to give you very good advice in this area is Dr. Bruce Evans, the new president of the Foundation for Economic Education at Irvington-on-Hudson, New York 10533. I recently met him and was most impressed. He has an academic background, having served as president of a couple of evangelical colleges. I think he would be eager to help. Moreover, don't hesitate to ask him about grants to attend some of the seminars he sponsors. Not only would it be good orientation for you, but I think you would make some excellent contacts. Don't hesitate to mention my name when you are writing to him.

You might also drop a line to Dr. Ronald Nash, Western Kentucky University, Department of Philosophy & Religion, Bowling Green, Kentucky 42101. He is a leader among evangelicals who are expert in economics. We have used a couple of his books here in the Club. I think he will be able to give you good advice. Mention my name with him too.

If these leads don't work for you, please write again. I may be able to come up with some other names. Come to think of it, you might also drop a line to Lew Rockwell, The Ludwig von Mises Institute, 322 Massachusetts Avenue, N.E., Washington, DC 20002. He too sponsors seminars and may be able to offer something. Mention my name, and mention your religious background. As with many of these libertarian groups, Lew gets many people who are, to put it gently, not excessively religious. I suspect he may be glad to redress the balance.

I must say that I doff my cap to anybody with heavy family responsibilities who is willing to risk a change of career. It could well be that you are able to combine your present profession with your new interests. As evangelicals grow more interested in politics and economics, somebody with your background could wind up doing important work. The likeliest place for foundations like FEE and Mises to find new blood is among evangelicals. You might think about something like that and, when you gain some expertise in economics, pioneer some such program at some such foundation.

Thank you again for your wonderful letter and please let me know if I can be of any small use to you.

Kindest regards,
Neil McCaffrey

ᘓ

April 18, 1989

Dear Murray:
That was a fine piece on Rushdie. I'm sure that most libertarians will

profit as you recall them to the real world. You are one of the few commentators that saw the real point of this incident. I must say that I enjoyed the discomfort of the liberals; but then, I always enjoy their discomfort. Among other things, this is further evidence that the only peace in the Middle East will be the peace of the grave.

Penny Lernoux enjoys a distinction of sorts. She is the Latin American authority for *The Nation* and—the *National Catholic Reporter*. Would such a thing be conceivable a quarter of a century ago? Now it hardly bears mentioning. She uses a technique that the Left perfected half a century ago. They cast Dewey or Ike or Nixon or Reagan or any of the recent popes as conservatives or even reactionaries. Thus, when these people do their bidding as they usually do, this is simply taken for granted as normal behavior among all "right-thinking" people. Then everybody to the Right of these pseudo-conservatives becomes consigned to outer darkness. So they manage to keep most of the debate on their terms. The pseudo-conservatives are usually intimidated, and many conservatives are fooled into defending their false friends and their often liberal positions.

But you know all this.

Incidentally, I saw a small item in the paper the other day where our Pope, addressing the Italian army, looked forward to the day when all national armies would merge into one "world army". No, I'm not making this up. I may have an evil mind, but some thoughts are simply beyond my imagining.

Life goes well here. Gene will have a baseball article in the next issue of the *Village Voice*, of all things.

Best,
Neil

ᘉ

October 26, 1989
MEMO TO: Lew Rockwell, Jeff Tucker
CC: Murray Rothbard
FROM: Neil McCaffrey

Thanks for letting me see your articles, most of which I agree with. Because they both say much the same thing, my few comments can serve for both.

One of my three fundamental problems with libertarianism (hereafter L) is that it scants original sin. From this follows a dizzily optimistic view of man and society, though your articles do move part of the way back to reality. And from this underplaying of original sin follows a) the L view of the state as evil incarnate and b) a vision of man and society happily free and cooperating in a dreamlike social order that never was and never can be: in fine, utopian.

I think a more balanced view of the state, the theory of it, sees it as inevitable, invariably more or less of a burden, always potentially a burden, and *meant* to be a burden, if not a curse, for fallen man; but for all that, a necessary institution—or, if you will, a necessary burden. I join you most of the way in seeing the modern state as the monster state, but I find your theory of the state too sweeping.

You make sensible points about the need for authority in church, family, society and private groups. But why quit there? We have seen in our lifetime the collapse of authority in all these institutions; demonstrably, they aren't enough. Something more is needed. Is it the virtuous state?

Of course not. But the state that fails in its policing duties—its proper duties—hastens the collapse of the other institutions that can't go it alone. We need the state far less than most people think; but we *do* need it. Private cops? Fine—up to a point. Private armies? Up to a point. But this ain't 1776. An armed militia, and *only* an armed militia, would be but a few steps short of Fidel—or maybe Jesse—in the White House. Let's be sensible.

(Which leads me to digress. A worldview not rooted in common sense and the common experience of mankind is doomed from the start. *Universal* law!) My third radical problem with L is the awkward matter of the Bible and Christian tradition. I am not confident enough to shrug off all that. Like it or not, our faith takes the state for granted, a given where it does not explicitly enjoin the institution. You don't have to go overboard, but you *should* render *something* unto Caesar.

I've always been troubled, by the way, with Acton's dictum, a glaring confusion of end and means. It seems plain that liberty is a means to, or a condition for, the good society. But the end of society? This is like calling good digestion the end of health. The end of society is, well, civility, order, stability. Liberty, properly ordered, is a means. Liberty absolutized is the libertine idol—which you rightly deplore.

Acton, no philosopher, made a fundamental mistake, aided I'm sure by the stable society he took for granted. We all did, till criminals and libertines assumed their privileged status.

Yet as you distance yourselves from the barbarians and the libertines, the distance between us narrows. All the better. Libertarians have a lot to teach us. They will have more when they shuck the utopian baggage.

Bravo for your remarks on egalitarianism, which I regard as an even greater menace to liberty than the state (in our society) because it pervades every institution. I see you went easier on its twin bastard, democracy; but one thing at a time, everything in its season.

Along that line, a few distinctions. We are drugged by the cliché "equal before God." Of course it's blasphemous. You and I can see that *none* of us is equal. We are all different, hence unequal. Is God less perceptive than we?

To be sure, man considered abstractly has certain strictly limited common features. We are all creatures—but each of us is a unique creature. We share equally a few human rights: to life, to worship, to marry, to own property. But even these rights are conditioned to a degree by such circumstances as our duties, our station, our age, our behavior. At best, "equal before God" blurs more than it explains.

Especially for a Christian, who understands that God invests each of us with a different destiny. Though we are all to have the opportunity to achieve heaven, nobody will occupy the same place there. More is given to some of us; more is expected of some of us; the same is expected of none of us. Does this sound like equality? It is the crudest sort of equality, an equality that obscures our real situation, to insult the Lord who wrought a creation infinitely various. To hear today's religious leaders talk, God made a terrible mistake creating men and races so plainly unequal, so they busy themselves trying to make good His cosmic blunder. When I said blasphemous, I meant just that.

The same remarks apply, of course, to equality before the law. It is a severely limited equality, and should be. Even the law (or such provisions of it that have so far escaped the levelers) acknowledges this. If Smith takes a poke at me and Jones takes one at my wife, the law is likely to deal more harshly with Jones, and should.

Drug laws are debatable. No one has a *right* to harm himself, and these laws are meant to support the authority of church, family and society. (Whether they do is another question.) Individual parents and clerics and teachers have long since learned that they may be no match for the drug pusher outside—or within—the schoolyard. I see nothing intrinsically wrong with making this a part of the state's mandate to preserve order. Quite the contrary, it's what the government should be doing. But as a prudential matter, of course there's room for debate about how best to marshal the forces against this scourge.

By the way, Vic Gold has an amusing piece in the current *American Spectator* on why drug laws are indeed needed.

ॐ

November 25, 1991
MEMO TO: All Concerned
FROM: Neil

Back around 1970 I had one of my premature inspira-
tions. It took no genius to see that the future lay with private
schools, whether nonprofit or for profit—that is, if we are
to have any decent future at all. Around that time the fran-
chising business was picking up. So it struck me that there
might well be a future for franchised schools, whether for profit
or not for profit. Indeed, it seemed and seems that there could be
two models.

Anyway, nothing ever came of this and I didn't get much
encouragement to pursue it. But other people did, here and there. I
understand that there are a few pre-school franchisers around, and
maybe even a school chain or two. Still, the movement, if it is to
become a movement, is still in its infancy, and there is a lot of room
for entrepreneurs.

As with my other idea, private package and magazine and later
first class mail delivery, I think the way to go is to do a dry run
with one school. That way, you learn the ropes and work out the
problems; or you learn that the thing presents too many problems
to pursue. But if it turns out that the project is workable, either for
profit or not for profit or both, then it has dazzling prospects as
a franchise operation. Do you realize that the explosion of private
schools, largely Christian, and the stunning growth of home school-
ing both came about without an ounce of promotion? Each one is
truly a grass-roots phenomenon. People did all this on their own,
usually after much agonizing. They only did it because they saw
their children being destroyed. But think how many parents see the
same thing but can't cope with the problems or simply don't want
to. In other words, the market is much larger than we have yet seen.
If once the millions of parents on the fence can be shown that a
private school is good and doable, the movement will grow. And this
is where good promotion comes in. Nobody has ever promoted a
private school. This is part of the service the franchiser will provide.

Here again, this is not a ball I care to seize and run with. But I
think everybody getting this memo, at least everybody who likes
the idea, will have some thoughts about it. I would like to be part of
anything you get going, but simply as a consultant and in a minor
way, the guy who helps where he can and who provided the original
idea. But somebody should run with it. I don't guarantee success,
but it cries out to be tested.

ʊ

May 17, 1993

Editor
National Review
150 East 35th Street
New York, New York 10016

Editor:
I find Robert A. August's view of abortion ("Letters," May 24) twice as sound as yours but not half as slick. Take, for example, your ringing phrase, "Despite the monumental injustice of the unlimited abortion license." That foxy "unlimited" qualifier opens up a hole big enough to accommodate Hillary herself. "Underlying Mr. August's complaint," you go on to say, enfolded in Old Glory, "is the conclusion that the American constitutional order is not morally legitimate. We do not share that conclusion . . ." What, I wonder, would change your mind—forty million legal murders? Fifty million? As for the comparison to Stalin and Hitler, at least we have to concede one point to the pioneers in mass murder. They felt sufficiently edgy about the opinion of mankind to hide or lie about their crimes; whereas here in the Land of the Much Too Free, vice need no longer pay lip service to decency. We have, instead, discovered the human and civil "right" to slaughter the innocent. Could this be the patina of moral legitimacy you discern in our system?
Neil McCaffrey

ʊ

FIFTY YEARS OF CONSERVATIVE BOOKS
By Neil McCaffrey
[*Human Events,* September 30, 1994]

When Tom Winter asked me to produce a list of conservative books to coincide with HUMAN EVENTS' 50 years on Earth, my first instinct was to stick to the acknowledged classics, the most popular conservative books, the most influential—in short, the ones everybody would pick. Easy as pie. But Tom suggested that I stretch a bit and go beyond the obvious. On thinking it over, I see that this is a more interesting idea—even if it takes longer and, paradoxically, involves tougher choices.

First of all, what would constitute a conservative book for

purposes of this list? The definition should be broad enough to include books that were important to conservatives, though not written by conservatives and indeed not avowedly conservative. Thus, I include several (e.g., *Nineteen Eighty-Four, Atlas Shrugged, The Rosenberg File*) whose absence would render the list too narrow. I also include books—not necessarily classics, or not all that popular—on *themes* that are or have been important to conservatives. And I even sneak in a few personal pets that I wish were better known.

The list makes no claim to be comprehensive, much less complete. It aims rather to be *representative*. If, therefore, I've left out a few books you think belong, I may indeed have overlooked them; but equally, I may have omitted them because it seemed to me that one or another book on the list covers the subject adequately. And remember, books published before 1944 fall outside the scope of this selection.

MARTIN ANDERSON
The Federal Bulldozer

HANNAH ARENDT
The Origins of Totalitarianism

EDWARD BANFIELD
The Unheavenly City

PETER T. BAUER
Equality, the Third World, and Economic Delusion
Reality and Rhetoric: Studies in the Economics of Development

ALLAN BLOOM
The Closing of the American Mind

ARNAUD de BORCHGRAVE and ROBERT MOSS
The Spike

ROBERT BORK
The Tempting of America: The Political Seduction of the Law

DAVID BROCK
The Real Anita Hill

ANTHONY CAVE BROWN and CHARLES B. MacDONALD
On a Field of Red: The Communist International and the Coming of World War II

PATRICK J. BUCHANAN
Right from the Beginning

WILLIAM F. BUCKLEY, JR.
Did You Ever See a Dream Walking?: American Conservative Thought in the Twentieth Century (editor)
God and Man at Yale
Up from Liberalism

WILLIAM F. BUCKLEY, JR. and L. BRENT BOZELL
McCarthy and His Enemies

JAMES BURNHAM
Congress and the American Tradition
Suicide of the West
The War We Are In
The Web of Subversion

CLARENCE B. CARSON
Basic American Government
Basic Economics
A Basic History of the United States (five volumes)

JOHN CHAMBERLAIN
The Enterprising Americans
The Roots of Capitalism

WHITTAKER CHAMBERS
Witness

PETER COLLIER and DAVID HOROWITZ
Destructive Generation

CHARLES COLSON
Against the Night

ROBERT CONQUEST
The Great Terror
The Harvest of Sorrow
Stalin, Breaker of Nations

LEO DAMORE
Senatorial Privilege: The Chappaquiddick Cover-Up

Politics and Economics

MICHAEL DAVIES
Liturgical Revolution (The trilogy includes *Cranmer's Godly Order, Pope John's Council, Pope Paul's New Mass*)

CHRISTOPHER DAWSON
Christianity in East and West (expanded version of *The Movement of World Revolution*)
The Crisis of Western Education
Religion and the Rise of Western Culture

MIDGE DECTOR
Liberal Parents, Radical Children

ALLEN DRURY
Advise and Consent
Capable of Honor
Preserve and Protect
A Shade of Difference

T. S. ELIOT
Christianity and Culture (includes *The Idea of a Christian Society* and *Notes Towards the Definition of Culture*)

M. STANTON EVANS
The Liberal Establishment
The Politics of Surrender

ROWLAND EVANS and ROBERT NOVAK
The Reagan Revolution

DON FEDER
A Jewish Conservative Looks at Pagan America

CONSTANTINE FITZGIBBON
When the Kissing Had to Stop

MILTON FRIEDMAN
Capitalism and Freedom

MILTON and ROSE FRIEDMAN
Freedom to Choose

GEORGE GILDER
Sexual Suicide
Men and Marriage
Wealth and Poverty

VICTOR GOLD
So You Want to Be a Liberal

BARRY GOLDWATER
The Conscience of a Conservative
Why Not Victory?

IGOR GOUZENKO
The Fall of a Titan

GEN. SIR JOHN HACKETT
The Third World War: August 1985

BENJAMIN HART
Faith & Freedom: The Christian Roots of American Liberty

F.A. HAYEK
The Constitution of Liberty
The Road to Serfdom

HENRY HAZLITT
The Conquest of Poverty
Economics in One Lesson
The Failure of the 'New Economics'

MARGUERITE HIGGINS
Our Vietnam Nightmare

DIETRICH von HILDEBRAND
The Devastated Vineyard

JAMES HITCHCOCK
What Is Secular Humanism?

PAUL HOLLANDER
Political Pilgrims

J. EDGAR HOOVER
Masters of Deceit

BRYAN HOUGHTON
Mitre and Crook

PAUL JOHNSON
Modern Times

HERMAN KAHN
Thinking About the Unthinkable in the 1980s

WILLMOORE KENDALL
The Conservative Affirmation
Willmoore Kendall Contra Mundum

ROGER KIMBALL
Tenured Radicals

RUSSELL KIRK
The Conservative Mind
Decadence and Renewal in the Higher Learning
The Portable Conservative Reader (editor)
The Roots of American Order

JEANE KIRKPATRICK
Dictatorships and Double Standards

IRVING KRISTOL
Reflections of a Neoconservative

ERIK von KUEHNELT-LEDDIHN
Leftism Revisited
Liberty or Equality?

VICTOR LASKY
It Didn't Start with Watergate
JFK: The Man and the Myth

C.S. LEWIS
The Abolition of Man
God in the Dock
That Hideous Strength

RUSH LIMBAUGH
The Way Things Ought to Be

CHARLES A. LINDBERGH
Wartime Journals

EUGENE LYONS
Workers Paradise Lost

DOUGLAS MacARTHUR
Reminiscences

SAMUEL McCRACKEN
The War Against the Atom

FORREST McDONALD
A Constitutional History of the United States
Novus Ordo Saeculorum: The Intellectual Origins of the Constitution

FRANK S. MEYER
The Conservative Mainstream
The Moulding of Communists

LUDWIG von MISES
The Anticapitalistic Mentality
Human Action (Third Edition)
Socialism

THOMAS MOLNAR
Utopia: The Perennial Heresy

CHARLES MURRAY
Losing Ground

GEORGE H. NASH
The Conservative Intellectual
Movement in America Since 1945

RONALD H. NASH
Social Justice and the Christian Church

JOHN HENRY NEWMAN
Newman Against the Liberals (sermons from 1833-41 selected by Michael Davies and published in 1978)

ROBERT NISBET
Prejudices
The Quest for Community

PEGGY NOONAN
What I Saw at the Revolution

OLIVER L. NORTH and WILLIAM NOVAK
Under Fire

MICHAEL NOVAK
The Spirit of Democratic Capitalism

MICHAEL OAKESHOTT
Of Human Conduct
Rationalism in Politics

GEORGE ORWELL
Animal Farm
Nineteen Eighty-Four

KEVIN P. PHILLIPS
The Emerging Republican Majority

RICHARD PIPES
The Russian Revolution

NORMAN PODHORETZ
The Present Danger
Why We Were in Vietnam

RONALD RADOSH and JOYCE MILTON
The Rosenberg File

AYN RAND
Atlas Shrugged

RONALD REAGAN
Where's the Rest of Me?

JEAN-FRANCOIS REVEL
How Democracies Perish

PAUL CRAIG ROBERTS
The Supply-Side Revolution

WILHELM ROEPKE
The Economics of the Free Society
A Humane Economy

MURRAY N. ROTHBARD
America's Great Depression

WILLIAM SAFIRE
Safire's Washington

MICHAEL SCAMMELL
Solzhenitsyn

FRANCIS A. SCHAEFFER
Complete Works

PHYLLIS SCHLAFLY
A Choice, Not an Echo

HERBERT SCHLOSSERG
Idols for Destruction

IGOR SHAFAREVICH
The Socialist Phenomenon

WILLIAM E. SIMON
A Time for Action
A Time for Truth

ALEXANDER SOLZHENITSYN
The Cancer Ward
One Day in the Life of Ivan Denisovich
The First Circle
The Gulag Archipelago (three volumes)

THOMAS SOWELL
Civil Rights: Rhetoric or Reality?

Politics and Economics

The Economics and Politics of Race in American Education
Marxism: Philosophy and Economics

LAWRENCE STEPELEVICH
The Capitalist Reader (editor)

CLAIRE STERLING
The Terror Network

LEO STRAUSS
Liberalism Ancient and Modern

JARED TAYLOR
Paved with Good Intentions

JOHN TOLAND
Infamy: Pearl Harbor and its Aftermath

RALPH de TOLEDANO and VICTOR LASKY
Seeds of Treason

ADAM B. ULAM
Stalin

ARMANDO VALLADARES
Against All Hope

ERIC VOEGELIN
Science, Politics and Gnosticism

JUDE WANNISKI
The Way the World Works

EVELYN WAUGH
Brideshead Revisited
The Essays, Articles and Reviews of Evelyn Waugh
Helena
Sword of Honour (trilogy of World War II novels includes *Men at Arms, Officers and Gentlemen, Unconditional Surrender*)

RICHARD M. WEAVER
Ideas Have Consequences
Visions of Order

And Rightly So

ALBERT C. WEDEMEYER
Wedemeyer Reports!

ALLEN WEINSTEIN
Perjury: The Hiss-Chambers Case

GEORGE F. WILL
The Pursuit of Virtue & Other Tory Notions

WALTER E. WILLIAMS
The State Against Blacks

PETER WITONSKI
The Wisdom of Conservatism (editor)

TOM WOLFE
The Purple Decades

∞

2

Reformation and Deformation in the Catholic Church

December 7, 1959

Dear Brent [Bozell]:

I thought that was a very good rundown on the birth control business; but may I niggle on a couple of points?

I don't think you can state categorically that a Catholic must veto such a bill. There are circumstances under which he would not be obliged to, and I think they can be subsumed under the lesser-of-two-evils principle. E.g., Congress might pass a sound foreign aid bill with a birth control rider. I would sign such a bill on my way to Communion, and so, I think, would you.

I was startled by your statement that Kennedy was as free to re-examine his religious commitments as Stevenson; and again, that a Catholic's allegiance to the Church is an open question. Surely not. A Catholic is no more free to reject his faith than he is free to murder. I grant that you can make a theoretical case for following one's conscience, even out of the Church; but theologians generally reject the possibility of a blameless apostasy on the grounds that it is a contradiction in terms. Faith is a necessity for salvation and a free gift of God; therefore, God would not withdraw the gift without reason. I think you confound the temporal meanings of freedom with its metaphysical meaning. Here, of course, we are on the frontier of mystery, but I think we can infer the ultimate meaning of freedom aprioristically from the nature of God: He is infinitely free—and incapable of evil.

I much enjoyed your observation that a harder Catholic line on communism would involve Catholics in many internal embarrassments. Indeed, it would, and I am indecently eager for the day. Apropos of this, I think we can safely predict that this birth control business, and the UN's role therein, should dampen the ardor of most Catholic apologists for the UN. It's a pity that they had to have their faces rubbed in the UN's aggressive secularism before seeing what elementary prudence should have revealed to them.

Bill and I were talking around this subject the other night, so I am sending him a copy of this.

Sincerely,
Neil

⋈

January 12, 1960

Mr. Neil McCaffrey
Doubleday & Company, Inc.
575 Madison Avenue
New York 22, N.Y.

Dear Neil,
I very much appreciated you dropping me a line about my birth control piece. You deserved a quick answer. I hope you will forgive me.

Shortly after the issue broke, the *Times* ran an article by a Jesuit maintaining that while a Catholic could not sign a birth control bill, neither would he, in every case, have to veto it. He, too, used the "lesser evil" argument, and added a fillip: the possibility that the Constitution's framers envisioned a situation where the President might want to abstain and accordingly provided that a bill might become law after a certain amount of time without the President's signature. However, I do not believe that either you or he comes to grips with my argument that the President has an integral role in the law-making process and thus has a powerful opportunity, in virtue of his veto power, to influence the content of the legislation. My view is that a Catholic must do everything he can within that role to promote his moral beliefs. In the veto situation, I do not understand that a Catholic President would be confronted with the necessity of choosing between two evils. There is a third possibility—namely, that he vetoes such a bill as you describe because of the birth control rider, that the bill then goes back to Congress where the rider is detached and comes back to him for signature. Surely the President is required to use such powers as are needed to explore this possibility. And I guess I think you would use the power in this way—at least *after* you had gone to Communion.

On the second point you raise, I agree that "we are on the frontier of mystery." I think it is possible, however, to accept both your doctrine of a "blameless apostasy" and mine of religious freedom. I don't see that they are inconsistent. Moreover, I don't believe you could deny my statement about freedom and at the same time affirm the essentially free nature of man. God cannot do evil, but surely man can. Surely the meaning of man's freedom is that he is free to do good or evil. My statement that Kennedy is free to re-examine his religious commitments is simply a description of Kennedy's powers over against the cosmos. Both Kennedy and Stevenson may incur God's displeasure for the choice they make—and Kennedy may for even permitting himself to examine the question—but it remains that freedom thrusts this power on both men equally. Another way of saying this is that faith is a continuing commitment. One does not make an act of faith on Monday and forget about it for the rest of the week and for the rest of his life. Rather, one's faith is reaffirmed, assuming he stays in the Church, at every conscious moment; and therefore at every conscious moment a free choice is made between rejecting faith or affirming it; and therefore the process of re-examination of which I spoke is at least potentially forced on the Catholic as a matter of course.

I don't think we are too far apart on this. I also don't think we can make too much headway toward closing the gap by letter. Let's have an evening on it soon.

Best regards,
Brent
6108 Kennedy Drive
Chevy Chase, Maryland

ઝ

March 14, 1960

Dear Brent:
Now it's my turn to apologize for tardiness in replying; but I won't bore you with excuses.

I think you have me on the business about a birth control rider on an otherwise blameless bill; certainly a Catholic should veto such a bill and give his reasons—*unless* a veto would mean that a largely necessary bill could not be passed at that session of Congress.

But there is more to the freedom question than our everyday definitions would suggest. Yes, a man is free to do evil; but ascetical theologians agree that this is the lowest form of freedom—indeed, almost the negation of freedom. The human beings who are most free are those who have reached the highest level of sanctity; and then, it seems, they have long since passed the point where they are "free" to do evil. Thus it is in Heaven, where we are all perfectly free—to choose only the good. Of course, it's a mystery, and by all means let's have an evening on it when you're in town. (Our home is strategically located halfway between New York and Stanford; blow in anytime.)

Did you see this interesting item in *The Wanderer*? This is the same Gerard Sherry who addressed a Catholic audience some months back on the theme that a Catholic could be neither anti-Negro, anti-union, nor anti-Communist. Of course, he later qualified the latter by saying "not *merely* anti-Communist"; but the

damage was done—as I'm sure he had intended.
Sincerely,
Neil

ᑳ

April 17, 1961

Dear Bill [Buckley],
You can't tell from looking, but the enclosed monstrosity is published by Maryknoll, no less. The last time you gave ten dollars to the missions you didn't know you were subsidizing this, did you?

This brings me to a cherished old idea of mine; I hope you admire its new dress. What would you think of doing a special issue in which a Protestant, Catholic and Jewish conservative did articles on liberal trends in their respective faiths? Morrie or Ralph for the Jews; Merrill Root or Russell Kirk or John Chamberlain or someone for the Protestants; and, hopefully, I for the Catholics. Everyone would get "equal time"; you would be probing an urgent issue, one very near the hearts of practically every one of our readers; and you would be putting it in *responsible* terms—unlike virtually all of the conservative protests against Liberalism in modern religion.

It goes without saying that I hope you will do this whether or not you think me a suitable candidate for the Catholic article; and if you give me a crack at the article, you can feel perfectly free to edit it for style, argue with me over content, or reject it entirely. Naturally, I would also have it checked by my Catholic confederates.

Regardless of any role I might play in it, this issue cries out to be done.
Best,
Neil

ᑳ

December 26, 1962

Dear Bill:
[…] I think the Vatican is behaving according to form. It's the Italian style. Why issue free handouts when you can pass out an unlimited number of rumors, all for a price? The rich Anglo-Saxons must produce so many hundreds of words a day; why shouldn't they pay when we can feed them 'news' by the hundredweight? The Vatican officials are underpaid, Italian fashion; and they are expected to supplement their incomes, Italian fashion. Yet the devil you know is better than the devil you don't know. I'm not convinced that the

Church would be run better with the Germans or the French or the Americans. [...]
Best,
Neil

C8

June 1, 1965

The Wanderer
128 East 10th Street
St. Paul 1, Minnesota

Editor:
I found much to disagree with in Garry Wills's "On the Present Position of Catholics", but nothing to justify Robert G. McCauley's groin-and-eyeball attack. He impugns the motives of Dr. Wills, assuming the prerogative of the Godhead to give the world a reading on the state of Wills's soul. (At another point Mr. McCauley comes out four-square for the Ten Commandments: something of a *tour de force* in light of the Eighth's strictures on rash judgment and the imputing of base motives.)

When McCauley leaves off his personal attacks, it is only to rise to travesty. Wills pleads for a more expeditious handling of marriage cases; McCauley's sensitive (and charitable) pen transmutes this into an appeal that Rome ape Reno and grant quickie annulments. Wills is, I think, too sanguine about the present ferment in the Church. But McCauley assembles a showy batch of Liberal Catholic demons and lays them all at the feet of Wills—including the same Chardin whom Wills has been attacking for upwards of five years.

One of McCauley's targets, decentralization in the Church, is a strange one for a conservative. Mr. McCauley sees decentralization as an attack on authority. This is the same argument used against the advocates of states' rights: we are accused of attacking the Presidency. (The other parallel, the attacks in totalitarian states on anyone who resists deifying the leader, is also worth pondering.)

In the first place, authority is not the Pope's alone. Christ established the Papacy, yes; He also chose twelve Apostles. The Church did not begin in 1870, and Catholic history will give the Rome-is-everything thesis some awkward moments. Until only yesterday, the Church was largely decentralized, even under strong Popes. Were we languishing in heresy for 19 centuries?

The drive for decentralization merely recognizes the obvious, that the Pope and his Curial staff cannot know everything and do

139

everything. The Pope knows less about conditions in Podunk than the Bishop there, and if we ask the Pope to involve himself too intimately in Podunk, the universal Church must suffer—and then the authority and prestige of the Papacy will indeed be undermined. Decentralization, by placing the Pope above certain mundane concerns that can be handled by lesser officials or by priests or by the laity, should really enhance the prestige of the Papacy.

This discussion suggests a larger problem that I believe is misunderstood by some Catholic conservatives. When the Pope agrees with us (e.g., on the right-to-work), some act as though debate is thereby closed. But when Papal remarks suggest a warmer endorsement of the UN or the welfare state than conservatives would give, how do these same people react? Often disingenuously, I am afraid. They look the other way. They blandly misread the obvious. They desperately search for one favorable sentence in a sea of hostile ones. (Needless to add, the Liberals are just as adept at the Papal Quotation game when they confront remarks on Communism or Socialism that make them squirm.)

How should loyal Catholics escape this dilemma? I think the dilemma is a false one. it grows out of a misunderstanding of Papal prerogatives. The authority of the Pope, not to say his infallibility, is not all-embracing but limited. The Pope doesn't know whether it will rain next Tuesday, doesn't know if the Mets can get out of the cellar this year, doesn't know how Italy can lick its balance-of-payments problem. He knows less about economics than Ludwig von Mises, less about politics than Dean Manion, less about the cold war than James Burnham, less about Communism than Frank Meyer.

I hope no one is shocked at this. I don't think our Lord would be (or the Holy Father). Christ might have picked Aristotle to start His Church. Instead, he chose a fisherman.

But this is a large question. I have never seen it better treated than in a respectful, profoundly conservative book called *Politics and Catholic Freedom*—by, of all people, Garry Wills.
Cordially,
Neil McCaffrey

ଔ

September 30, 1965

Dear Bill:
I have checked with Monsignor Cohalan, Father Clark and Father Pryor on your notion about birth control and the Religious Liberty Schema. I don't know any other priest nearby in whom I have

enough trust and confidence to confide the problem as you posed it.

Monsignor Cohalan stresses that this is only the first draft, comparable to a first reading of a bill in Parliament. He is of the opinion that the final conciliar statements on both issues will give the Liberals much less than they expect. He thus urges you "in the name of the Holy Undivided Trinity" to hold off commenting until the Council closes on December 8th. He sees nothing to be gained by haste and fears that you might be going out on a shaky limb.

He believes that the Religious Liberty Schema is not concerned so much with subjective sincerity as with limiting the civil authority's forays into the religious order. If it were only a question of subjective sincerity, what would we do with the snake worshippers and the polygamists?

He does not look for any relaxation of the ban on birth control, not even for *this* kind of pill.

As is usual in discussions of this kind with him, he fled from the realm of the abstract into the practical. He believes that the trend in Rome is now all against the Liberals—the worries of *Commonweal, America* and *The National Catholic Reporter* tend to confirm.

This is only a small part of what he poured into my ear. You might want to get the whole negative argument firsthand. Why not give him a call. His private number is RI 9 4659, and he is usually in from the late afternoon on.

Father Clark thinks you should wait until the Council closes. He believes we should continue to protest the use of public funds for the dissemination of birth control information, but that if we are outvoted we must go along. When I spoke to him he did not seem to expect a change in our position on birth control, although on another occasion both he and Father Pryor thought that we would probably wind up with an approval of the pill.

Father Clark believes, with me, that the Catholic retreat on corporate opposition to birth control legislation is already under way. Your stand, in short, will hardly seem revolutionary except to the *Wanderer* types.

Father Pryor likes your reasoning and thinks you are taking the right stand.

I think you have everything to gain and nothing to lose by waiting. Garry does not speak *ex cathedra*. Father Clark thinks he prepared a clever lawyer's brief for an untenable position. I think I agree, on the grounds that we cannot dismiss lightly or at all what was until yesterday the *universal* teaching of the hierarchy on what they regarded, to a man, as an urgent matter of morality.

Best,

Neil

 og

November 15, 1965

Dear Bill:

Thanks for sending on the letter from Farley Clinton which I enclose. It makes me a little nervous. Is he a somewhat saner and more stylish John Wisner? Could he fill a book with anything *relevant*? Who would be his readers?

I think you stayed just this side of innocence on the Viking-Putnam negotiations. Viking must clear with Putnam's, and I think you might have made your acceptance of their offer contingent upon their getting clearance. It is indeed a nice offer, but they are not throwing the money away. They will get it back and probably several times over.

The birth control controversies and sub-controversies make a tangled web for a Catholic. Of course there is no question of the subjective rightness of practicing contraception if you think it is okay; and the same holds true of snake worshipping. The question rather is, should Catholics (assuming the Church continues to damn contraception) try to make this a matter of public policy? Here I agree with you that there can be no "Catholic line". But this must work both ways. Catholics should feel free to take any side on the public policy question. In doubtful matters, liberty.

Do I read unjustly into your letter a disposition not only to tolerate the practice of contraception among those who do it in good faith, but to invest it with a kind of sacramental aura? I hope I am reading you wrong, because I think this notion romantic, the sort of thing I attribute to Planned Parenthood ladies who are the granddaughters of suffragettes and prohibitionists.

Yes, let's by all means get together for a long talk. I await your convenience.

Best,
Neil

og

January 5, 1966

To the Editors
National Catholic Reporter
P.O. Box 281
Kansas City, Missouri 64141

I am curious to know why you omitted my affiliation when you published my letter in your January 5 issue. When one of your loyal readers writes to complain that nuns are still being denied the rights of Lesbos, you are always careful to note that she is an instructor in ethics at East Dingle State Teachers.
Neil McCaffrey
President
Conservative Book Club

 catholic

January 20, 1966

To the Editors
National Catholic Reporter
P.O. Box 281
Kansas City, Missouri 64141

As you say, there are no hard-and-fast rules about whether to give a correspondent's professional identification. If I were editing a newspaper and printed a letter on Catholic peaceniks from the Publisher of N.C.R., I would deem his affiliation relevant. When the President of the Conservative Book Club offers a conservative view of your ventures in political morality, his affiliation is equally germane. In this case, your journalistic touch went dead.

As for the free plug, I would assess its value, among the zealots who subsist from week to week on N.C.R.'s intoxicating fare, at about 98% less than your ad rates.

I am glad you have discovered the problem of good taste, and I can only apologize for taxing your urbanity. But to identify yourselves, in all Homeric innocence, with the renewal of religious life—well, as everyone says, we've long needed a Catholic humor weekly.
Neil McCaffrey
President
Conservative Book Club

catholic

June 16, 1967

Your Eminence [Francis Cardinal Spellman]:
I am enclosing a copy of a letter [see below] I just wrote to Mother Mary Cleophas of the School of the Holy Child. It covers a matter that is likely to concern you, since it deals with a problem that seems now to be present, more or less, in every Catholic high school in America.
Yours respectfully,
Neil McCaffrey

ભ

June 16, 1967

Dear Mother Cleophas:
It is my sad task to advise you that we are transferring Maureen to Pelham High School next year. Mrs. McCaffrey and I took this decision after long thought, and I think we owe you an explanation. Though we have what seem to us serious criticisms of the education Maureen has been getting, they should not be read as reflecting on you or on the faculty. Quite the contrary. Though I have not myself had the pleasure of meeting you, Mrs. McCaffrey and Maureen assure me that you are a charming, gentle lady and an admirable Christian. So this letter is all the harder to write.

We ask ourselves four questions about a school. First and foremost, does it give a child a good grounding in Catholic doctrine? What are its intellectual standards? What about its social tone? What of the moral atmosphere?

Holy Child's performance as a Catholic school is what disturbs us most. In this it is, I am sure, no worse than the others; though also no better. Doctrine is diluted. Morality becomes equivocal. There is no enthusiasm for Catholic culture, Catholic history. There is none of the—dare I utter the discredited word?—old-fashioned Catholic élan.

You are entitled to specifics. At one point in religion class, the question of diabolism came up. The resident expert on the Black Mass was called in for a long, vivid description of the whole horror. Was this voyeurism necessary from a nun, for fifteen-year-old girls? If a question about prostitution came up, would Polly Adler become required reading? If someone asked a question about homosexuality, would the girls be given Cenet?

The juniors spent a good part of the year discussing abortion in religion class. In college ethics we covered the matter adequately in about a half hour. Maureen's class was told that the Consecration is not the most important part of the Mass. It seems the Consecration has been supplanted by something called the "Great Amen". Our Lord would be surprised, if I may be pardoned an anthropomorphism. A girl asked in class about French kissing. Sister temporized, declined to condemn it. Would Sister be quite so casual if she had a daughter of fifteen who came to her with the same question? How would she feel about what is euphemistically called petting? How about fornication? Would "love" make everything all right?

Then there is the politicalization of religion. Martin Luther King is hailed as a prophet. The girls' reading list includes James Baldwin, a homosexual revolutionary who describes Christ as a "sun-baked fanatic". The luminaries of Catholic letters in the English-speaking world—Newman, Chesterton, Waugh, Greene, Belloc, Knox, Philip Hughes—found no place on Maureen's reading lists. They had to make room for *The Cross and the Switchblade*, *Black Like Me*, and *The Junkie Priest*: all titles on the *religion* reading list. This is *education*? *Catholic* education?

I think a public high school would be better. There they are frankly secularist, and a child is on his mettle. The most immediate danger to the faith of our youngsters is a Catholicism without content, without doctrine, without objective moral standards—and all served up by priests and nuns who are posing as spokesmen for the Church.

Holy Child maintains reasonably good scholastic standards. So does Pelham High School. A standoff.

As for social tone, I fear that Holy Child has lost faith in its mission, which is to train girls to become young *ladies*. To be sure, good manners still prevail at Holy Child. But so many of our clergy and religious are infected with guilt feelings about the pursuit of quality, especially in its social manifestations. The Holy Child faculty seems to think it must condemn a system that makes it possible for anyone to live outside the Inner City. They should be made to memorize Newman's reflections on what makes a gentleman, and why gentlemen are important. The social classes are the repositories of excellence. Leveling is its enemy. The pursuit of excellence is what education is all about. And *noblesse oblige* is Christian charity at work.

As for morals among the student body, I understand that the line is being held pretty well but that soft spots are showing up (as seems to be the case in Pelham High School). Once again, a standoff. But are you aware that a noticeable percentage of the girls are casual about Mass and the Sacraments? Surely this isn't surprising, with the cues they are getting from the faculty, who in turn take their cues from the Catholic revolutionaries who have discovered how to make the headlines.

What is pitiful is that so many priests and religious are being taken in. Lunches with John Cogley, cocktail parties with John Leo, black-and-white orgies with this month's civil rights hero—how glamorous they all seem, until you have been to a few of them. How nice to get a write-up in the *Times*; except that the *Times* exacts its price. How easy to mistake novelty for renewal, revolution for reform, camp-following for relevance, sentimentality for charity, emotion for reason. And how pitiful to see our priests and nuns so tired of the faith of our fathers.

Have you ever read Ronald Knox's *Enthusiasm*? It is *the* book for our times, and therefore much neglected by today's pied pipers. Yesterday's quackery is today's New Religion. I think you will experience the shock of recognition when you read this book.

Thank you, Mother Cleophas, for the nice things you have done for Maureen over the past two years. I hope that the reasons for our taking her out of Holy Child soon vanish, for all our sakes. And God's.
Kindest regards,
Neil McCaffrey

P. S. The cry goes up for honesty in the Church. Here, surely, is a crusade we can all join hands in. I put this to you solemnly: don't you owe it to parents to make clear that Holy Child is committed to radical Christianity? That it preaches the gospel according to Teilhard de Chardin, U Thant, Jack Kennedy and Stokely Carmichael? Granted, more than a few parents would balk at coming across with $500 a year for Harvey Cox. But they are entitled, in strict justice, to know what they are buying. I'm sure you would be quick to condemn a businessman who made his sales budget by mislabeling the merchandise.

☙

July 13, 1967

Dear Monsignor Rigney [New York Archdiocesan Superintendent of Schools]:
Thank you for your letter of July 7. I think you have chosen to miss my essential points, which are:
1. Are the incidents set forth in my letter of June 16 accurate?
2. If so, do you regard them as defensible?
3. If defensible, do you consider it a school's duty to advise

parents that it is featuring the New Look in Catholic education?

Your letter suggests that you would answer yes to the first two questions, and no to the third. If so, I guess the matter is closed.

But not quite. Because I decline the role of defendant, and insist that our discussions can indeed be pursued by letter—the better to assure that His Eminence does not fall victim to what you describe as "lack of proper communication." An exchange of letters is not, after all, an unheard-of form of communication.

To reinforce this point, I asked Maureen to write out what Mother Campion had told the girls in class about the Black Mass. Maureen blushed. (Nuns now make teenagers blush.) I insisted. This is how Maureen wrote it out: "This is how she described the Black Mass. The altar is the body of a naked woman. A consecrated Host is placed in her vagina and all the men in the congregation have intercourse with her. They then urinate on her. All the girls I spoke to found this lecture sickening."

Now, Monsignor, let's make sure we are communicating properly; *What do you think of this—from a nun, to a class of fifteen-year-old girls?* (Am I getting through?)

When you ask why I did not communicate with Mother Cleophas first (i.e., why did I have to bring His Eminence into this), I realize that you don't expect, or want, an answer. Nonetheless, you asked:

1. I recognize the odds against convincing avant-garde Catholics that they are reeds in the wind. They have already experienced traditional Catholicism, and have turned on it with hatred.

2. Nor did I want to be drowned in a sea of marshmallow.

3. Nor do I need an exegesis of the avant-garde position, and of my benighted ways. I too read the *National Catholic Reporter*.

4. Nor did I want Maureen vulnerable to reprisals. (I still believe in original sin, and human imperfectability.)

5. Nor, above all, did I have any confidence that this swarm of novelty seekers could be approached on any commonsense level. Have events not borne me out?

I undertook this correspondence in the conviction (also borne out) that His Eminence cares about kookery; and that he may be dogged by authority's age-old problem of functionaries who decide for him what he should hear, and how and even whether his own wishes should be carried out.

I know you want to de-escalate this, Monsignor. I know you want to reduce it to something manageable like "the McCaffrey problem," then file it away. (You see, we understand each other. We are Communicating.) But I view this one school as a microcosm of Catholic education today.

So I urge you to pause for a few minutes of eschatological meditation. You owe me no explanations; your responsibilities are far more solemn than that. After your pondering, if you still think the girls should be getting more of Martin Luther King than John Henry Newman, if you still think Mother Campion on the Black Mass squares with your ideal of Catholic education, then I hope you will consider asking for a new assignment; or, perhaps better, to be laicized.
Cordially,
Neil McCaffrey

ॐ

July 21, 1967

Dear Gene [Clark]:
I just had a call from Monsignor Doherty. He was speaking, a little nervously, for The Boss. He said he had been authorized to invite me to a meeting, but that he will be gone for three weeks and Mother Cleophas is out of the country for a couple of weeks.

It was a cordial enough chat, but he seemed nervous, as if he was afraid to depart from the script. I asked him what purpose he thought a meeting could serve. He mumbled something about clarifying the issues, and added that he had been authorized to offer me a meeting. I said that I had nothing really to add, and that I thought the matter now rested with him. He replied that he had only been authorized to invite me to a meeting. I said that I knew less about the matter than Joan and Maureen and that I thought any meeting should include them. He said that he had been authorized to invite only me. (Incidentally, I'm glad I didn't go on for the priesthood.) I asked him if I might think about it and drop him a line next week. We left it there.

So now I'm thinking about it and solicit your advice. Does a meeting accomplish anything? It isn't I they have to placate—as I pointed out to Doherty. What can I say but what I have already said? The notion of arguing with them strikes me as being as fruitful as milking a bull. And we are *not* sending Maureen back to Holy Child.

Please call me and advise.

On my letter to Rigney, Bill writes: "You were on top of your argument with Monsignor Rigney until that last sentence—which was fatally inept." Joan agrees. No doubt you do too. In the face of all this authority I'd be hubristic not to feel sobered. I do; yet I'm not entirely sure I was wrong. There is something to be said for righteous indignation, especially when it cuts through cant. Maybe

this is one of the little mysteries whose solution will have to await the Last Day.
Best,
Neil

Ↄ

July 31, 1967

Dear Monsignor Doherty:
I've been thinking about your call of July 21. I'd be glad to meet with you, provided only that you deal straightforwardly with me.
I asked you the purpose of the meeting, the subjects to be discussed. You would not answer in specifics.
I explained that I had nothing to add to the information I gave in my letters of June 16 and July 13; that I consider it supererogatory for me to lecture you and patronizing for you to lecture me; that the responsibility for correcting—or, God forbid, endorsing—the teaching at Holy Child lay with you, not me; and that I therefore could not divine your objective. You would not reveal it.
I asked if Mrs. McCaffrey and Maureen might be present, since they know more about Holy Child Academy than I. You refused—on what grounds I cannot guess; surely you don't expect the discussion to get gamier than Mother Campion on the Black Mass?
As of now, we do not have the basis of a fruitful talk. I have raised serious questions. Neither you nor Mother Cleophas has replied, and Monsignor Rigney's letter was merely a generalized defense that shrank from answering my specific points or grappling with the larger implications.
Yet you want to talk. Can *this* be what you mean by "dialogue"? Before we can talk to any purpose, you will have to come up with straight answers:
1. Why do you decline to discuss these matters by letter? Why should you shrink from committing yourself?
2. To assure that His Eminence gets an uncolored report of our talk, are you prepared to let me bring my tape recorder?
3. Are Mrs. McCaffrey and Maureen welcome? If not, why?
4. Are you prepared to discuss each point raised in my letters of June 16 and July 13? If not, why?
And since you decline to provide an agenda, let me add to the above:
1. A discussion of Matthew XVIII, 6 and Mark VIII, 36.
2. A resolution of this question: Is a Catholic high school meant to give a student a knowledge of the Faith as it has been held for upwards of 19 centuries? Or is your aim to wipe out the past?

3. If the former and not the latter, will you explain why Holy Child girls read nothing (at least through sophomore year) of Newman, Knox, Undset, Chesterton, Waugh, Belloc? Will you explain why the four *required* books in sophomore religion are, rather *The Junkie Priest, Black Like Me, The Cross and the Switchblade* and a book on charm? (I include a few choice pages from two of them.)

4. If you approve of the Holy Child style, is it your settled policy to pursue it in the other diocesan high schools? Are the parents to be so advised? If not, why?

5. Alternatively, would you consider organizing some schools on the principles of radical Catholicism and others on the principles of traditional Catholicism? Will you so advise the parents and thus give them a choice? If not, how do you justify keeping parents in the dark?

6. What advantages do Holy Child and other radical Catholic schools offer over public schools?

7. Since radical Catholicism by definition makes the individual conscience the norm of faith and morality, is it possible to endorse radical Catholicism and at the same time, consistently, to maintain that a Catholic is obliged to support Catholic schools that violate his conscience? For that matter, is it possible to retain any absolutes while espousing radical Catholicism?

Monsignor Rigney wrote me a little lecture to the effect that you educational experts will not tolerate interference from us amateurs. In light of this expertise you lay claim to, surely you have ready answers for my perhaps naive questions. And since these will be Expert Answers, you will have no reason not to put them in writing or on tape, will you, Monsignor?

Because unless you are prepared to, Monsignor, don't bother to write or call. I am president of two companies and consultant to five national organizations. I haven't time for bureaucratic maneuverings. If you feel ready to reply *to the points I have raised in this letter*, then we can talk. Otherwise, please spare me further messages from the Friendly Sons of Port Royal.
Cordially,
Neil McCaffrey

ભ

November 28, 1967

Dear Brent:
What with closing the deal to buy the Club, I have been busy beyond all reason over the past month. That is why I only now have a chance

to reply to your fund-raising letter. I am enclosing $200: the same as my last contribution, not double it. And I want to tell you why.

The same, because *Triumph* should be kept alive. Not double, because I want to register some disquiet about the course it is taking.

In a word, I object to Wisnerism—or should it be Bozellism? With orthodox Catholic doctrine and morals under attack, and with the shepherds deserting their flocks in the face of it, surely *Triumph* has enough to keep it busy. Must the defense of orthodoxy involve alienation from American values? Spanish Catholicism is fine, for Spaniards. I can't accept the notion that there is little to choose between Washington and Moscow, or that America—non-Catholic as well as Catholic America—is the capital of Satan's empire. And if we must look abroad for inspiration (and there is no reason why we shouldn't), I suggest pre-1960 English Catholicism.

I was especially appalled when I read that you exhorted the faithful at the *Wanderer* Forum to "vomit out of your mouth and being, the word, approach and mood of Conservative." Everyone who sends you money will be a conservative of one sort or another. Shouldn't you tell your contributors that you despise them?

What is going on in the Church now is not merely a struggle. Those of us who love the Church (however feebly we might serve her) are in the position of watching a gang of thugs take our Mother and turn her into a harlot. And much the same is happening to our country. So Catholic conservatives must live with two kinds of heartbreak. You share only one, and seem to rejoice in the other.
Best,
Neil

 C3

December 11, 1967

Dear Brent:
Would you like to publish this? Even though you might not agree with every sentence.

An Alternative for Conservative Catholics
Neil McCaffrey

It all happened so fast. The disintegration of the Church in America can now be measured in months, not decades. Last night we went to sleep at peace. Today the cockle is choking the wheat. Small wonder we were unprepared.

Traditional Catholics bring to the battle certain psychological impediments. We have tended to assume that the old safeguards would operate. They're taking away the Latin Mass? Well, Latin is not *de fide*. Father McGillicuddy is saying strange things about Teilhard and original sin? Surely the old Monsignor will take care of him. Sister Patricia has canonized Martin Luther King? Reverend Mother will never stand for *that*. Priests are saying Mass in people's living rooms? Now they've *really* gone too far. The bishops *have* to crack down. The Dutch hierarchy have actually sponsored a catechism that throws off the whiff of heresy? This is the last straw. Now, finally, the Pope will move.

After the first thousand shocks, it is beginning to dawn on the most sanguine that Monsignor and Reverend Mother and His Excellency and His Holiness are *not* going to move. Or, if they do, they will move clumsily, ineffectually, too late. And so traditional Catholics find themselves bewildered, in disarray. Part of the disarray, I suspect, springs from an error most of us fell heir to. Not much burdened with a knowledge of Catholic history, we have assumed that Authority could do no wrong; well, very little wrong; well, at least nothing *seriously* wrong. And so we found ourselves disarmed. We were sure Authority carried a good swift sword. It turns out to be made of celluloid.

Let us review, briefly and informally, how we fashioned the paper tiger that bore a banner marked "Father says no." The Church is infallible, yes: but *only* in matters touching the deposit of faith. The Pope is infallible, yes—but only when he speaks *ex cathedra*. and this he has done but three times in 114 years. The bishop is infallible? No, except when he speaks with his colleagues in council, with the pope ratifying. Father is infallible? Never. No one, I assume, will quarrel with the above as doctrine. But who will deny that *as a practical matter* we tended to give Authority more authority than Christ gave it? Our Lord Himself chose the Twelve; yet one of the Twelve was a traitor, and ten of the others deserted Him. I cannot believe that our Lord meant all this as anything but a lesson for us. And for those bearing authority.

Not only have we exaggerated the authority of Authority. More to the point in our present crisis, we assumed that Authority was wise in areas quite outside that of Christ's promise. Christ promised that the Church would endure—not that His successors would always rule wisely, or with resolution. (Peter himself blundered badly about the Gentiles in the Church, and it took nothing less than a special revelation to set him straight.)

I stress all this not merely because Authority is now behaving suicidally. It is also behaving heartlessly. Authority has in effect said: We can take you *good* Catholics for granted. We can tear from your bosom the faith of your youth, the consolation of your suffering years. "You won't complain—you never have. You'll swallow anything. You'll keep coming, and keep contributing. You are sheep. Our right flank is covered.

"So we'll move to the left. The future lies with Kosygin and U Thant and *The New York Times*. We'll ride the wave of the future."

I don't mean to say that the shepherds are *calculatedly* harsh; and neither do I think we can let them off the hook by simply saying that they "mean well." At the least, I think they have shown a massive insensitivity to the needs and desires of their flock. We are suffocated with prattle about "democracy" in the Church. But did the hierarchy ever ask *us* whether we want an English Mass? Whether we want to jettison the Baltimore Catechism? Whether we think open housing and coexistence should be articles of faith?

Far from it. The changes that had to be noticed were decreed. Others, like the scuttling of the old catechism, were introduced without a by-your-leave, while we were looking the other way.

But the radicals will counter, we are diehards. We have not yet found our way into the 20th Century. The bulk of the laity *have* been heard. Michael Novak, Dan Herr and Robert Hoyt are their spokesmen.

Perhaps. But even if these avatars of the Brave New World can speak for the majority (which I doubt; they bleed too profusely for the residents of the Inner City to have much plasma left over for their despised suburban neighbors), we traditionalists also have souls. Assume, for argument's sake, that we make up only 10% of the American Church. Are we then to be left to die by the wayside while the majority march on toward Progress, to the beat of twanging guitars?

So it would seem. And this is why I find it hard to let our leaders off so easily. This is why I greet with vast cynicism their "moral commitment," their discovery of Love. You see, I've heard that song before: "You have to break a few eggs to make an omelette."

Fortunately, we conservatives have an alternative. Oddly, it is the radicals who have presented it to us. Which may be why we have been slow to grasp it. This is the age of the laity, we are told. A new age of freedom has come for the Latin Mass? On a *real* altar? With his *back* to us?

If "floating parishes" are to proliferate like floating escape games, can't we find some gutsy pastor who still yearns to preside over a *real* parish? With a school that is not ashamed to be Catholic? I think he'd draw families from miles around. (Granted, most pastors are conditioned to Go Along. But I can't believe they've all lost their manhood. Who knows, maybe there's one near you who is just waiting for your invitation to the adventure of orthodoxy.)

As for schools, if your parochial school has deserted you and your CCD classes are hopeless, all is not lost. Have you thought of neighborhood religion classes? My wife started one—small, modest—when we discovered that Eileen, after four years of parochial school, didn't know the Commandments. So far, it's working fine.

For that matter, if you despair of both parochial and public schools in your neighborhood, have you thought of launching a small independent school? It needn't be confined to Catholics. If the school is open to children of all faiths (or none), arrangements could be made to break up the classes just for religious instruction; for those parents who want it for their children.

The alternatives are there if we shake ourselves and wake up to the fact that it's going to be up to *us*. Anything goes in the Church today, say the wreckers; and the bishops assent by their silence. Of course we don't agree with the wreckers; but if they have created an atmosphere in which just about anything seems to go, then surely we can maneuver within that framework to see that orthodoxy stays alive. And we have precedent, as Newman reminds us. The Arian heresy won most of the hierarchy. The laity kept the faith alive.

If, as I believe, many members of the hierarchy are prisoners of radical "public opinion", the best way to bestir them would be just such manifestations of grassroots orthodoxy. I suspect that many bishops would dearly love to be convinced that Robert Hoyt does not speak for you.

I have written here mostly in terms of long-term projects. They will be the most constructive. Meanwhile, short-term projects should not be overlooked. Archbishop Cousins has been getting buttons in the collection basket from Catholics who believe that open housing works both ways, that neighborhoods should not be sacrificed to ideology. May the buttons continue to pour into the Archbishop's residence.

Closer to home, if your parochial school no longer allows the children to call themselves Catholic (in ours, the children may say only "Christian"), and if the parish magazine rack enthrones JFK and Chardin, should you be contributing to their support? Should you, as Lenin said of the capitalists, vie to sell the rope that will hang you? If your alma mater boasts it is no longer Catholic, why keep writing that annual check? Did you make your usual donation to Catholic University? If so, why? If not, did you write your pastor and your bishop a polite note telling them why? Certainly, we have an obligation to support the church; and a corresponding obligation to withhold support from those who, we believe, distort her message. There are orthodox Catholic causes still worthy of your dollar. If you search hard enough.

I hope no one will read this as an invitation to schism, even an oblique invitation. This is *our* Church. Like a family, we may not always be proud of its elders or its members. But it is still ours, we owe it filial love, it is our hope. We owe it loyalty, too: and not just in fair weather. Once the loyalty came easier. Once the yoke was sweet, the burden light. Now we are in a tunnel—or, rather, a madhouse. The consolations are gone. Our home is in the hands of strangers. Strangers who hate us, who tell us to conform or die.

Let us turn their own non-conformity against them. If they have the freedom to preach contempt of the Church we know and love, surely we have the freedom to defend, to resist, to cherish what is part of ourselves. As Americans we are accustomed to exercise generous freedoms in the temporal sphere. We are not used to having to use them in the Church. Now we must, or be swept away. And the radicals do mean to sweep us away. They preach freedom—but only their own brand. They leave in their wake a totalitarian stink.

ߜ

August 18, 1969

Dear Father Mahoney [S.J., Dean of Studies, Fordham Prep]:
My son Neil just received his outline of the Junior religion course. Neil and his mother and I have discussed it at length and have a request.

We are Catholics of the traditional sort and feel that this religion course is not merely useless, but misleading and dangerous. I realize that you disagree and I would not presume to argue the point with you. And since I have weighed the point of view that is reflected in this course and find it a disaster, I think it would be a waste of your time and mine if you attempted to convince me otherwise. Let us agree to disagree, and go from there.

Our request is simply that you excuse Neil from religion this year. Since he takes six courses anyway, credits will not be a problem. We would like him to be excused because of the aforementioned reason; and because since Neil feels obliged not only to resist the thrust of what we consider to be pseudo-theology, and moreover to argue his traditional principles as best he can, an antagonism is built up between Neil and his teacher which is reflected in below-average marks for him in this course.

I think we should be granted this request because, primarily and ultimately, we are responsible for the education of our children. We

155

take it as our first obligation as Catholic parents to do our best to pass on the traditional faith to our children. So far I think Neil's has not been undermined. If I thought it had been, I would naturally withdraw him immediately from Fordham. But a religion course should not be a battle for him. He should not be exposed to indoctrination that chips away at his principles. He should not be asked to waste his time.

If Neil were a campus revolutionary, I have no doubt that the authorities would ponder and agonize over his demands, and probably meet most or all of them. Is it too much to ask that Catholics who subscribe to the Nicene Creed and other definitions of orthodoxy be accorded the same privilege?

Given our views, you are entitled to wonder why we keep Neil in Fordham. First, he likes it. Second, he can take Greek there. Third, it is not yet coed, and we think coeducation is inferior. Finally, since Catholic parents in general are more concerned about behavior than about orthodoxy, they cling to the Catholic schools as lesser evils. The Catholic high schools cling to their constituency by maintaining a measure of their traditional discipline. Thus, another plus for Fordham—at least for the moment.

Could you let me know your decision by return mail? I'd be grateful.

Kindest regards,
Neil McCaffrey

ભ

October 3, 1972

Dear Dan [Dan Mahoney, Esq.]:
We've had a chance to review *Glory in Exile*. Before I comment on the manuscript itself, a few words about the market.

As far as I know, there are three fairly recent orthodox catechisms: St. Joseph's, the one from the Daughters of St. Paul, and Msgr. McGuire's. Not to mention the best, the Baltimore Catechism.

As I understand it, all of these catechisms are finding it tough going. The catechetical Establishment has a horror of sound doctrine. So I don't see any market, for the moment, for yet another catechism that pays its respects to orthodoxy.

As to the work in question, all praise to Msgr. Fowler for hewing to the orthodox line. But I'm afraid I'm less enthusiastic about the pedagogy. It is an effort to reconcile the current cant about love with orthodoxy. But because the Christian ideal of love is today reduced to vulgar sentimentality, the effort is doomed.

The idea of Christian love is not easy to grasp, and I'm certainly not the one to set it forth with any authority. But it is easy enough to spot its counterfeit, that vague, generalized good will that turns people to mush. Humanitarianism, that bastard child of charity, has all but conquered the Church, and this catechism carries it along on a sea of ooze.

Love is hard. It doesn't necessarily make you feel good. It has to be motivated by faith, informed by intelligence and tested in the will. It has nothing to do with feeling benevolent. This catechism, in trying to teach love, caricatures it. It flees from the concrete problems in favor of vague benign sentiments. This is the surest way to make love unreal and impossible to the child. Do you expect your daughter to turn around and smile at the brat who just pulled her hair? This is about all the catechism would suggest (if it dared to confront such a tough question).

The catechism we learned from in the bad old days was on the right track. Never mind the cant about respecting the child today: the old catechism had real respect for him. It set things out in logical fashion, and paid you the compliment of expecting you to be able to follow logic, be able to memorize it, and eventually come to understand it. So, in your impressionable years, you memorized an awesome body of doctrine. And much of it stuck. Today we feed the children a diet of molasses. And they die of malnutrition.

The prologue is an embarrassing attempt to be with it. It sinks in a tidal wave of clichés. The austere, no-nonsense, downright, winning, fiery God of the New Testament comes out sounding like Adlai Stevenson as Eleanor Roosevelt might have described him.

Where is St. Ignatius, now when we need him most?

Best,
Neil

ೞ

November 2, 1972

Editor
The Wanderer

The Archdiocese of New York has just issued a survey on Mass attendance. Based on reports from 343 of the 410 parishes in the Archdiocese, the survey reveals that 824,475 Catholics attend Mass on a typical Sunday in 1965. For 1970, the figure dropped to 627,235. This is a decline of twenty-two percent.

Any Catholic with eyes in his head has noticed the decline in

Mass attendance. Now it's official.

Isn't this where we came in? A decade ago, the Hierarchy set about to pick apart Catholic teaching and Catholic practice. It was all, you will recall, done in the name of updating religion, making religion more relevant, making the faith more meaningful to Catholics and non-Catholics, bringing religion into everyday life—pick your own cliché.

Now that the Hierarchy can see the shambles they have created (or rather, the first fruits of the shambles), will they move to repair the devastation by restoring traditional Catholic practices and teachings and emphases?

I doubt it.

Will they at least learn the lesson that conservatives keep trying to teach Liberals, that it is much easier to destroy than to build?

I doubt that, too.

Neil McCaffrey
Pelham Manor, N.Y.

&

January 15, 1973

Dear Gene:

Did you see the Firing Line last night on which Bill had Garry pontificating on the collapse of the Church? It's pretty bad. It was bound to be bad, the way Bill set up the program. Garry was mouthing tired modernism, misinterpreting Newman, misinterpreting everything in his own self-serving way. But there was no conflict. Bill was merely a gentle, polite interviewer. He was quite incapable of puncturing Garry's nonsense—yet he didn't bother to have a counterforce on the program. He described Garry's arguments on birth control as "entirely persuasive". With friends like that . . .

Best,
Neil

&

April 3, 1973
MEMO TO: Gene Clark
FROM: Neil

Do you find it hard keeping up with the flood of converts in this springtime of the Faith?

It may indeed be that the carelessness and bad example of parents are causing the drop in Mass attendance among Catholic students.

But since Catholic education is now giving our children so much more than they ever got before, I'm confident that the dedicated priests and nuns will ultimately prevail. But what a tragedy that the parents are stabbing them in the back.

ଔ

June 27, 1973

Mr. Neil McCaffrey
Arlington House Publishers
81 Centre Avenue
New Rochelle, New York

Dear Neil:
Enclosed are the rosary beads which were blessed by his Holiness, Pope Paul, on Saturday, June 23rd. The beads are a gift from me and our mutual friend, Monsignor Eugene Clark. The beads were blessed when the Pope entered the American Art section of the new Vatican Modern Art Museum and had an audience with the 50 people who were there.

As I understand it, Monsignor Clark played a very substantial role in making the arrangements for the group to come to the Vatican and spend five days in celebration of the opening of the Modern Art Museum. A portion of time that we spent together was in the small hotel bar. I was drinking Dubonnet. I think the Monsignor was drinking something harder.

After a while in my left-wing egalitarian manner I started to call him "Rev". I thought this was appropriate, ecumenically speaking, since I do the same with representatives of other major faiths who happen to be friends of mine.

In the course of our quasi-serious discussions surrounded by quiet and not so quiet guitar music, the Monsignor characterized his old friend Neil as follows: "Whenever a conservative position is taken generally, Neil has already been there and is already two steps to the right."

During one of the evenings the guitar player came over to our table and played Ave Maria for the Monsignor. It was cornball as hell but really very effective. I was really very moved.

I was delighted to hear that your son Eugene was named after the Monsignor. It is indeed a pleasantly small world.

Needless to say, I was in absolute and complete awe of the power and majesty of the Vatican. St. Peters is unbelievably beautiful, second only to the Sistine Chapel. On reflection, however, this power is demonstrated to me in still another way. The Museum of Modern Art that the Vatican is setting up has only one requirement in the works that it acquires and that is that the works have a religious theme. This being the case, the Vatican has acquired works by persons who have in the past and who may still presently have views antithetical to the established Church. Thus, for example, works of Picasso, Siqueiros, Shahn and others, all of which are of a deeply religious theme, are hung side by side with works depicting traditional Catholic themes. This demonstrates to me a subtle power whereby the Church feels itself sufficiently secure to accept the spiritual nature of the works even though the artist may have specific views contrary to the views of the Church.

Another example of the point I am making is the Grace given by Cardinal Cooke at our farewell dinner. In apparent recognition of the fact that a substantial minority of the people there were Jewish, the Cardinal said Grace without specific reference to Christ. He could have done so if he wished but in my view he, too, reflects a feeling of security that comes only with power.

In thinking about it I truly believe that this is a most beneficial use of power, i.e., the ability to be flexible and to tolerate differences. This posture can only be taken if the power does not feel threatened. Obviously the Vatican is not threatened and thus it can move forward with a true goal orientation.

A second conclusion I have drawn, which is a perfectly obvious one, is that the Vatican thrives on symbols. Of course, this is true with all religions because if you do not have symbols and short hand methods of obtaining desired spiritual responses, one would have to constantly repeat the litany.

An example of this was the concert given by Leonard Bernstein and the Newark Boys Choir in commemoration of the Pope's Tenth Anniversary. Picture, if you will, the stage of the huge auditorium, seating approximately 8000 people, with the Newark Boys Choir made up of substantially all black children from Newark. Beneath them and still on the stage is Leonard Bernstein, a world recognized conductor who is Jewish. Directly below them in the center line, seated by himself, was his Holiness. Throughout the performance and during the comments afterwards the Boys Choir and Leonard Bernstein were facing the Pope and the Pope was facing them. The drama and symbolism of the occasion was surely intended and at least to me achieved the desired result.

A final view. I was so much in awe of what I saw that I asked myself with some amazement how the Jewish people have managed to survive in view of all this majesty and panoply. I mentioned this to the "Rev". His response was: "Well, we are in there trying anyhow."

I really hope you get to the Vatican soon, Neil, and I thank you for listening to my comments.

Best regards.

Sincerely,

Martin Bressler

P.S. —Obviously the meter is not running on this one.

୧ଓ

June 29, 1973

Dear Martin:

I was fascinated by your perceptive letter. Your reactions are remarkably acute.

And I'm doubly grateful for your thoughtfulness in sending me the rosary blessed by the Pope (Gene's excellent crack notwithstanding). I take as my model vis-à-vis the Pope, the attitude of St. Catherine of Siena. When several popes left Rome to dally for decades in France where they had no business, St. Catherine went to see one of them at Avignon. Her first act was to enter and abase herself before him as the Vicar of Christ and the successor of St. Peter. Then she arose and gave him hell for flouting his obligations as pope. This is the way popes should be treated.

I rejoice in Gene's description of me. It is one of the nicest things anyone has said in a long time.

My reaction to the welcome of Picasso, Shahn, Siqueiros and the like into the Vatican was less than grateful. But your interpretation of it is at least as valid as mine—and, ironically, more in the Catholic tradition. There is truth in *both* reactions. That is one of the interesting things about being a Catholic. It is a world of paradox.

Your remarks about Church power and symbolism are comparably acute. But the Church *is* threatened; and in the past decade it has done more to destroy its own symbolism than anyone but her enemies who periodically lay waste to churches.

I got a little shock when I read your remark about how amazing it is that the Jews have survived over against all this majesty; not a distasteful shock, just sense of being caught up with a way of looking at something that is so different from my own. *We* think of the Church as our mother, not threatening to anyone; and (when we are thinking as we should) we think of ourselves as the guests who were invited to the wedding feast at the last minute, so all that food shouldn't go to waste. You have the prior claim. But there must be some reason in the divine economy why it isn't the Jewish Catholic Church. Maybe then it would be too easy. Maybe it is in keeping with the posture of humility that Christ adopted that he chooses to work with us second-string people.

Yes, I must get to the Vatican. Meanwhile, I can't tell you how grateful I am to you for sharing your visit with me.
Best,
Neil

ↄ

March 7, 1974

Dear Mrs. [C. W.] Baars:
Your letter was a tonic, to all the family. We know there are other families like our own, but it is always a tonic to share experiences. The most ominous note in your letter is your observation (largely correct, alas) that most of the parents are willing to accept the present state of the schools and the Church. I suppose we shouldn't be surprised. Most people *want* authority. But when authority leads them astray . . .

Our son Neil goes to Dallas, and Roger will be joining him next year. We are delighted with the school. Everything you say about it is true: not all the professors there can be trusted. But that was always and everywhere true. Though of course not in the same menacing context we have today. At any rate, the school has been wonderful for Neil and I think it will be for Roger too.

But would you ever have dreamed, ten or fifteen years ago, that we would today be reduced to one good Catholic college (along with a few others that aren't as bad as most, and a few others barely beyond the embryo stage)? I can only think of the speed with which Henry VIII and Cromwell all but wiped out the Church in England.

Yes, we will surely remember your family in our prayers. And thank you for yours. And for your wonderful letter.
Sincerely,
Neil McCaffrey

ↄ

May 14, 1975

Editor
Our Sunday Visitor
Noll Plaza
Huntington, Indiana 46750

Editor:
Mr. Whitehead gets all the better of the argument with Msgr. McHugh, and for a wonderfully simple reason: Msgr. McHugh can't get around the explicit condemnations of sex education by Pope Pius XI and Pope Pius XII. A more disturbing question: how can Msgr. McHugh ignore these condemnations and still continue in the responsible position he holds?
Neil McCaffrey

ଔ

May 21, 1975

Dear Ken [Kenneth Whitehead]:
Now that you mention it, conservative Catholics don't give CUF the reception it deserves. I'm not sure I know why. Probably there is no sovereign reason, but many individual reasons. Among them might be: some are generally discouraged; some prefer not to look the scandals in the face; some are afraid to venture from the official line (or non-line); some prefer a more militant stance; some are more interested in temporal affairs; some have no appetite for painful, plodding work that involves little immediate return and no glamor; and many have never heard of CUF.

I'm sure this catalog doesn't exhaust the reasons.

I think you are wise to resist the temptation to hire just anyone. I assume you have let reliable people know that you are looking for someone. I hope you find him (her?).
Best regards,
Neil

ଔ

August 8, 1975

Dear Neil:
Thanks so much for sending me the copy of *The Remnant* with all the information about Econe.

About two weeks ago a young priest newly ordained by Archbishop Lefebvre came to Oklahoma City and celebrated three Tridentine Masses. Archbishop Quinn, for the first time in living memory, exercised his authority. No Catholic was to attend these rebellious Masses under pain of sin. Several hundred ignored him.

For the past five or six years Oklahoma City has lived with the scandal of The Community of John XXIII, an "experimental parish," where Protestant ministers openly "concelebrate" with the priest in charge. Intercommunion is commonplace, as is the priest asking the parishioners to stretch out their hands toward the altar during the consecration, while repeating the words of the Canon with the priest. His favorite trick is to consecrate a loaf of bread, which is then passed on a platter among the congregation. None of this has ever elicited a squeak from the Archbishop.

Still, all was not lost. The Vicar General opined that this young traditional priest was doing the Devil's work. Last year, during an interview on *The Exorcist*, this same Vicar General told his radio audience that "Catholics don't believe in the Devil any more."

This traditional priest will be coming through Oklahoma City every two weeks from now on. Do you think I would be sinning by attending his Masses? I was able to stand the new liturgy as long as our parish had an orthodox pastor. Now he has been transferred, and our new pastor is a liberal and effeminate to boot. When he told me he was instituting The Green Bay Plan next year instead of the Daughters of St. Paul, I of course resigned as Religious Education Director.

What do Neil and his new wife need in their home? I haven't gotten their wedding present yet, and I don't want to duplicate something they already have.

Sincerely,

[————]²

છ

August 13, 1975

Dear [————]:

Your question is one I've pondered these many years. Needless to say, I have no authority to decide this tough one. Beyond that, I don't even have a firm opinion. I find the arguments justifying attendance at the old Mass persuasive but not compelling, and the same for the arguments against attending. They checkmate each other, so I find myself diffidently occupying both sides of the fence. No need to

---

2 The author's name has been omitted for privacy's sake.

review all the arguments, which you know as well as I. But I do have a few thoughts, on both sides.

The bias must always be on the side of authority—any sort of authority. The alternative dissolves authority. But authority isn't absolute. Even Church authority is subject to doctrine, law, tradition—and charity. The spiritual writers speak with one voice on the need for obedience. But we might pause for a closer look at this. These people were nearly all religious, writing for religious whose lives in virtually every detail are meant to be regulated by obedience, and who have vowed themselves to obey. Even where the spiritual writers are not writing directly to their fellow religious, their thinking is naturally colored by their own way of life.

Not that the laity are exempt from obedience. But the degree of obedience to which we are bound is not to be compared to the obedience under which even the diocesan clergy must live, much less religious.

I know of no precedent in Catholic history for banning not simply a devotion, but the form of the Mass that was established by the higher authority, that grew if possible more venerable over the centuries, that was offered millions of times by our greatest saints, that was made even holier (if we may speak loosely) by the blood of thousands of martyrs who have died for it. When a Church that subsists on tradition bans this Mass, abruptly and even ruthlessly, we are faced with a phenomenon that ought to unsettle a high-grade moron.

There are rationalizations for this act of brutality, to be sure. There always are. In the light of our Lord's words about evil trees bearing evil fruit, we can dismiss them with the contempt they deserve. By their fruits you shall know them. Only the Father of Lies could pretend that the fruits of the new Mass are anything but bitter.

But [Father Andrew] Greeley tells us that the new Mass is overwhelmingly popular. I have no doubt of it. The same surveys also reveal that the same Catholics reject, in equal numbers, key points in Catholic morality. The new Mass, the attitude it fosters, makes them feel comfortable. They receive Communion in roughly the same proportion as they reject Catholic morality. But when was the last time you heard a bishop mention this? He is too busy stamping out the infamous Mass of St. Pius V.

If it were simply a matter of experimenting with a new liturgy, it would be bad enough. One does not use the sacred for a plaything. But now we have seen the experiments, and their ashes. If the innovators were no better than pragmatists (they like to think of themselves that way), they would have long ago consigned their experiments to the rubble. Again, if pastoral considerations persuaded them (against all experience) that this exercise in vulgarity would somehow redound to the honor and glory of God, the same pastoral considerations would have obliged them to move slowly, to test cautiously, and above all to leave those Catholics undisturbed who had built their spiritual lives around the traditional Mass. In the event, prudence was the first victim. Does God bless enterprises that scorn one of the cardinal virtues?

But this was not merely an enterprise that spat on prudence. Any suspicion that this was simply the work of kindhearted nitwits is dispelled when we look at the brutality with which they war on the old Mass. Never forget, they are warring on the Mass hallowed by centuries and saints; the Mass which presumably formed the center of their own spiritual lives until yesterday; the Mass they were ordained to offer; the Mass by which they exercised their own priesthood; the Mass loved by most of the people who loved them, who gave them life. Are we talking about men, or monsters?

Okay, they don't act like monsters. I think we are moving closer to the mystery of iniquity. No human calculation can explain this: they are doing the work of the Devil. Remember, they didn't drop the old Mass with tears of regret, as simple human decency would demand. They dropped it with relish, and they pursue its remaining devotees with hatred. Hatred. The same hatred that Satan feels for anything holy. The master hand of the Devil can seldom be demonstrated, but I can see no other explanation that comes close to fitting the facts.

In case you think I've gone nutty, read that old extremist Newman. Read "The Antichrist of the Fathers" in *Discussions and Arguments*. Then read "The Antichrist of the Protestants" in *Essays Critical and Historical* (which isn't quite as good). In fact, read everything of Newman, especially his lesser-known works. They are a lifeline.

Which brings us to the question of authority. A lot of work remains to be done here. The proper exercise of authority obviously doesn't depend on the worthiness of the person exercising it. One could even adopt a narrow focus and read the whole history of the world, including the Church, in terms of the abuse of authority. But the proper exercise of authority does indeed depend on the object on which it is exercised. When a medieval pope conducted a dynastic invasion, I find it hard to persuade myself that his Catholic subjects on the other side were obliged to lay down their arms.

We all know that authority cannot oblige us to sin. What we are talking about here is something that stops well short of that—otherwise we would have no problem. We may be brushing up against the question of legitimate freedom. I know, I know—we are perishing of freedom. It is hard to sort out all the cant that poured forth from Vatican II, but one strain of it had to do with freedom. Suddenly, we were told, Catholics could be free. In point of fact, the Catholic world before the Council was a model of ordered freedom. We knew what we could do, we knew what we couldn't do, we knew what was doubtful; and all of it made sense. So the cant about freedom gave off an odor. Nevertheless, it was encouraged by these two disastrous Popes, and their minions.

But they forgot one thing. They forgot to tell us that their new freedom didn't apply to orthodox Catholics.

Now it became possible to identify the odor. It was sulphur. What are we to make of a hierarchy that tolerates and even encourages every sort of doctrinal and moral and liturgical aberration, yet breathes hatred on the old Mass? The way they are handling the seminary at Écône tells us all we have to know. The Devil has to be busy here. If there is one thing he can't abide, it's holy water.

So I think a powerful case can be made that legitimate Church authority is in suspension, precisely as it was during the Arian heresy. They were, you will recall, too busy pursuing Athanasius to worry about heretics.

I don't buy the theory that we cease to be human when we become Catholic. As Catholics, we have *rights* to go with our duties: above all, a right to the Faith of our fathers. Sometimes, to be sure, it is better to suffer quietly under the arbitrary exercise of power. But would anyone make that a universal law, especially for the laity? And especially in this grotesque age? What would we say about a mayor and a police chief who gave the keys of the city to killers while they busied themselves enforcing their new ban on Sunday church attendance?

Perhaps we can educe a principle (if someone hasn't already): to the extent that authority acts unjustly as a matter of policy, to that extent it loses legitimacy. E.g., a Communist regime. E.g., present practice in most organs of Church authority, wherein evil is fostered or winked at, while the orthodox are hunted down. Reason rebels.

Thus, though I think I know where right lies, I don't feel easy enough in my conscience to act upon my theories. So I avoid the problem and search out churches where the new Mass is offered less offensively. But you are in a somewhat different situation. Here you have this heroic young priest, for all we know sent from heaven. What should you do? You don't want to abandon him, and thus imitate the brutality of the hierarchy. Yet you don't want to disobey a legitimate command. At the very least, I think you should consult one or more priests whom you rely on. Obviously, you will consult orthodox priests. But be tough on them (or rather, on yourself), no matter which side they come down on. If they tell you it's okay to go to the old Mass, rejoice—but also make sure their reasons are convincing. If they take the timid way out, make sure they have confronted the problem manfully and starkly.

Make sure they aren't like the majority of (theretofore orthodox) priests who went along with Henry VIII. (The orthodox Catholics who take an uncritical view of authority have never faced up to the anomaly of their position. They deplore what is going on in the Church. But logically, they have no right to deplore it. Authority has ordained it. So they adopt the shabbiest of delusions. They keep telling themselves that the Pope and the bishops are the salt that hasn't lost its savor—except that in effect they also consider them imbeciles who can't see what is going on, can't draw the right conclusions, can't protect themselves from scheming underlings, etc. They are actually saying that we must obey authority even when authority is too dumb to come in out of the rain, and really not capable of exercising authority. It is a pitiful subterfuge they resort to, and it exacts a price on their integrity. It also has its sadly comic side: they fool themselves, but do they really expect to fool God? This is what I mean by facing up to our problem, starkly. It is tempting to slip out from under the cross, but better to bear it.)

We are just back from the wedding, which went off famously. Father Miceli was able to make it, on his way back from the Coast. A grand time was had by all. You are very kind to remember Neil and Maureen, and I'll pass your letter on to them.
Best,
Neil

P.S. Suarez was asked whether a pope could be a schismatic. His response must have struck contemporaries as another exercise in dry Scholastic speculation, but it hits us today like the kick of a mule. Yes, he said, if a pope moved too radically to change Catholic traditions.

ଔ

September 10, 1975

Dear Bill:
It's tough to know what to say—for publication—about *Triumph*. Especially after the patient has expired. Off the record, I call it a case of unfocused alienation, being a charter member of the club. But Brent and his flock seemed to have a genius for missing the

boat. They were always dashing off in six different directions. And how they loved to feast on illusion: the IRA, the vigor of the Church in Latin America, the political muscle of the Church in America, the hero in the Vatican. They even made a pass or two at Belloc's economics. Whereas nothing serious held their interest for more than a few issues. A sophisticated defense in-depth of Catholic doctrine and morals, tradition and old usages; and all this coupled with a sober, unflappable, Olympian, more-in-sorrow-than-in-anger critique of the Pope and the hierarchy—these are the crying needs. Brent blew it. He certainly had the brains, but not the temperament or the background. (Our ranks are so thin. Is God trying to bring this home to us, so that we finally realize there is only One Hope?)

So this leaves only the *Wanderer*. With much less, they are doing much more. Not nearly enough: Brent could have carried the heavy end of the stick.

I'll miss *Triumph*. An issue never went by that didn't have something worth reading, after you picked your way through the underbrush.

Poor Brent. What is to become of him now?

Best,
Neil

ങ

October 8, 1975

Dear Mrs. Martinez:
Thanks so much for your fascinating letter. I'll be watching with the keenest interest to see if Al Matt runs your column. There is really nothing he should object to, since you were careful not to mention the Pope. I don't know him well enough to know where he would stand if you did, but at least some of his readers would object: the ones who suffer from papolatry.

I bet you could do a fascinating book on Spain. You write well. Your fund of information is amazing, and presumably your sources. Your writing is tough yet you manage to stay this side of shrillness.

I have just a couple of fears. One is commercial. With so much looking inward and plain exhaustion among the American Right, it is tough to sell them a book on a foreign country. On the other hand; I suspect that the prospect of the collapse of Spain, and above all the way it will have been accomplished, may shake up the brethren.

Then there is also the problem of timeliness. Since you probably have never written a book before, I must warn you of a few things. It isn't like stringing together a batch of columns. It is a project. An average book runs about 100 times as long as your column on

Spain. If you are as fast as most journalists, it will still take you somewhere between six months and one year. A rare writer can do it in less, and more than a few take longer, sometimes much longer.

Then, when you deliver the manuscript, you begin to get itchy. But it is going to take us about the same amount of time to get the book out.

And finally, you won't make much money on the book, if your book is typical. Some writers strike it rich, but they represent a tiny percentage of the whole. Least of all do writers build huge sales on the sort of book you have in mind. So, if you are figuring your time on a per-hour basis, I doubt that the book will reward your efforts.

On the other hand, there *are* compensations. The feeling of accomplishment. The satisfaction of having created something permanent, and useful. The growth of your reputation and therefore your marketability as a writer and, if you are so inclined, perhaps as a lecturer or teacher. I have seen many instances where the writer nourished romantic hopes about the money he was going to make from a book; but the same writer was agreeably surprised when he found that the book had led to other things he had never dreamed of.

Another possibility is a book on the pontificate of Paul VI. Here you will have a good deal more freedom than you enjoy in the pages of the *Wanderer* (not that your columns sound inhibited; but I know there are land mines you must avoid). We *need* a Xavier Rynne of the Right. Would there be a market for such a book? Probably as much as for a book on Spain, not much more, not much less. Would it fall between two stools? The liberals yawning because they are interested in other things, the conservatives nervous because you might sound less than reverential about this Pope? Perhaps. But I think that your style and your sources would combine to command attention. And it is long past time that Catholics (especially in the English-speaking world) learned something about the human side of the papacy. Yes, they will give a notional assent to the idea that such exists; but then they will go on as before, banishing the unpleasant thought from their minds. Or, if they do, they cherish the fiction that the Pope is in chains, a prisoner of the knaves around him (the knaves whom, they forget, he selected, and can fire tomorrow). Heaven knows I'm not suggesting a treatise on papal authority. But a good journalist's account of this pontificate will bring the question in the back door, inevitably. I don't mean to go on and on about this; but it is an aspect of the Church that exercises me these days. I see nearly all of our current problems in terms of the failure of authority. Yet most orthodox Catholics prefer to look at the other side of the problem and blame the people who disobey. Of course they are not wrong; if men were angels, the problem wouldn't exist. But men aren't angels, and any organization that claims to speak with authority must have a strong hand at the helm.

But that's not all. Many Catholics assume that, because the pope is protected from teaching error in a solemn declaration of faith or morals, he is somehow protected from errors and mistakes and weaknesses on a less solemn level as well. It would be useful if they could be disabused of this nonsense. They are clearly impervious to Catholic history, indeed of the behavior of Peter in the Gospels and in Acts. Now, under the hammer blows of John and Paul, they are beginning to open their minds to the possibility. But they have only begun to think about this, and about the consequences. (They should all be required to take a course in the behavior of the papacy during the Arian heresy, not to mention the Great Schism.)

What am I getting at? Well, it won't make them any happier when a pope joins the wolfpack on Spain, but at least they can put the behavior in context.

It might even suggest to them that, even with the extraordinary guidance of the Holy Spirit, a pope must cooperate with grace. Yes, of course he is protected from promulgating heresy (*Humanae Vitae* may be a classic example: it certainly went against all the human instincts of the present Pope). But short of that, everything turns on the mysterious collaboration between grace and the individual. To put it simply, a pope, too, must think with the Church. Not every pope has. Not this one, I believe. Otherwise, how explain his infatuation with so many modern aberrations? How explain his preoccupation with what are absurdly called human values, in clear opposition to the counsels of the Gospel? How explain his utopianism?

But I'm running on and on. I apologize. To bring our discussion back to the concrete, please think about whether you want to do a book, and if so, on which subject. If you have the time; if a book would not cause you unbearable inconvenience in some other area of your life, then I would certainly encourage it. The ranks of orthodox Catholics are thin, so thin that, just offhand, I can't think of another journalist who gives you any competition.

Kindest regards,
Neil McCaffrey

൙

December 17, 1975

The Wanderer
128 East 10th St.
St. Paul, Minnesota 55101

Editor:
My daughter is a sophomore in one of the less objectionable Catholic high schools in the Archdiocese of New York. The other day in religion class somebody mentioned the Act of Contrition. Several of the girls asked what that might be. Most did not know. Two of the girls and the teacher knew part of the prayer. One of the girls knew most of it. Out of 21 girls and one teacher, my daughter was the only one who knew the prayer all the way through.

Cardinal Cooke has referred to this period as the springtime of the Faith in New York.
Neil McCaffrey

ↄ

January 12, 1976

Dear Roger [Msgr. Donald Pryor]:
Now you see the dangers of loyal service. [Fr. Donald Pryor was made a Monsignor.]

I would offer congratulations, if only I could keep irony from breaking through. Yet condolences would be out of place too, because you have a chance here to do a great work. I suppose your first problem boils down to one of strategy. *L'audace, toujours l'audace!* You might as well be hanged for a sheep as a goat. That way, you either accomplish something or get an early reprieve to that nice little parish upstate. The other way, you probably will be harassed just as much, since nobody is happy with the schools these days (except those who have an interest in propagating good news); and you will be less happy with yourself.

In this connection, I just read something striking in Newman. He points out that we should not select, much less tailor, our message with a view to making it acceptable, since that is not our business, but God's. Citing Scripture, he goes on to point out that Christ was not so much concerned with making converts, but rather with bearing witness to the truth; that He did not *expect* most people to accept His words. I hadn't thought of that before. (I can hardly read a page of Newman without finding something I hadn't thought of before.)

I hope you make the seminary your first priority. If you find

yourself needing some orthodox profs with good academic credentials, I have some good names for you.
If a few shabby prayers from Pelham will make the difference, you're home free.
Best,
Neil

ભ

February 25, 1976
MEMO TO: Fr. Berbusse [S.J.], Fr. Bradley [S.J.],
             Fr. Miceli [S.J.], Dr. and Mrs. von Hildebrand,
             Dr. and Mrs. [William] Marra
FROM: Neil McCaffrey

Bill asked us to contribute a memo about our discussion. I'd like to offer mine on the subject on which we seemed to show the least consensus, criticism of the papacy.
1. Scripture makes no bones about the weaknesses of the Apostles and especially of Peter; which in any case were well known to the early Christians, whose faith survived the knowledge. Catholic history, from the age of the Fathers on down, provides us with the model. It was only in the 19th century that some Catholics found it necessary to refine the policies of the Holy Spirit.
2. The papacy is given primacy from the earliest years, yet there is little evidence of papolatry until we get to the last century. The papolaters of our day would have been regarded with astonishment by the Fathers, by Dante, by St. Catherine, by Bellarmine, by Suarez, by just about anyone you can name.
3. We can see papolatry in perspective when we put it beside its kin; and we can do that with a flying visit to Moscow or Peking. There too we are allowed to criticize underlings. *Pravda* does it every day. But the Leader, never.
4. Those orthodox Catholics who feel most comfortable with the spirit of Vatican II are least comfortable with its encouragement of free speech. John [XXIII] and Paul [VI] told us to relax and speak our minds. Perhaps they meant us to make an exception about speaking of themselves, but in fact they didn't say so. So their admirers hasten to protect the Popes from themselves. (It seems, then, that popes *can* make mistakes; but only a privileged few are allowed to notice them.)
5. In this connection, the favored few allow themselves, and even an occasional unwashed Catholic, one indulgence. We are permitted to disagree with Paul's *Ostpolitik*. I haven't yet been able to divine why the Pope can be criticized about this but not about

173

Church discipline or the liturgy or ecumania. So paradox piles upon paradox. It is possible to make a plausible (though far from compelling) case for papal policy toward Communism. We might argue that the Church expects to outlive today's tyrants; that she is trying to make life a bit easier for Catholics behind the Curtain; that she no longer has any confidence that the West will defend itself; even that life in Eastern Europe is less lethal to souls than life in the West. Whereas I have never heard a good argument for the new liturgy or for the new laxity in discipline. Even the papal cheerleaders can't muster an argument, for the excellent reason that there is no argument that would commend itself to the orthodox. All the arguments, such as they are, come from the infidels. The papal cheerleaders can only repeat their incantation: obedience, obedience, obedience. By which, ironically, they don't really mean obedience. They mean something else. They mean: shut up. Is it necessary, in this circle, to spell out the distinction between obedience and calling black white? (By way of underscoring the bankruptcy of papal policy, have you remarked that nobody ever talks these days about devotion to the Mass? There are no more courses on the Mass, no more books, no more private studies so that we might assist more knowledgeably and devoutly. In fact, if you so much as call it the Mass, you are a reactionary. There is a message here for the apologists of the new liturgy. But they don't want to hear it. That would be "disloyal". As long as we polish up the reputation of the present Pope, it would seem, we can forget about what happens to the Mass.)

6. Which leads us ineluctably to the question of charity. I suggest that the papal cheerleaders are pursuing a policy that has the effect of destroying souls, but that masquerades as charity. They want to deny this Pope, or any living pope, the blessing of constructive criticism and never mind what its absence may do to his soul. Never mind what the spiritual writers tell us about the duty of fraternal correction. Above all, never mind what its absence will do to the Church, and to the souls of the faithful. The caricatures that pass for charity in the Church today may be Satan's most spectacular recent victory.

7. We heard a lot of talk Sunday about the importance of faith when authority misbehaves, all of it sound. I think faith involves a corresponding devotion to truth, even unpalatable truth. What does a Catholic have to fear from truth? Shrinking from the truth is an indecent posture for a Catholic. Granted, tender souls need not concern themselves with high policy, and with the blunders of those in authority. That does not exonerate the mature Catholic. Moreover, if nobody concerns himself with these blunders, nobody will criti-

cize them; and evil will flourish, unopposed.

Not only that, but the papal cheerleaders are naive if they suppose they can silence criticism. All they succeed in doing is suppressing it among the orthodox. So the only criticism the Pope hears (except for coarse abuse from the unbalanced Right) is from the enemies of the papacy. When we reflect that this Pope is obsessed with public opinion ("human respect," the spiritual writers used to call it), it becomes double folly to choke off constructive criticism from the loyal orthodox.

What makes the papal cheerleaders that way? Partly, as we have seen, a counterfeit charity. Partly, I think, an unappetizing elitism that makes them think even mature Catholics can be affected in their faith if they admit to themselves that popes can suffer from the worst human weaknesses. And partly, it is fair to suspect, their own faith may not be seasoned enough to cope with this.

Neurotics make lousy parents. Sometimes they try to make their child healthy by giving him a germ-free environment. Which only makes him prey to the first disease he encounters. Do the papal cheerleaders really suppose that stomping out every whisper of criticism is going to fortify the faith of the people they presume to speak for? It only leaves them vulnerable. They have built up no antibodies. The intelligent and charitable policy is to show innocent souls that true devotion to the Church, and to the papacy, is not incompatible with constructive criticism; indeed, demands it.

The answer to immaturity is not perpetual childhood. A better cure is to grow up.

P.S. What the cheerleaders are really telling us is that this Pope (any Pope?) is too vain, too irascible to accept even constructive criticism; that he is incapable of growth; that he is a crippled human being; and that he must be treated not like a father but like an Oriental despot. Q.E.D.

ଔ

March 19, 1976

Dear Bill [Buckley]:
I have pondered your letter and the accompanying material from Mr. Perrone. In the present climate, I think the project foredoomed. [The proposed project was a Novus Ordo booklet missal in Latin and English.]

Let us step back first and review the strategic situation. At least for this generation, Latin is out. Young priests know little or none. The efforts of the present Pope, with the national hierarchies indecently eager to cooperate, have been spent in introducing and indeed forcing the use of the vernacular. Not long ago the Pope, reviewing the wreckage, remarked that he hoped that Latin wouldn't disappear, and he had a good word to say for Gregorian chant. But—and this is the crucial point—he did nothing to implement what must be taken as little more than an *obiter dictum*. If Rome seriously wanted Latin revived, Rome would set about doing something serious about reviving it. They haven't, and there is no prospect that it will be done in this pontificate.

Bear in mind that it would take a strenuous effort by Rome to unscramble the eggs. The national hierarchies like the vernacular. It removes them that much farther from Rome. It contributes to the general slackness. It is one less subject they have to burden their feeble seminarians with.

Without pressure from the American bishops (which will not come without an enormous effort from Rome), the introduction of a Latin Mass in the new rite stands as much chance as a revival of burning at the stake.

Here I think you (and Mr. Perrone) ought to be made aware of the ways of the higher clergy. Of course, they give a verbal pat on the head to everyone with a "worthy project". Sometimes they are being polite; sometimes they are just getting rid of cranks; sometimes they even mean it. Whatever, laymen tend to misinterpret this, especially when they want to. They think it means the Church is going to get behind their project. No such thing—as the bankruptcy records can testify.

Not only that, but even when the Church does get behind something (way back when), that is no guarantee of popular acceptance, much less of commercial success. Let me flaunt my expertise here. I worked in this field from the late 40s until the early 60s. My father worked in it from 1930 until his death.

When officials express their approval of a project like this one, it is merely pro forma. If it were anything more, be certain of this: they would either be publishing this work themselves under the auspices of the Liturgical Conference, or they would see that it was published by friendly publishers, with their backing. The most revealing sentence in Mr. Perrone's letter is the one where he admits that Catholic publishers aren't interested. This says it all. If the market were there, they would be interested.

The market isn't there because the infrastructure isn't there. And most Catholics are probably less bored with the new Mass than they were with the old. The minority who prefer Latin prefer the old Mass. The whole point of the new Mass is verbal "participation". But that makes no sense with a Latin Mass, for the excellent reason that most people don't know Latin. Nor would the new Mass in Latin have the old associations; and certainly not the old reverence. Reverence, I'm sure you've noticed, is out. Silence, private prayer, genuflecting, even kneeling for Communion are discouraged when they are not positively forbidden.

Publishing this book, therefore, would be a suicidal enterprise for Arlington House. But I would go further: I'm afraid it would be a waste of time for any private group or foundation to spend its funds here. I just can't see it evoking any response worth mentioning. The mere existence of such a book would not force the hand of pastors. The new Mass is already available in Latin. Catholics United for the Faith (CUF) makes it available in inexpensive pamphlets. But nothing happens.

I happen to think that the old Mass may come back some day. But not in the foreseeable future. And not, probably, by edict from on high. I think it will have to take a roundabout route. I think there will have to be a serious call for a Tridentine Rite, something like one of the Eastern rites: in other words, a rite devoted not just to the old Mass, but to the old *Church*, and all that it stood for. This Pope would never countenance such a thing, but the next? Or the next? By that time, they may be willing to try almost anything; and more important, some pope down the line will have no investment in today's wreckage. If it is to happen, these little men are no match for God. If He doesn't want it to happen, well, then of course it shouldn't. But from where I sit, it looks to be worth a try. And I mean to take some small steps to start the ball rolling. But more on that anon.
Best,
Neil

Cʒ

August 31, 1976

Dear Mr. Nelson:
How very nice of you to take the trouble to write. I sent a copy of my letter to *The Wanderer* and also to *The Remnant*, just in case it was not run in *The Wanderer*. So far it hasn't been, so I'm glad Walter Matt ran it in *The Remnant*. And I'm glad you liked it.

Yes, I think we must all pray hard for the Archbishop [Lefebvre]. This whole situation is so unnecessary, and certainly not provoked by him.

Although I am not often given to optimism, I believe that the battle over the Mass is already won. "By their fruits you shall know them." Not only that, but the arguments in favor of the old Mass are unanswerable. Whereas nobody has ever come up with a good argu-

ment for the new Mass, beyond the obligation of obedience. So, in time, I think this experiment will be recognized as the failure it is, and some future Pope will restore the Mass in its classic form. Meanwhile, we must all watch and pray.
Kindest regards,
Neil McCaffrey

႙

December 1976

Dear Father Lyons [Rev. William D.]:
Thanks so much for your nice note. I couldn't agree with you more. In fact, I think the decline of Western civilization can be laid in a measure to the decline over the last 15 years of the Mother of Western civilization, the Church. And I think the surgery will have to be just as drastic in the Church. I would not presume to read the mind of God, but the pattern of His dealings with men seems to be that in times of mass apostasy, man must first see and acknowledge his sins (for convenience, we can lump them all under the signs of liberalism, or self-worship), and then reach for the sackcloth. We do not seem to be even close to reaching our first step on the road back. Where are the prophets calling on us to repent? I pass over the hierarchy, from the Pope on down, not one of whom begins to recognize our parlous state. For the moment, they are part of the problem, not part of the solution.

So I think that little people like ourselves must just watch and pray. Relief will come in God's good time and in *His* way, not ours. Meanwhile, thanks again for your nice note.
Kindest regards,
Neil McCaffrey

႙

December 20, 1976

Dear Father [Rev. Edward Berbusse, S.J.]:
It was kind of you to send me your article on papal infallibility. So I hope I don't sound ungrateful if I report that I found it unconvincing. What it seems to do is to stake out an extreme position, the same one we associate with Manning and Veuillot and Ideal Ward. It is a bit late for that. I don't think anyone serious holds that any more.

The difficulties in your analysis are several. First and foremost, Honorius. You strain to exonerate him, but it just doesn't work in view of the double condemnations by Third Constantinople and Second Nicea. And once we face up to that, a more modest definition of papal infallibility becomes mandatory.

The second weakness I find is almost as radical: a persistent confusion of terms. You are naturally at pains to cite evidence for papal primacy through the centuries. Quite properly. But all the evidence you cite is in favor of papal primacy and authority. *None* of it has anything to do with papal infallibility. And it is important to understand that the terms are *not* synonymous. They were never considered synonymous in Catholic history. And why should they be? They mean different things. One might have authority, primacy, and never dream of having infallibility. One does not demand the other. As it happens, we have both; but not as you define infallibility. For example, the Council of Florence certainly did define papal primacy. I think you will search long and hard for any definition of infallibility at that Council.

You also ignore evidence that disagrees with you. The Pope himself, and his spokesman right after *Humanae Vitae* was issued, were both explicit in saying that it was *not* infallible. How could you discuss the whole question and overlook this? (Note that I am not saying that I think this is not infallible doctrine. I rather think that the teaching on contraception will one day be recognized as infallible. Indeed, I would be mildly surprised if it weren't. But I would certainly not be shocked or shattered. I wonder, however, whether the same can be said for those whom we might describe as premature definers.)

I understand your objective with this article, to help reaffirm and restore papal authority. This is praiseworthy. But I think you do your case a disservice by trying to prove too much. This sort of thing weakens a good case. In the case of papal infallibility, the doctrine would be destroyed if it attempted to encompass too much. There are too many papal errors to be explained away, and your explanations are unconvincing. We simply cannot have papal infallibility if it encompasses all you say, and then *not* have it when this or that incident proves too awkward to rationalize. I am trying to find a tactful way of saying something that I think can only be put candidly. I think your argument lacks rigor and carries the whiff of special pleading.

The Pope does not, after all, have to be infallible in his ordinary teaching for us to be obliged to obey him. Nobody else in authority is infallible, yet we are obliged to obey legitimate authority regardless, except in special cases. What is the difficulty?

And by the way, the present Pope is disobeyed not because people no longer believe in papal infallibility, but because he does not rule as one having authority. Even if your article were entirely true, it would not have any practical effect. You would still have a weak Pope. The papal powers have always been the same, at least implicitly. The difficulties have always arisen from bad behavior by popes, not from any theoretical limitation on their authority or infallibility.

Have a wonderful Christmas.
Kindest regards,
Neil

ᳺ

December 30, 1976

The Remnant
2539 Morrison Avenue
St. Paul, Minnesota 55117

Editor:
One of my few acts of heroism is to keep an eye on *The National Catholic Reporter.* Since most of your readers have surely found even sterner penances, let me share with them an interesting item that ran in the Dec. 17 issue, from the National Catholic News Service:

> VATICAN CITY. The pope said Dec. 6 he is maintaining for the time being a "thoughtful silence" on the Detroit Call to Action conference in October, but said the conference, which produced recommendations to ordain women and married men and ban nuclear weapons and U.S. arms sales abroad, was one of several events of "extreme interest in the life of the Church."

My guess is that His Holiness will carry that "thoughtful silence" to his grave, if past performance yields any clue. Meanwhile, should his statement be read as quiet approval? Tolerance? Or is he really not sure which side of the fence to come down on?

In any case, his response is miles away from the horror felt by traditional Catholics—of whatever hue. Those who embrace the pope-can-do-no-wrong school of latter-day theology have so far resorted to their tried but not necessarily true tactic, the Averted Gaze. I searched in vain for this item (as for so many others) in *The Wanderer.*

Whatever view one takes of the Averted Gazers (I think they are more to be censured than pitied), this latest embarrassment calls attention again to the corner they have painted themselves into. The

Pope's ambiguous response (or nonresponse) to the Detroit conference is only the latest of many such. What becomes of the Averted Gazers if the Pope breaks silence and, after his fashion, comes down firmly on both sides of the fence? Then, despite years of practice, even they will have a problem pretending he agrees with them.

Fortunately, this trauma need not make a shipwreck of their faith. The problem has already been confronted, and Catholic tradition holds the answers. I hope they will acquaint themselves with its riches.

Neil McCaffrey

ভ

January 13, 1977
MEMO TO: Gene[3], Roger [Msgr. Donald Pryor]
FROM: Neil

There is another argument available on the question of popes being able to commit their successors in perpetuity on matters of discipline. At the Council of Constance, Martin V did indeed commit himself and his successors, in perpetuity, to seven limitations on papal power. Note that these were exclusively matters of discipline, much more so than anything to do with the Mass. They dealt with papal appointments, tithing and such.

Note that these are the *only* decrees of this Council that were signed by the Pope: therefore the only reason the Council is held to be ecumenical.

ভ

---

3   The letters concerning the powers of the papacy are part of an exchange between Neil and one of his oldest friends from minor-seminary days in New York, Msgr. Eugene Clark, both protégés of Msgr. Florence Cohalan, noted New York archdiocesan historian and pastor. Both men rather quickly succeeded in their chosen paths—Neil as an executive at Doubleday and Macmillan publishers before founding his own companies, and Gene as secretary to Cardinal Spellman and then communications director and aide de camp for Cardinal Cooke. Vatican II liturgical changes were embraced by neither man at first, but Clark eventually took up the party line, and the two old friends quarreled, eventually committing their thoughts to letters. The reference to *The Wanderer* was to the way that newspaper leveled criticism at traditional Mass partisans like Michael Davies while not, McCaffrey complained, giving equal time for responses.

And Rightly So

January 19, 1977

Dear Neil:
Back to the question of Pope Pius V and the Tridentine Mass.

What you said about Paul VI acting *ultra vires* in establishing the new order cannot be maintained, I am sure, without damage to the essential commission of Christ to the Church. I am saying this on the principle that there is no way in which the commission of Christ given to the apostles can be any different in one age and another.

That steadiness and permanence of the Church's basic constitution and commission require not only a constant principle but the assurance that no one, not even a Pope, can, in fact, diminish or contract the operational commission of Christ to Peter.

We all accept that the custody, protection and regulation of the Sacraments and Mass are part of the commission Christ gave to Peter and the Church. The question you are posing is whether or not a Pope anywhere down the line of history can, by anything he says or does, restrict or reduce the jurisdiction and responsibility that Christ gave to the Church. Parallels are poor, but could one Pope decide that no future Popes will have the right to absolve the sin of theft or the right to annul marriages of certain categories? It is inconceivable precisely because no Pope has the power to reduce the area of competence of the Head of the Church, no matter what he said or implied or planned to do.

It is unhistoric to suggest that Pius V could have *intended* to do what he certainly knew, and what all Christian theology recognized without exception in his time, was beyond the power of any man, i.e., deliberately to revise by reduction the original commission of Christ to the Church. If, *per impossibile,* he adopted a unique and eccentric view of his powers, it matters not at all what he said or thought. He could not invent, much less exercise, a power he did not have. This would be true also of a Pope who attempted to enlarge Christ's commission. We are more familiar with that. A Pope who announced that he was in charge of economics (a few have hinted it) is quietly and constitutionally ignored.

What is binding on our consciences is the final product of the Church's direction. There is nothing infallible in a Pope's believing, if he did, that he could restrict or enlarge future Popes' jurisdiction.

There is no parallel here with final infallible doctrine which, of course, reduces the options of doctrinal interpretation. The regulation of the Mass is a jurisdictional and regulatory matter, and forever open to revision since permanence and infallibility are alien concepts in the area of regulations.

182

What do you say?
Kindest personal wishes,
Gene

ଔ

January 25, 1977

Dear Gene:
I suppose I should be grateful for your letter. It isn't often that you give your debating opponents a standing target. But really, sometimes you are impossible. I made it clear, four or five times, that I do not dispute the right of any pope to concoct a new Mass. I finally raised my voice to underscore this. And now, your letter. You argue like Kingsley (though here, I regret to say, the analogy breaks down).

Very well then, Dr. Kingsley, let me give it one more try. I do not dispute the right of a pope to concoct one new Mass, or a dozen. My point was and is altogether different. You will discover it if you haven't burned your old Roman Missal. Pius V, in establishing the Tridentine Mass, made two points. He established this Mass as standard for the Latin Church for all time, and he decreed that no priest should ever be penalized for offering it. I did not address myself to the first point, the permanent validity of which is I suppose arguable. I did insist, however, that no priest can be banned from saying the Tridentine Mass in view of the second decree. You scoffed, but I take papal prerogatives more seriously. What a pope binds on earth is bound in heaven. If a pope says, with due solemnity, that a grant is perpetual, I'm afraid I find no way of making it shorter than that. If a successor pretends to be able to, I think he is acting *ultra vires.*

Did Paul VI have the right to concoct a new Mass? No question. Was he imprudent? By their fruits you shall know them. Was he heartless? Without a doubt. Was he barbaric? Quintessentially. Was it an act of pristine liberalism, either malevolent or utopian (if there is any difference) or both? The question answers itself. But for all that, it was not quite illicit. But your letter does raise another, trickier question. May one pope bind or limit another in matters of discipline? You put the case well for the principle that he may not. Yet I see arguments for the other side. If a pope may not bind in such matters, what you are really saying is that every pope's works die with him. This is profoundly untraditional and unCatholic. (As you say, doctrinal matters are not, indeed cannot be, in question here.) The genius of the Faith, even on the level of discipline and administration, is continuity. *Tradition.* If we cannot always and necessarily be bound by the customs of an earlier century, neither are we free to toss them away like a used kleenex.

So we should look for guidance in Catholic history. And sure enough, your aprioristic statements find no resonance there. Quite the contrary. Papal power, while in theory absolute in its own sphere and in all that is not sin, is in fact hedged in by law and prescription, custom and usage. Newman circled around this point in his reply to Gladstone. The Vatican just admitted as much a couple of weeks ago when it protested that all that Roman property was owned not by the Pope but by religious orders. (Ain't nobody here but us chickens.) And it was decreed in marble by Martin V and the Council of Constance.

I think this Council will give you more problems than you can handle. Not that I mean to line myself up with the papal enemies, though reform was long overdue. (I never line up with enemies of the papacy: least of all with its worst enemy, bad popes.) The Council was called under auspices that were doubtful at best; and it soon turned into something like an antipapal, and therefore anti-Catholic, orgy. The parallels between Constance and Vatican II, and especially the "spirit" of each, are too obvious to need laboring. At least the liberals are consistent in embracing both. But when the papolaters of the Right (among whom I know better than to number you) bow down before Vatican II, heedless of its resemblance to Constance and the latter's grave consequences for the papacy and the Church, I can only think of Cleopatra clasping the asp to her bosom. (Except that Cleopatra *knew* it was poison.) Constance is ranked among the ecumenical councils because Martin signed seven decrees. Now watch closely. Every decree he signed disciplined the papacy. Every decree undertook to limit the papacy: not just his papacy, but that of his successors, *in perpetuity*.

Poor Kingsley is in trouble again. These decrees have nothing to do with infallibility, so leave that red herring by the roadside. But the Pope, and the teaching Church in solemn assembly, apparently saw this as a perfectly legitimate exercise of papal and Church authority. It was only after more than five centuries that Dr. Kingsley was able to put them right.

And note that this Council is doubly awkward for you. Not only do Pope and Council formally circumscribe many papal powers; they do so in perpetuity.

Thanks to good Pope Martin, I think we now may amend the terms of the dispute. Not only is there little question that Pius V was quite within his powers to give every priest henceforward the right to say the Tridentine Mass. We have at least an interesting argument that that Mass itself must be normative. Not perhaps a conclusive argument, but one that must give sober men pause.

And here, I think, we may be on to something. Forget for a moment the narrow question of liceity. Do we seriously suppose that the Holy Spirit is informing a Pope who scorns prudence, overturns tradition, and abandons souls? A Pope who flouts the solemn prescriptions of a sainted predecessor? To say that is to flirt with blasphemy. (That they canonized Pius V is impressive but, I grant you, not finally germane to this discussion; though when they canonize the present Pope, figs will whistle and pigs will fly.) Our Lord told us what sort of fruit to expect from poisoned trees. (At Mass Sunday one of our priests, several leagues more enthusiastic for the New Church than you, admitted that he would be surprised if he had more than ten confessions a year—ten a *year!*—from people between eighteen and thirty-five. (But, he neglected to add, thousands of Communions.) And yet there are bishops who can look out over this devastation and pronounce it the springtime of the Faith.)

One interesting thing about your letter: it puts you in company you will welcome like the itch. Or do you relish having *The Wanderer* for an ally? *The Wanderer* cannot bring itself to state the arguments of its adversaries without travesty: much less to let the adversaries state their own arguments for themselves. This does not, I'm sure you will agree, argue for the strength of one's case. You do not belong, certainly, among the papolaters; but your letter reads like one of theirs. (By the way, I think it is time we stopped treating the papolaters as pious but misguided. Why do we assume that simple folk must be virtuous? How does one serve the truth by refusing to confront serious arguments from men of good will? We are accustomed to think of the papolaters as infantile, or unlettered, or sycophants. We ignore their radical lack of charity. They deny a bad pope the grace of fraternal correction. They turn away from souls abandoned by faithless or frightened shepherds. And if these strictures don't apply to you, at least you should know something about your new friends.)

All these legalistic arguments are interesting, and so important in their own right that we are in danger of missing the real point. Pope Frankenstein made a monster, and you are trying to fix it up with cosmetics. On a certain level, I view with alarm, just like the next anguished soul. But on another level, I view with something like equanimity. God is not mocked. And God's will is done, somehow. The hydra of liberalism is the quintessence of man's rebellion against God. For God to let us see it in all its vileness, perhaps He had to let it invade and moreover corrupt the Church. Perhaps we need to be scourged with it (for a season, or a century, or more). But none of this will begin to have its ultimately benign effects until we see the evil for what it is. And abase ourselves for our part in it.

So maybe the next archbishop will be a divorcee. And maybe your job will be to look after her bastard children. If that happens, offer it up. For Lefebvre.
Best,
Neil

P. S. Is the form of the Mass wholly a matter of discipline? The Mass pushes up against doctrine at every point. So score another big one for the Old Mass.

ભ

February 8, 1977

Dear Mr. Fraser [Hamish]:
Many thanks for your kind letter. By all means, feel free to quote me and identify me as you suggest. My only concern was that Msgr. Clark be not identified.

The Benelli argument would almost have to parallel Msgr. Clark's. I can think of no other defense either might adopt. And this suggests an important point. Not only did the architects of change not do their homework. So suffused are they with the spirit of liberalism that they simply took change for granted. They did not even bother to confront the claims of tradition. Which in itself condemns them.
Kindest regards,
Neil McCaffrey

ભ

February 21, 1977

Dear Gene:
The other day I chanced upon a quote from Pius XII: "What the Church has established, the Church may change or abrogate." This is very strong. Though it does not refute the point I made about Martin V and the Council of Constance, it does run counter to it.

I wondered if there might be an exception to what is clearly a sound principle. At first, I thought of the Commandments of the Church. Here and there they can be changed, of course. But can they *all* be changed?

Another example, much stronger, is infant baptism. It took the Church several centuries to make it mandatory. But having done so, could she ever abrogate this, in view of the indispensability of baptism for salvation? I don't see how.

It then struck me that we have here a textbook example of *exceptio probat regulam*. Pius V and Martin V and the Council of Constance all understood the general principle enunciated by Pius XII. Because they understood it; because they realized that future popes might in normal circumstances change the edicts they had issued, they went out of their way to underscore that these edicts might not be changed. They issued them in perpetuity, thereby acknowledging the general principle while they took pains to make exceptions to it.

Last year the Pope sneered that Lefebvre "opposed the old tradition to the new tradition". The remark is grotesque, and betrays a liberal's ignorance of what tradition means. As if today's tradition could refute yesterday's; as if tradition were not a seamless garment. But the point is that Pius V and Martin V and the Council of Constance were conscious of the requirements of tradition and continuity, and took pains to accommodate them. I wish I could say the same for Paul VI.

Best,
Neil

ଔ

February 22, 1977

Dear Neil:
Thank you for your letter of January 25th. As an ancient admirer of your letters, I am disappointed by this one, perhaps your worst. I have never read you so mistaken (a small fault among mortals), so rhetorically uncontained, and so dangerous in the direction in which you seem to be heading. You touched many subjects, so let me answer in sections.

I) Your response to my original argument:
Your gaucherie of shouting is based on the assumption that I missed your point. You seem unable in your sixth decade to accept that anyone could understand you and find your argument inadequate which, *salva reverentia,* I find it to be. I may not convince you, but allow me to try.

You write as if doctrinal and disciplinary acts of Popes operated under the same rules. Your subliminal guilt for so serious a blurring appears in your "P.S." when you try to identify the two by saying the Mass "pushes up against doctrine at every point." So does life—but regulations regarding Mass are disciplinary by every definition, and you know it. Fearful of more shouting, let me spell it out. You can skip the next few paragraphs if you don't need the argument.

187

In a shameful phrase you recognize that a Pope may always "concoct a new Mass." But you create a novel position that a Pope may grant a disciplinary privilege (the right to say Mass according to one rite) in such a way that no other Pope may rescind it. In saying this you base your argument on one misapplied principle (that what a Pope binds on earth is bound in heaven) and one illogical principle (that such a grant of privilege or right to priests does not, in fact, limit the prerogatives of future Popes as does a declared limitation of jurisdiction).

You apply your theological principles as if they had neither purpose nor context.

Regarding your 1st (misapplied) principle:

What binds a Christian to specific acts of a Pope is the authority given by Christ to Peter for the spiritual safety of Christians. But the authority does not bind in the same way for different purposes. Papal authority can, in ultimate acts of jurisdiction, define doctrine and morals in a way that binds us to intellectual assent, to witness to it creedally, and to obedience to its consequences in our lives. In this area the essential subject of definition becomes immutable and reduces future options. But Papal authority functioning to protect and regulate the sacraments and other spiritual activity binds us to obedience only. Here the act of obedience is the stable and permanent factor. What binds us here is, of its nature, always open to change since it is not anchored in Revelation or Apostolic Tradition. (I am allowing your Scriptural quotation—"binding on earth and in heaven"—to serve for the basic indefectibility of the Church. It was directed primarily toward the forgiveness of sins.)

All this to lay out that you are wrong to say that a rite can be an imputable subject of earthly-heavenly bindings. All that can be mandated is obedience as long as the rite remains subject to Church law.*

On your invented second principle, that the grant of an inalienable right or privilege does not limit the Christ-given prerogatives or jurisdiction of future Popes:

You make a fundamental error regarding jurisdiction and power. Like any other right, a grant given and irretrievable is a jurisdiction lost. I skip the obvious examples. The inalienable grant of a privilege needs no further declaration to limit the grantor's future powers and options. If the Pope cannot rescind a disciplinary right once granted, he would have, to that degree, lost a power granted by Christ—which is absurd.

What is wholly confusing about your argument is that on page 1, paragraph 3, you insist that Pius V established the Tridentine rite against future rescinding by any Pope. But in paragraph 5 you admit that it is probably true that one Pope may not bind or limit another in matters of discipline. We both know that the substance of the sacraments can never change. But surely you know that the form of liturgy, of rites, of sacraments, however sacred in their purposes, are matters of discipline, however much it may touch doctrine.

The arguments you pose against this do not stand up against such a central fact.

I have not implied, as you suggest, that every Pope's works die with him. Not at all. A Pope's disciplinary regulation stands indefinitely as the law of the Church until it is rescinded, which is almost the opposite of saying a Pope's works die with him. Having indicted me for so eccentric a principle, you conclude that I am opposed to continuity! Of course, I know that continuity, even in discipline, is an important part of the genius of Christianity. What a strange thing to write to me.

You write of the Council of Constance and Pope Martin V. But you are wandering from the point. The limitations (reforms) of Papal activity urged and enacted by Constance and in part approved by Martin V were a matter of great celebration—however unsound the power of the Council, and meant to last. But neither the fathers of Constance nor Pope Martin, who ratified most of their decrees, thought their acts literally irrescindable. They were in the very act of rescinding laws, customs and traditions that had become baleful influences in the Church. How could they have thought, in the act of rescinding, that their laws were irrescindable?

You ignore a human factor. Men making great reforms and full of enthusiasm for them may assume that no man of good sense would ever rescind laws of such manifest goodness. But that is no reason to think that they, any more than you, failed to know that a law, marvelous for one age, can become a vehicle of corruption for another and need to be withdrawn. You may find many examples of reformers besides Martin V and Pius V who could not imagine why anyone would want to alter what they were legislating, but would never have denied to future Popes the very powers they were exercising over disciplinary matters.

References to "perpetuity" belong to the language of continuity which you esteem. Church affairs are expected to remain stable, they are not to be trifled with, and the phrase "in perpetuity" belongs to that style, but was not intended to mean that no other Pope, ever, could change the law. Nor did Pius V mean in his decree to limit his distant successors when he wrote that no one could forbid a priest to offer the Tridentine Mass; he was forbidding his contemporaries to offer Masses or require Masses to be offered in rites previously approved by Church authorities. His strong language conveyed a long-time plan to the bishops and religious superiors telling them strongly not to block the new Mass [sic] or continue older rites. But there is no way to resolve this on a purely literary basis. Roman style tends to the immemorial, universal and undisturbable. And add to that the classical tone of Renaissance language. Am I not right to say that before you started on this indictment of Pope Paul VI you would not have been so literalist about phrases and oblivious of the context and style in which they were used?

On page 2, paragraph 3, you use the solemnity and importance of Martin V's decrees to obscure once more the critical difference between faith-and-morals and discipline. I don't know why you think I have trouble with Martin's important but not irrescindable decrees.

You conclude triumphantly, on the bottom of page 2, begging the question and making the Mass "normative," whatever that means. And your final "conclusive argument" is wholly below your standards. You say let us forget the narrow concept of liceity. Holy Lord! That was the whole point of our discussion—liceity—since neither you nor I challenged the validity of the Tridentine or the new Mass. And then you descend into a dreadful *ad hominem* argument, dreadful because you know that Popes have been unworthy and did not, by that, act *ultra vires*. "Poisoned fruit" and all that is just dreadful rhetoric—a total red herring relative to our discussion of whether or not Pope Paul had the right to forbid priests to say the valid Tridentine Mass.

The good and bad pastoral results of all this belong to another discussion and you, unworthily, mix the question of liceity and your estimation of results. I put aside all you say about vague association with the *Wanderer,* "papolatry" and all that. This is just high irrelevance to the specific disagreement we had.

II) Since you have written about the significance of my comments, let me return the compliment.

I think you must consider where you are and what you are doing. If I were to assume—as I do not—that your every charge against the intentions and integrity of Pope John and Pope Paul were true and verifiable, I could not concede that your reaction to them is soundly Catholic. You write and speak often of the perduring ways and attitudes that are the inner spirit of Catholicism and Catholic traditions. You know they enrich and bind us. But your latest letter seems far removed from a central Catholic attitude, an interior sense of the Church as the Mystical Body. You write—and I think mainly of a third party reading what you wrote—of the Church as doomed to disaster which you view with detachment, even satisfaction, because, as you see it, the hierarchy and its allies have brought all this destruction on themselves.

I am considering the spirit in which you write. You indicate that no amount of destruction is too much to expose the hydra of liberalism. Besides being without compassion for sinners, you seem detached from the fate of millions of Catholics who will suffer loss of the creed and sacraments in that destruction. Ninety-nine percent of your interest now seems devoted to indictment. Perhaps I misjudge your tone. I hope so. Our part of the Mystical Body has always been semi-disastrous or worse because of sin and mismanagement. But no low point in Church conduct ever, I believe, permits us the alienation which you seem to accept.

I am disturbed by the wild rhetoric with which you fill you letter. Your Popes "concoct" Masses, the present Pope is Frankenstein, barbaric, malevolent; Archbishops are divorcees with bastards; naiveté is papolatry. I am loathe to suggest any comparison that will lead you to a long list of counter-comparisons. But, in my loyalty to you, I must say that your position reeks of Port Royal. You are withdrawing into a tight circle of the real Catholics where alone orthodoxy and the true spirit of Catholicism will be preserved. Dear friend, have you lost your copy of *Enthusiasm*? You talk the language of a *petite eglise*. The final preservation of orthodoxy is never accomplished so. Final guaranteed orthodoxy is the work of the Holy Spirit, fulfilling in His unfathomable manner the Petrine guarantees. It makes no difference if you should be correct in your every denunciation of the contemporary hierarchy. The *petite eglise* must always fail, sooner or later, even when it is begun in total rectitude. It is not the locus of the action of the Petrine guarantees which worked through and in spite of the 4th and 9th century Popes, and Alexander VI and Clement XIV.

III) Another matter. Perhaps more important still.

You must forgive my continuing obtuseness in the face of some of your unexplained allusions. You call me Kingsley. (Have I been put down by a 20th Century Newman? Really, Neil!) Are you suggesting that the reasoning of my letter—which was theological— was directed towards "ends" rather than honestly held? I do not know. But Kingsley was also a defamer and that frightful role, if it is consciously pursued, is sinful. And that is the point I bring to you.

You seem to be so passionate in your hatred of Pope Paul, Vatican II and its sponsors that you have put aside your Christian relationships with the rest of mankind. You plunge into arguments with a mean anger and stab away at persons like an avenging angel. I am not writing just of attitude. I am speaking of defamation so cruel and unmeasured and scandalous that if it is conscious it is sinful. Forgive my directness. You have somewhere run across a story without witnesses, proof or even reasonable probability—excepting a Birchite disposition to believe anything that will indicate a conspiracy for evil—that Pope Paul committed some unnamed 'indiscretion' in Milan and is being blackmailed out of his sworn duty by the left-leaning possessor of that secret information. (Copy enclosed.) It is the sort of thing we read in murky depths of a degenerate press. But you, an honorable Christian, apparently have no sense of sin in reproducing, circulating, this soiling speculation and giving it currency among excellent people. Surely you know the crime of calumny against a person who can offer no defense, and among people who have no means to challenge or verify it. Need I tell you the effect of a similar scurrilous suggestion, printed and privately circulated, about the private life of any friend of yours? I would rip to shreds anyone who wrote such things about you, not because you are impeccable, but because no one should be subjected to such deeply unfair and harmful treatment. Do you think because Paul is a Pope and your enemy that you are exempted from the 7th and 8th commandments and the code of a Christian gentleman? Have you forgotten Dr. Hyde? Dr. Hyde wasn't wrong because Damien was saintly. The shocking fault was in the defamation itself and Damien's defenselessness. Our relaxed libel laws for public figures do not reduce Christian standards.

Without a shout and with kindest personal wishes,
Gene

* For your interest, Canons 4 and 6 of the Code of Canon Law treat specifically of vested rights, indults, privileges, etc., in effect prior to the Code (Canon 4) and of prior ecclesiastical legislation (Canon 6). The Code and the commentary are legal and not theological documents, but I thought the documents would be useful to you as an indication of the formal point of view of the Church.

☙

March 2, 1977

Dear Lily [Dr. Alice von Hildebrand]:
I think you might be interested in the enclosed from *The Wanderer*. My first reaction when I heard about Bugnini, you may recall, was skepticism. I think skepticism is always called for by such stories, until proof is forthcoming. But proof of a convincing sort was forth-

coming, from your husband and you. The fact that the source of the story was a friend of yours, and you knew all the details, seemed all but ironclad to me. And then it was confirmed by Father von Straaten. Whereas this article, purporting to be the facts, is actually more fantastic than the original charge. This priest is the one who did the hatchet job for *The Wanderer* on Archbishop Lefebvre. And his former piece was no more convincing than this. He merely asserts. He doesn't prove. And what he asserts is a story that taxes credulity. Franzoni's motivation, as advanced by Father Flanagan, is preposterous. And the article is not helped by the "proof" in the form of a universal negative. It has the paradoxical effect on me of strengthening my belief in the original charge. A rebuttal should be more convincing than this. What do you think?

Kindest regards,
Neil

ဢ

March 14, 1977

Dear Neil:
Your letter of February 21st crossed mine to you. I also have your letter of the 25th.

Regarding the first:
If the Pope and other agencies of the Church have the right to change Church law, then there can be no qualification in principle of that right. Consequently, there is no principle forbidding the Church to revoke *all* Church law including even the Sunday obligation. You realize I am talking of rights and lawfulness and not speaking of the effects of making changes that might harm the spiritual health of Christians. If, which God forbid, the Sunday obligation were lifted officially we might bind ourselves to Sunday Mass but we could no longer say we were bound by the Lord *through Church law*. I believe Pope Pius XII's quotation ("What the Church has established, the Church may change or abrogate") must stand as a universal principle. You know it does not apply, of course, to Apostolic revelation or Apostolic tradition or the defined doctrine drawn infallibly from them since the Church did not *motu proprio* "establish them" but serves as their vehicle.

It applies in principle—again putting aside pastoral wisdom—to infant baptism. The Church has the legal power to forbid Baptism before, say, the age of reason. It could not declare infant baptism null. That would touch doctrine. But it could surely make such baptisms henceforth illegal.

Your hypothesis about Martin V and Pius V knowing the perduring principle of undiminishable jurisdiction and making an exception to it is logical internally and could possibly have been their own thoughts (which I do not think credible historically); but I do not think it obtains here as an argument because their intention would have been superseded by the fact that the principle of undiminishable jurisdiction is part of the Church's constitution as established by Christ. Making an exception to it (diminishing future jurisdiction) would have been an act *ultra vires* whatever they thought.

History often reflects legal principle and gives shape to its practice. But we cannot always argue safely from one to the other. We cannot know precisely—unless a document is discovered—what was in the mind of historical figures like the Fathers of Constance, Martin V or Pius V when they spoke of perpetuity. *Whatever* they meant historically and the presumption is on the side of tradition and rule—theology will not tolerate a literal definition of perpetuity. If by exception they meant it literally they were wrong and it cannot stand.

If you disagree with me, and wish to answer—do so. Labeling an argument as scoffing or institutional or obdurate is a light mile from answering or modifying it. In my two letters I was honestly interested in responding to your original verbal arguments, not in challenging or answering any of the numerous points you raised later.

Regarding your letter of February 25th:

I have enough trouble fielding all the balls that you hit on January 25th. Please don't speak of subliminal messages. If you wish to stop writing you are certainly free to do so, but please don't say I suggested it. I did not. You have, in this letter, dropped the original subject of discussion. So I stand on what I said earlier and above as an open, reasoned position. I believe it sincerely and, barring a pointed answer to where my facts or reasoning fail, I have no choice but to speak so. You hold this against me, associating it with a life-long refusal to listen to you *or anyone else.* In view of that I do not write expecting credibility. I write only for the sake of truth which has its own rights.

You burlesque the meaning and tone of my words when you write that I scoff and wrote in a white rage, called you depraved and indifferent to souls. None of this is true. Far from scoffing I *initiated* this correspondence with a calm dull letter of theological reasoning which I offered to you openly for your criticism. You answered but appended a page of unsupportable statements about the Pope and my alleged allies, which had nothing to do with my thesis.

I was and am alarmed by what you wrote on January 25th. It

is not institutionalism (?) or intellectual obduracy or disregard for an old friend that causes me to be concerned about several of your statements which do not fall under the category of entertaining zinging to which you refer. You wrote on January 25th:

> "Do we seriously suppose that the Holy Spirit is informing a Pope who scorns prudence, overturns tradition, and abandons souls? A Pope who flouts the solemn prescriptions of a sainted predecessor?"

This is not zinging.

A careful exegesis might allow you to say this means that you believe the Pope was not guided by the Holy Spirit *in particular sub-magisterial decisions* which you believe are harmful to souls. But a person reading it would have to know you as well as I do, not to accept this in its first ordinary meaning to a reader: that this Pontificate lacks, in effect, the credentials of the Petrine guarantees.

This brings me immediately to the point of readership. I wholly appreciate your style of *obiter dicta* and shorthand marginalia. I have enjoyed it for years and, knowing your undilute faith, creedal anchors and loyalty to the Church, I received the license of your commentary within that context. Nor did I think the other few names on your old encyclical list thought any other way.

But I discovered before I wrote on January 25th that you had circulated the dangerous and misleading statement above and much else in circles where the assurances you require of me cannot exist. I discovered two persons who know me not at all and know you only slightly had received copies of these letters and also the unjustifiable calumny of the Pope as a man blackmailed out of his duty.

I did not write to accuse you of defection or depravity or literalism, as you say. I wrote to cry alarm of statements that can be interpreted by friends as strong opposition to particular Papal decisions but to others must suggest open contempt and alienation from a Catholic relationship to the Pope. I objected to what you wrote on principle and in the context of your circulation of your January 25th letter to literal interpreters and the circulation of the Milanese calumny to persons who cannot receive it as I did, as just another wild story like the one stating that all the Cardinals are Masons. You have circulated the calumny to people who receive it seriously because you sent it. (Indeed you continue to justify it as a creditable document—an unnamed author retailing an unnamed crime used by unnamed blackmailers causing the Pope to fail his duty in unnamed instances! In my Catholic Worker days in high school I would not have credited such ridiculous evidence. Why limit it to the Pope? Just change the city and fill in anyone's name.)

You are not on reliable ground to speak of the Pope as 'unguided' by the Holy Spirit and controlled by blackmailers on the grounds that I should understand you are winking. Neither fits under that heading, especially when you are circulating them among people who will take them literally and seriously, to the vast danger of their relationship to the Church and perhaps the faith.

Is it institutional or obdurate or scoffing to say such things to a friend when I believe you are doing something harmful to others?

My adherence to our consensus of assumptions has not been altered or undone, however ineffective it may be at the moment. What you are requiring now as a basis of discussion is not really shared assumptions but shared conclusions about particular points of law, theology, history and the Pope's personal integrity.

As a personal matter I have not in the past viewed your commentary with suspicion or literalist misinterpretation, charges you assert gratuitously. Quite the opposite. And over the years I have often, very often, changed my appraisal of people and situations based on facts and judgments to which you had attended more carefully than I. In areas where I had no competence at all, I accepted your judgments as wholly reliable and was not misled. But you say this cannot have been so, because in 1977 I disagree with you on the matter of this correspondence. From that, you discover that I have never listened to you *or to anyone.* Your personal perceptions are not what they should be.
Yours,
Gene

Cʒ

March 18, 1977

Dear Mr. Fraser:
Just a line to compliment you on the February issue. Your remarks on Lefebvre are prudent, brave and sophisticated. You may get flak from both sides; but that can be a sign that one is on target.

A small point I want to quibble over, I think there is a tendency around these days to telescope history. One reads, in the February issue and elsewhere, that the Modernists simply went underground from the early years of the century until Vatican II. I think this unsound. One long generation (or even two short ones) were quite untouched by these errors. The firmness of Pius X carried the day. So much so that when *Humani Generis* came out, the best-informed

Catholics in this country honestly wondered what all the fighting was about. I think the same was true throughout the English-speaking world. Apparently it was not true on the Continent; but even there the Modernists were so well isolated that it was not obvious even to the well informed. I think the point should rather be not that they went underground but that no battle is ever finally won. Eternal vigilance is necessary, and never more necessary than when we start congratulating ourselves that we have finally put the bad old days behind us. I believe you are a convert who was not a member of the Church during the years I refer to. Speaking as a cradle Catholic, I can assure you that Modernism and its effects seemed as remote to us as Nestorianism. We even regarded the oath against Modernism as an historical curiosity, a quaint throwback.

Somewhat along the same lines, I also think you have telescoped the history of the Church in France. Powerful conservative elements survived in the French Church, and indeed were in the majority, despite the condemnation of Maurras. They emerged and asserted themselves in 1940. They were definitely in the ascendant during the Vichy years—including, and this is revealing, many who would later be associated with the Left. Opportunists? Of course. But we did not realize that then. I think the turning point for the French Church came after the war. *Humani Generis* attempted to deal with the problem, and so did the crackdown on the priest-workers. As we see now, the mild measures were not tough enough. (Pius XII looks like a giant now. He looked like a bit less then. And that is *not* hindsight. I *remember*.)

France is an abiding problem for the Church. I don't wish to oversimplify, but conflicts between Rome and the French hierarchy (or at least rivalry) go back to Charlemagne. And they never really disappeared. Regularly, they became acute. Once they expressed themselves in a feudal context, then in a monarchical, then in a monarcho-nationalist, now in a left-liberal. And then there were the French heresies: first the Albigensians, then the Jansenists and Quietists, then the forerunners of today's heretics in the 19th century, and now the present crowd (by far the worst). I do not mean to overlook the great chapters in Catholic history written in France, but only to suggest that the powers of darkness are never idle, and our battle with them never done until the Second Coming.

Kindest regards,
Neil McCaffrey

CB

And Rightly So

March 19, 1977

Dear Gene,
I had thought that my last letter would have spared you another laborious reply. I'm really not interested in pursuing this debate, for reasons you will find hard to grasp. In the first place, I prefer to discuss. It is a more appropriate posture for learning, or teaching. And if it must be debate, then each party must signify truth, not victory, as favorable. Rules of courtesy must be observed. Each party must swear off personal attacks. Each should have a veil of distance, and if possible, of humor.

You bring none of this to a discussion. Instead, you stake out a position (right or wrong; it hardly matters) and never move. And seldom listen; and then only to refute, never to enter into another's mind. It becomes a crude exercise in ego, the cruder in your case because you are plainly riddled with guilt, which you don't confront in the Classicalist fashion but with what Freud called projection. The classic instance came the night you laughed with your visitor image, Ken Whitehead: two deaf men shouting back and forth, oblivious to the inconvenience they are causing everyone else.

My first instinct, then, was not to reply. Then I thought about one point you raised. I think I should remark on that.

You mention scandal—to my amazement, as when Brezhnev attacks on human rights. With him it is cynical, with you that flight from the real world that marks off the men in the bunker.

Last time you were here, Joan remarked that the teachers at St. Clare's denied the Virgin Birth. Without missing a breath, you were ready with reply 47. You defended them (badly). Were Joan and I scandalized? Not really. We have come over the years to expect these pleasantries from Father Glib (to our shame, I now realize). But I wonder about the children. We make (poor) efforts to pass along our faith to them. But are we any proof against people like you? I do know this: we have been blessed in the last few years to make friends with a few *good* priests. They have filled the hole which we used to assume would be yours and Roger's. They impart a glow of grace. They live below the surface of life. Whereas one of the children remarked after your reply to last letter: "Father Gene is about ready for the hierarchy." Even more perceptively, Joan observed a few weeks ago: "I never remember Gene talking about God, or our Lord." I was thunderstruck. I had never thought of it with that penetration. What a terrifying thought about a priest, a hundred times more terrifying because it is the simple truth.

Scandal? I wish you knew how many times we have tried to

answer the question: "Isn't there *anyone* down there who knows what's going on? What's Monsignor Clark doing there?" Our alibis grow ever less convincing. Lately, we just shrug, and tell the truth.

Scandal? You write, or endorse, letters raising money from innocent Catholics for that graveyard of the Faith, Catholic U; not to mention all the archdiocesan graveyards.

But when you write about the pope, I realize that you use Catholic language the way a man who has lost his larynx has to work a voice box. "A Catholic relationship to the Pope"? I know about that. I learned about it in the Church you and your associates lose no opportunity to disdain. Like every other man who has lost his spiritual bearings, you strain at the gnat and swallow the elephant. You are mightily exercised over a few remarks by an unimportant layman. Nowhere do I see any concern over the derelictions of the worst Pope in history. Speaking of right relationships, *he* has betrayed us, his flock, uncounted thousands of times. But you are silent. The father comes home roaring drunk, and you scold the baby for taking a cracker. Could it be that you are expecting a favor from this Pope? Or does your unconscious sense that my strictures about him apply to all those who conspire, if only by silence, in his policies?

You don't begin to see where the scandals lie because your Catholic sensibilities are blunted. When a Catholic of only average intelligence sees papal policies like those of this Pope, and papal permissiveness like Paul's, he *knows* it's wrong. But then, if he only hears Father Glib, he mistrusts his instincts. He *needs* to hear truth and decency reaffirmed, needs to see good fostered in the Church and not rebuked. The Church is greater than the Pope, or your boss. But when the average Catholic compares your message with what he knows to be Catholic truth, his faith is likely to be weakened, even shattered. You owe these little ones bread, not stones.

Whereas if they see faithful Catholics who are able to distinguish between our Lord's body and its unworthy leaders, they see a way out—a way out of their dilemma that you would deny them. Not only do you have contempt for their intelligence, but indifference to their spiritual plight. It comes from that odd, unspeakably crude error of Churchmen identifying the Church with their administrations. And always, of course, with corrupt administrations. Churchmen worthy of their office have a keen sense of their unworthiness, and would suffer death before identifying their unworthy selves with our Lord.

There is, of course, your indifference to the truth. God is Truth. Yet you use language for your own purposes—as if you could ever serve God by bending the truth. By pretending, for instance, that the Catholic schools are Catholic, or that the Pope is not a disaster.

At the most radical heart of his being, every man must confront truth and its demands. And how do you confront it? Glibly. If at all. All through the years, your response to anyone who says something you dislike has been to go for the jugular. You dismiss his arguments by attacking the man. 'They' and 'crook' are two of your favorites. Thus, you are quit of the need to confront what he says—or so you think. I cite this as one example of a person who fails to take ideas, and therefore truth, seriously, who shirks from confronting truth and its demands on a serious level. Small wonder you dislike the drift of my remarks. Because we *don't* operate on the same level, or from the same premise. You have long since ceased to be a serious person.

Why, then, do I address you in words meant only for a serious person. I used to applaud your apostolate of charm (for that is what I thought it was). I think differently now. It is a dangerous game, courting popularity. Now that I think of it, I can't think of a saint who played it. And certainly, if it is played at the expense of your interior life, your spiritual and other reading, it is one of the classic roads to ruin. Your training—and, I used to think, your tastes and your values—was meant to make you proof against the lies of Madison Avenue, and Park Avenue. Well, what do you know, it didn't. The bright, attractive young man from the Bronx was swept off his feet. As to when, it is not my place to venture. But I'm going to guess that the reasons aren't exotic. The old warnings about the world probably apply here. Pre-conciliar warnings, needless to add.

So does the warning of St. John Chrysostom, that it is almost impossible for a bishop to save his soul; would he apply that to bishops' functionaries? I bet he would.

So now you know why I bother to answer. You keep inferior company. They flatter you. You like it. That is why you react with fury to me—even in an argument. So the opening you unintentionally offered me may have been divine providence. Who am I—or you—to spurn that?

What I think you should do is take a month off. No, make that six months, Get thee to a monastery—one that hasn't thrown out the old Mass, the spiritual writers, Newman. Find yourself a good (better?) director. Find *yourself*—in Him.

Then come back to your present job, and do what you should. You may not last twelve days, but that doesn't matter, does it?

By the way, we do pray for you.
Best,
Neil

ଔ

April 18, 1977

The Remnant
2539 Morrison Avenue
St. Paul, Minnesota 55117

Editor:

I find myself in broad agreement with Michael Davies' remarks on religious freedom (*The Remnant*, March 31), but I do pause when he asserts, then assumes it is proved, that Pius IX's teaching in *Quanta Cura* is infallible doctrine. Doctrine is defined infallibly in one of three ways: a) a pope defines it; b) a general council defines it, the pope assenting; c) the Church's magisterium teaches it universally—not just today, but at least implicitly from apostolic times.

In this case, Mr. Davies must be relying on the third contingency, since the pontificate of Pius IX saw the first two also at work: the first in 1854 when the Pope himself defined the Immaculate Conception, the second in 1870 when Vatican I and Pius IX defined papal infallibility. The manner in which the Pope restated the traditional teaching on religious freedom was obviously of a different order of solemnity from the first two. Are we entitled to call it infallible teaching? The question recurs in different contexts and always will, so it is worth exploring.

Most of the arguments revolve around one question: has this or that teaching been *infallibly* defined? Where any doubt exists, theologians will naturally differ (as they do on religious freedom). While differences remain unresolved, Catholics are free to accept any opinion that boasts a decent pedigree.

How do these differences get resolved (*when* they get resolved)? Not by any team of theologians. Not by even so solid a writer as Mr. Davies. They get resolved by a pope, or by a general council.

Since the question of religious freedom was at least reopened by Vatican II, I think it idle to pretend that nothing has changed. So I believe Mr. Davies would make his point better if he put it in the form of a dilemma: If the teaching of Gregory XVI, Pius IX, Leo XIII, Pius X and Pius XI on religious freedom is infallible, then Vatican II made grave errors in its (admittedly noninfallible) teaching on the subject. If the teaching of the earlier popes was not infallible and Vatican II's was a legitimate variant, it is nonetheless an abuse of authority to condemn anyone for holding the traditional view, heretofore held unanimously.

How could it be otherwise? The traditional view traces back to the Apostles. St. Paul urged excommunication, and no liberal nonsense about error having equal rights with truth. Likewise other general councils, most notably Third and Fourth Lateran, and Trent. Popes and bishops have always acted on the same conviction, have restated it implicitly or explicitly through the ages, and would have heaped scorn and anathemas had they foreseen any successor rash enough to try to overturn nineteen hundred years of Catholic practice and, in their view, Catholic teaching. (The liberals will tell us, patronizingly, that this is doctrinal development, ignoring the seven notes by which Newman distinguished between true and false development. But then, liberals are defined by their lust after novelty and their corresponding hatred of tradition.)

Leaving aside religious liberty as such, we can learn something about the Council by the way it handled the question. If the Council Fathers had simply been bemused by liberal ideas on the subject, Catholic habits would have checked their rush to embrace these innovations. They would then have inched up to the novelties, flirted, but left themselves an exit; because *tradition would have slowed them down.* Instead, they behaved like liberals. They thought a few paragraphs could dispose of nineteen hundred years of Catholic teaching and practice. Without saying so, they displayed a contempt for their Catholic forebears that is unprecedented in the history of the Church. Up until Vatican II, the Church had always insisted upon continuity. It was her guarantee of authenticity—the mark our Lord and St. Paul told us to look for.

And now we find an archbishop under ban—for disapproving new "orientations" that would have been condemned, *indeed often were*, by every pope until the present one (and possibly John XXIII). I can think of no parallel in Catholic history. The Church has been blushing over the Galileo case for upwards of three centuries. Yet given the state of scientific knowledge in the 17th century, the Church's conduct was defensible. The condemnation of Athanasius? We don't know to what degree Pope Liberius was coerced into condemning him; and in any case he repented (as Paul VI may; as we should pray he does). It was the abuse of papal authority that prompted Dietrich von Hildebrand to state, sorrowfully, a few months before his death: "The Lefebvre case is one of the worst scandals in the history of the Church."

A scandal can of course be rectified; if not by the present Pope, then by a successor. At the very least, Archbishop Lefebvre may yet be granted a hearing—the sort of hearing Church authority did offer to Hans Küng. And to Galileo.

The supreme irony will surely be remarked by historians, however it is ignored by present commentators: an archbishop of

the Catholic Church stands under ban for following his conscience and questioning the brand new views of one general council on— freedom of conscience. Pity for him he isn't the Archbishop of Canterbury.
Neil McCaffrey

Cℰ

June 8, 1977

Dear Roger [Msgr. Donald Pryor]:
I got your note, scanned Msgr. Kelly's presentation, and immediately began to think up names. Meanwhile, I had passed the letter on to son Roger, who pointed out to me the paragraph in the presentation wherein Msgr. Kelly embraces the Council and all that. Now I have second thoughts.

Among the names I had thought of, some would agree with Kelly, some would disdain the New Church, and others would come up with mixed reviews. Quite apart from my own views, I think an organization of this sort would be better advised to gather in Catholic scholars, regardless of their views on the Council and the last two popes. To make their views on the latter the touchstone of the organization belies its very name. There is as yet no party line on the Council (though I have no doubt what it will be, a year or ten years or twenty years from now). And even if there were a party line, it would have nothing to do with Catholic scholarship.

I'm afraid that what Msgr. Kelly wants is not scholars but cheerleaders.
Best,
Neil

Cℰ

January 16, 1978

Dear Mary [Martinez]:
I appreciate your keeping me up to date on your disagreements with Walter Matt. I won't comment directly on them, however, because I doubt that anything I would say hasn't already occurred to you, and been rejected, more than once.

But I do want to make a few comments as your potential publisher. As you know, from the start I have stressed that you should write a journalist's book, not a partisan account. You assure me that it will be so. I wish I could feel as confident. The article that Walter Matt rejected sent up warning flares.

In the first place, the article itself is not up to your standard. It in fact isn't journalism at all. It reads like one of those chummy mimeo-graphed papers that people enclose with their Christmas cards to bring their far-flung friends up to date. Even worse from the stand-point of good journalism, there was no disposition to dig, to ask tough questions, to give us the real situation. Instead, the column was all gratitude and sweetness and light. In other words, it read like a club bulletin.

To take one startling example, your visit to Cincinnati. No Lefe-bvre priest was available, so you and the group contented yourselves with a tape of the old Mass, a rosary and a talk. In other words, a prayer meeting. This, you were careful to point out, occurred on a Sunday. You obviously thought nothing of it, because you presented it as the most normal thing in the world when a Lefebvre priest is not available.

And this is why I worry about your book. You have bought the extreme line so fully that you take it as normative. Whereas a journal-ist with her Catholic antennae in good order would have pounced. The right sort of journalist for doing the book we have in mind (and, in my judgment, for writing a column in *The Remnant*) would have immediately begun asking some tough questions. Do these people consider that the state of the Church today emancipates them from the obligation to hear Mass on Sunday? Did any priest or anyone connected with the Archbishop presume to "dispense" them from the Sunday obligation if an old Mass should not be available? On what authority? Is this not a denial of the authority of the Church? Is this not to say that the new Mass is invalid? But if the new Mass is invalid, what becomes of the infallibility of the Church and our Lord's promise to stay with the Church for all time?

So you had a juicy story here, if you were doing your job as a Catholic journalist. I'm afraid you weren't. I don't want to get into an argument with you about what should be the proper Catholic response to this situation. Clearly you do not agree with me on this. But that is not the point I am trying to make. I am trying to point out to you that you are not responding to these situations as a Catholic journalist but as a press agent for Lefebvre. (I am not arguing with you as a friend not because I am indifferent to the position you have argued yourself into. But I consider this a matter for prayer, not argument.) Good journalism on the part of a Catholic would in this situation nose about and get the full story of all the attitudes. A good journalist would do the same wherever she found herself. Are you doing this? Are you digging out the stories of dissension at the Mich-igan seminary, in other parts of the movement here and abroad? Are these only nasty rumors? That is what you should be exploring, both for readers of *The Remnant* and for readers of your book. But do you have the stomach for this? You are a tough, brainy reporter when you are after a story that interests you. But can you be tough and brainy about the movement next to your heart?

For that matter, to do a good book on Lefebvre and his movement, you must not only talk to his people—and ask them hard, awkward, embarrassing questions: you must also talk to his critics. And I mean all his critics. Not only his critics who follow the papal line, but his friendly critics among the traditionalists, people like Hamish. You must dig out the skeletons. Have you talked to any of the seminarians who quit? Have you talked to that priest (I forget his name; he writes for *The Remnant*) who left Écône? What about rumors of trouble in the English movement? Are you exploring these?

My point is, you *must* explore them in order to do a good book. I'm afraid you don't have the stomach for this. I do hope you are able to prove me wrong; but I won't be surprised if I turn out to be right.

To encourage you, I remind you of a point I have made all along. The Lefebvre movement will not be helped by a piece of puffery. If your assignment was to cover the Vatican today, you would be tough and resourceful and not afraid to ask hard questions. I am suggesting that you must treat this subject exactly the same way. Will this wound something you hold dear? Perhaps. But here you must be detached—both as a journalist and as a Christian. Remember, if this movement is from heaven, it will accomplish its objectives. If not, you don't want to put yourself on the wrong side.

I guess what I am saying is this: it is not up to you, or me, or Lefebvre, or Paul to decide. This is *God's* decision. If you dig out the truth, you are doing your job.

But I hasten to add: I'm not preaching to you. I'm talking to you as a *publisher.* If the book is good, it will make its way. If not, if it is just a piece of press agentry, it will be a commercial failure. Not all such books are, to be sure. But the Lefebvre movement by itself is not big enough to sustain a book like this commercially. It must make its way well outside this little circle. If the book is so obviously a piece of puffery that even somebody like Walter Matt can't swallow it, then it has no chance of success. You would be better advised to take it to the Lefebvre people and have them publish it privately.

Along these lines, I hope that you and Walter Matt will not sever relations. I say this for several reasons. First, if even Walter Matt finds your copy unacceptable, then it is a sure sign that you are writing just for one clique. (Incidentally, and parenthetically, I think he is perfectly justified in keeping anything out of his journal that he deems unacceptable. Remember, *The Remnant* is one of the last specimens of *personal* journalism around these days. He has every right to publish what he wants and reject what he doesn't want. He also has every right to turn his journal into a house organ for a particular group—or *not* to.)

I also think it a small tragedy if a journalist of your talent should lose her outlet. Needless to say, I'm not speaking for him. But I suspect that he will continue to be glad to get your reports from Rome and elsewhere, as long as they are good journalism and not just press agentry. In this respect, his position may not be far from mine. For my part, the fact that you go much farther with the Lefebvre movement than I would is of no concern to me as a publisher. I am only interested in the sort of book you turn out. I suspect he would feel pretty much the same about your articles. (But in this connection, I don't think you should take offense because he puts in a disclaimer dissociating himself from the views and outside activities of his writers. In the first place, he did not specify you. But even if he had, why is he wrong to do this? Granted, it shouldn't be necessary to do it. People should understand that byline articles do not necessarily reflect the views of an editor. But they seldom do understand this, especially if they are not sophisticated in the ways of the media; especially if they are readers of a "cause" journal that is also a personal journal. Actually, by issuing this disclaimer and at the same time welcoming the views of other writers, he is safeguarding the independence of the writers just as much as he is protecting his own. He does not want to have to answer for all the views and activities of all his writers. But by the same token, I'm sure many of the writers do not want to have to answer for all of his views.)

Journalists are like other souls. Their duty is to find the truth, and then conform to it. But in human affairs, the truth is never simple. The best a good journalist can hope to do is to focus on such parts of it as he is able to dig out. Then he must write it up, even if some of what he writes goes clear against the grain. He may find himself writing things that hurt his friends. That is one of the hard parts of a writer's vocation. But it is also liberating. The truth *does* make one free. And also makes for good journalism.
Best regards,
Neil McCaffrey

P.S. Along these lines, anyone covering the Lefebvre movement *must* report on the tragic suicide of the deacon last summer, just a week before he was to be ordained.

 G3

June 7, 1978

Dear Bill [Buckley]:
Thanks for your note from Dennis Brown, on his errand for Father Hardon. The terms of his commission may be revealing. Father Hardon is orthodox, but within the limits imposed by Vatican II. Hence his assumption that it is possible to find fifty decent Catholic books in the popular vein (or in any other vein) since 1975. This assignment is somewhat more difficult than finding ten just men in Sodom.
Best,
Neil

෴

November 16, 1984

Dear Mr. [George] Will:
Now and again your columns leave me grumbling. But after the one on the bishops, all is forgiven. May it live a thousand years. It is definitive, and the tone is just right. Tattered, flyweight ideas are not improved by posturing, and the proper response is exactly the note of disdain that sounds all through your column.
Kindest regards,
Neil McCaffrey

P.S. I just unburdened myself on the same subject, in a little column I do for our Club Bulletin. See the last half of the enclosed. Newman is just the one to put the vulgarians in their place—if, that is, they've ever heard of him.

෴

19 August 1985

Dear Neil and Joan:
It was a pleasant surprise to receive letters from you both in May. You are probably not expecting replies until November on the current six-month delivery time basis. I much enjoyed the little snippet in the Newsletter. I received a letter from a lady in Portland, OR, today, which took thirteen days to arrive by air. She wrote to tell me about Archbishop Power's 14 Commandments for implementing the Indult. One is that only those named in the petition can be present, and another that petitioners must be over thirty years of age. It seems that those below that age could not have *remained* attached

to the old Mass! A regular gay Mass is celebrated in Portland. I have written to ask the lady whether one must be over thirty to assist at this. It may well be that no danger is envisaged if young people mix with homosexuals, but that their faith would be endangered by being present at the Tridentine Mass, which, presumably, is now a sin crying out to heaven for vengeance.

We were very sorry not to have met your friends the Sullivans. They couldn't contact us as our phone is not listed. I sent them a card saying how sorry we were to miss them.

Sorry about the "go-situation"! I now lapse into what I consider to be my fluent American as soon as I start writing for an American publication. My one reserve so far has been a reluctance to use adjectives in place of adverbs. I am still saying "did well" instead of "did good"—but I have no doubt that I will eventually overcome this scruple.

I spent ten days in Texas this month getting five pamphlets ready for printing. I am particularly pleased with what will be a totally new version of my pamphlet on the Tridentine Mass. Carlita Brown decided to re-set it, and so I made some extensive revisions, and also added the text of the indult + a short commentary. There are also some new and very attractive pictures. I hope that it will appear in September.

The Browns have had a lot of family problems lately. Mrs. Brown was rushed off to hospital with what was thought to be cancer. She phoned to give me a cheerful Texas farewell in case she didn't return. It transpired that what she had was a very severe ulcer which still gives her continual pain. Mr. Brown was rushed off a month later with what was thought to be a heart attack, but was found to be diabetes. Carlita also looks after her very lively grandson all day. It amazes me that *The Angelus* is appearing at all now. I could not stop off in New York as I had a special cheap direct flight to Houston with Continental.

It is unlikely, but not impossible, that we might get over next year. At the moment I am struggling to complete my Religious Liberty book. I am beginning to think that I shall never do so, and that it will remain with me like some sort of curse for the rest of my life. This week I shall be writing a review of Roger's new edition of Von H's [Hildebrand] *Devastated Vineyard*. I am delighted to see this back in print.

Maria sends her love and hopes, as I do, that if we don't see you in N. Y. next year perhaps we shall see you in London.
All good wishes,
Michael [Davies]

CB

Christmas Eve 1985

Dear Michael [Davies]:
Not to shatter the post-Christmas peace of your home, but you are hopelessly out of date. Either that or it's the overflowing of your charity, the waves of which obscure your vision. The bishops aren't afraid of trendy liberals. That was in 1966. Now they *are* the trendy liberals. If you object that they're too dumb, I remind you of the useful old Communist jape at the lumpenliterati. (Was it from Trotsky? He could be witty.) The bishops and their epigones are the new lumpenliberali.

Led by their boss, who however permits himself an occasional atavistic protest, no doubt to keep the boat in some sort of balance. He reached a new low the other day when he assured the Red rioters of South Africa that "the Catholic Church supports their protests." By the way, check out Joe Sobran's *Pensées* in the new *National Review*, the 30th anniversary issue. He's talking about liberals, but note how accurately most of what he says describes the hierarchy. Your Christmas card found us just in time, and we are gladdened at the prospect of a visit. *Please*, plan to spend a few *leisurely* days here. Hell, I may even break down and invade your shores for a few days of self-indulgence. What gives me pause, as always, is my growing aversion to travel. Like certain fine wines (and many cheap ones), I don't travel well. Joan and others try to shame me by reminding me that my hero Waugh was a great traveler. I reply that one of his trips led him to hallucinate and almost did him in. Newman also hated to travel, and Knox steadfastly refused to go even to Rome. The defense rests—at home, whenever possible.
Best,
Neil

CB

January 17, 1989

Dear Mr. [Colin] Cain:
I'm sorry that Mrs. McCaffrey and I will be unable to join you in your tribute to Walter Matt. Nobody deserves it more. When darkness descended on the Church back in the middle Sixties, Walter Matt lit a candle for the remnant. With nothing in the way of resources to draw on, he began publishing anyway, a living demonstration of the

three theological virtues and one of the cardinal virtues, fortitude.

Heaven must have smiled on the enterprise. If Walter Matt and *The Remnant* had merely managed to survive, it would be a success story worthy of your tribute. But Walter Matt did more. For over two decades now, Walter Matt and *The Remnant* have given us the best record in the English-speaking world of the fight to keep our Catholic traditions alive: indeed, the only complete record. Month after month he provided the principal forum for the ablest reporter and commentator on the traditional scene, Michael Davies. When historians of tomorrow seek to record the desperate rearguard struggle of Catholic traditionalists during these grey decades, they will need a complete file of *The Remnant*. And, remarkably, that is all they will need. What an achievement for one man and his family, operating on a prayer and a shoestring!

We can never repay him. Fortunately, there is a world beyond this one where rewards are handled better.
Kindest regards,
Neil McCaffrey

ℭຘ

Archbishop Lefebvre, Pope Paul VI, and Catholic Tradition
[Circulated to friends, c. 1975]

The Lefebvre case is bringing orthodox American Catholics to a boil. The dispute, long simmering, centers on Pope Paul VI, but it concerns not only the merits of one individual pope. History is full of such *ad hoc* squabbles, and history deals with them in its own good time. The present dispute raises more basic questions. What, if any, are the limits of papal power? What does a living pope owe not merely to the doctrines of the Church but to its traditions? To its usages? What does he owe to the ideas and policies of his predecessors? What should be his relations to a world hostile to the Faith?

To one group—let's call them the conservatives—the questions exist not as subjects for exploration but simply as points for affirmation, slogans for the troops. The pope can do no wrong (or, if he can, don't mention it till he's in the grave a safe century or so). Ours not to reason why, or question; ours but to rally round the papal flag, with the conservatives establishing the ground rules for Flag Day.

The opposition have no such simple formula to counter with. The opposition are groping—and bleeding. And the dispute is the more poignant, the more bitter, because most of the opposition until yesterday ranged themselves with the conservatives.

But then, reality broke through. For some years after the Council, the conventional line had been: the Pope is isolated/misled/uninformed/captive/what-have-you. This position always depended on a vast innocence of Church and human affairs, and moreover needed occasional tokens that the Pope was really on their side. The pressure of catastrophe had to eat away at that position—particularly when the Pope was at pains to show that he does indeed know what is going on, that he is indeed the author of these policies, that he is no fool, and that he is not at all pleased with Catholics who oppose him.

When these facts began to hit home, less balanced Catholics reached for new explanations, and came up with kookery: the Pope is a Communist/Freemason/imposter...or was invalidly elected...or is drugged; and so on. Sensible Catholics, rejecting all this nonsense but still confronting the cruel fact of a pope hostile to much of what they hold sacred, had to enter upon what may be called, at least analogously, their dark night of the soul.

But if God is there, dark nights of the soul can be illuminating. Troubled Catholics began to consider seriously what had once been mere abstractions to them. Not every papal or conciliar statement is infallible, or even wise. Not every papal policy is prudent, or in the best interests of the Faith. No pope, St. Peter himself knows, is beyond error, and no humble pope refuses to correct his error. And, as Dante and St. John Chrysostom once told us, some popes do go to Hell.

These truths had almost to force themselves on many a conscientious Catholic. But once they did, these Catholics made a wondrous discovery: the truth had set them free. They found to their delight that they had at last joined the Catholic mainstream of centuries. Now the traditions they revered meant so much more to them as they became more deeply a part of those traditions. They drew strength from those traditions. To be specific, they found in Catholic tradition almost universal respect, even reverence, for the pope as St. Peter's successor—but nothing of the pope-can-do-no-wrong aberration. They found some courtier flattery of popes, but none from Catholics who had a decent respect for the pope, and for themselves. They found among real Catholics a widespread love for the pope as father, and almost no papolatry. (A good son loves and respects his father—but he doesn't praise him for coming home drunk. Refuting Stephen Decatur's "My country, right or wrong," Chesterton once remarked that it was like saying, "My mother, drunk or sober.")

God writes straight with crooked lines, and when disaster strikes the Church, Providence invariably seems to draw good from it. And why not? Christ, after all, has already conquered. Thus, the derelictions of the present papacy have forced thoughtful Catholics to reconsider the papolatry some had succumbed to in recent decades:

a corrective badly needed in many quarters—-just as, in the opposite direction, the Councils of Florence and Vatican I helped to right
the balance after the Council of Constance had heaped indignities
on the papacy. (Incidentally, I wonder how many edicts of Constance
those council buffs among today's conservatives would subscribe to.
Or is the most recent Council the only one that counts?)

But enlightenment of the sort that squares with Catholic tradition does not bestow on the loyal opposition the easy one-dimensional formulas generated by the Vatican cheerleaders. Loyal to the
pope? Of course—but not to Honorius I when he errs or Sergius III
when he murders. Peter must be corrected by Paul, and Gregory XI
did not lack for courtiers to assure him that he was doing right by
staying in Avignon. But the girl who told him bluntly that his place
was in Rome, and just as bluntly urged him to resign if he would
not exercise his authority, is honored as one of the great women in
Catholic history, St. Catherine of Siena.

My disagreement with some in the conservative Catholic media is
twofold: they distort our present crisis, and are not even true to their
own murky principles. They distort by suppressing news about the
Pope—which is to say, they fail as Catholic journalists. They never
report when the Pope receives a Communist leader, or Women's Lib
pioneer Betty Friedan, or mass murderer Idi Amin. They do not tell
us that he refused to meet with an international pilgrimage of traditional Catholics even though they kept an all-night prayer vigil in
St. Peter's Square—though at the same time he was receiving three
Portuguese revolutionaries. We could never have learned from them
that the Pope joined with the international Left to condemn the
Franco government for executing the Spanish terrorists. In papers
that proclaim admiration for the Pope, why is news of so many of his
key activities carefully excluded?

The answer may be that the conservative Catholic press finds
these activities shameful. But doesn't this repugnance really speak
well for it? I think not. First of all, Catholic newspapers must print
Catholic news honestly, or they fail in their first duty. But more than
that, suppressing news about the Pope says something interesting
about one's professed admiration for him. If it cannot bring itself to
report activities it finds shameful, why does the conservative Catholic press at the same time pretend that the Pope is blameless?

There is one other alternative: the conservative Catholic press
shares the Pope's penchant for revolutionaries, but dares not let on
for fear of losing its readers. But this explanation is absurd on the
face of it. The first alternative is the only one that rings true. The
conservative Catholic press is the prisoner of its own inconsistency,

trapped in it by a liberal Pope.

Of course, they don't have to be trapped. What they can do, what I hope some day they will do, is to subject their premises to a good dose of Catholic history, swear off papolatry, and take the cure. It may pinch, but adversity is the price of growth, and a channel of grace.

The situation of papal-loyalist organizations differs in one way from that of the press: they are not newspapers. They therefore have no obligation to report awkward facts—though they do have an obligation to face them. I believe they, and the likeminded Catholic press, resist the facts, and here also fall short of their own principles.

Their position is familiar: the conciliar documents are blameless; the Pope is just as blameless as guardian of the Faith and tradition; everything bad that has happened has happened in spite of the Pope and the Council.

Who can deny the enormous emotional appeal of this position? Almost every orthodox Catholic used to hold it, if he doesn't now. Every orthodox Catholic wishes he could hold it. There is only one argument against it: it isn't true.

Among other things, the argument is jejune. As if Church councils are only judged by their documents! People who think this have no sense of the texture of human affairs, hence of history. If we judge the Council of Constance merely off the handful of disciplinary measures it passed and Martin V signed, we would yawn and give it a paragraph in Church history. How different was the reality—an anti-papal orgy the like of which the Church has never seen (save perhaps in the last fifteen years), whose effects dogged the Church for more than four centuries.

Not surprisingly, Pope Paul VI understands his Council far better than his conservative admirers. He has never disguised his conviction that the Council was the gateway to change in the Church, and was meant to be. And he has underscored this, pointing out that *Gaudium et Spes* was a break with the old Catholic view of the world held by many of the saints. (He could with greater accuracy have said *all* of the saints—not to mention the authors of the Epistles, and our Lord Himself.)

As for the conciliar documents themselves, they require an exegesis that could fill a bookshelf. But they do breathe a spirit, especially where they deal with temporal problems, that clashes with the strictures of earlier popes on liberalism and humanism.

It is no accident that liberals the world over sang hymns to the Council. Were they all wrong? The children of this world are wise in their generation. The liberals know their own. In particular, they know that the Council moved their way on religious liberty—

whereas they despised the views of earlier popes (who, in turn, were simply repeating what had been the unvarying attitude of the Church since the Apostolic Age). If the Council did not offer a wholly novel view of religious liberty (novel, that is, for the Church; it is old hat for liberals), then words have lost all meaning. This, I suspect, is one reason why Archbishop Lefebvre is denied his hearing. The Vatican is loathe to defend a hopeless case, even in its own court.

But the Pope himself has given us the final refutation of the conservative position, in condemning Archbishop Lefebvre. Among other things the Pope demands that the Archbishop accept the post-conciliar "orientations" of the Church—which are, by definition, new, or else the Pope, the Archbishop, and the rest of us would be arguing over—nothing.

Which leads to my point that the conservative axis is here again betraying its own position. Why do they decline to follow the post-conciliar orientations? The Pope has endorsed them. Why do they resist the pentecostal wave? The Pope smiles on it. Why do they shy away from the revolutionary activities of papal appointees in the Third World? Why do they quarrel with theological ideas that are taught in Rome's pontifical seminaries? Why do they argue with catechisms imposed by nearly all the bishops of the world? These bishops, after all, are answerable to the Pope; most are appointees; and the caliber of the appointments has remained constant over fourteen years.

I think I know why. Scratch a conservative—and more often than not you'll find a traditionalist. But a traditionalist who shrinks from resolving the ambiguity of his own position. This is not surprising. It hurts to change.

Which is just what we've been telling our father, the Pope. Who isn't listening, and doesn't care.

℣

A Little Help from Pope St. Pius X
By Neil McCaffrey (*Wanderer*, 1970)

Breathes there a beleaguered Catholic today who hasn't had recourse to Pius X's epochal encyclical on Modernism? *Pascendi Dominici Gregis* was issued in 1907—and I suggest that there isn't a papal document extant that is more contemporary, or more consoling. It is directed against the Modernists who had surfaced in the Pope's day—and their heirs all around us today.

Perhaps you've put off reading it because you find the mock-Ciceronian prose of latter-day papal documents impenetrable. Not to worry. Pius X writes directly, bluntly, sometimes with a bite that will make you blink. Hardly a page passes that you won't want to mark, maybe memorize.

To give you a sense of what's in store, let me offer a handful of quotable passages. But I offer them with one caveat: for every one here, there are literally a dozen more, just as choice, in the encyclical. In fact, you'll undoubtedly find at least a dozen that you like better than my own favorites.

Before quoting some of the Saint's own words, let me cite parts of the encyclical wherein he quotes from other popes and councils. First, from a decree of Vatican I:

> ... that sense of the sacred dogma is to be perpetually retained which our Holy Mother the Church has once declared, nor is this sense ever to be abandoned on the plea or pretext of a more profound comprehension of the truth.

He quotes from *Singulari Nos,* that neglected 1834 encyclical of Gregory XVI:

> A lamentable spectacle is that presented by the aberrations of human reason when it yields to the spirit of novelty, when against the warning of the Apostle it seeks to know beyond what it is meant to know and when, relying too much on itself, it thinks it can find the truth outside the Catholic Church, wherein truth is found without the faintest shadow of error.

To condemn those who sneer at the church of yesterday and genuflect before the spirit of change, he cites the condemnations of two general councils, including Nicea II:

> For Catholics nothing will remove the authority of the second Council of Nicea where it condemns those *who dare, after the impious fashion of heretics, to deride ecclesiastical traditions, to invent novelties of some kind… or to endeavor by malice or craft to overthrow any one of the legitimate traditions of the Catholic Church ...* [Italics in the original.]

As befits the head of a Church grounded in tradition, Pius X often invokes his predecessors. But most of the encyclical is original with him. Does this passage strike you as dated?

> It remains for us now to say a few words about the Modernist as reformer. From all that has preceded, it is abundantly clear how great and how eger is the passion of such men for innovation. In

all Catholicism there is absolutely nothing on which [Modernism] does not fasten. They wish philosophy to be reformed, especially in the ecclesiastical seminaries. They wish the scholastic philosophy to be relegated to the history of philosophy and to be classed among obsolete systems, and the young men to be taught modern philosophy which alone is said to be true and suited to the times in which we live . . . . Dogmas and their evolution, they affirm, are to be harmonized with science and history. In the Catechism no dogmas are to be inserted except those that have been reformed and are within the capacity of the people. Regarding worship, they say, the number of external devotions is to be reduced, and steps must be taken to prevent their further increase . . . .They cry out that ecclesiastical government requires to be reformed in all its branches, but especially in its disciplinary and dogmatic departments... [They insist] a share in ecclesiastical government should therefore be given to the lower ranks of the clergy, and even to the laity, and authority which is too much concentrated, should be decentralized. The Roman Congregations, and especially the Index and the Holy Office, must be likewise modified.

The Pope calls Modernism "the synthesis of all heresies," then goes on to analyze why people succumb to it. He finds three reasons, but one stands out:

It is pride which exercises over the soul incomparably greater power to blind it and lead it into error, and pride sits in Modernism as in its own house, finding sustenance everywhere in its doctrines and lurking in its every aspect. It is pride which fills Modernists with that self-assurance which puffs them up with that vainglory which allows them to regard themselves as the sole possessors of knowledge, and makes them say, elated and inflated with presumption, "We are not as the rest of men," and which, lest they should seem as other men, leads them to embrace and to devise novelties even of the most absurd kind.

What must the hierarchy do when they confront this spirit? The Pope addresses the bishops of his day in impassioned words; how many of their successors are now heeding them?

It will be your first duty to resist such victims of pride, to employ them only in the lowest and obscurest offices. The higher they try to rise, the lower let them be placed, so that the lowliness of their position may limit their power of causing damage. Examine your young clerics most carefully . . . when you find the spirit of pride among them, reject them for the priesthood without

216

compunction. Would to God that this had always been done with the vigilance and constancy that were required!

It is worth noting that the papal Saint made no exceptions for a shortage of priests, or any other reason. No, his order is delivered in the imperative, with no hedging: "reject them without compunction." Period. We can be sure that Pius was not indifferent to shortages of priests; but he was a saint, not a clerical bureaucrat. He understood that God is not thwarted by (temporary) shortages.

The Pope pauses to note the hatred that Modernists pour on the orthodox. Anyone who has seen today's breed in action will have to conclude that nothing has changed:

> There is little reason to wonder that the Modernists vent all their bitterness and hatred on Catholics who zealously fight the battles of the Church. There is no species of insult which they do not heap upon them, but their usual course is to charge them with ignorance or obstinacy. When an adversary rises up against them with an erudition and force that render him redoubtable, they seek to make a conspiracy of silence around him to nullify the effects of his attack. This policy towards Catholics is the more invidious in that they laud with an admiration that knows no bounds the writers who range themselves on their side, hailing their works (which exude novelty on every page) with a chorus of applause. For them the scholarship of a writer is in direct proportion to the recklessness of his attacks on antiquity, and of his efforts to undermine tradition and the ecclesiastical magisterium. When one of their number falls under the condemnation of the Church, the rest of them, to the disgust of good Catholics, gather round him, loudly and publicly applaud him, and hold him up in veneration as almost a martyr for truth. The young, excited and confused by all this clamor of praise and abuse, some of them afraid of being branded as ignorant, others ambitious to rank among the learned, and both classes goaded internally by curiosity and pride, not unfrequently surrender and give themselves up to Modernism . . . . What efforts do they not make to win new recruits! They seize upon professorships in the seminaries and universities, and gradually make of them chairs of pestilence. In sermons from the pulpit they disseminate their doctrines, although possibly in utterances which are veiled. In congresses they express their teachings more openly. In their social gatherings they introduce them and commend them to others. Under their own names and under pseudonyms they publish numbers of books, newspapers, reviews. It is also a subject of grief to us that many others who, while they certainly

do not go so far as the former, have yet been so infected by breathing a poisoned atmosphere as to think, speak, and write with a degree of laxity which ill becomes a Catholic. They are to be found among the laity, and in the ranks of the clergy, and they are not wanting even in the last place where one might expect to meet them, in religious communities. If they treat of biblical questions, it is upon Modernist principles; if they write history, they carefully, and with ill-concealed satisfaction, appear to cast a stain upon the Church. Under the sway of certain *a priori* conceptions, they destroy as far as they can the pious traditions of the people, and bring into disrespect certain relics highly venerable from their antiquity. They are possessed by the empty desire of having their names upon the lips of the public, and they know they would never succeed in this were they to say only what has always been said by all men. Meanwhile it may be that they have persuaded themselves that in all this they are really serving God and the Church. In reality they only offend both, less perhaps by their works in themselves than by the spirit in which they write, and by the encouragement they thus give to the aims of the Modernists.

Pius understood that it wasn't enough for a pontiff to instruct and even exhort. (What, after all, would we say of a parent who periodically quoted the tenets of the moral law to his children, pleaded for their obedience, but refused ever to discipline them?) The Pope knew that words weren't enough. He must *act*. Pius X did just that; and I think we may see in his determination one mark of that heroic sanctity that earned him the saint's crown. He certainly laid it on the line to the bishops:

> We exhort and abjure you to see to it, in this most grave matter, that no one shall be in a position to say that you have been, in the slightest degree, wanting in vigilance, zeal, or firmness.

Plain enough? Yet the Pope doesn't stop there. He has a program. He *acts*. He "strictly ordains that scholastic philosophy be made the basis of the sacred sciences"; and, following Leo XIII and indeed the whole of Catholic tradition, all the arts and sciences are to "serve [theology] and wait upon it after the manner of handmaidens."

But that's *still* not all. This saintly Pope understands that there must be sanctions aimed at those who rebel against Catholic teaching—sanctions that

> are to be kept in view whenever there is a question of choosing directors and professors for seminaries and Catholic universities.

> Anyone who in any way is found to be tainted with Modernism is to be excluded without compunction from these offices, whether of government or of teaching, and those who already occupy them are to be removed. The same policy is to be adopted towards those who openly or secretly lend countenance to Modernism either by extolling the Modernists and excusing their culpable conduct, or by carping at scholasticism and the Fathers and the magisterium of the Church, or by refusing obedience to ecclesiastical authority in any of its depositaries; and towards those who show a love of novelty in history, archaeology, biblical exegesis; and finally towards those who neglect the sacred science or appear to prefer the secular to them. In all this question of studies, Venerable Brethren, you cannot be too watchful or too constant. . . Equal diligence and severity are to be used in examining and selecting candidates for Holy Orders. Far, far from the clergy be the love of novelty!

Next come a series of papal edicts that give liberals the shakes. What would their soul brothers in the American Civil Liberties Union make of all this?

> It is also come duty of the Bishops to prevent the writings of Modernists, or whatever savors of Modernism or promotes it, from being read when they have been published, and to hinder their publication when they have not. No books or papers or periodicals whatever of this kind are to be permitted to seminarians or university students. The injury to them would be not less than that which is caused by immoral reading—nay, it would be greater, for such writings poison Christian life at its very fount. The same decision is to be taken concerning the writings of some Catholics, who, though not evilly disposed themselves, are ill-instructed in theological studies and imbued with modem philosophy, and strive to make this harmonize with the faith, and, as they say, to turn it to the profit of the faith. The name and reputation of these authors cause them to be read without suspicion, and they are, therefore, all the more dangerous in gradually preparing the way for Modernism. . . We order that you do everything in your power to drive out of your dioceses, even by solemn interdict, any pernicious books that may be in circulation there.

But isn't all that hopelessly out of date? What would enlightened types say if they saw bishops behaving that way? The Pope, it seems, had anticipated the public relations problem—or what the spiritual writers used to call the temptation to human respect:

> We will . . . that the Bishops, putting aside all fear and the prudence of the flesh, and despising the clamor of evil men, shall—gently by all means, but firmly—each do his own part in this work . . . Let no Bishop think that he fulfills this duty by denouncing to us one or two books, while a great many others of the same kind are being published and circulated. Nor are you to be deterred by the fact that a book has obtained elsewhere the permission which is commonly call the *Imprimatur,* both because this may be merely simulated, and because it may have been granted through carelessness or too much indulgence or excessive trust placed in the author, which last has perhaps sometimes happened in the religious orders.

Finally, leaving nothing to chance, local option, ecumenism, or public relations, the Pope spells out still more specifically the steps that must be taken to defend Catholic doctrine and protect the faithful. Again he addresses the hierarchy, and again he doesn't hesitate to give them their marching orders:

> Of what avail, Venerable Brethren, would be all our commands and prescriptions if they be not dutifully and finally carried out?... We decree, therefore, that in every diocese a council of this kind, which we are pleased to name the "Council of Vigilance," be instituted without delay. . . .They shall watch most carefully for every trace and sign of Modernism both in publications and in teaching, and to keep it from the clergy and the young they shall take all prudent, prompt and efficacious measures. Let them combat novelties of words, remembering the admonitions of Leo XIII: *It is impossible to approve in Catholic publications a style inspired by unsound novelty which seems to deride the piety of the faithful and dwells on the introduction of a new order of Christian life, on new directions in the Church, on new aspirations of the modern soul, on a new social vocation of the clergy, on a new Christian civilization, and on many other things of the same kind.* [Italics in original.]

Does this give you the flavor? It does; but it's only a taste. To get the full impact of a Pope who speaks—and acts—as one having authority; who cares nothing about his reputation among the worldly, and everything about the souls of his flock, you must read the whole, great document.

Read it *now.*

 CZ

3

Philosophical and Theological Musings

March 22, 1963

Dear Bill [Buckley]:

The Hoyt correspondence so fascinated me that I put aside a massive and possible epochal proposal I'm reading for a VIP friend of yours (a copy of which I'll send you in, I hope, a few days). Let me just dash among the paragraphs and drop a few comments.

To begin with, you should order a copy of the Knox translation of *Humani Generis* from the *Tablet*, 14 Howich Place, London S.W.1 or from the Catholic Truth Society, 36 Eccleston Square, London S.W.1. Knox all but makes it readable. By the way, it isn't a bad encyclical, and certainly a gem beside M. and M. [*Mater et Magistra*]. I was not aware it was directed against Murray [John Courtney Murray, S.J.]. Are you sure?

Not having been vouchsafed the discernment of spirits, I can't say whether Hoyt is nasty, narrow, or naive. But I wonder if he'd hold John Cogley to the same standard in passing on the Fund's pamphlets, or Schuster in entertaining the views of the assorted atheists, agnostics and leftists he welcomed at Hunter, or Bob Giroux in deciding what should appear under the Farrar, Straus imprint. Logically, the force of his argument would condemn us all to editing diocesan newspapers.

Yet I am far from dismissing his argument. If we swim in the East River we must expect to encounter garbage, and each of us has to determine his own gagging point. The waters are clear at 35th Street.

Nat's [Nathaniel Weyl, ex-communist] review forces the inference that *he* disbelieves our common descent from Adam. So what? NR is for adults; we have confronted the notion before, and not abandoned the Sacraments. Coon's finding, which Weyl endorses, are susceptible of other readings. E.g. *after* Adam mankind divided into races. (The question of when man became *homo sapiens* is answered by faith: with Adam. Not before, and not after. Science cannot teach us this; neither can it teach us anything that will demolish a truth which has a warrant that science can't disturb.)

Hoyt was fatuous to cite an encyclical as his justification for chiding you. The doctrine has a hoarier ancestry: cf. the New Testament—not to mention the Old.

I'm afraid I must part with you on the theoretical possibility that Adam was not our common father. The doctrine of original sin then dissolves, does it not? And with it, the basis for the Incarnation and Redemption.

The only alternative I can even conceive is a generalized, "worldwide" original sin committed by *all* our ancestors; and this strains credulity, nor does it seem reconcilable with doctrine.

Your remarks on why, as a Christian conservative, you prescind from Christianity in the forum are as prudent and trenchant as any I've read on the matter.

Do I detect that the race question has you a bit uneasy these days? No reason why it should. Even if God made one race measurably and even permanently inferior, it wouldn't jeopardize their dignity as His sons. God delights in variety. Look at the animal kingdom. Should He be any less creative with His favorite (temporal) creatures, His adopted sons? A blinding genius towers over me: we are both as insects to God. Our norms are not His—and we should not presume to make His *eternal* norms ours *in time*. Christopher is not your equal now; Maureen and young Neil are not mine. And if, God forbid, their development should be stunted and they should remain children till eighty, they might be better according to their capacities than you and I but you and I would be justified—indeed, obliged—to treat them as children. Just so, civilization has its imperatives. We do children no kindness to pretend they are ready for adult responsibilities.

I might add, by the way, that this attitude is not only compatible with Christian charity but, I am convinced, demanded by it. Charity does not overleap justice, and justice gives to each his *due*—no more, no less.

As usual in these matters—as we conservatives alone know—we should be dealing in prudential judgments, not abstractions of (often spurious) ideals.

But enough. Welcome home! And thanks so much for your thoughtfulness in sending that $200. I'm preparing an affidavit for Thurston Davis to the effect that you *do* love your neighbor, and practice the works of mercy.

Thanks also for *Rumbles*, which just came yesterday.

Best,
Neil

Ꮕ

September 18, 1968

Dear Brent:
Your article on the encyclical [*Humanae Vitae*] was, along with [Will] Herberg's, the only impressive defense of it I've seen. It called up your finest powers of advocacy.

I stick on one point that you seem not to have grappled with. The encyclical finds its intellectual justification in the natural law only, and indeed gives scant attention even to that, merely repeating the familiar argument without attempting to explicate or defend it. Now there is an interesting point about the natural law. It is, by definition, accessible to right reason, to clearheaded men of good will regardless of faith. But if this is so, as it is, then we have here a wonderful exception to the natural law: a doctrine that is intellectually convincing to relatively few Catholics and practically no non-Catholics.

I have not seen anyone tackle this dilemma, much less resolve it. Can you?

Best,

Neil

ᙏ

November 12, 1968

Triumph
927 - 15th Street N.W.
Washington, D. C. 20005

Editor:

Triumph seems to have involved itself in an internal contradiction. Your editorial hails Salazar as a great Christian leader (I agree). It notes that he owed much to Maurras. It fails to note, however, that Maurras was anathematized by Pope Pius XI. Since *Triumph* appears to hold that papal decisions of this sort command assent, it would seem to have painted itself into a corner. Does *Triumph* believe that Pius XI erred on Maurras by intruding in what was really a political quarrel? Sub-question: would the Pope therefore have exceeded or misused his authority? Or did this admirable Pope simply err? Sub-question: to what extent, then, do you acknowledge the possibility of error in a pope?

Alternatively, I am afraid you are left with a great Christian leader who learned his statecraft at the feet of a heretic.

Incidentally, I think you are wrong in stating that "the Church teaches it has no power at all to dissolve a marriage." Not so. The Church claims the right to dissolve any marriage, even a valid one, unless it is *both* a sacramental *and* a consummated marriage. Check your friendly theologian.

Neil McCaffrey

ᙏ

225

April 12, 1971

Book Forum
Saturday Review
380 Madison Avenue
New York, New York 10017

Editor:
Without undertaking an elaborate rebuttal of Markus Barth on papal infallibility, I can offer a clue to his credentials by noting one error of fact, one travesty of Catholic teaching and one exercise in hubris.

Fact: The doctrine of the Immaculate Conception was defined in 1854, sixteen years before Vatican I defined papal infallibility.

Travesty: Dr. Barth writes that "the encyclicals of the Pope, no less than his dogmatic utterances, call for unconditional faith, acceptance, and obedience." This is crude. An encyclical calls for just that degree of acceptance that is required by the subject matter itself, its relation to faith or morals, and the solemnity with which the pope intends to treat it. Dr. Barth, by equating a solemn proclamation of doctrine with *obiter dicta* on, say, economics, manages to trivialize all papal pronouncements; as he no doubt means to. For a sophisticated study of this complex question, *Politics and Catholic Freedom* by Garry Wills is the most searching book, at least in English.

Hubris: Dr. Barth adjudges Hans Küng "a good Catholic Christian." It is enough to note that only God has any business making quite so categorical a judgment. But even short of that, Dr. Barth of all people has no competence. The Elks have their rules, and reasonable men know that Elks are the best judges of whether Jones lives up to the code of Elkdom. So when Dr. Barth calls someone a good Catholic Christian, he really means a good liberal Protestant. Dr. Barth's is the kiss that scarifies.
Neil McCaffrey

ൠ

January 2, 1973

National Review
150 E. 35th Street
New York, New York 10016

Editor:
Mrs. R. J. Schroeder's letter reminds *NR* [Jan. 5] of the moral dimension to the pot controversy, which as post-Christians your editors had

no trouble ignoring. Your reply ("The divine sanction is not the business of Congress") is one of those quarter-truths one expects from secularists, or from individualists of the godless sort. It is no part of the Christian tradition of government. That tradition holds that government derives its authority from God, whose authority it shares in the temporal order (in its bumbling fashion). To the extent that government seeks to legitimize an offense against the divine law (e.g. murder, or drug-taking), it clashes with the Source of authority and renders itself illegitimate. And people who foster a government's sins of commission or omission are the scandalizers upon whom judgment was pronounced in the Gospels, in words that burn.
Neil McCaffrey

⊗

February 5, 1973
MEMO TO: Bill Buckley
CC: Bill Rusher
FROM: Neil McCaffrey

Notwithstanding the item in the current letters column that you will run no more letters on the pot controversy, I think you owe it to me to run this one. It's shabby to take the cheap shot and run; and it does the magazine (and truth) no service to leave as your last word the vulgar argument that there is no difference between liquor and dope.

National Review
150 E. 35th street
New York, New York 10016

Editor:
If the editors of *NR* can't see the difference between dope and alcohol, and therefore the difference between repealing Prohibition and decriminalizing dope, they would do well to leave off commenting on moral matters.

Alcohol is a good that can be abused. The state therefore has the right to regulate its use and guard against its abuse, but no right to ban it. Most people who take a drink have no intention of reducing themselves to a subhuman condition. They drink because they like the taste, or to be sociable, or to relax. The minority who drink in order to get drunk have no business drinking; but their abuse of a natural good is no justification for denying the majority the proper use of that good.

With dope it is otherwise. The *only* possible motive for taking dope is to get high: to "liberate" man from those moral, intellectual and physical restraints it is his obligation to cultivate, if he would be fully human; in short, to reduce himself to a subhuman state. Taking dope is a form of mutilation, and mutilation is forbidden by the natural law.

If the editors of *NR* are still puzzling over the difference between having a drink and taking dope, it's time they quit drinking.
Neil McCaffrey

ങ

May 2, 1973

New York Magazine
207 East 32nd Street
New York, New York 10016

Editor:
Dorothy Rabinowitz never disappoints, but her portrait of the estimable Dr. Abend was something of a *tour de force*. She portrayed him vividly, and justly—in a magazine most of whose readers must be charter members of the Hate Abend club. One small slip, however. It is hardly accurate to characterize the Oxford Movement as a 19th century effort to reconcile science and religion. That supposed conflict has never been a major problem for believers. I suspect it is more a rationalization for unbelief. Newman, Keble, Pusey and Froude understood the importance (and the unimportance) of science, above all understood its pretensions. They were embarked on a more serious enterprise, to recall the Anglican Church to what they conceived to be its Catholic origins.
Neil McCaffrey

ങ

June 12, 1973

Dear Mr. Keeler:
Thanks for your searching letter. I think it would be useful if I expanded a bit on my premises. I approach the problem from Roman Catholic theology and natural law ethics. In that system, the prohibition against mutilation is seen as a corollary of the prohibition against murder. A common example would be that it is forbidden to cut off one's toe in order to avoid the draft. More broadly, it is forbidden to abuse one's natural powers. Under this would come the prohibition against drunkenness and the use of dope.

Of course, it is possible to use cannabis in exiguous amounts in order to achieve a mild and harmless high. This would be akin to having a drink or two: harmless morally. In practice, of course, dope is never taken to achieve such a limited objective. There is simply no reason to take it unless one wants to get *high*. Getting high involves in some way or other releasing inhibitions, making a person less responsive to his reason and his will, and (secondarily) more or less harming his health.

Seen in this light, the use of dope contrasts with the reasonable use of alcohol—not merely in its effect, but more important in its intention.

Very well, but does that mean that its prohibition should be enforced by law? Here we get into the area of prudential judgment. Granted, human law is not intended to be a perfect reflection of the moral law (or more precisely, divine law). But it should reflect it to the extent that prudence permits. Since the use of dope is pandemic, socially devastating, demoralizing, and dangerous to health, I take it to be not merely legitimate but a crying need for government to outlaw dope. Moreover, in the climate of a post-Christian society that has so departed from traditional morality that positive law is almost the only sanction remaining, as a practical matter I regard it as disastrous to decriminalize the use of dope.

On the point of principle, I don't subscribe to the notion that the state should be indifferent to what is (erroneously) called private morality. This is one of the ideological fantasies of liberalism. It has no pedigree in history or experience, nor in my judgment in reason. Up to a point the state represents society, and society cannot be indifferent to morality. Where society is indifferent to morality, as in fact it is in large areas today, social and personal demoralization is swift and deadly. A fair description, wouldn't you say, of the world today?

And when a reputedly Christian and conservative journal advocates such indifference, I believe the cancer is reaching the terminal stage.
Kindest regards,
Neil McCaffrey

CB

Mr. Marshner's Catholic Mathematics
[*Triumph*, July, 1973]
Neil McCaffrey

I'm not sure, but I think Mr. [William] Marshner is still missing my point (*Triumph*, July). But this may be as much my fault as his; so, back to the typewriter.

For most of my 48 years, I've been hearing Catholic spokesmen talk as if something they call "papal social doctrine" is the sane man's alternative to the isms of the century. If we understand papal social doctrine, as Mr. Marshner sometimes seems to, as an elucidation of the natural law in a modern context, I would enter no protest. Part of the Church's mission, always, is to help men apply the law to concrete situations.

But all too often these spokesmen get swept away. They begin to equate political and social and economic programs with "Catholic social *doctrine*." And a more subtle error: they convince themselves that something called "Catholic social doctrine" will usher in the golden age. This nonsense is seldom stated outright, since it will not withstand explicit statement. It is rather implied, suggested, encouraged. It is an effort to baptize a golden calf—really, an opiate of the people.

I believe *Triumph* encourages these illusions, more than any contemporary voice. Mr. Marshner is more cautious, and if his remarks provoke a nicer sense of the possible among his colleagues, our little exchange will not have been in vain. Certainly, he subjects my own remarks to rigorous analysis. A few comments on his:

I think we should be chaste in using a term like Christian economics, lest we seem to accord it a place of honor beside that other eminent discipline, Christian mathematics. If we mean that the economic order should be structured in accordance with justice and open to the practice of charity, then we should say so plainly, and not tease people with the hope that Christianity somewhere contains the answer to our balance-of-payment crisis.

Truth, however, is a unity. Moral sentiments do not create good economics, but good economics must be an economics of justice. Not, however, a sectarian economics, the very thought of which is ludicrous, an oxymoron.

Moreover, somewhere in all this lies a religious imperialism. It is no service to our faith to invest it with sham authority. Such a practice can only bring scorn on that faith when, sooner or later, the truth comes out that fiscal authority is not one of the gifts of the Holy Ghost. And because truth *is* a unity, it will come out.

It should be (but apparently isn't) unnecessary to add that the Church does indeed have valuable things to say about economics, but on the level of principle. For example, Catholic tradition has always considered debasing the coinage a high crime. Good economics, sticking to its proper technical sphere, calls the same thing a hidden tax. So the one sphere complements the other: again, the unity of truth.

What troubles me about some *Triumph* editorials is not that they start from Christian beliefs and seek to work these beliefs into the secular arena. That, after all, is part of living one's faith. What I find off-putting is the tendency to short-circuit temporal problems with jolts of 'religion,' as if 'religion' rendered expertise unnecessary and one's temporal judgments unassailable. Religion as shibboleth, as amulet, as club, is religion abused.

I sense that *Triumph* editors may have an ingenious view of Catholic journalism—the view that every problem must somehow be solved by Catholic doctrine. Such single-mindedness makes for bad religion and worse journalism. Relax, fellows. A sacramental view of life let's you enjoy a ball game without seeing it as an analogue of the struggle between darkness and light.

And don't worry about scanting religion. You can—*must*, as Catholic journalists—bring your faith to bear directly on a beehive of problems like crime, abortion, dope, divorce, the abdication of authority in church and state, education, porn, astrology, contraception, sodomy, attacks on the family—but I've hardly tickled the surface.

As to whether the world is good, an elementary distinction: God created the world and found it good. Of course. Then came sin. Then came redemption. Thus we should avoid both extremes and say: the world is good but wounded, and will be until our Lord returns. Government, like the world, will always be more or less good, more or less bad. Governments run by Christians and informed by Christian principles will be—*better*; but not *good* in any absolute sense. If we haven't learned this from experience, we have the word of our Lord. Yes, His kingdom is *not* of this world. Mr. Marshner may find this an inadequate commentary on the secular order; I can only say it's good enough for me.

This matter of whether the world is good or bad—isn't this another example of that dualism that permeates Catholic thought? The Triune God is absolutely One; predestination and free will are *both* realities; and so on. Catholic thought is hostile to easy one-sided answers. We live with paradox, and panaceas strike the Catholic ear as off pitch.

That the popes quote Scripture and St. Augustine and St. Thomas is no discovery. Whom better to quote? But they find no panaceas in these sources. St. Paul has no blueprint for a new Roman Empire. Augustine was concerned (living in an age like our own) but ultimately detached. Aquinas mentioned the three just and the three unjust forms of government but fashioned no constitution.

No, I don't think the modern popes have given us political

programs; and, taking them at their word, I don't think it is their business to. They have more serious work to do. The problems come when we descend from high principle to depressing areas like the UN. We are awash here in a sea of gray. The popes can blunder here like the rest of us (just like they blundered in some of their medieval wars); they are, after all, grappling with contingent temporal affairs. What I object to is the equation of papal temporal policy, much less the policy of any writer or magazine, with Catholic social *doctrine*. We have nothing to fear from modesty.

I should reiterate what I take to be basic: politics and social problems and economics should be guided by natural justice. Natural justice is not exclusively the province of the Church, though the Church has the preeminent role in interpreting it. But the Church has no monopoly on political and social and economic wisdom; and the children of this world are wiser in their generation than the children of light.

ᘓ

August 20, 1975

Dear Bill:
About your Princeton column, Jim Burnham identified the phenomenon in *Suicide of the West* but did not explain it; in fact could not, from his spot on the epistemological turf. It is the persistently suicidal note that marks this behavior as a phenomenon. We aren't used to seeing humans above the level of imbecile acting against interest. So, because we expect people to behave rationally, we keep trying to *explain*.

I think it a vain enterprise—because we seem to be dealing with something whose explanation lies outside the natural order. Modern man, even within the Church, has dethroned God and enthroned himself. That is to say, he has given his soul to the Devil. If we can trust the observations of Screwtape (I do) and those of traditional theology, Satan may dangle rewards here and now, but even here and now he is niggardly. He has nothing to offer, and nothingness is what we get. So his works tend to nihilism. Hence, modern man's suicidal drive.

Extravagant? Mindful of the words of our Lord and Sts. Paul and Peter and superstitious writers like Newman, I don't expect a more plausible explanation.
Best,
Neil

ᘓ

November 26, 1975

The Atlantic
8 Arlington Street
Boston, Massachusetts 02116

Sir:

Barbara Tuchman correctly notes that she encountered land mines among the "Hazards on the Way to the Middle Ages" (December *Atlantic*). There were more than she realized, and I'm afraid they are going to keep cropping up.

Mrs. Tuchman is taken with the researcher who compared the number of homes in a town with the number of Communion hosts sold over a period of two years, from which he inferred the Mass attendance— "about once or twice a year". Alas for scholarship, there is no connection between the two. Reception of Communion was indeed less frequent in the Middle Ages, and probably did average once or twice a year for the typical Catholic. Most Catholics, however, did attend Mass, but with no thought of receiving Communion except at Easter and probably at Christmas.

Mrs. Tuchman equates "absolution for sin" with "what we would call freedom from guilt"—and thereby commits an historical anachronism. Moderns go to their shrinks to lose some of the burdens of guilt; whereas Catholics really do believe—*know*—that their sins are wiped away in the sacrament of penance; which absolution, however, cannot be bought. I do not dispute that here and there some wretched priest may have tried to traffic in forgiveness (for which act he would have incurred automatic excommunication). But to take such an abuse as typical is grotesque. What Mrs. Tuchman may be confusing is the remission of what the theologians distinguish as the eternal punishment and the temporal punishment for sin. The eternal punishment, which refers to one's condemnation to hell if he dies in the state of mortal sin, is most usually remitted by a worthy reception of the sacrament of penance. The temporal punishment, which refers to the added debt we must pay to God to completely atone for our sins, means temporary suffering in purgatory for such debts as we do not make good by prayers and good works in this life. Indulgences were and are sometimes granted for these prayers and good works; this led to abuses in the medieval Church; and these abuses were undoubtedly what Mrs. Tuchman was referring to.

It does get involved, and I'm afraid nuances like these may trip up Mrs. Tuchman before she gets far into the medieval world.
Neil McCaffrey

ᛒ

March 24, 1976

Dear Sister [Rose Marie Larkin, OSB]:
Now it's my turn to acknowledge that you caught me in a clumsy statement. I was *trying* to say something like this. Everyone needs authority. We need it in our personal lives and in our intellectual lives. In our personal lives, we are not cut out, most of us, to stand apart from and indeed up against everybody else. In our intellectual lives, we likewise accept most of what we believe on authority. It is the same in the Church as in everyday life. Indeed, it is more true in the Church. Our Lord meant us to be part of one Body, intended us to draw our beliefs from a revealed body of truth we should seek to understand better but never to question, did not expect us to have to go back to the beginning and figure everything out for ourselves. In support of all this, it occurs to me that one psychological attraction of the rule for religious is the very security it provides. But I should not have implied that this precludes religious from being good leaders. I guess the percentage of good leaders among religious is at least as high as it is among the general population. Probably higher. But nevertheless, good leaders are always a small minority, in or out of religious life. And (this is what I was really getting at) it is particularly cruel to force freedoms on religious who have vowed themselves to a radically different sort of life.

Of course, I didn't mean that religious can't be good thinkers. Here again, what I was fumbling to say was simply that religious, when they started out, did not want to be forced to come up with a whole new set of answers. They were right in this. But they have been told now that they have to. They have been set loose from their moorings. And, because they have never been trained for this, they probably flounder about even more helplessly than the rest of us. Which is going some.

I don't know if I have explained myself any better. But I'm grateful to you for forcing me to try. I think the Rule is one of God's great gifts to mankind, and that of St. Benedict one of the greatest of the great.

I don't know too much about Fr. Fenton. I rely for most of what I know about him on a priest-mentor (very conservative himself) who took a dim view of Fenton's heresy-hunting. Or at least he used to, back in the good old days. I suspect he would be rather more tolerant of it today.

I don't know the Fenton brochure *On Communism in the Church*, so I can't really comment. It is certainly true that Marxism has

conquered an alarming percentage of the clergy. If this is what he says, I agree wholeheartedly. If, however, he says that the Communists planted people in seminaries, I'm not so sure. I don't deny the possibility; I just wonder if it actually happened that way. We would need evidence on that point. I tend to think it unlikely. A more plausible explanation is that the softening that liberalism brings makes a person easy prey for Communism, especially somebody who tends to what is misleadingly called idealism.
Kindest regards,
Neil McCaffrey

Thanks again for writing.

CB

[February 23, 1977]

Dear Rog [son Roger McCaffrey],
The problem of true charity is—the problem. Some random thoughts.

There can be no charity without justice, in this sense: charity may go beyond justice, but never at the expense of justice.

Von Hildebrand makes a useful distinction between injuries done to me and injuries done to God; the latter either directly or indirectly [because] to others. *I* cannot forgive an injury done to God, or to another.

We owe charity to our leaders in the Church, yes. But this does not extend to forgiving what in fact *we* cannot forgive, their offenses against God and the souls in their care. We should pray that they acquit themselves of these sins, but we do them no charity by pretending that their sins are virtues. Indeed, we do them the gravest disservice with such lies; and a worse disservice to those they harm.

We delude ourselves, and insult God, when we act as if God can be served by suppressing the truth, or by lying. This is an amazingly crude notion, but widespread. God is truth.

We may hold ourselves to a high standard of truth, and still offend if we lack charity. "The greatest of these is charity." So we must somehow find a way to serve truth *and* charity.

It is a commonplace that charity doesn't oblige us to *like* someone. We must treat him as we would want to be treated, do him no harm, wish him well.

Pseudo-charity is a kind of cowardice and damages both subject and object. All lies do.

There is also a place for righteous anger, especially anger at

235

offenses against God or our neighbor. This, surprisingly, is also an aspect of *charity*. But it is also tricky, and can easily deteriorate into personal anger.

Nothing, *nothing* in the way of charity can be accomplished without God's help.

Terrible sins are committed in the name of charity.

Newman insisted on charity—and insisted equally on measures that should be taken against bad people: ostracism, avoidance, censure, etc.

The motive for charity is imitation of and union with God. His life is love, and he lives it not only with Himself but with His creation. If *He* loves His creatures, we should and must, if we are to imitate Him and become His.

We can judge objective evil—objective guilt if you will—with great accuracy, if we use God's norms. As to subjective guilt, we can make informed *guesses* but can never really know. It is in that sense that we "cannot judge." Hell, we barely know ourselves, let alone others. Who but God *can* know, in this sense? But in the former sense (objective guilt), we *can* judge, and indeed our Lord instructs us to, often. He even tells us: "By their fruits [ye shall know them]…" He tells us to watch out for false Christs, to shun evildoers, etc. What are all those but *commands* to judge? Judging, after all, is the pristine act of the intellect. It is a sham piety that would have us act contrary to our very nature. Sure, we must rise *above* nature to reach heaven; but in that process we are to *use* nature, not do violence to it.

Those of us who have some grasp of the truth yet yield little fruit are barren, I'm pretty sure, because and to the extent that our charity is cold. Prophets, remember, are men *of God*.

One point Newman insists on: that false ideas of religion *harm* people. Of course. Otherwise, why Revelation? Faith is no mere adornment. It is *the* way.

Be patient. Every individual has his own rhythm. Grace too has its own tempo. That is why converts are made—but often over long periods. It took Augustine and Newman about a decade each.

I wish I knew more about charity.

Love,
Dad

P.S. The classic Gospel and Epistle remarks on charity refer mainly to our fellows, not to Church authorities. Although charity must obtain here, too, the *governing* problem deals with good shepherds, scandal, etc. "Charity" should not distract from the real issue—which, paradoxically, is *charity*. But charity rightly understood: the charity owed to the faithful, not the mock charity bestowed by feeble Christians on feeble shepherds. This false charity, in other words, is a device of the Devil to distract from the real charity being denied to the faithful.

Ponder the Pharisees in light of today's hierarchy. The parallels are overpowering. Was our Lord charitable to the Pharisees? Of course, He was—*and* He excoriated them. So we see that charity *must* subsist with righteous indignation, contrary to what the caricaturists of charity like to pretend.

Rog—Read First Corinthians, chapter 5, in the Jerusalem Bible translation. It gives *the* rules for how we are to treat bad Catholics. And *we* are right. Moreover, Catholic tradition follows St. Paul. Today's practice is the aberration. Dad

ᘓ

December 12, 1977
MEMO TO: All Concerned
FROM: Neil McCaffrey

I am trying to work out some ideas about charity. If you have any comments on what follows, whether agreeing or disagreeing, I'd be grateful for them.

False charity, it seems to me, is pandemic, and encouraged in the highest places. But if current excesses are travesties of travesties, the travesties were always there. Which is why modern Catholics, even the orthodox fragment, are helpless when confronted with this solvent of all standards.

Our Lord warns us to beware of false prophets; St. Paul bids us reject even an angel who departs from traditional teaching; Peter is at least party to, and clearly endorses, the striking dead of two followers who had lied to him; and the Apostle of Love instructs us to ostracize heretics, and himself refuses even to go to a public bath frequented by one. It is more than clear, therefore, that the virtue of charity is not only compatible with but actually requires sternness, punishment, many kinds of *judging*. (The ultimate judgment can of course only be rendered by God, and we sin if we pretend to such a power. But we must make a host of *ad hoc* and provisional judgments every day: as parents, as priests, as people in any kind of authority. We must judge [in order] to avoid bad companions, to keep from being cheated, to advise, etc. Indeed, to live is to judge, and to pretend not to judge is to deny our very nature. Judging is intrinsic to the act of thinking itself.)

The practical consequence of fake charity (if we need an example, when the very stones cry out) was seen a year or so ago, when the faculty and parents of a midwestern "Catholic" high school named after JFK were no longer able to ignore stories of Jack's whoring. They met and, what do you know, they voted to keep the great name. "We can't judge," they intoned virtuously.

This example may seem grotesque, but it is in fact the all but universal response of pseudo-Christians and, shockingly often, of serious Christians.

Von Hildebrand has pointed out that sin, any sin, is *first* an offense against God, which only He can forgive. Yet most spiritual writers of the better sort urge on us instant forgiveness, quite overlooking a serious problem. For a sin to be forgiven, God requires repentance (necessarily. Repentance is no mere grace note. God *cannot* forgive without it). The spiritual writers ask no such requirement. Nothing short of automatic forgiveness is what they demand of us.

What they are really saying, if they only realized it, is that their version of charity *improves* on God's!

It follows, of course, that the sort of charity preached to us *over the centuries* is often counterfeit: or so I read the logic of the case. Am I missing something?

On the other hand, I squirm when I find myself on the wrong side of centuries of spiritual writers. Could most of them have erred on this central point? And yet, from what we know of Scripture, what reasons can you offer to show that they have *not* gone wrong?

ob

April 10, 1980

Dear Murray and Joey [Rothbard]:
In spite of all our tribulations, a wonderful evening. And a very nice way to celebrate thirty years.

On the question of election and free will, I think my understanding of it is a shade less fuzzy than it sounded last night. The infinite intelligence of God sees all the possible choices we might make. His Providence *elects* to give us this series of circumstances rather than that series of circumstances or the other series of circumstances. He also foresees the choices we will make. Perhaps under this series of circumstances we will choose the good path, while under another series we might choose the bad path. Hence, election. But our *decisive* choices will always be, *must* always be free. Otherwise, we could not in justice be held accountable for our salvation, nor could we make a voluntary offering of our obedience to God.

Is election therefore simply a matter of words? No. We accept it as real, first on the authority of Christ, later on that of Paul and the great Fathers like Augustine. And our reason is not offended. *This* set of circumstances will incline a person to make the right choices and therefore to earn salvation. Other circumstances might lead him to make the wrong choices. So everyone who is saved owes his salvation in part to the general conditions God has given him for his life; but also to the particular helps God gives him all through the struggle (which helps, I believe, always go well beyond the bare minimum necessary).

So I think the formula is true, even if obscure: no salvation without grace and election, and no salvation without free will.

We must pursue this further. But the only time and place that will enable us to do full justice to the question is some Tuesday soon at the Red Blazer Too. We'll call you.

Best,
Neil

☙

Jan. 1984

Dear Neil:
Thanks a lot for the clippings you've been sending me. Also, I appreciated your notes on the Vineyard Vintage Jazz Band. Sounds like a lot of fun. As for *Critique*, I have never seen a copy; for some obscure reason, it has never made its way to the Stanford or Columbia libraries, nor to any of the worthy but leftish book and magazine stores that I frequent. Why, for example, do all these stores carry every conceivable variety of Trotskyite and Maoist publication, but not *Spotlight*, which now bills itself as "right-wing populist"? Somehow, despite its reasonable price, I can't seem to bring myself to subscribe to *Critique*—or to *Spotlight,* for that matter. There used to be a similar publication called *Conspiracy Digest,* which billed itself, like *Critique,* as open to any conspiracy theory whatever. *Conspiracy Digest* was edited by young Peter McAlpine, who was a rather shaky ally in the fight at the 1975 LP convention to convert the LP from a pro-war to an isolationist position, shaky, because, before the convention was over, McAlpine had become convinced by the LaRoughian analysis that I was a conscious, dedicated agent of either the Rockefeller or the Zionist world conspiracies—time has clouded which one (or does it make any difference?).

Neil, did you ever get to see the 1981 Canadian documentary film on Bix [Beiderbecke], produced, written, and directed by Brigitte Berman? I saw it with Joey in San Francisco the other night and found it a wonderful emotional and esthetic experience. Before leaving for California, I had played and loved the complete Bixology that Joey had gotten me for my birthday. What a great musician and great man! My old friend, Christopher Weber, the investment writer, who is a leading opera buff, after I told him about Bix and played him some of my tapes, exclaimed: "Bix is like Mozart—the simplicity, the clarity, the flow." I've now started to read the great Sudhalter book.

One moving moment in the film came when someone reported (there are a lot of interviews with colleagues of Bix) that when Bix came down once to play with Louis Armstrong, Louis handed Bix his cornet, Bix put in his mouthpiece, and played "Coquette", after which Louie had tears in his eyes. As Louis concluded afterward, "Ain't nobody played like him yet!"

Have you ever heard of the British poet and critic, Philip Larkin? He sounds great, from a review of his new *Required Writing* book in *Newsweek* (June 25). In poetry, "he regards directness rather than ambiguity as a virtue, believes in the emotion-enhancing efficacy of rhyme and meter and has a positive loathing for poems that require academic interpretation." In jazz, he states that "Charlie Parker wrecked jazz," by stressing the chromatic scale, and that "the chromatic scale is what you use to give the effect of drinking a quinine martini and having an enema simultaneously." Larkin's three pet hates of 20th century modernism are Parker, Picasso, and Pound. The guy sounds terrific! (He also likes James Bond, and Cole Porter.)

As you know, one of my great esthetic loves is Bavarian baroque (or rococo) churches of the 18th century. They were a magnificent, beautiful, integrated expression of the religious faith of the Bavarian peasantry. It now turns out that the reason for the abrupt decline of these magnificent churches (all built in the short span between 1720 and 1770) is that at the latter date, the Elector of Bavaria had become influenced by the deist-atheist Enlightenment, and seized the power of church renovations and architecture from the monasteries and parishes themselves and put it into the hands of a central government board. The Elector wanted to eliminate "silly ornaments" and stucco, and create churches which had the austerity which he felt was appropriate to religion. These churches were the final great fruits of the Counter-Reformation, which set out to show that esthetic beauty can be used for the glory of God.

So! I have long known that Protestants, steeped in the view that reason and sense enjoyment were hopelessly sinful, destroyed religious art wherever they could. Now it turns out that the Enlightenment in a sense moved in the same direction. Also it turns out that I can blame the decline of my favorite art on &*#)@ government! Catnip for a libertarian!

Also, as we mentioned last time I saw you, Leo Steinberg has demonstrated (in his new book on the sexuality of Christ, and in his previous work on Da Vinci's *Last Supper*) that, contrary to positivist-secularist myth, Renaissance art was steeped in ultra-Catholic theology, and was meant to exemplify it. So, that means that what I consider the finest art in world history—Renaissance-Baroque—was not only created by Catholics, but as a direct result of Catholic theology and esthetic values.

Hey—do you think it is possible to construct a general field theory of esthetics in which Catholicism will hold a central place? I don't know exactly where Bix and Cole Porter fit into this theory, but it's something to work on.

Warmly,

Murray

P.S. Have you ever heard of Alan Dale? He's a British dj who's on San Jose's 24-hour nostalgia music station, KLIV, on Wednesday nights. He plays a lot of Al Bowlly. The other night he played Jessie Matthews' "Dancing on the Ceiling". Lovely. M.

ဢ

Tom Paine Day, 1984

Dear Murray,

It must be overpowering to meet all of Bix at once. I envy you. Should we be glad he died young? I can't see him in a swing band, much less leading one. Could he have kept swing from its excesses? I doubt that any one man could have thwarted the Gresham's law of music and art. Nor did his temperament and weaknesses make him any sort of leader.

I've never caught up with that documentary nor has cable TV. I did make a few passes on getting people to use the Sudhalter book as the basis for a play or, better, a movie. Quixotic of me, needless to say. Yet his life has all the ingredients: the comet of genius flashing across the sky, fated to expire because of one flaw that kills.

I was delighted at Larkin's candor. I reviewed his book, *All What Jazz?*, for NR, favorably of course [attached]. I have to agree with him and you about Charlie Parker, though I confess I'm not immune to *his* genius. But on balance it was I'm afraid an evil genius, the more evil I suppose because it *was* genius. So much firepower, turned loose to destroy. We see that more clearly now, as we view the wreckage. But it's easier to despise his acolytes, like that mountebank Miles Davis. Whereas Bix left us nothing but glorious creations and shining influence.

That's an acute accusation of yours, how Protestant theology chills esthetic expression. The wonder is that it didn't kill the arts outright. (Bach was after all a good Protestant.) The raw, radical Protestant belief, articulated and stressed by Luther and refined by Calvin, is the absolute depravity of man. What follows directly is a contempt for man's works. Yet the grand Protestant error *does* grow (lopsidedly) out of the Christian tradition of tension between the claims and attractions of this world and the next. Augustine catches and grapples with the dilemma, doing justice to both horns and never quite resolving the question neatly. St. Thomas writes about it somewhere, followed by Maritain in *Art and Scholasticism*, which I blush to confess I haven't read and never will. The best thing I've seen on it is in Newman, who doesn't address the question directly but still disposes of it. In the sections on literature in *The Idea of a University*, his observations can be applied to all the arts. From which I draw my own esthetic: a) art is of *man*, and may or may not serve God; b) but it can indirectly without being in the least "religious" because an attribute of God is beauty (so there is plenty of room for Bix and Cole Porter).

This is, as you sense, the Catholic esthetic, and of course derives from a theology that sees man as a) corrupted by original sin and by his own sins but b) corrupted *from* what was once good and is by original design good, and c) redeemable by grace—*only* by grace, as the Protestants correctly say, but with the *necessary* cooperation of man with God's grace (free will)—which is where Catholics and Protestants part, leaving an abyss no ecumenist can ever bridge. (Isn't it preposterous, by the way, to herald the Reformation as the beginning of political or indeed *any* freedom, with that theological pedigree? The large role of Protestants in the history of freedom was played *in spite of* their theology—really in reaction against it.)

But don't misunderstand me. Protestants soon found the inhuman theology of their founders too hard to live with, so they mostly ignored it, England being the classic example. It didn't turn out the way Cranmer planned. Then, for the Protestants, the real trouble began. Luther and Calvin were impossible, Rome unthinkable, so we got the YMCA and creeping unbelief. Then came secularism, night following twilight. Now, in the darkness, Protestants are turning back to *their* roots (e.g., the Moral Majority)—and I am far from scorning them. Twilight is better than [line missing]. I could never nourish myself on their thin gruel, but when famine stalks the land, gruel will look like a feast. Victorian America may not be Renaissance Baroque, but it beats Sodom.

The only Alan Dale I know is that corn ball Fifties singer.

We saw Vince and the band at their new refuge, Buster Long's on East Tremont Avenue in the Bronx (*way* east; seems safe). Acoustics great, dance floor huge, food okay, prices not bad. But I miss the Blazer ambience.

Please give us plenty of advance warning of your return to Babylon. We must have another music night. But this time you don't have to bring dollar bills. There will, however, be prizes for those who earn them. All stolen property, of course.

Love to Joey.

Best,
Neil

ALL WHAT JAZZ by Philip Larkin (St. Martin's. $6.95). When British poet Philip Larkin was asked to do a jazz column for the Daily Telegraph in 1961, he had one worry: his taste for trad and mainstream jazz and his dislike of the modernists ("With Miles Davis and John Coltrane a new inhumanity emerged") might cost him a nice assignment. So, like a Waugh anti-hero, he set out to play along, editing his copy to replace "insolent" with "challenging," "excruciating" with "adventurous." Yet his articles, reprinted here, treat the modernists tartly, the classicists warmly, and everyone stylishly. His book can thus serve as a reliable primer while still offering the buff insights enough to keep him from dozing. What sets Larkin apart in the dreary literature of jazz is his iconoclasm. E.g.: "the term 'modern,' when applied to art, has a more than chronological meaning: it denotes a quality of irresponsibility peculiar to this century, known sometimes as modernism, and once I had classified modern jazz under this heading I knew where I was." And: "From using music to entertain the white man, the Negro had moved to hating him with it." To understand what the lumpen-jazzmen and their scribes are doing to jazz, this breakthrough book is essential reading.
— *N. McCaffrey*

ଓଃ

10/1/84

Dear Murray,
Aren't you taking liberties with Thomas Aquinas? Like many of his fellows, he followed Aristotle in believing that ensoulment takes

place on the 40th day for males, the 80th or 90th for females. He therefore held that abortion wasn't *murder* before ensoulment—which doesn't mean he endorsed it, even though his view of when human life began was inaccurate.

I assume you know that the opinions of theologians—even of St. Thomas—don't constitute Catholic doctrine, but simply contribute to it, by explication or inference. And surely you know that the opinions of modernists who still lay claim to the name of Catholic, shouldn't be taken seriously. They remain nominally Catholic only because the modern papacy shirks its plain duty.

As for pluralism, you can't be serious. St. Thomas opposed the theocratic view of temporal society, but of course presupposed a Catholic society. By the way, what you *meant* to say was "the imposition of *any* religious views on secular [is there any other kind?] politics. The trouble with you utopians is that you want it both ways. You want democracy, but only your kind.

The band is now at Buster Long's in the Bronx on Wednesdays (easy drive) and the Carlyle on Sundays and Mondays (hopelessly expensive). When will you be back for a visit?

Are you aware that some old-time musicians have found refuge in Vegas? Charlie Teagarden was (is?) an officer in the musician's union. Will Yaner, lead alto and clarinet with Isham Jones and then lead alto with Jimmy Dorsey, is another—among many. Why don't you drop in at the union hall and get a copy of the address list? Then mail it to me and I'll annotate it for you.

Love to Joey.
Best,
Neil

ↂ

April 1, 1986

Dear Dan [Rosenthal]:

[…] Absent a higher sanction in the form of a lively belief in God and eternal punishment and eternal rewards, I've never been able to understand why *everyone* doesn't go in for sex, drugs, crime, or whatever strikes his fancy. To be sure, in the twilight of belief when social sanctions still count for something, as in Victorian England and in pre-modern America, some form of public and even private morality can prevail for a generation or three. But when even the social sanctions crumble, as now, what incentive is left? "Quarry the granite rock with razors or moor the vessel with a thread of silk; then may you hope with such keen and delicate instruments as human knowledge and human reason to contend against those giants, the passion and the pride of man."—John Henry Newman.

೭३

April 11, 1986

Dear Dan:

[...] I think you misread my observation. I simply said that *I* don't see how anyone can avoid the shoals without a lively conviction of a divine judge and a divine law. In other words, both are necessary for *me*. I also said that society can live off moral capital for a few generations. But you know what happens to capital when heirs are careless with it. The Newman quote is of course not meant to describe everybody. It is a general observation, richly borne out by history and experience.

I too find surprisingly little correlation between creed and conduct. In my younger years I discerned a higher moral standard among Catholics. I'm afraid that has melted away at roughly the same pace that the Church has. At the same time, some people are better than their creed. Some of my best friends are agnostics. And I've been screwed by Protestants, Catholics and Jews; and, far worse, by close friends. That was the unkindest cut of all. And yet, I have no right to be surprised even at that. After all, think of the tens of millions of husbands and wives who have done terrible things to each other.

Best,
Neil

೭३

August 25, 1989

The Freeman
The Foundation for Economic Education
Irvington-on-Hudson, New York 10533

Editors:
Jeffrey A. Tucker does well to correct a simplistic reading of the history of liberty (August 1989). Permit me one carp in an otherwise valuable letter, where Mr. Tucker identifies "the Renaissance [as] a Catholic Counter-Reformation." Not only were they not coterminous, the Renaissance having emerged a couple of centuries before the Counter-Reformation; they were not the same. The Renaissance was both a revival of classical studies and an explosion of creativity

in the arts the like of which the world had never seen before and has never seen since. The Counter-Reformation was the reform movement within the Catholic Church.

What surprises me about Mr. Tucker's important letter, however, is that Nick Elliott—a *Freeman* contributor, no less—brushes aside the authority of the great historian of liberty, Lord Acton. On Mr. Elliott's Good Guys vs. Bad Guys reading of history, the Levelers somehow become the forerunners of the classical liberals. I can hear Macaulay and Acton and Mill moaning from the world beyond, "What have we wrought?" The real heirs of the Levelers are Abbie Hoffman and his Yippies.

Mr. Elliott goes on to tell us that "The Glorious Revolution of 1688 enshrined religious toleration in law." Well, up to a point. Nonconformists could practice their faith in peace but had to subscribe to the 39 (not 37, as in Mr. Elliott's letter) Articles to serve in Parliament or enter Oxford (and Cambridge too, is my guess, though I don't know that for a fact). Roman Catholics and Jews were not so lucky. They had to wait another 144 years for comparable relief.

Mr. Elliott's next venture into history informs us that the Reformation in England led to the rejection of the divine right of kings, by which kings had previously justified their excesses. This would come as a surprise to James I. This eminent Protestant monarch, who assumed the throne 86 years after Luther posted his theses, produced the classic defense of the divine right of kings. It led to controversy, and his leading opponent was Robert Bellarmine, Jesuit, cardinal and later canonized saint.

Mr. Elliott is now warming to his peroration: "The immediate response of the Catholic Church to the Reformation was the inquisition and the index, religious purification by burning, and a clampdown on dangerous books." Of course—but why does Mr. Elliott quit there? Alas for his Villain Theory, there were Catholic martyrs to match the Protestant martyrs, and Protestant censorship to ban those dangerous Catholic books. It was the mode of the time, and to condemn retroactively what people on both sides then saw as a religious duty is historical provincialism. Rare indeed were the contemporary voices that spoke out for toleration. Erasmus and Thomas More come to mind: ironically, one a Catholic maverick, the other a Catholic martyr.

In truth, Mr. Elliott subjects the Reformers to the ultimate indignity: he refuses to take them seriously. Not that Mr. Tucker didn't warn him when he noted in his letter that Luther and Calvin had no use for the Renaissance. Right or wrong, there they stand. Mr. Elliott notwithstanding, if the Lord had vouchsafed to Luther and Calvin

and Zwingli and Cranmer a vision of the Enlightenment—even its prettier side—all of those divines would have died of apoplexy.
Neil McCaffrey

ℭ

Neil McCaffrey
President, Conservative Book Club
[Undated]
Recommended Catholic Books

This is not meant to be a list of the best Catholic books (a task beyond my competence), nor is it even confined to books by Catholics. It is simply a list of many of my own favorites, books that I think will be instructive and heartening to Catholics in these grey days.

JOHN HENRY NEWMAN

The most original religious thinker and the finest preacher in the English-speaking Catholic world. Of some forty volumes of Newman's works and another thirty hefty volumes of letters and diaries, these stand out:

Parochial and Plain Sermons. These eight volumes, written in Newman's Anglican days, were reissued decades after his conversion and required only a few footnoted corrections to flag beliefs he no longer held. Extraordinary for their insight into our weaknesses and their prescriptions for how we might improve—the whole flavored by an astonishing ability to cite the apt Scriptural text at every step. Michael Davies has collected in *Newman Against the Liberals* twenty-five of these that are particularly good for Catholics today.

An Essay on the Development of Christian Doctrine. Liberals claim this seminal work as their justification for dismantling Catholic doctrine. Either they haven't read it, or they're playing loose with the truth. Newman was fiercely orthodox, and showed why orthodoxy requires that we distinguish defined doctrine from its corollaries and from pious beliefs. Most important today, he gives the seven norms for distinguishing true and false developments.

The Idea of a University. Why these interminable conferences on the meaning of education? This is the definitive book on education, and on Catholic education.

And Rightly So

Apologia Pro Vita Sua. Not to be read as a complete autobiography (it isn't detailed enough, and in any case, Newman lived another twenty-five years), this is rather an extraordinary revelation of a subtle, mind and a sensitive soul.

The Pillar of the Cloud/The Light in Winter. Meriol Trevor's two-volume life of Newman, though sometimes argumentative, is much the liveliest, best researched, most detailed biography.

A Newman Treasury. An anthology of Newman's writing by category, along with the essential biographical background. The best Newman sampler for those who want to see whether they'd like to read more of Newman.

EVELYN WAUGH

Brideshead Revisited. My choice for the richest Catholic novel ever written, this powerfully recalls a Catholic culture now in ashes. The characters are as unforgettable as those of Dickens—and more deeply drawn by far.

Helena. A novel about St. Helena and the finding of the True Cross, under Waugh's hand it becomes a tour de force mingling modernity and the Age of Constantine. Waugh's portrayal of the Arians foreshadows the behavior of their heirs in the post-conciliar Church—uncannily, because he wrote the book in 1950 and never dreamt what was in the offing.

Sword of Honor. Waugh's trilogy about World War II is based, loosely of course, on his own experiences and is by common consent the finest novel to come out of the conflict. And certainly the most satisfying, because the themes are Catholic, conservative and anti-Communist.

Ronald Knox. Waugh's life of his good friend, the stylish writer and eminent preacher of the pre-conciliar English Church, is not only a fascinating biography but also, in retrospect, the evocation of a golden period in the history of the Faith.

RONALD KNOX

Enthusiasm. Knox's masterpiece, a learned, sophisticated study of what in 1950 seemed a curious byway of Christianity, the religious emotionalism and quackery that flares up periodically over the centuries, always claiming the inspiration of the Holy Spirit—and which today in the charismatic movement is back to provide some future Knox with a new chapter.

Let Dons Delight. Another tour de force, and one only Knox could have written: conversations in an Oxford common room, every fifty years from 1588 to 1938. They capture the religious and political currents of each period—in the language and style of each. A dazzling performance.

The Mass in Slow Motion. Msgr. Knox was Newman's heir as the great British Catholic preacher. Always the choice for great occasions at Westminster Cathedral, he was equally at home, as here, preaching before teenage girls. These are graceful, enlightening talks on each part of the Mass. (The Old Mass, needless to say. Such sermons on the New Mass would be inconceivable.)

Memories of the Future: Being the Memoirs of the Years 1915-1972 Written in the Year of Grace 1988 by Opal, Lady Porstock. Yet another tour de force, actually written in 1922, as Knox becomes an upper-middle-class English lady selecting from her diaries toward the end of our century. Delicious spoof, and sometimes remarkably prescient about social and moral trends.

MISCELLANEOUS

Theology and Sanity. Frank Sheed's best. The first third is probably the clearest exposition of the Blessed Trinity and the nature of God ever written.

The Moulding of Communists. Frank S. Meyer. Probably the best analysis of how and why they get that way. Nobody who must deal with them, from popes and presidents on down, should dream of undertaking the chore without having mastered this book. Frank *knew.* He was a Communist in the 30s and early 40s, in charge of training recruits. (Later he became literary editor and keeper of the tablets at *National Review* during its best years, and friend to a thousand conservatives of every shade. He was received into the Church on his deathbed in 1972.)

The Screwtape Letters. C. S. Lewis' most popular, and deservedly so. No book offers keener insights into our frailties, and how the tempters prey on them.

The Teaching of the Catholic Church. Edited and reassembled in 1948 by Canon George Smith from the earlier, prestigious "Treasury of the Faith" series, this two-volume compendium by some dozen solid British Catholic writers like Fathers D'Arcy and Martindale is weighty, reliable and comprehensible.

The Church in Council. Philip Hughes. A popular survey of all the councils, written on the eve of Vatican II by the great British Catholic historian. Useful for those tempted to think that all the pronouncements of all the councils are the work of the Holy Ghost.

By What Authority?/The King's Achievement/The Queen's Tragedy/Oddsfish/Come Rack, Come Rope. These, some of the better and better-known historical novels of Robert Hugh Benson, are wonderful stories that give a vivid picture of English Catholics in the centuries of persecution.

The Man on a Donkey. H. F. M. Prescott's superb novel of English Catholics in the reign of Henry VIII.

Kristin Lavransdatter. Sigrid Undset. Powerful, earthy three-volume Catholic novel of medieval Norway that won its convert author the Nobel Prize.

Suicide of the West. James Burnham. Not a religious book, this is incomparably the best analysis of the liberal mind—in politics, religion, whatever. Essential reading for a world blighted by liberalism.

Catholicism in England. David Mathew. Stylish, sophisticated, historical survey by a remarkable man—*and* an archbishop. Will the English-speaking Church ever produce men like him again?

Liberty or Equality/Leftism. Erik von Kuehnelt-Leddihn. Challenging and original ideas (thousands of them) by the provocative Austrian Catholic conservative. He ranges across theology, politics, history, economics, sociology, just about everything, with a vision permeated by the Faith and illuminated by travel and wide-ranging reading.

Mitre and Crook. Bryan Houghton. An imaginative, boldly original novel about the crisis in the Church. Unlike so many books on this theme, Fr. Houghton's is a work of style and verve, more than a touch of wit, and deep feeling.

4

Writers, Publishers, and Friends

3/19/58

Dear Garry [Wills],
I suppose this would be more edifying if I headed it "Feast of St.
Joseph". That is only slightly less ghastly than that liturgical statio-
nery you have no doubt been subjected to. I suppose it's a banal
thought, but it occurred to me today that St. Joseph was quite a
man: how would you like to be married to the most wonderful girl
in the world, a girl who loves you—and you can never go near her:
a prodigy of grace, of course; but grace works through nature.

Thus, my Thought for the Week. Make sure you save this letter.

It's tedious but true to say I've been too busy to write. Each
Sunday as I escape from the little monsters by retreating into my
room under the pretext of working, your letter goes on the pile of
things to do. But then the fiends arrange some domestic crisis, and
you (and others) get put off another week. Nor has there been time
in the office, until today.

And thereby hangs my tail (damn, I knew it would come out
spelled that way). We are launching a big, vulgar "Know-Your-Bible
Program" later this year, and I'm editing the Catholic half. It consists
of 64-page booklets which are issued monthly and sold by mail. We
plan to do 60 on key themes of the Old and New Testaments. They
are geared for 12-year-olds—and hence enormously popular among
adults. At any rate, our other similar programs are. You see them
all the time in the Sunday supplements: the Nature Program, the
Around-the-World Program and the Know-Your-America Program.
I'll send you samples.

We have already assigned the first year's booklets, and I thought
it best to concentrate on Catholic authors, of proved popularity, for
a number of selfish reasons—principally that I don't want to crash
first time I solo. Later, this won't be necessary, so would you like to
take a crack at one? The money is interesting: $750 for an 8,500-
word manuscript. Don't worry because you've no degree from the
Biblical Institute. We want popular *writers*. Can you write on the
teen-age level? All the emphasis is on narrative. I know you'd be
incapable of writing without insight, and hell, we're broadminded,
we tolerate *ideas*, just as long as you weave them into the kind of
narrative that drags the morons into the next paragraph.

I do think that this kind of thing can be done interestingly and
be intellectually presentable, on its own level. If you're at all interested, you'll surely have some questions. Fire away.

Sorry to learn that you sent your Knox piece to *The Epistle*. Seems
a pity to bury it. Never fear about sending too much to *Modern Age*:

253

you can't. Don't you find it blighted with academic dullness and third-rate prose? Kirk should read *National Review*! Anyway, why don't you send the Knox to *The Month* or *Dublin Review*? The latter has just reverted to the old quarterly schedule, and my guess is that they'd be most receptive.

Forgive me for being forward, but please quit burying your light.

We found your Christmas card the most distinctive we've ever received. Joan immediately preempted it for her missal.

I must compliment you as warmly as I can for your recent contributions, especially the Christmas editorial, the UN piece (best I ever read on the subject) and the one on the *Partisan Review*.

This threatens to degenerate into a mash note.

"Mrs. McCaffrey" says to say hello, and for heaven's sake to stop that nonsense and call her Joan.

The Chesterbelloc peddler is A. C. Prosser, 3118 N. Keating Ave., Chicago 41. He also carries other Catholic authors; mention if you want that list. You might also try Aquin Bookshop, Box 454, Cranford, N. J.

If you don't come to dinner next time you're in town (when?), we'll spread compromising stories about you.
Best,
Neil

ଓ

August 15, 1958

Dear Garry,
A good time—a very good time—was had by all. Glad you could come.

For the booklet, "Famous Men of the Old Testament", we thought of including Isaias, Jonas, Josias, and Amos. Can you think of two or three others? Incidentally, no Deutero-Isaias!
Best,
Neil

P.S. I just spoke to Bill and he told me that you were going to help with the copy. This is no work for a nice young man of hitherto blameless life, but since you have chosen the path to perdition, let me help smooth your way. Bill suggested that I go over your first effort. I made the point that there are certain tried-and-true principles to be observed in this nefarious business, and why didn't I initiate you into these dark secrets? He agreed, so when can I begin to soil you?

Marilyn [Rubino, his secretary] will be gone for the next two weeks, so I am now incommunicado about *anything* except the Bible Program. If you want to say anything about *that* magazine, please write to 452 Fourth Avenue, Pelham.

In all conscience, I must advise you: make a closed retreat before you undertake this huckstering!

ॐ

November 10, 1958

Dear Garry:
This hurts me more than it hurts you. I worked on the first five pages of your manuscript [for the Doubleday *Know Your Bible Series*] for half of yesterday afternoon, then realized that it would take about a week's work in the office to get it into shape—if the balance of it is like the first five pages: I haven't read the former.

I am returning the manuscript so that you can see what I've done on the first five pages, especially on page five. Five in its present shape is by no means the best of all possible versions, but merely a patch job. Yet it will give you an idea, and I hope you will take it from there.

A pattern is beginning to emerge. What caused most of our trouble on Elias as on Jonas is, I think, your failure to think this out and sweat enough. This hack writing is in its own craven way a discipline. You can take nothing for granted in the reader. Everything must be spelled out one-two-three. You have to lead him by the nose in order to evoke any desired reaction. But I do not suggest that your writing is too sophisticated or too subtle; I think it is just plain careless.

Part of thinking and sweating these manuscripts out, a very important part, should be a more adroit handling of narrative. You will go along with a man's thoughts or with an incident for a paragraph or two, being careful to give due attention to the details that distinguish a living from a dead narrative. Then suddenly you'll transport Jonas to the docks in a clause. The reader is bewildered and unsatisfied: because the writer has not handled the material professionally.

You also change the narrative's point of view disconcertingly as you go along. The way the initiative is shared by the captain and the crew acting collectively is wholly unconvincing, both literally and nautically. This is what I mean by "thinking it out".

I could not write to anyone but a dear friend so bluntly; and I would not write in such terms to anyone who was not capable of doing better.

Friday's great debate was something less. Cogley spent half of his time reviewing the bygone meanings of 'liberal' and 'conservative'. The balance was devoted to a careful delineation of the conservative stereotype, after which he boldly did battle against this man of straw. He rounded it all off with a number of unexceptionable Catholic platitudes, most of which he contradicted when he attempted to apply them concretely. Altogether, he sounded like a baptized Kreuttner cartoon.

Bill declined to wrap himself in the Encyclicals, so that they were really debating about two different issues. In its own right, Bill's talk was naturally very good, though he appeared tired. He did rebut Cogley brilliantly, pointing to their agreement on essentials and disagreement on nonessentials, and suggesting that people like Cogley spend less time making common cause with Liberal secularists on secondary matters, but rather devote themselves to converting them on first principles. "If he does that, I predict that Mr. Cogley will be busy enough," Bill concluded.

Later, Bill, Faith and Jim, Thomas Molnar and his date and Joan and I went to Condon's. Enjoyable, but too noisy to talk satisfactorily; and the quality of Dixieland has declined at the joint.

It is six days since Black Tuesday, and I am only now beginning to emerge from a state of shock.

Don't hurry with the manuscript. And don't feel that you have to rewrite the whole thing. I haven't read the balance of it; maybe most of it is good as is. I was just overwhelmed by page five.

Best,
Neil

P.S. The welcome mat is still out, and Joan adds that you and Natalie should make it for dinner. She can now swing it.

P.P.S. The crude masculine handwriting on your manuscript is mine, the dainty feminine script is Marilyn's. Marilyn read it all the way, so any comments beyond the top of page six are hers.

ᘓ

April 24, 1959
Dear Mrs. [Benjamin] Heath [Aloise Buckley]:
I have not had the pleasure of meeting you, but I am a friend of Bill's, the magazine's, and your contributions to it. I recently received a bunch of juvenile books that were particularly egregious for their "social significance". They are both published by the Beacon Press (one under an allied imprint). Beacon, as you may know, is the

publisher of such classics as Blanshard and Rorty.

At any rate, these books, and the trend they represent in juvenile literature, cry out to be pulverized; and so I thought of you. I hope I am not being brash to send them to you. If the idea does not appeal, please just consign these masterpieces to the nearest wastebasket.

And *please*, would you keep this letter entirely confidential? Bill will explain.

Sincerely,
Neil McCaffrey

ଓ

April 18, 1960

Dear Garry,

Thanks for your comments on Father Anselm's. I tossed a couple back to him. Thanks also for the recommendations on the Psalms to quote.

Yes, we are still planning a booklet on the wisdom of the Bible. You may have some overlapping between this and the Solomon one. I suggest, therefore, that you get as much of Solomon's life as you can into the booklet on him.

We don't include advertisements in our booklets because a) everyone who gets the booklets already belongs to the Program, and b) yes, we flee from the least hints of commercialism here on the Avenue. But enclosed are a few samples of our advertising—in case someone *insists* upon joining.

I enjoyed W.F.B. [father of Bill Buckley] immensely. The big section on his Mexican adventures is a revealing microcosm of Liberal foreign policy— and a definitive portrait of one of our more repulsive presidents.

I read the Lewis and found it excellent—so good that, with your permission, I plan to circulate it among several friends who would like it. The chapter on "Lilies that Fester" is the best, don't you think? I think you and he are both awry (you for implicitly agreeing with him) on the absorption of humanity into the Godhead. This is not what Sister taught me about the Hypostatic Union. Among other things, it is a metaphysical impossibility.

There are a few things in the current *Critic* that might interest you, including the "Letter From England," which had some observations on the Waugh book that I found objectionable.

Best to Natalie and Smilin' Jack.

Sincerely,
Neil

೪

April 5, 1961

National Review
150 E 35 St
New York 16

Editor:
Dr. Prezzollini's defense of Machiavelli stands out as a paean to posi-
tivism, the one really scandalous lapse in *National Review's* brilliant
history. Out of the depths of my bewilderment I ask: *how* could you
bring yourselves to print an article that so brazenly flouts the moral
consensus of the West; an article, moreover, whose intellectual level
never rises above that of an undergraduate magazine? One example
can serve as a paradigm of the author's slovenly mental habits: "The
concept of evil implicit in human nature is not extraneous to *early*
Christian thought." (Italics mine.) Does Dr. Prezzollini think this
concept died with Gregory the Great?

Not without reason has Machiavelli been the *Bedside Esquire* of
tyrants; nor should anyone be surprised that immoral principles are
welcomed on the Columbia campus, and intellectual imprecision
honored. But to find these in America's most distinguished magazine—heralded with extravagant editorial fanfare, at that—is both a
shock and a disgrace.
Neil McCaffrey

೪

April 17, 1961

Dear Bill:
You've pulled it out. The Welch article was exquisitely balanced,
masterfully executed—flawless, really. How rare to find a piece, of
any sort, that challenges hyperbole. Name your favorite adjectives and
they're yours.

Interesting to find it cheek by jowl with Waugh, who must, I think,
be regarded as one of the real giants of English prose, in this or any
period. It is no offense to observe that Waugh's style has achieved
dimensions that yours has not yet reached, and perhaps never will.
And yet, piquantly, in this issue at least, the master meets his master.
Best,
Neil

CB

April. 17, 1961

Dear Garry:

Warmest congratulations on the fellowship [to the Hellenic Institute at Dumbarton Oaks, Washington, D.C.]. I hope—though I continue to doubt—that it will be the better thing for all of you. I doubt it with much greater conviction after having read your editorials, which are in a class by themselves. I think the discipline of getting down to cases and writing for the Broad Street merchants has done wonders for your style. And Lord, with what obscene ease you adapt to this medium! As you know, I am the only one who feels that your place is in Richmond; but I can report, triumphantly, that Joan has weakened considerably after reading your editorials. I intend to pass them on to Bill and Frank, and order them under the gravest penalties to see that you get them back eventually.

I found the [Evelyn] Waugh review not as deadly as I had been led to expect. Unfavorable, yes, but in an offhand way he does give you some breaks. The real trouble with his criticisms is not that they are outrageous, but that they are not overbalanced by the plaudits you deserve. The fact that I find the book plodding is no fault of yours, but of the subject. Well, largely: I did find Waugh's lecture on Chesterton dazzling. But so far (I haven't had time to read much of it), you have done a conscientious, sensitive, perceptive and readable job. Apply the same kind of treatment to an author who interests me and I'll be singing hosannas.

Bill was superb on Birch, don't you think? And cowardly on Machiavelli, the way he buried Frank's letter and ignored mine and Carol Robinson's.

Love to Natalie and John.

Best,
Neil

CB

July 13, 1961

Dear Bill,

On the eve of the annual editorial meeting, may a voice cry out from the wilderness?

My recommendation is more general than specific, and can be summarized in six words: editorial enterprise, editorial enterprise, editorial enterprise. It would be tragic, and a cruel irony, if the journal that provided the dynamism for the conservative revival should succumb to tired blood. We should be far more alert to domestic issues; since Brent's departure, I get the feeling that our coverage in this area would disappear if the *Times* went out of business.

And we should, occasionally, be outrageous. Perhaps the time has come to replace Willi Schlamm.

And finally we come to that sensitive area, the articles section. I always fear it will become a depressed area. I know full well that you can't give it the time it needs; nor, perhaps, does it offer you the same challenge as the editorials. Do you suppose you could find an assistant whom you had confidence in, and who could make the planning and assignment of colorful articles his major chore— subject to your approval, of course?

In sum, the movement is on the rise. NR must always lead it, or lesser breeds will snatch the banner.

Best,
Neil

P.S. In case you ever need a local attorney, I attach Martin Armstrong's card. He is the son-in-law of Fulton Oursler, the Stamford Republican mayoralty candidate, and is a good friend of the magazine and of your brother-in-law, with whom he serves in the Connecticut legislature.

CR

September 11, 1962

Dear Bill:

Enclosed are copies of Garry's latest editorials [in the *Richmond News Leader*]. He is still free-lancing for Jack [James Jackson Kilpatrick, editor]. Note especially the three-part series on Liberals and Conservatives: a seminal piece, and brilliantly written.

A couple of years ago Garry would not have been my leading candidate for the best editorial writer in the country, but time and experience work wonders. Why don't you use him for the front of the book? Why should all this talent be lavished on a few counties in Virginia?

He can do a piece in no time; I'm sure if you called him with an assignment or two on Monday you would have a copy on Wednesday.

Gold is where you find it—sometimes in the backyard, or the back of the book.

Best,
Neil

CR

June 17, 1964

Dear Garry:
Be glad for attacks from any quarter. They sell books.

I'm not sure I understand what Tom Molnar believes either. It changes often. I don't think he has a consistent philosophy. I would describe him as an eclectic and somewhat volatile conservative.

You haven't captured the spirit of the new liturgy. The trick is to say Amen with your tongue out.

The *Library Journal* review is good but not worth a bellyband around the book. It is worth quoting in toto in *Library Journal* and excerpting in other ads, only.

Many thanks for the book ideas. Some I had thought of, some are impractical, some I hadn't thought of and some I'd like to talk about with you. On the idea of conservative classes, that may come later if we get into original publishing. Meanwhile, I have been thinking of including excerpts in omnibus volumes. But I know that you dislike these selections. Nonetheless, since money transcends principles think about this. Would you like to go through some of the classic conservative authors and pull out the quotable passages? In some cases you would have to write a brief-as-possible lead-in. You would get no credit line. I think the price should be somewhere between $100 and $200 for each author, depending on how much work it involved. We would run one author in each quarterly omnibus volume. It would be conservative classics without tears; though some percentage of the readers might be prompted to go more deeply into an author.

I had thought of doing this myself but if I try it will never get done. No time.

The mechanics would be simple. You could pick up one or two of the books you would need (we'd pay) and just cut out the sections you want to use. The only typing would be the lead-ins. We could work out the exact methodology.

I think you'd have fun.

I suppose the first one should be Burke, though Johnson and Newman will be better. Then I suppose we should go to Tocqueville, the Federalist Papers and probably Acton. This could be done over a couple of years. Perhaps you would only want to do some of them. What would you think about Adam Smith?
Best,
Neil

ന്ദ

August 20, 1964

Mr. Turner Catledge
Managing Editor
The New York Times
229 West 43rd Street
New York, New York

Dear Mr. Catledge:
In light of your campaign to revive objectivity, and common decency, among *Times* reporters, the enclosed letter will call your attention to a new innuendo, this one in the long-discredited *Book Review*. In all fairness, don't you think they should print my reply, in full? Yet the methods of Messrs. Markel and Brown over the years leave me less than sanguine.

I wish you well in your campaign for journalistic integrity. Certainly, it is no less than a great newspaper owes to its reputation, not to mention its readers. But I fear you have an uphill fight.
Sincerely,
Neil McCaffrey

ભ

August 20, 1964

New York Times Book Review
229 West 43rd Street
New York, New York

Editor:
Mr. Lewis Nichols seems to find something amusing, or maybe sinister, in the Conservative Book Club's unlisted phone number. Perhaps he means to suggest that we are somehow operating under cover—though he doesn't bother to explain how a book club can remain in the shadows and yet survive. In point of fact, in four months we have advertised twelve times in four national publications and have sent out just over 500,000 mailings announcing our existence and our address at 542 Main Street, New Rochelle, New York.

Our motive for having an unlisted phone number is limpid, though perhaps idiosyncratic. We have a small staff, and I regard the telephone as a great enemy of efficiency. With a quiet office we can handle our members' queries with dispatch—and not be forced to give unfair preference to local members at the expense of distant ones.

All this Mr. Nichols might have discovered; *he* has our phone number. But how many *Times* reporters will deny themselves a smear in the interests of accuracy?
Cordially,
Neil McCaffrey

ॐ

June 28, 1965

The Wanderer
128 East 10th Street
St. Paul 1, Minnesota

Editor:
I appreciate N. N.'s kind words about the Conservative Book Club, the more so because he includes them in a letter that takes us to task for offering Robert Kendall's *White Teacher in a Black School*. I want to assure N. N., and your readers, that my associates and I were conscious that the book is "raw and shocking" when we decided to offer it. Indeed, we described it in those very words.

Would an expurgated variation have been as effective? N. N. thinks it would have been. This is a matter of literary and editorial judgment. The author did not think so. The original publisher, Mr. Devin Garrity, did not think so. Nor do we.

Is the book immoral? I could not in conscience have offered it if I thought it were. Would some readers find it morally offensive, or distasteful? (They are not the same thing.) We knew some would, and we went to great pains to make this clear, even to urge those members *not* to take this selection; just as we were convinced that other members would find it a powerful and important document on problems the Liberals have cloaked in a conspiracy of silence.

Our Club operates on the principle of freedom of choice. No member is obliged to take a selection he thinks he may not like. Two distinctions must be made. First, there is the distinction between morality and taste. We sometimes tend to make them synonymous. Second, there is the question of morality itself: in the area under discussion, the morality of occasions of sin. We are all obliged to avoid them. But my occasion of sin need not be yours. For that matter, my occasion of sin at 19 is no longer one at 39. I must avoid what would lead me into sin, but I have no right to make you avoid it. If I am an alcoholic, I must avoid the first cocktail; but I have no right to forbid you to have one.

N. N. believes we took a "snide left-handed jab at all persons with true Christian moral sensibilities" when we pointed out that this book was not recommended to all. Quite the contrary. It was precisely because we respect these sensibilities, and also respect the fact that they take different forms in different Christians of equally sensitive conscience, that we emphasized that not everyone would share our high opinion of the book. My own wife is a concrete example. Despite my enthusiasm for the book, she declines to read it. No one would accuse her of being "ostrich-like" or "closing her eyes to realities", and there is no one in the world whom I respect half so much.

I would be a monster of arrogance if I looked down on those who don't share my opinion of this book. I hope N. N. will allow the same freedom to those who don't share his.

Because there were many. Some of our members shared N. N.'s view and told us so. Others praised it to the skies. So did several critics who reviewed the book warmly, including Mr. Don Raihle in *The Wanderer*, Miss Priscilla L. Buckley in *National Review*, and Miss Rosalie Cordon in *America's Future*. Clearly, this is a book on which good and intelligent people may differ honestly—and, let us hope, with "the freedom of the children of God."
Neil McCaffrey

ര

September 1, 1965

The Village Voice
Sheridan Square
New York, New York 10014

Dear Editor:
The invective directed against "something called the Conservative Book Club", by someone called William H. Honan, consoled me (*Voice*, August 19). We must be doing something right. So I hope I don't seem ungrateful if I question Mr. Honan's easy description of Robert Kendall's "White Teacher in a Black School" as "scurrilous". Mr. Honan will discover, if he ever reads the book, that it deals with the author's experiences in two Negro schools in, of all places, Los Angeles.

The recent fun and games in Watts seems less surprising to one who has read Mr. Kendall's grim story. He describes his own efforts to give them a sense of dignity and accomplishment, the bitterness of the many and the friendliness of the few. We've heard that song before; when Baldwin and King sing it is it also "scurrilous"?

The real villains of the piece, the masochists among your readers will be glad to hear, are the white liberals in the school system. Kendall wanted his students to study and learn; the progressive educators wanted them promoted, graduated, out of their hair. Kendall paid his students the compliment of expecting them to work and behave and comprehend; the liberals regarded him as quixotic, a menace.

But that is the sort of writing you run into, over here on the Right. What more can you expect of people possessed of these quaint notions of human dignity?

Neil McCaffrey
President
Conservative Book Club

ଔ

May 24, 1966

Dear Gerald [Gidwitz]:

My friendly memo of April 21 to you and Randy [Richardson] was followed by an equally friendly exchange between Randy and me. I was therefore unprepared for yours of May 20; indeed, it leaves me astonished.

I am gratified that you recognize the company's "phenomenal growth", and correspondingly surprised, therefore, that you seem to regard my compensation as excessive. It should be unnecessary to point out that this growth followed from my concept, my organization, my direction, the staff I hired and trained (in part with Marvin's help), the books I selected, the tone I set, the promotions I launched and pursue; the stature I enjoy in the conservative movement, which has opened the door to mailing lists and manuscripts nobody else could have gotten; the 90- and 100-hour weeks of tender care and follow through that show in an operation which is very likely the best-run book club around; the prudent way I managed a modest investment, repaid it, and turned it into what Randy has publicly termed "better than an oil well".

Perhaps my failure has been not to turn the moon into green cheese.

You mention as one of the objectives of the business the promotion of conservative literature outside the "hard core" market. I do not disagree with this in principle; I have made, and will continue to make, experiments to reach outside the hard core. But I became aware, months before we started the business, that Randy and presumably you (for I had not met you then) had inaccurate notions about how to do this, and unrealistic ones about whether it could

265

be done. I was therefore at pains to iterate and reiterate to him, both verbally and in writing (a thick file exists on the subject, dating from both before and after we organized), that our main thrust had to be to the avowed conservatives. I made it plain that this was the *only* condition under which I would launch the firm with you; and indeed, on several occasions when I detected resistance or lack of understanding, I urged Randy to withdraw, in which case I would seek financing elsewhere. He would then assure me that it would be done my way. I even agreed, on the initial test, to split the mailing in order to determine whether a more neutral approach would prove more successful. This test, and later events, proved me right.

I had always assumed that Randy kept you advised of my conditions, and that his subsequent agreement with my policy had your approval.

I have therefore not at all "lost sight of our objectives". They were not "explained" to me at "our first meeting" (which, you may recall, took place some weeks after the company was launched). Rather, they were explained *by* me to Randy (and, therefore, I assume, to you) time and again before we ever started; and repeated insistently, in every promotion piece we have ever issued, since our launching.

Let me assure you, once again, that we do not write off the uncommitted. We'll continue to try to reach them, especially through Arlington House—with how much success I don't know, at this writing. Even if we fail to reach them, the Club stimulates conservative writers and general publishers—and who knows how many individuals. (Only the other night the Minister from South Africa told me that the books he got from England's Old Right Book Club had inspired him to make a career in public life.)

Moreover, we expect to diversify in the area of self-help books, as I explained in an earlier letter.

I can appreciate your not wanting to reduce your holdings in the company. Since it is probably desirable to have some stock available, and since you did not reply to my question about how to distribute present and future profits, I would be happy to sell mine (and continue as President, if my job is not made too difficult). I mentioned my modest circumstances and my large family that needs educating, in the hope of some friendly understanding from men who face these problems with real wealth. I was disappointed. I repeat my question, to which I am surely entitled to an answer: what do you and Randy propose to do with the profits—since my equity is difficult to market? And with you and Randy apparently aligned against me, my equity seems of dwindling value.

I agree that the pension plan is not essential. It *is* helpful. Most solid companies have one. The company without one is at a disadvantage—especially in this highly specialized, highly competitive publishing business. Good men, here as elsewhere, are very hard to find, and are paid accordingly—or change jobs.

How is equity in the business of any value to me if there are no dividends? How would it benefit my heirs? I asked you to make provision for my heirs (and for your own and Randy's) by a simple agreement that the company buy back the stock of anyone who dies. Doesn't this deserve an answer?

You make a large assumption that a diversified company would grow faster. What diversified book club or publisher *has* grown faster? None. What more dramatic vindication of my policies than the figures for the past two years could anyone reasonably ask? Praise and gratitude would be the just response.

And how do you propose to carry water on both shoulders? How do you avoid changing the character of the company, breaking up a winning combination? You are a stranger both to politics and to publishing, and I am afraid you have little understanding of the emotions a strong position can evoke: deep loyalty, but also tough opposition. Whereas an attempt to play it several ways would be speedily—and scornfully—exposed: by *all* sides.

The quickest way to spoil the image of our company (and therefore its profit picture) is for you and Randy to attempt roles in directing it that your background does not equip you for. Randy assured me, at least a hundred times, that I would have a free hand (as, so far, I have had—with the present results you acknowledge). Please, I beg of you, don't complicate matters by changing the rules in the middle of the game. it would make for a diffusion of my energy— and I simply have none to spare. It would make our company less attractive to our employees, because of increased tensions, divided counsels and dwindling profits.

Above all, it would be a disservice to the conservative community. If they detect (as they would be sure to) a lessening of the quality of our books and promotions (a certain result of my dissipating my energies in unsound projects, or of hands without the right touch entering the picture), the Club and AH [Arlington House] would suffer in profit and esteem. I would go further: the conservative community, to whom the Club stands for something they cherish, would simply not sit still to see the Club's character changed or its thrust blunted. I wish you could be at a YAF convention and hear the roar of enthusiasm at the very mention of the Club. This Club has *obligations* to its members. We have promised to stand for certain principles and policies. We cannot betray them and be faithful to our proclaimed principles. We would be blistered from Maine to Alaska.

But mainly, I find it hard to believe that anyone would want to tamper with triumphantly successful policies; would want to upset the hard-pressed employees who devote themselves so unstintingly to these policies.

Please try to appreciate another point, a deeply personal one. We are a dedicated crew. Virtually all of our people give their jobs much more than 9-to-5 service. They *believe* in this company, to a degree that money can't buy. More is expected of me, of course, and I give more. I eat and drink and breathe this business—because it is *worthy* of it, and because so much of me is in it. But so do the others, most of them way beyond their responsibilities.

This morale is a precious—*and a delicate*—thing. *It is perishable.* Randy has often commented on how remarkably well everything went, right from the start. Gerald, it was no accident. But now it stands in jeopardy. Rocking the boat will do that. So I beseech you both to let well enough alone: not merely as businessmen but as sympathetic human beings. Because of our personal involvement, our people and I have a stake in stability and good morale that affects us in our day-to-day peace of mind and zest for living. Randy will remember this, and confirm it. Not merely do we deal here with an abstraction called company policy. We are talking about 20 human beings, *now* smiling. Let us cherish it for the prize it is.

The pension matter *was* taken up with you and Randy, and was *not* discussed with the employees. We *did* have preliminary approval to review the question, since Randy and Stan and I had often discussed it; indeed, at Randy's suggestion, I authorized an earlier survey. And surely a President has the right, indeed the duty, to investigate these matters.

I continue to hold that pension plans help a company's employees—and therefore its stockholders. Most of American management agrees. But if I'm outvoted—well, I play by the rules.

I could not agree with you more when you say there need not be disagreements between partners. I sought none and seek none. I wrote you a courteous and friendly note asking for a review of our long-range objectives. You slammed the door in my face—often with harsh language gratuitously added. (Randy followed with comparably harsh language when I later phoned him.) Lest you think I am unduly sensitive, I should add that my secretary (whom I have *instructed* to read all my mail) was horrified by your letter. My wife was horrified. Anyone would be.

I don't deserve this, Gerald. Our executives and employees don't deserve it. Search your heart: why should a friendly request provoke such a cold and unresponsive no? If I have sometimes disagreed with you, I have *never* written or uttered a discourteous word to you. Civilized discussion is poisoned by invidious words. I raised legitimate questions. Against the background of my record, and the repeated expressions of approval from you and Randy, I had no reason to expect anything but a congenial exchange of views.

For my part, I would like nothing better than to forget your letter ever came. I will try to. Let us, then, start over and discuss my letter of April 21, and this one, in cool and reasoned and friendly terms. If you disagree, please give me reasons, and please suggest alternatives. (It is not enough to say that I am being paid well. So is Jim Linen. But he and all the employees get more as *Time* prospers; that is *why* it prospers.) And please look back on my April 21 note and observe the unanswered questions. Notice, for example, that I devoted five paragraphs to Marvin and the other executives. You made no comment. Yet we have no business without them and our other people.

Let us, please, continue this—graciously.
Best regards,
Neil

P.S. Randy charged me on the phone with not keeping you informed. Randy often forgets. When he was leaving here in November, I asked him if I should send a monthly report to you and him. "That's not necessary," he was kind enough to assure me. "Every three months will be plenty." I was and remain grateful to this consideration, and I have given you comprehensive reports every three months. So, as you can imagine, I could hardly believe my ears when I heard this strange about-face.

P.P.S. When I discussed with Randy, just before he left, the problem with bringing in talent, and the related problem of my own tenure and contract, he replied: "Don't you think you can come and discuss this with your partners, and get a sympathetic hearing?" So I did; and I'm still in a state of shock.

ߐ

June 15, 1967

Dear Bill:
I had not thought of your book on style as an anthology, nor even as a collection of your own miscellaneous writings that might fit under that rubric. No, I was thinking of an original. It occurred to me that

the subject is one that absorbs you; one about which you would
have oceans to say; and one which would demand very little of the
research that, I suspect, you find inconvenient and a drag.

There is no reason, however, why you can't use individual chapters from such a book either for lectures or magazine articles.

Isn't it the sort of book you can see yourself scribbling away at, if
only mentally, when you are sailing?
Best,
Neil

 cs

July 21, 1967

Mr. F. M. Flynn, President
New York Daily News
220 East 42nd Street
New York, New York 10017

Dear Mr. Flynn:
On Wednesday night I watched *The Knute Rockne Story* on WPIX.
If you saw the picture, you'll readily recall the two dramatic high-
lights: George Gipp (played by Ronald Reagan) breathing his last
and saying, "Win One for the Gipper!"; and later, Rockne giving the
team this message at halftime during a game they were losing.

Would you believe it, those two scenes were missing from the
picture Wednesday night! It got me to thinking. Either the film
editor at WPIX is so bankrupt of dramatic judgment that he should
be working in a grocery store, or he is a fanatical Democrat who
would not hesitate to gut a picture to deny the Republicans' best
candidate for 1968 his high spot in the movie. In either case, I think
you may want to take a hard look at the man who was responsible
for hacking up a pleasant old movie.
Kindest regards,
Neil McCaffrey

cs

September 12, 1967

Dear Gene:
The *Wanderer* has now reprinted the second of your columns. So I
revert to an earlier suggestion and urge you to syndicate them. You
might use either the *Catholic News* or some syndicate that serves

the Catholic press.

I'll be sending you a clipping of the second *Wanderer* reprint, which appeared on page 1. I think the columns have been better lately. But you still have not wholly conquered your major vice: obfuscation and imprecision. I cannot argue down the suspicion that you sometimes resort to these not just out of laziness, but from an urge to make the banal sound sophisticated. This may impress the Altar Society, but it doesn't help them; and it embarrasses your friends and peers.

Best,
Neil

ભ

October 19, 1967

Dear Bill:

Many thanks for your hospitality the other night. I just received, and enjoyed, the *Commonweal* article. But it makes me repeat a point I made the other night. You are too unassuming to realize that you can now command top dollar from the major media even if you just write a piece about mowing your lawn on Sunday afternoon. I think, too, that you may be underestimating the interest these days in things Catholic; especially, something on a Catholic theme that is, *mirabile dictu*, fresh. If Lois [Wallace, literary agent] couldn't have sold your liturgy piece in forty-eight hours to the *New Yorker* or *Esquire* or some magazine for $500-$1000, you need a new agent. (I prescind from the fact that *Commonweal* proposed the article to you. I think that makes you honor bound to give the article to them. On the other hand, does a magazine have a right to ask a high-priced author to work at its scale, unless the author has personal or principled ties to the magazine?)

Anyway, the moral is that you can make a good living as a writer.

Best,
Neil

ભ

March 27, 1968

Dear Bill:

Assume Nixon wins the election. Not a bad bet at this time. Wouldn't you enjoy doing a book to be called something like *A Conservative Writes to President Nixon*? I think it is the sort of thing you would find easy and pleasant to write. It wouldn't take much research. Just let your constructive imagination run free. Part of the book, I suppose, would consist of the old recommendations in a new package. But I know you would have many fresh ideas too. In some ways the book would be akin to your position papers in the mayoralty race.

And incidentally, this could serve as a nice campaign document if you have any political plans.

One thing: the book would have to get out pretty soon after the inauguration, before the novelty wears off. You can write fast, and in a pinch we can publish fast.

Of course, you don't have to say yes or no right away. But would you just toy with the idea?
Best,
Neil

ༀ

April 10, 1968

Wall Street Journal
30 Broad Street
New York, New York 10004

Editor:
When a liberal writer spends 564 pages on a book attacking the House Committee on Un-American Activities, that's not news. When the *Wall Street Journal* disfigures its pages praising the book, that is. The *Journal's* editors might ponder Lenin's prediction that capitalists would vie with each other to sell the rope that would hang them.
Cordially,
Neil McCaffrey

ༀ

May 3, 1968

Dear Bill:
I don't know who to suggest for the *National Catholic Reporter.* They were spoiled by Garry. How many write that well? Certainly none of their other contributors. And how many would write for the piddling amount they offer? (I feel strongly that authors shouldn't write below scale, except for overriding personal reasons. The laborer is worthy of his hire.)

You could offer a choice of columns, but do they want that?

Brent [Bozell] is the one who comes most readily to mind. Even if he would give them gray hairs about deadlines, John Leo did the same. I suspect the reason they haven't asked him is that they have set the limits on what *they* consider responsible conservatism.

Fritz [Wilhelmsen] is another possibility. But does he have the discipline to make a weekly deadline? Would he spoil it all by winding up every column with a toast to the Carlist Pretender?

Why not suggest Russell Kirk? He is no more ponderous than some of their writers and he might be able to use the dough.
Best,
Neil

ᛦ

May 15, 1968

Dear Neil:
I am terribly distressed at your correspondence with Garry. I don't really see the necessity for it. I don't see that there has been any substantive change in Garry's position—or for that matter in mine. Correct the latter; I have changed as regards what I see as accomplishable—not as regards what I see as paradigmatic. But on no account, repeat no account, must you damage your fine friendship with Garry which has meant so much to both of you.

I am off to Miami and Garry is sailing up with me on Cyrano. If he brings up the matter I'll express myself frankly.
As ever,
Bill

ᛦ

May 17, 1968

Dear Bill:
I appreciate your letter. You will be even angrier with me when you read the letter I wrote you earlier this week.

Am I going to write bluntly to *close* friends? Isn't candor one of the privileges of friendship? When you don't care about a person, you let it go. I always like to have the air cleared. I think candor is a duty as well as a privilege of friendship.

I sense a sea change in Garry and some even in you. That in itself is no crime; but doesn't it open the way for discussion—among friends? And are you aware that in Garry's NCR article, I was the "so-called conservative" he laid into?

I feel desolate when you mention damaging a friendship. I hope I haven't, at least not irreparably. Please give it to me straight: is it better to sputter behind a friend's back and pretend all is well to his face, or to speak out? When you think a friend has made a mistake, isn't it an act of friendship to tell him so? I know you have chided me on several occasions. I have taken your words to heart (as I always do; as I do now) and been grateful that you took the trouble and were candid with me.

Best,
Neil

ᗵ

October 10, 1968

Boston Magazine
125 High Street
Boston, Massachusetts 02110

Editor:
F. Peter Model's article on books about Presidential candidates was not only partisan but inaccurate. Victor Lasky's *JFK: The Man and the Myth* was published in 1963, not in 1960. It was reissued by Arlington House in 1966. His new book on Robert Kennedy was not published in 1966. It is due to be published next month by Trident Press.

Mr. Model goes on to describe Allan Ryskind's *Hubert: An Unauthorized Biography of the Vice President* as a book that "carries the distinctly subtle imprimatur of the John Birch Society." I suppose it is silly to ask for accuracy from a man who could perpetrate that sort of prose. I am even driven to wonder whether Mr. Model is capable of a working definition of the word "imprimatur."

Cordially,
Neil McCaffrey

ᗵ

January 27, 1969

Mr. Richard W. Clarke
Editor
New York Daily News

Dear Mr. Clarke:
I had an idea for a continuing series in the *News*: a series that would start a lot of talk in New York, be a public service, and not hurt the circulation. You should assign someone to the federal, state and city courts to tally up all the felonies, perhaps give a brief description

of them—and then list the sentences and the judges who handed them out.

The idea came to me when I read the other day about the disposition of the case against the man who stabbed the boy to death in one of the city parks. He got ten to twenty years. He will be out in five years, stabbing again.

The *News* should be doing things like this as a matter of course. Alas, your wonderful paper is growing fat. As a longtime admirer, I have to say that it is getting dull.

And yet, never has the city been in greater need of a crusading, plain-spoken newspaper. When the *News* gets tired, New York's days are numbered.

Kindest regards,
Neil McCaffrey

ೞ

July 28, 1969

Dear Brent:

Come on now. You called on July 1st and asked if we wanted to publish a collection of *Triumph* articles. I replied the same day with a letter spelling out various things we would look for, schedules and such, and winding up by underscoring that the big consideration here would be how many books you could guarantee to buy.

You came up with an interesting book but an uninteresting guarantee. The reason I did not encourage you to raise your guarantee is that I know of your financial squeeze. Would I be wise to encourage you to overpromise, when this would leave us waiting a long time, perhaps forever, to be paid?

So I did not "encourage" you except to the extent that I told you, honestly, that we would be receptive under certain conditions. You were not in a position to meet those conditions, so that should have been that.

But I went on to offer what I thought was a useful suggestion for publishing the collection on your own. This is the way *National Review* published its collections when *National Review* was as small and as poor as *Triumph*. But I got no thanks. And in truth, I wasn't expecting any.

You seem to be under a delusion about our profits, even if you could prudently guarantee to buy 3,500 copies. They would be modest, and we would then publish the book as much in the nature of a service to you as out of our capitalistic lust after profits.

About which, a few words. Although I run this company, I don't own it. I am charged with running it at a profit. I try to fulfill that obligation. It is not mine to dispose of our company's resources and energies in unprofitable ventures.

There is a common type in Catholic history, the person who dedicates himself to the Lord, and then assumes that everybody else has taken the same vow; assumes, moreover, that everybody else must serve the Lord *his* way, fit into *his* plans. Monsignor Cohalan calls this regimental pride, the notion that you can bend everyone to your will provided it is all done for the honor and glory of the Franciscans. These people used to venture forth behind Roman collars or wimples; now I see one wearing a sports jacket. It is not the most sinister form of pharisaism, but it is one that people doing the Lord's work should be aware of.

Part of my apostolate is to sound the alarm.
Best,
Neil

ଓଃ

August 13, 1969

Dear Don [McClane]:
How rare to be asked for advice. How irresistible the invitation.

First, to dispose of the book, I don't think it would have been all that much of a breakthrough. But if you disagree, I can't for the life of me understand why you don't publish it as a paperback after the style of *An Evening with National Review*. You simply paste up your articles and photograph them. Very cheap. And as I mentioned to Brent, if you want the book reviewed, you can arrange to have 100 or so copies bound. It isn't essential to have copies bound in order to get reviewed, but it helps.

I agree that there is no easy solution to *Triumph*'s problems. But *Triumph* hasn't done badly. It has survived. It is as big as *National Review* was at the same stage in its life, and remember that *Triumph* is drawing on a market only 25% as large as *National Review*'s.

I agree with you that *Triumph* is not likely to enjoy a major breakthrough. Which doesn't mean you shouldn't keep trying for one. But more than likely, what you will have to settle for are minor breakthroughs. For these, you have to attack on many fronts:

1. Never let an issue go by that you don't run a house ad for gift subscriptions, or for laymen who will try to get the magazine put in the parish magazine rack, or for priests who will put it in their own parish magazine rack, or whatever. Keep chipping away at this.

2. Ask your readers for the names of prospects.

3. To get the magazine out of the magazine rack and into the hands of new readers, never let a cover go through that isn't a *selling* cover. Try to entice the editors down from Cloud Nine.

Triumph's larger problem is, in my view, pretty much out of your hands. It may even be out of the hands of the editors—in the sense that they won't, or can't, make the editorial changes that might wake up the Catholic market, get them excited, get them writing checks.

Triumph is alienated, and not even *productively* alienated (in the sense that somebody like Welch can turn his alienation into money). *Triumph* is aiming at patriotic American Catholics who are either articulate or inarticulate conservatives. So what does *Triumph* do? It kicks America in the groin in every issue. It kicks conservatives in the groin. It often carries articles that manage to be unreadable without being profound.

And of course, there are also the good things. These are mostly the exposés and the journalism. People read these pieces. They talk about them. They get sore; and when they get sore, they are likely to reach for their checkbook. *You cannot raise money without arousing the emotions.* And the most effective, the most obvious way to arouse the emotions of a conservative Catholic is to give blow-by-blow accounts of what is going on at Catholic U., Dayton, the Liturgy Club, etc.

Triumph has proved that it has the talent and the resources to do these exposés. But they stop short of riding the winning horse, and I believe the fault lies with the editors and their alienation. Unconsciously perhaps, they refuse to *just* defend the status quo. Rather, they hate the status quo, or the status that was quo ten or fifteen years ago in the American Church. And I doubt that anything can be done about it.

The Catholic businessmen of Dallas had a message for you. I doubt that these men *really* wanted [George] Wallace in the White House. But they wrote big checks for him because he was telling the bastards off. People will pay good money to anybody who tells the bastards off. *Triumph* could get rich tomorrow, if it wanted to.
Best,
Neil

ও

August 19, 1969

Dear Bill:
Maybe you score on Jarrell. But maybe not. Joan read him first. Or a good part of *Pictures*. She gave up in despair because of what she

described as overwriting. Joan and I often agree on writers, but not invariably, so I decided to try it. What do you know, I found the first few pages over-written. Since I agreed with Joan on the first few pages, and since she assured me that things didn't improve, and since I have only read 7% of the books I should have read and therefore quit early when a book seems unpromising, I decided to save all that blood.

Then too, if a writer bogs down in the first few crucial pages, doesn't that say something about his skill?

Please, please, don't put me down as an Enemy of [Whittaker] Chambers. He wrote one of the great autobiographies. Much of his other writing comes up to *Witness*. For the rest, I have no business arguing style with you. So let's just say that to my semi-tutored mind he is sometimes purple or solipsistic, pompous or misty. To push this opinion just a step further, I bet if we could poll all the good writers and good critics and good readers over the past half century, we would find that the consensus thinks of Chambers the writer more as I do than as you do. The sales of *Cold Friday* are not definitive, but they tend to bear me out. Which is not to say that you should go out and burn everything you've written on Chambers.

Sure, Chambers has written more profoundly on Communism than Waugh. But do I understand you to say that he has written on greater themes than Waugh? I hope not—because that would mean you had forgotten all that Waugh has written about Catholicism, sanctity, sin, behavior, humanism, and the old values. Take Chambers beyond Communism and he flounders.

Or put it another way (though here we are treading on Holy Ground, and see only opaquely). Waugh's odyssey carried him to Catholicism and conservatism, Chamber's only to anti-Communism.
Best,
Neil

ങ

September 8, 1969

National Review
150 East 35th Street
New York, New York 10016

Editor:
I remember when *NR* used to call itself, with justice, the keeper of the tablets. After an article like Philip Ardery's on the Woodstock zombies, that proud old claim sounds Aesopian.

First there is the awkward matter of Christian morals, which most of your staff espouse and which these moral aborigines flout as no one in the West has flouted them since the Adamites. Mr. Ardery's antinomianism belongs in *The Village Voice* or *The National Catholic Reporter.*

Then there is the question of sophistication, real and ersatz. The ersatz sophisticate affects neutralism as between decency and its enemies, as between civilization and its wreckers. The ersatz sophisticate dominates the media. The ersatz sophisticate was just published in *NR*.

One mark of real sophistication is the instinct for sniffing out con games and mythmaking. *NR* used to be adept at it. Now it joins in fashioning the instant myth of Freaks' Virtue. We are asked to bow down before the degenerates because, stoned with drugs and exhausted from barnyard sex, they lacked the energy for mayhem.

Did *NR's* old editorial stance sometimes make it sound out of fashion, quaint, square? So be it. The alternative is a journalism of corruption.

Neil McCaffrey

ларо

April 2, 1970

Twin Circle
86 Riverside Drive
New York, New York 10024

Editor:

I see where that croaking old voice of the Catholic Left, Msgr. George Higgins, is embarked on a vulgar effort to impute anti-Semitism to *Twin Circle*, in part because you ran our advertisement for Nathaniel Weyl's *The Jew in American Politics*. Although Msgr. Higgins is careful to exonerate Mr. Weyl of anti-Semitism, he goes on to remark "that doesn't mitigate the fact that some portions of the advertisement of his book in TC are calculated to fan the fires of anti-Semitism by creating the impression that Jews have been consistently soft on Communism, etc. Again, shades of Nazi Germany!"

Here is the passage in this long ad that Msgr. Higgins is referring to. I leave it to your readers to judge his accuracy, his fairness, his intelligence:

> "Plainly, American Jews stand out as our great national achievers.
> Yet, for a generation and more the majority of them have been

pulled toward a Liberal-to-radical stance. Many have sympathized with the Soviet Union and fought anti-Communists. *Why?*"

Having done such a blatant job of quoting out of context—indeed, misquoting—Msgr. Higgins goes on to charge that the advertisement "is deeply offensive to many Jews." I hate to embarrass Msgr. Higgins with facts, but our review files show that this book was praised by seven Jewish reviewers. One was neutral. Three panned the book, but only because they disagreed with some of Mr. Weyl's ideas. Nobody so much as hinted that the book and its theses (which the advertisement simply encapsulates) are in any way anti-Semitic.

Nor did Mr. Weyl, who is half Jewish, find the ad offensive. Nor did Mr. Theodore Lit, who served as his editor for this book and who is Jewish. Neither did our Jewish advertising agent, Mr. Alan Rosenberg. Our former sales manager, Mr. Daniel Rosenthal, found the book and the ad to his liking.

More to the point, we advertised this book in *Commentary*, easily the outstanding Jewish magazine in America, and indeed published by the American Jewish Committee. *The New York Times*, which was founded by an American Jew and is still published by his heirs, found nothing offensive in our advertisement.

If there is any anti-Semitism here, I think it can be found in Msgr. Higgins, with his arrogant assumption that American Jews must inevitably share his knee-jerk Liberalism and shun Mr. Weyl's thoughtful conservatism. If I were Jewish, I'd be sore at Msgr. Higgins.
Cordially,
Neil McCaffrey

ભ

May 12, 1970

Voice of the People
New York Daily News
220 East 42nd Street
New York, New York 10017

New York politicians are right to turn out in force for the Israel Day Parade. But how come most of these liberals don't show up for our own Loyalty Day Parade?
Neil McCaffrey

 timeless

July 16, 1970

Advertising Age
740 N. Rush Street
Chicago, Illinois 60611

Editor:
I have just seen the new Olin doublespread four-color ad that pictures
Washington and carries the headline, "A monument to disastrous
city planning." I should say, rather, that the ad is a monument to the
vulgarity and insensitivity of some smartass Madison Avenue types.

To scorn what is universally acknowledged as one of the world's
most beautiful cities is the act of a barbarian. And to mock our
national capital tells us something about the instincts of the people
who prepared the ad, not to mention their sensitivity to the instincts
of most Americans (whom they probably hold in contempt).

I am glad I'm not an Olin stockholder. If I were, I'd move fast
to replace the present chief executives with people who were less
alien to the feelings of their fellow Americans, and to the opinions
of civilized men.
Cordially,
Neil McCaffrey

July 1, 1970

Newsweek
444 Madison Avenue
New York, New York 10022

Editor:
Your choice of six contributors pretends to cover the spectrum yet
reveals a bias that is, even for *Newsweek*, overt and disingenuous.
Hofstadter and Schlesinger "centrist liberals"? If they're honest they'll
sue you; and if they *are* anywhere near the center, then depend upon
it, four out of five Americans are screaming right-wingers.

Pushing along with the charade, you reveal that Andrew Hacker
and Daniel Boorstin "are, relatively speaking, conservatives." They
are, but thanks only to the sleight of hand you work with the adverb.
John Lindsay is also, relatively speaking, a conservative—relative to

Mao Tse-tung. Conservatives would describe Hacker and Boorstin as moderate liberals, a description neither would deem inaccurate.

Thus you manage your little game so that no conservative gets to play. Scared to mix with kids your own size? A pity. We have some tough ones. To cite only three, James Burnham was a ranking interpreter of the modern world when Hacker, Genovese and Lynd were still worrying about long division; Ernest van den Haag has academic credentials and an intellectual range matched only by Dr. Boorstin's; and Will Herberg would have given you not just wisdom, but the spiritual insight whose absence left your 16 solemn pages two-dimensional.

Neil McCaffrey

ᴄʒ

October 23, 1970

Dear Garry:

Belatedly, thanks so much for the copy of your book [*Nixon Agonistes*]. I know I'll find it wicked, but I also know, off the several excerpts I have already read, that I'll enjoy many of the more salacious passages. I'm much less hard on Nixon than you, and when hard often for different reasons, but there is a merciless accuracy in some of what you say.

Nice review by Leonard. But did you notice—he cribbed the whole thing from the excerpt in *Washington Monthly*? Bookreviewmanship.

I'm yearning to read it, but I don't know when I can. My schedule is almost comically crowded. In order to keep up with work and/ or reading, I've become a near recluse. Not that I mean to sound the martyr. I enjoy it. What I really miss is time for off-duty reading. Business, especially Arlington House, is growing by leaps, and a good part of the important work can't be delegated. It just grows. I remember you were once hugely amused, about ten years ago in my little office in Doubleday, when I think you likened it to a command post; whereas in fact Doubleday was a six-year vacation.

There are a few things I *think* I'll want to write to you about in your book, but I don't think I should on the strength of excerpts. So I'll wait.

Best,
Neil

ᴄʒ

April 22, 1971

Dear Frank [Meyer]:

For upwards of ten years I have listened to you make a travesty of my attitudes. Bad luck for me, or rather bad judgment: I shouldn't have. To be sure, I have protested and explained. All to no avail.

On occasion, I have experienced this incomprehension from other people. They were ignorant more often than malicious. Either way, I broke off talking to them because it accomplished nothing.

In your case, I guess I have tolerated it partly because we have both profited from what is now a fairly long friendship, partly because I kept telling myself that you meant no harm. I think I was wrong.

A month or so ago, when you had launched an old tirade about why I hadn't backed Reagan, I finally blew up. I pointed out to you what I had pointed out many, many times in the past: that I began supporting Reagan for the presidency before the 1964 elections. I thought I had begun to make an impression on you, because I thought you had been behaving for the last month or so. Then you started in again last night about my "hero" Wallace. It was once too often.

The victim of this sort of misrepresentation has three responses. He can do as I did for so long and turn the other cheek. He can fight back and reply in kind. But since I regard such behavior as barbarous, and only slightly less barbarous when it is in reply to similar barbarism, I have no appetite for that response. The other alternative is to walk away. I'm walking.

Apart from ignorance, the conduct I describe can have only two roots. Either the perpetrator has such contempt for his victim's words that he doesn't even bother to listen to them, or he knows them but twists them in order to denigrate his victim. Either way, I've had quite enough of this abuse from you.

When you learned to be a Communist, you learned how to upset, one-up, defeat and destroy adversaries. And when you were learning to be a Communist, I was learning to be a Catholic. One of the things I learned was called, a little fatuously, the Golden Rule. A little later I understood its roots: we do unto others because God made the others and left His image in them, which they more or less retain and which they can always enhance.

The Golden Rule can do wonders for human conduct. It makes you want to give every man his due, build him up, help him grow, put the best face on him. But it forbids one to deny any man what is his, or to misrepresent him, or to want to see him cheapened or destroyed. It is no exaggeration to say that to attack another man is to attack God. To misrepresent a man's attitudes or to make a travesty of them, or even to show such contempt to them that you don't bother to get them straight, is a personal attack no less cruel than rape.

As I say, my response is to walk away. Please note, and for once pay attention: I do *not* say to become your enemy. I wish you everything good. What I propose instead is simply benign neglect, which may or may not be a lesson for you but will surely be a relief for me. We'll have lots of business to do, and most of that can be done by mail. When a phone call is essential, I'm here at the office till six or after on most nights; and, incidentally, I really prefer to take calls at the office rather than at home, where for a few precious hours I like to talk to the family, or read quietly, or relax with television, having borne the burdens of the day.

But no more playing the foil or the fool. It's bad for both of us.
Kindest regards,
Neil

ɔʒ

May 3, 1971
MEMO TO: Gene Clark, Bill Buckley
FROM: Neil McCaffrey

I suppose you noticed the enclosed story from the *Times*. Focus on paragraph eight. Have you noticed how the media have been getting away with more and more ridiculous stories and statements about the Church lately, as witness that preposterous one about the tablecloth?[4]

For centuries the mythology had priests growing horns, the better to pose as satyrs for their orgies with nuns. When Catholics began to get a little more outspoken—or was it more numerous?—in the early part of the century this nonsense began to die down. Now, as part of the demoralization of the Church, the media can again pretend to take seriously every psychotic and freak who has a bloodcurdling story about his Catholic childhood back in the dark ages, before good Pope Porcine.

4   The Times article had said: "As a girl, Miss Bacon attended the Sacred Heart School, a Roman Catholic elementary school in Atherton. It was a strict school, according to an account that she gave a friend in Washington, who said: 'They were taught, for instance, that you don't put a white tablecloth on the table when a boy is coming to dinner because it might remind him of bed.'"

In your new job I think you ought to muss them up a little, Gene. And I think that you, Bill, ought to be conscious of this, because you never know when you might be able to use it.

I'm not recommending an ADL reign of terror or paranoia, Italian style. In general, I think it is good to relax these taboos about ethnic and religious groups. But I *also* think the groups in question ought to send up a bitch when fantasies are offered as facts in respectable newspapers.

&

July 8, 1971

New York Times Book Review
229 West 43rd Street
New York, New York 10036

To the Editor:
When Ward Just describes Martin Gershen's *Destroy or Die* as "considerably over priced," he is venturing out beyond his competence. The book contains 325 pages plus 8 pages of photographs (which Mr. Just neglected to mention) and sells for $7.95. Many comparable books are today priced at $8.95. I found these prices for the other adult non-fiction reviewed in the same issue: 218 pp. - $6.95, 585 pp. (illustrated) - $12.95, 278 pp. (illustrated) - $7.95, 256 pp. (illustrated) - $7.95, 367 pp. - $8.95, 116 pp. - $5.95, 332 pp. - $12.50, 224 pp. - $6.50, 465 pp. - $15.95, 196 pp. - $6.95, 239 pp. - $6.95, 220 pp. - $5.95, 224 pp. - $6.95, 165 pp. - $9.95, 248 pp. - $9.95, 436 pp. - $8.95, 363 pp. - $8.50. On a cost-per-page basis, *Destroy or Die* is the fourth best buy, in a virtual tie for third, among these eighteen titles.

Two or three years ago, *Destroy or Die* would have cost $6.95. In the early Sixties it would have been priced at $5.95. I'll gladly sell Mr. Just any number of extra copies at $5.95, if he will sell me his house for the price he paid for it in 1962.
Neil McCaffrey

&

And Rightly So

September 17, 1971

Dr. P. A. Doyle, Editor
The Evelyn Waugh Newsletter
c/o English Department
Nassau Community College
State University of New York
Garden City, New York 11530

Editor:

I found Mr. Martin S. Cohen's article ("Allusive Conversation in *A Handful of Dust* and *Brideshead Revisited*") a study in misinterpretation. But just to confine myself to factual errors, in the order of their appearance:

Mr. Cohen calls *Handful* and *Brideshead* "the only Waugh novels based on potentially tragic situations". What about *Sword of Honor*?

Tony is established as a "fully pathetic figure" in *Handful* not because of the double-entendres that Mr. Cohen discovers, but because he has just lost his only son and been cuckolded.

Bridey is a plain, blunt man, anything but "Jesuitical".

Julia is not "alone of all the Flytes... able to temporarily put her religion and its obligations aside". Sebastian put his aside for many years, and Lord Marchmain put his aside for some twenty years. Nor did Julia put her religion aside "in order to win Ryder". She had put her religion aside years ago when she married Rex outside the Church.

Poor Lady Marchmain fares badly in Mr. Cohen's heavy hands. She is simply the symbol of Orthodox Catholicism. Lord Marchmain, Sebastian and Julia profess to rebel against her, but Mr. Cohen should have seen behind their protestations and realized that they were actually rebelling against their religion.

Brideshead's marriage may have been "grotesque", but Mr. Cohen misleads us when he leaves it at that. The novel makes clear that the marriage was a happy one.

Cordelia is not guilty of "turning to the total escapism that her religion affords". Cordelia became a nurse in the Spanish Civil War. Some escapism!

Mr. Gene D. Phillips, in his review of the Kellogg book, is right to score the author for omitting *Sword of Honor* in his consideration of Waugh as a Catholic novelist. Equally egregious is Mr. Kellogg's omission of *Helena*.

But enough of criticism. Your *Newsletter* is valuable, and a joy to read.

Kindest regards,
Neil McCaffrey

ભ

November 3, 1971
MEMO TO: Vic Gold, Stan Goldstein, Dan Mahoney
FROM: Neil McCaffrey
                    Super-Confidential

Let me try to put down on paper, in rough draft form, an idea I have talked about with each of you. The idea is for a "silent majority" but not rigidly ideological newsmagazine, most closely approximating *Newsweek* in that it would have a few columnists as well as all the news departments. It would be more ambitious and more readable than *U. S. News* because the latter doesn't cover religion, culture, sports and leisure, and is spotty on education as well.

But before going into detail about the magazine, a word about how it might be launched.

As an investment, it would have to be called highly speculative. In general, this is not the best time to start a magazine. A newsmagazine is expensive to get out and staff. To be sure, there seems to be a market for this magazine: the *Reader's Digest* type (and there are 18 million readers of the *Digest*). Still, in sheer investment terms, this would take at least 10 million dollars just to start, and it would be crapshooting money.

But with the new tax law as it applies to private foundations (most of them are private, I believe), we might uncover a likely source of big capital. Most of the private foundations are going to have to spend many millions of dollars more than they are spending now. Much of what they spend even now is of doubtful value and effect. A *big* project like this might appeal to them, under the rubric of educational publishing.

I believe the magazine could get away with this as long as it was not identified as partisan. That doesn't mean it couldn't take positions on issues. If it came under dispute, this would happen down the road, and by the time the issue was litigated, the magazine would be well launched and, if the foundation lost, it could probably just dispose of the property. (Here, obviously) I speak with all the authority of the village idiot; but I think a case can be made for this position, and the right tactic is to run for daylight, and worry about litigation if and when.

But I am profit-oriented, and I think that this magazine has a chance to turn the corner in a few years. What then? I gather that the foundation would then either have to pay taxes on the magazine's profits, or perhaps dispose of the enterprise. In either case, so what? The foundation would have done its work. This isn't the place to try to staff the magazine, but a few thoughts occur to me. Among authors I know (many of them on our list), we might build the nucleus of a good magazine. A few top-of-the-head possibilities: editor - Vic Gold, Stan Evans. Managing editor - either of the above, Don Rogers, George Carpozi. Columnists - Burnham, Vic Gold, Vic Lasky (Washington gossip). Military affairs - Frank Johnson, General Thomas Lane, Hanson Baldwin. Economics - Larry Fertig, D. T. Armentano. Books - Peter Witonski, John Chamberlain. Business - Don Rogers. Movies - Francis Russell. Music - George Simon. Broadway - Stanley Green, Ted Sennett. Religion - Harold Brown, Bill Marshner.

This certainly doesn't exhaust the possibilities. I merely rattle off these names to show that we can staff a good magazine. But the talent hunt would go far deeper than names that just occur to me now.

The magazine would need one or both wire services. It would use stringers all over the world, as good ones present themselves. (Stringers are vastly cheaper than full-time employees, complete with office and secretary and expense account.) For that matter, many of the departments would use freelance writers. There's no reason at all to put people like George Simon or Peter Witonski on your staff. They have other ways to make a good living but would be delighted to pick up this extra money.

Production and circulation would have to be staffed. I think you can buy printing at pretty good prices these days. Many printers are hurting.

You would need advertising reps, probably supervised by a few sales executives. Most of the circulation would be sold by direct mail or coupon space ads (mail order). I think it not outlandish to project one million readers within one year, at a cost of not more than ten million dollars and probably not less than five million dollars. I want to handle this. I also want to be the publisher.

The thrust of the magazine is hard to reduce to a memo. But let me try. Most of the coverage would be similar to that in *Time* and *Newsweek*. But it would have a different slant. Almost as important, some of the coverage would be what *Time* or *Newsweek* would rather overlook: outrages in Communist countries, weakness in our defense posture, welfare scandals, terrorism in our schools, and everything we could unearth about Leftism in our schools and churches.

Under culture, we should rough up the media good. We should make a point of documenting their distortions. (Idea: Edith Efron to cover TV.)

Very important: to show that we are big boys and care about

the truth, we should not be afraid to look squarely at scandals on the Right and the foibles of its leaders. It makes for good journalism, and builds readership like nothing else. I don't mind ruffling people, as long as they read us.

Possible title: *Mid-America*. Possible objection: it might suggest to some that it deals only with the heartland, or only with a certain segment of society. But I think that can be gotten over easily in the promotion.

I would like to be adventurous. I would like to use the talents of people in unusual ways. Example A: I would like Dan Mahoney to be the corporation counsel. But how many hours a day can he read Blackstone? Dan should spend his time developing political sources and informants all over the country. That way, we can dig up offbeat political stories and trends. Dan is not a journalist, but he sure as hell can dictate a memo and turn it over to the rewrite man. Example B: Stan Goldstein is our accountant, but informally he spends a lot of time nosing around Wall Street for interesting business ideas, success stories, scandals.

Once the magazine attracts a minimum of half a million readers, it would be no trick at all to start a book club. It would not be another CBC. It would be a lot looser ideologically and cover a lot more ground. But, like the magazine itself, it would be mid-America oriented.

I think we could muster just about enough talent to staff one *good* "silent majority" newsmagazine. We would be enormously influential, because we would have this huge vaguely-right-of-center audience entirely to ourselves. We could literally mobilize them. For example: it's one thing to say that the networks are Left-leaning. How much better journalism to interview the people who put, say, the Carson show together, to lay out their ghastly opinions for the world to look at, above all to *photograph* them and show them for the freaks they are? Again, instead of talking in abstractions about how soft the judges are, we zero in on one or a handful of judges and follow them for a period. We *spell out* what they let thugs get away with.

I may have touched on this above, but I'd like the magazine to take on most of the media establishment. We would get lots of criticism, lots of bad press—*but we would get press*. That way, we could become a kind of rallying point for everyone with a grievance. This, after all, is the whole point of the magazine. We will carve out a market among those who have no voice. They number tens of millions.

To come down to earth, where do we go from here? Whom do we talk to? How do we go from here to there? How do we approach people and still keep this idea in strict confidence? The idea can easily be stolen; besides, I have personal and professional reasons for not unveiling my plans until something concrete shapes up.

I'm in touch with each of you, but shouldn't, as Stan suggests, we all get together? Vic will probably be coming up in a few weeks. Shouldn't we arrange an evening among the four of us and Marvin Nagourney? Please let me know. We can make plans as soon as Vic tells me when he will be up.

ଔ

May 2, 1973
TO: Roger Pryor, Gene Clark, and Jim Mahoney
FROM: Neil

I am enclosing a set of editorial fact sheets covering the Summer and Fall list of Zondervan, one of the bigger evangelical Protestant publishers.

This is an enterprising publishing house, commercially successful, as big as many of the medium-sized general publishers. Nor is Zondervan unique. There must be another four or five evangelical Protestant houses just as big, just as profitable; and many more that are smaller.

The moral is clear enough. They put out a big, impressive list offering both popular and scholarly books and covering a whole range of conservative Protestant concerns. The conservative Protestant market is able to support several impressive publishing programs on this scale. People write these books in abundance, and people read them. It is a strong indication of the vitality, and the growth, of conservative Protestantism.

Need I even mention the disgraceful contrast orthodox Catholicism presents? I can't think of a more dramatic demonstration of how moribund the Church in America is these days. Catholic publishing has never had the size and vigor of Protestant publishing in America. We don't, after all, have the numbers, the talent or the readers. But at least Catholic publishing was alive in the thirties, forties and fifties. It was alive in the sixties—having an orgy before the climactic murder of the Church in America, and its own suicide.

I don't suppose you know any member of the hierarchy who would like to study this list, multiply it by ten or twenty, and then ponder its implications for American Catholicism.

ଔ

August 23, 1973

Dear Mr. Cowles [Robert Cowles, President, Publishers-Hall Syndicate]:
Congratulations on signing Vic Gold. You've scored the coup of the
decade. Three times a week, your wires are going to explode. By
Christmas, your papers will be demanding five columns a week.

On the working level, you and your papers can expect a not
insignificant bonus. You will be getting as tight, as accurate, as trou-
ble-free a writer as we have in the working press. My own editing goes back fifteen years, first at Doubleday. I've worked more or
less closely with over 200 writers: scores of unknowns, dozens of
semi-names, maybe a dozen lions. Nobody comes close to Vic Gold
for taking pains: rare enough in a writer, as you know, and all but
unique in a brilliant writer.

And brilliant he is. Veterans will be reaching back for compar-
isons with Mencken. Younger readers will be reminded somewhat
of Breslin (though the more perceptive among them will notice that
with Vic Gold the Middle American strain is not ersatz). But what
everyone will notice, pros above all, is the indecent fertility of ideas.
Maybe Vic Gold will start to sound tired around 1990, but certainly
not before.

I have a special reason to be grateful for Vic Gold. As a working
conservative in the media, I keep up my membership in the Viewing
With Alarm Society. Thank God for Vic Gold, our chairman of the
Wit That Bites Committee.
Kindest regards,
Neil McCaffrey

છ

December 10, 1973

Dear Gene:
I've talked extensively with John Mulloy. A nice man, and sound as
a Swiss Franc. But we have already been over this territory. We've
taken some soundings in the Catholic market and the prospects for
reissuing the classics are not bright. In fact, I think you and I talked
about this a year or so ago. But I'm still probing, because this is
obviously something that ought to be done if we can make it pay
even moderately well.

In this connection, one depressing fact: the conservative Catholic
press, in which we would hope to get most of our ad response, is
not a good book medium. It is only fair, and neither big enough nor
responsive enough to support in any significant measure a publishing

program of this sort.

Another point, even when Catholic books were flourishing in the forties and fifties, by and large the *good* ones were not successful. *A fortiori* . . .

We'll miss you Thursday. But how about Thursday, December 27? Dietrich and Alice von Hildebrand are coming for dinner. A great and appealing man.

Best,
Neil

ભ

April 9, 1974

Dear Bill:

Thanks for passing on the comment on Bernanos, which I guess is from John Wisner.

Bernanos murky? I was getting charitable in my old age. Inconsistent would be better, or opportunistic, unstable, or incoherent. He was for Maurras when it was fashionable. He was at best ambiguous, at worst pro-Loyalist during the Spanish War. During the Occupation, he hurled denunciations at Petain, having first taken the precaution of putting three thousand miles of ocean between him and the Germans. In that, he may have been one of the war's more stouthearted Frenchmen. In Brazil.

John Wisner acquitting Bernanos of murkiness is like Bella Abzug defending Jackie Susann's refinement [a fabulously successful novelist, Susann was a gifted self-promoter].

Best,
Neil

ભ

April 15, 1974

The Wanderer
128 E. 10th Street
St. Paul, Minnesota 55101

Editor:

Apropos of Bishop Rausch and those epigones of Loisy he so admires, I recommend "Modern Theology and Biblical Criticism," an essay by C.S. Lewis in *Christian Reflections,* a posthumous collection of his writings published by Eerdmans. Lewis vanquishes the pseudo-theologians; and, in demolishing their pretension, he gives

us new insights into our Lord's personality. Like almost everything Lewis writes, this essay is invaluable for beleaguered Christians today. If we neglect him, we impoverish ourselves.
Neil McCaffrey

ଔ

April 23, 1974

Dear Gene:
Thanks for the Augustine book. It resolves itself into two questions: a) is America ready for a book of his excerpts, and b) this book?

Books on Augustine never sold well, even when America had some Catholics. But I don't rule one out. After Newman, I think he is *the* Catholic writer for our age. After all, he lived through the same thing.

But this book? I confess I have let my Italian lapse. So I really don't know what is in it. But even if I did, there would be no point at all in our going to an Italian publisher and translating his book. Augustine exists in English. If we wanted to do a book, we would simply take existing translations in the public domain and use somebody's expert selection. A project for your retirement to the ivory tower?

On a more solemn note, we are to be the guests of Martin Bressler and his wife at that art affair at the Waldorf next Wednesday. Have you been roped in? I hope so: not sadistically, but in self-defense. Come. Minister unto us. Salvage the evening. (I don't know anything about art, but I do know what I hate.)
Best,
Neil

ଔ

December 17, 1974

Dear Mr. [James] Fitzpatrick:
Thanks for your nice letter. I continue to think *How to Survive* is a title that does the job just right. First and foremost, it captures your prime market; and that is the function of a title. More than that, it is riveting to both the Libs and the innocent. You can't ask for anything more of a title. I wish all our titles were as good.

Don't worry about putting off Lib educators. Dull titles will put them off even more. Your title puts them on the defensive, almost forces a fair-minded Lib to give you a hearing—if only so he can live up to his own principles. Others will find reasons for not giving you a hearing, and there isn't much we can do about that. But it is far better to challenge them in a polite way than to try to get cute with them. Look what happened to Nixon. People respect you more for candor. So, especially, do kids. If your book gives off a faint whiff of forbidden fruit, it might be that much more attractive to kids.

As for the titles you suggested, let me practice what I preach and be candid. They are deadly.

We definitely want you to write another book for us. Bob [Markle, editor at Arlington House] is high on your manuscript. I am impressed with your writing. We are both impressed with the professional, no-nonsense way you deliver on time. You write well and think well. You have everything going for you. Rest assured, you will come up with something we like, or we will find something you like.

All of which is a prelude to my passing up the Coughlin idea. Are you aware that there have been two (Liberal) biographies of him over the past decade? Nothing much happened with either. I say Liberal, but I have the impression that they were not unfair. May I again be candid and give you my real reasons? They are several.

First, the above. Your book would not fill any gap as far as libraries and students are concerned.

Second, there isn't much interest in Coughlin among our people. He still has a handful of diehards on the Right; but my impression is that they are old and are not readers. For most people on the Right, he is a figure who antedates their interest in politics and/ or religion; and is, moreover, an embarrassment. They don't much want to know about him; and they certainly don't want to have to defend him.

Finally, I don't think you are the man to do this book. First of all, you have no memory of him. More than that, I think you may have absorbed some misleading information about him from your *Triumph-Wanderer* reading. Coughlin was and is a mountebank. He is an economic illiterate. He is soft on Vietnam. And, of course, he is unreliable about the Jews.

In this context, I want to reiterate that I like your writing and certainly go along with the main thrust of your recent articles. I share with you a conviction that, if the American Right is ever to have any hope of exercising serious influence, it is going to have to change its complexion more than a little. Since I have a hierarchy of values, I am perfectly prepared to sacrifice something in economics in exchange for some moral and social conservatism. But when I make the sacrifice (if indeed I ever have the chance to), I propose to call things by their right names, at least in private. I have never attempted to deify the free market; but I'm not going to damn it in favor of some putative (actually nonexistent) "Christian" economics. I am not going to pretend that George Meany is a better guide than Mises. In short, I am not going to buy the *Triumph* hogwash. What they do (and what you do, perhaps under their influence) is to set up a straw man after the model of John Galt, and then tell us Christians and humane people may not buy this. But this is really a confession of weakness. If you have a stronger case, or something concrete to propose, you would not feel obliged to reduce free market economics to John Galt.

But I don't mean to argue economics with you. What I am doing is calling attention to the weakness of your stance. If you are going to seek some sort of coalition (and here you differ from the people at *Triumph*, whose slogan is always unconditional surrender), then you are going to have to acknowledge the soundness of the free market position—and then go on from there to offer a first-things-first sort of argument. *That* might carry some conviction (especially since events are likely to take the matter out of everyone's hands, since we are in a 1930 situation).

Incidentally, I think we should beware of canonizing Coughlin because of his enemies. That sort of thinking puts a Nixon in the White House. I hope you and your family have a blessed and happy Christmas and New Year.
Kindest regards,
Neil McCaffrey

℃

October 23, 1975

The Chattanooga Times
117 East 10th Street
Chattanooga, Tennessee 37401

Editor:
In his review of *Kissinger on the Couch* by Phyllis Schlafly and Admiral Chester Ward (October 19, 1975, the *Chattanooga Times*), Albert H. Bowman writes: "Arlington House specializes in publications of the far right, especially those of the John Birch Society . . ." Arlington House does indeed publish many conservative books, but whether most observers would characterize books by such authors as William F. Buckley Jr., James Burnham, Russell Kirk, and Kevin Phillips as occupying the far right is open to question. But what is not a matter of opinion is what Mr. Bowman states as fact, that Arlington House

"specializes in publications . . . of the John Birch Society." Arlington House has never issued a publication of the John Birch Society, and indeed has no connection whatever with the Society.
Cordially,
Neil McCaffrey

భ

August 18, 1976

Mr. Robert L. Bartley
Wall Street Journal
22 Cortlandt Street
New York, New York 10017

Dear Mr. Bartley:
The trouble with conservatives, as you correctly state, is that they haven't made the necessary demonstrations. The problem has many facets, and I'm afraid the *Journal* is not innocent of blame.

As you may know, we are the only publisher in the country that regularly and as a matter of policy publishes conservative books. We are a small publisher. Our conservative output numbers not more than two dozen books a year, an average we have maintained over a dozen years. That is to say, we have published upwards of 200 conservative books, and we will soon be pushing 300. Yet in all that time, I doubt that the Journal has noticed more than five of our titles (even though several of your writers are on our review list).

Not all of these books are worthy of your notice, needless to say. But many are, many more than you have noticed. Buckley, Burnham, Kirk, Hazlitt, Kevin Phillips, Murray Rothbard—these are just a few of the writers who grace our imprint, along with scores of others who might become better known if the nation's leading conservative newspaper would give them a break.

You can't, of course, act as a house organ for conservatives. But a little more sympathy, a little more attention, would hearten the poor wretches laboring out in the vineyard.

Another aspect of the problem will underscore some of your remarks. How many people see the *Journal* every day—upwards of two million? I should guess at least that many. Most of them are more or less conservative. Yet whenever we run an ad in the *Journal* (it is always a quarter of a page); that is, whenever I feel adventurous and we have a likely book, we are lucky to break even. And we *know* the responsiveness of the *Journal*, because we always run coupon ads and count the coupons.

Which points up a passing remark of yours, that conservatives tend to shrink from anything approaching the intellectual life. So it isn't all the fault of the communicators. As you well know, our side is not embarrassed with good writers. Yet even the good ones tend to dry up when they conclude that nobody is listening. Book clubs with a liberal bias number their members into the millions. Our sister company, the Conservative Book Club, has never gone higher than 36,000 members, and after the demoralization of Watergate, we are now struggling to get back over 23,000. Conservatives themselves must provide the social and economic and intellectual infrastructure for a lively conservative intellectual life and a conservative demonstration. So far, they haven't.
Kindest regards,
Neil McCaffrey

ભ

Via Sommacampagna 47
00185 Rome, Italy

August 13, 1976

Mr. Neil McCaffrey
Pelham Manor
New York, N.Y.

Dear Mr. McCaffrey,
I can't begin to tell you how *great* your letter to the *Wanderer* is—nor can Michael. Brilliant polemics in the best sense of the word.

Is it time for the world's first book on Econe? Putting people straight on the basic issue: one side, a changing Church in a changing world; the other, an immutable Church meant to change the world. A blow-up of my article for NR—no word yet about whether they will buy it or not. There would be no pleas or recriminations, not even conclusions. The documentary build-up is dramatic and revealing enough. All documentation is available to me. I have 80% of all articles and commentary on the affair in Italian, French and English and I can get the rest. Msgr. Lefebvre knows me and will talk to me. His sister here in Rome may well give me nice bits about his earlier life.

If I did nothing else, starting October 1, I think I could deliver 35,000 or 40,000 words in January. It would be a short, compact book that ought to sell like hotcakes (!) at your minimum price. Remember Americans are still waiting for "Un Eveque Parle," which has sold well in French and Italian. It is only a collection of his sermons and letters but can be drawn on for our book.

You can understand that the Matt-Mulloy attack puts me squarely at the crossroads. Up to now I have been able to explain away my *Wanderer* connection to traditionalists. No more. Of course, if NR prints my article, it will be Al Matt who boots me out of his paper. I note that Wm. Marshner has left.

But before I leave the *Wanderer* I *must* attach myself to another paper because our permit to stay in Italy is contingent on a correspondenceship. Roger kindly suggested *Human Events* to Michael. I might query them. *Wanderer's* $200 a month, which supplements my investment income (so that we can get along in inflation-crazy Italy), probably cannot be matched unless the new paper has a need particularly of news from Rome. Not likely. But the main thing is accreditation and a little work so that I can do the book.

So long away from the U.S.A., I have no idea what the conservative papers are. Might Roger be kind enough to make some more suggestions? Even American periodical indexes are unavailable to me right now due to the libraries being closed during August. (As are typewriter repair shops!)

To sum up, dear Mr. McCaffrey:

Bravo for your letter! (will they dare to print it?)

Shall I write the book?

Do you know what conservative paper might take me on?

With kind regards to you and to Roger,
Mary Martinez

∽

August 27, 1976

Dear Mrs. [Mary] Martinez:

How nice of you to write. I'm glad you liked my letter. By now you have probably seen the follow-up by Mulloy and me.

I see that they have not run my letter, but I am told that the 8/26 issue of *The Remnant* has. I haven't seen it.

I did talk to Al Matt the other day. He called ostensibly to talk about advertising, but really to test the water. He seemed loath to print my letter, or indeed to engage in any serious discussion. He is incurious about unfamiliar problems, and dislikes grappling with them. But I think he is beginning to feel the heat. He called a friend the other day, prominent in our circles, to see where he stood and perhaps to find a defender. He acknowledged that he was getting a lot of heat. Even more significant, he began berating Mulloy. It is always a good sign when your opponents begin squabbling and blaming each other. Then they are looking for scapegoats, and you only need scapegoats when you are losing.

Your letter sounds as if you are resigned to leaving *The Wanderer*. May I urge you not to move so fast? For heaven's sake, don't worry about your traditionalist friends. Unless, that is, one of them volunteers to support you and your son. Not only that, but are they so dumb that they don't see how valuable it is to have a writer like you on *The Wanderer*? Moreover, I think you misread the situation. The last thing Matt wants is more trouble at this point. Will he make a bad situation worse by firing you? I doubt it. Moreover, the fact that you have just appeared in *National Review* will undoubtedly sting him, since he should have run that article a year ago. Moreover, nobody can accuse you of partisanship or extremism in any form. The article was a model of sobriety, a fine job of journalism. That makes him look all the worse. But at the same time, it makes you look all the better. Even less reason for him to drop you now. And don't forget from your youth: the girl who gets three invitations to the dance can usually expect three more, whereas the girl who has no invitations generally gets none. The more you run elsewhere, the more attractive you become to *The Wanderer*.

At any rate, that is my assessment. You might as well act on it until you have reason to believe otherwise. The longer you are there, the better it is for you and for all of us. So please, don't do anything hasty.

If I am wrong and Al Matt gives you your pink slip, would you please drop me a line immediately? I will then get busy with *National Review* and *Human Events* and try to get them to accredit you as a correspondent. I think the accreditation will be no great problem, provided they are not committing themselves to accept any minimum number of articles. I suspect they will be glad to do it as a favor, just so long as they maintain their freedom of action about how often they ask you to write or accept one of your stories. So I think I can handle that end for you. But you can also get yourself named as *The Remnant* correspondent in Rome. Why not? The Italians don't know how small *The Remnant* is. Nor, for that matter, does it matter. But I will also try to get *National Review* and *Human Events* to use some of your pieces, not merely to accredit you.

I don't know about the book just yet. Shouldn't we wait until the dust settles? By all means, keep your notes. They will be priceless, not only now but in the future. This is going to be an important case, and its effects may extend into the next pontificate and beyond.

Incidentally, one of the things I pointed out to Al Matt when I was talking to him is that if he gives both sides of controversies like this, he can only enhance the reputation of his paper and get more people to read it. He seems never to have entertained this truism. He sounded as if he was wrestling with a new idea. And I don't think he gets new ideas that often.

In any event, don't lose heart. I think your position is a good deal stronger than you realize. But if the axe falls, please let me know right away.
Kindest regards,
Neil

☙

October 5, 1976

The Remnant
2539 Morrison Avenue
St. Paul, Minnesota 55117

Editor:
You are to be congratulated for publishing all those letters on the Lefebvre case that *The Wanderer* refuses to allow through its Iron Curtain. I refer particularly to the splendid letter from Michael Davies. That *The Wanderer* should publish an attack on him then deny him the right to reply is stupefying, the lowest sort of hit-and-run journalism. Even *The New York Times* allows people it criticizes the chance to respond.
Neil McCaffrey

☙

January 18, 1977

Dear Don and Georgeanne [McClane],
Thanks so much for your letter. About children's books, the main thing to do is to throw out all of them that are copyright after the early 60's. That applies to both Catholic and secular ones. Among the Catholic books, the Vision books are good. For that matter, any that predate the modern Church.

As for secular books, of course put in the classics. But also put in the so-called "trash" series. Kids love them; they are wholesome; they learn to read from them; and sometimes they learn things from them. I am referring to series like the Happy Hollisters, Nancy Drew, Judy Bolton, The Hardy Boys, etc.

Anything after the early 60's is wholly corrupt and is guaranteed

to produce mindless monsters, the sort who will soon be taking over the world.
Love,
Neil

P.S. I forgot to mention the superb C.S. Lewis series, *The Chronicles of Narnia.* I think there are seven of them, and they are available in a boxed paperback set from Macmillan. I think the whole set costs $8.95. There is no better buy in children's literature.

œ

April 11, 1977

Mr. Anatoli Kandalintsev
Information Department
Embassy of the Union of Soviet Socialist Republics
1706 Eighteenth Street, N.W.
Washington, D.C. 20009

Dear Mr. Kandalintsev:
[In response to a solicitation letter from the Soviet Embassy actually sent to Arlington House Publishers.]
I was glad to hear from you. For a long time now I've been nursing the dream of publishing the memoirs of Leonid I. Brezhnev. I've even come up with a working title: *Blood On My Hands.* But I am not wedded to this. If Mr. Brezhnev should prefer a less confessional approach, more of a success story, I suggest *The Slave Labor Way to Personal Enrichment.*

As to terms, I would not want to affront Mr. Brezhnev with the usages of a decadent capitalism. Royalties are only for exploiters. But since we pay them anyway (they are built into our system, like crop failures are built into yours because of that unfortunate 60-year drought), I propose an alternative use for the money: an extra crust of black bread for each citizen of the Greater Soviet Gulag Republic, to be distributed in Mr. Brezhnev's name on your next Festival of Proletarian Liberation.

How will we promote the book? I think a TV-radio tour would be best. Mr. Brezhnev will find friends in many a studio, as you know better than I. To be sure, we cannot afford to pay transportation for all the intimates with black hats that Mr. Brezhnev likes to bring along on his trips. Instead, I know many men in America—Poles, Ukrainians, Latvians, East Germans, Rumanians, Lithuanians, Hungarians, Jews, White Russians, Estonians, Bulgars, Slovaks, Ruthenians,

Czechs—who in a moment of weakness were lured here from the Workers' Paradise. They want to meet Mr. Brezhnev. They want to talk about the old days. They have messages for him. And they are eager to take care of his transportation. Free. At the crack of dawn, in the dark of night—it doesn't matter: their cars will be waiting.

Would you pass on my letter to Mr. Brezhnev? Or is that asking too much even of a Socialist Hero?
Cordially,
Neil McCaffrey

♋

August 30, 1977

Dear Bill:
Delighted you got the Davies books. In confidence, and in no particular order, I think the best choices for a perceptive review would be Auberon Waugh, Malachi Martin or Tom Molnar. I take that back: I have given you those three names in the order in which I would go after them, for reasons of style. Come to think of it, the perfect reviewer would have been Colm Brogan. He didn't write quite as well as Auberon, but he had made it his business to get closer to this subject. Nonetheless, Auberon would do a smashing job.

By the way, haven't you often thought that God was kind to take his father early in 1966? Sure, he was an irreparable loss; but I shiver to think of the state of his nerves and spirits after fourteen years of this Pope.
Best,
Neil

P.S. I just thought of a wild candidate for reviewer: Muggeridge.
♋

October 13, 1977

Mr. Al J. Matt, Jr.
The Wanderer
128 East 10th Street
St. Paul, Minnesota 55101

Dear Al:
I remind you that three issues have passed since you published Miss Surs's letter criticizing me. Even though you did not advise me that you were publishing an attack, I happened to spot it and sent

you a reply the following day. Needless to say, I expect my reply published. But not in the Christmas issue. Part of what you owe a person attacked is *timely* publication of his reply. Justice delayed is justice denied.
Cordially,
Neil McCaffrey

ᏣᎦ

November 30, 1978

Dear Bill:
I read somewhere that you haven't yet plotted your next novel. You have a great theme ready at hand. The central figure is a man named Johnson, first name not Lyndon. The only text you need consult is *The Banality of Evil.*

The challenge, of course, is to make the character convincing. Normal people, I sense, find the reality not quite credible.
Best,
Neil

ᏣᎦ

April 12, 1979

Dear Bill:
Garry's book just came but I have only finished three chapters. My impression is that he gets the NR situation about right, at least those strains of it that interested him. He always gets his facts screwed up, but so far I have not discovered the "heinous distortions" you referred to. He does distort our relationship, partly by omission. And he is simply wrong about our parting. I explained to him, not unkindly, that the nation's leading conservative publishing house could not bring out a book about the nation's leading conservative by a conservative writer who had become a pariah. So I told him to offer it elsewhere and return the advance when he was able to get the same offer from another house. (I did indeed argue with him about Wallace, as I argued with you and with many others, largely on the grounds that you were all being unfeeling about the legitimate grievances of his followers. Ho hum. Time marches on, and many of their gripes are today part of the received wisdom.) But it is always safer to travesty your adversary, especially when he drops you.

I've been speculating, you won't be surprised to learn, on why I get short shrift in the book—not, I hasten to add, out of my reserves of sour grapes. On the contrary, I might have come off far worse, given the poison in Garry's pen and his gift for selective recall. But I was probably his best friend from 1957 to 1968, not Frank: or, at the least, one of his two closest friends. But I emerge in this book in the same role as Waugh's man of business. Why? Let me float this as a working hypothesis. It does not do to get too close to one's man of business. In fact, it's infra dig; especially when the man of business comes to find one a bore, and worse.

So far, you don't come off badly. The real surprise of the book is—Natalie. One expects a certain chivalry; and it is fitting that the wife of a great man be herself a woman of parts. But Natalie as guru?

Which prompts a thought about our own situation. Have you ever noticed how talented people tend to underestimate mediocrities, their virtues equally with their capacity for mischief? Stalin in the early years was the toady, hardly worth noticing. Hindenburg, von Papen, the Right, the liberals—everyone found it distasteful dealing with the upstart Hitler, who however could be handled and, later, disposed of. Same with Johnson. Who could take him seriously? We forgot two cardinal lessons from Hannah Arendt: not only the banality of evil, but the hubris of the authentic megalomaniac, who sees himself as not only beyond law (of course) but even beyond normal calculations of self-interest. Thus, Stalin eliminates his senior officers on the eve of war. Thus, Hitler refuses to put off the Final Solution until after the war and use the Jews to build new bombs and run chemical plants, even declines to ransom them for $50,000 per head. These people are *above* mere calculation.

The collapse of the old company is accelerating [after Neil and his management team were fired]. The 'management' has now cut out virtually all advertising ("It doesn't work"), now dropping *Human Events* along with NR and all the minor conservative media. We of course see the deterioration many months before Sullivan & Cromwell, [arch reference to two men from Starr Broadcasting, in over their heads] because we know what *should* be happening and getting done. But even they are beginning to notice that, with all the 'economies', they are still getting in a bit more than half the cash they were getting in a year ago. I believe they can't sell now, while they are in effect in registration. So the value drains away, probably to the tune of $25-50,000 a month. If it had no liabilities, the company would be worth about $500,000 right now. But as best I can calculate, they owe about $400,000 on the note that Starr took out on the assets, which note the company is obligated to pay. So the real value may be something around $100,000. By the time they are in a position to sell, I would guess that this will have a negative net worth.

So, yes, it may then be available for a song. They will first try Richard Viguerie (already have, informally). They are assuming he is a sure buyer. They are assuming too much. If he passes, they will then probably shop it around, and get laughed at. At that point they *may* come to me. I would be interested, but only at a distress price. Anything more fails to factor in the blood and the sweat; so the hell with it.

Our present operation [Movie Book Club] is at the moment marginal. We have put in six months unscrambling the eggs and holding back the tide. Phase One is now largely accomplished. We are now on the threshold of moving from breakeven to profitable. But we are undercapitalized. So our alternatives are to crawl up the cliff by our fingernails, or to find some modest amount of outside cash with which to build the membership into a solidly profitable club. Stay tuned.

But this challenge (Operation Bootstrap *is* a challenge) does not exhaust our time or talents. We are busy hawking around half a dozen new business ideas—all of which regrettably require either the right company or the right venture capitalist.

Meanwhile, I fare well and the Lord treats me tenderly. I don't—*can't*—make enough here; but remember, I'm a huckster, a man of business. So I've been fleshing out my income, comfortably, with freelance assignments. I only wish I could say the same for Marvin, who is making less than two-thirds what he should be making. But talent is hard to come by, and that can't last.

Even my children, the Holy Innocents of the carnage, have come out not badly. Maureen is editing this Club, with half the responsibility she had at the old company and almost all the earnings (which however were a bit less than she should have gotten). Gene was running the warehouse at the old place and is doing the same here. (He is trying to become a rock guitarist, just in case you think God doesn't punish our sins here as well as hereafter.) Roger is working the conservative circuit in Washington, doing well enough for a beginner, and apparently happy to be flapping his wings away from the nest. Eileen, the only child not affected, was and is doing nicely at Bergdorf's and getting married in June. Susie, fired from her summer job, tried college, hated it, and is now doing well at a beginning job downtown.

Young Neil probably got the rawest deal, but will come out of it all just fine. He landed a stopgap job as associate publisher of *Change*, a "social science" boondoggle going to the academic community. He did a good job there, but *Change* is in the process of going broke, so just a week ago he lost his job. Fortunately, he foresaw this and had been looking around. I would guess that he will have a better job before the month is out. But even if he must wait longer, we can keep him in eating money with work around here until he finds what he should get. He has two young children (both admirable, I can't help adding) yet bears up cheerfully under his responsibilities and hard knocks, I guess because at the old company he had already proved to himself that he is good. (He kept AH sales at the same level in a period when we were cutting back our new books by one-third. He inherited one of the most chaotic order departments in the business, one that had been mishandled for all its life, and left it probably the best, with receivables down from 25% of sales to 10%: and no other publisher can make that statement. In two years as rights manager out of the fourteen years AH had been running, he sold 20% of all the rights the company had ever sold. He is not a literary type, but he just plain gets things done. Know anybody who needs a good administrator?)

For all that we have survived, and wonderfully well, the wound heals hard. We all left part of ourselves behind. When you spend fourteen years rearing a lovely maiden, you have to weep when you see her after nine months among the white slavers.
Best,
Neil

P. S. My last official act at the old company was to edit and do the jacket copy for *Mitre and Crook* by Canon Bryan Houghton. (I *hope* somebody proofread it.) Now it's out, the best book yet on the crisis in the Church, and, believe it or not, stylish. It's a novel of sorts, in the *Screwtape* vein, and may be the best book we ever published. You'll find yourself underlining on almost every page.

೮೩

May 21, 1979

Dear Bill:
I should now be ten months beyond being shocked at anything that comes out of Starr. But I confess to being stupefied at Alt's words. As to motivation, I doubt that he would do anything without orders from on high. The motives for this order are not hard to guess. Caliban knows that what you are told will get back to me, and perhaps also circulate throughout the Right.

As usual, this latest leaves me with conflicting emotions. I never fail to be dumbfounded that people can lie so shamelessly. I guess they get to enjoy it, a frightening state. But they must also regard you as a mark, because they take very little trouble to lie convincingly. If things are going so well, how do they explain dropping advertising in your magazine, and virtually everywhere else? Why do the bills date back to February? Why are books being held up because there is no money for paper?

If book clubs stop promoting, they can stanch their losses for a time. But the business runs down—while inventories swell.

The germ of truth in what Alt tells you is probably this. Last third quarter sales dropped sharply. We had high accounting fees (which Starr promised to pay and then characteristically reneged on). We had very high legal fees, an outgrowth of our trouble with the FTC (fees we would not have had had Caliban followed my advice; instead, he hired a fancy Washington law firm which, $40,000 later, came up with the same recommendation I had made from day one). We ran some big, expensive ads. When I saw that the third quarter was going to be bad (after the record-smashing first six months), I decided to take writedowns that I would normally take at year-end.

Result: a loss of $100,000. Therefore, by dint of freezing *all* expenditures that can possibly be avoided, they may well cut the loss for this quarter. But that is meaningless. A sophisticated observer would compare cash flow in the two quarters (down almost half this year), sales (down at least twenty five percent off our poor third quarter last year), size of membership, and of course inventory turnover.

If things are going so well, why have Starr and Disney auditors descended upon the place, a mere two months before the regular audit? But on the assumption that things are as Alt describes, may I suggest a journalistic coup for NR? It may be a departure for you, what the hell, blaze a trail. The article might be called "Recipe for a Tired Capitalism". Your reporter describes a small publishing complex that to the simpleminded might have looked successful: started on a shoestring in 1964, the $100,000 shoestring being redeemed with interest two years later; operated at a profit for thirteen of its fourteen years, with the loss in one year attributable entirely to expansion; operated all that time without a dime of outside financing, and with bills almost always discounted; operated at a profit in a field where *nobody*—in books or magazines or newspapers—had *ever* shown a profit—the innocent, it smells of success.

Enter a dynamic manager, unencumbered by inhibitions or knowledge of the field or the care and feeding of quirky subsidiaries and their managers. This man happens to have a precious number two man earning $81,000 a year who nonetheless can be dispensed within a matter of days. Very well, but what *are* the talents of this marvel? Character? Intelligence? Experience? Sensitivity? Drive? Marketing sense? Does he work sixteen hours? (No, not sixteen hours a week.)

But maybe something else explains the sudden blossoming of what was once thought to be a successful company. Could it have been the New Methods? The nice clean Break with the Past? The marvel fires or drives off most of the key people. Their ragtag replacements have one refreshing quality in common: *no* publishing experience. (The pattern begins to emerge: away with the old management team, with their hidebound half-century of experience. *Anyone* can publish and sell books!)

The work habits of the new team? *Relaxation* is the watchword. Work just happens, doesn't it? And if it doesn't, we'll call a meeting (between three and four—between lunch and the cocktail hour).

But I have given you enough. You must do the rest of the legwork. After you do, I hope you will follow up with a piece on Idi Amin's economic breakthroughs.

On second thought, do that story first. Leave the publishing story to *Fortune*. If Alt and his master are telling you only half the truth, they rate a *Fortune* cover.

Best,
Neil

ગ

December 15, 1982

Dear Mr. Selig [Commissioner of Baseball]:
I would like to propose a name for your commissioner hunt. The chances are good that you have heard of Victor Gold, though you may not think of him in this context. As it happens, however, Vic covers every base you will want to touch.

If you know about him, it is undoubtedly in connection with his roles on the national political scene over the past two decades: assistant press secretary in the Goldwater campaign; press secretary to Vice President Agnew; speech-writer for Vice President Bush.

If these jobs seem to place him too much on the Republican side for the baseball commissioner, a few points should allay any fears you might have about that. Vic is a Southern Democrat by heritage, and that may be why he has always been singled out for his friendly and straightforward handling of the Washington media corps, who are mostly Democrats. Many books on the Goldwater campaign and the Agnew business mention him, and always favorably. Check him out with the big guns: [Washington journalists] Jack Anderson, John

Chancellor, David Broder, Theodore White, Bob Novak, just about anyone. I think you will discover that nobody will give any Republican higher marks both for professionalism and for character.

So Vic is a master at keeping a generally hostile media purring. Heaven knows baseball needs a man like that. It comes from his background in public relations, where he was an account executive for a major national agency before hanging out his own shingle.

But please don't expect a conventional PR man in Vic. He is easily the most creative and savvy one I have ever encountered, and that takes in some names you would recognize.

And along with his inventive ideas goes a rare ability to articulate them, both verbally and in writing. Vic has heavy experience as a television commentator, where of course he must think fast, come up with the right answers, and state them persuasively. He was a syndicated columnist, has several books to his credit, and has published in a good share of the prestigious national magazines. If part of the problem of the present commissioner is a wooden manner and a clumsy way of expressing himself, baseball can leave all that behind with Vic.

But let me circle back over a point I just touched upon, because it shows why baseball would recapture some lost respect with Vic. When the Agnew trouble started, the media people smelled blood. They were out to get Agnew—and as events proved, they were right. Where was Vic Gold in all this? Being loyal—and almost singlehandedly getting his boss whatever good coverage he was getting. But then, no sooner did it come out that Agnew had been lying than Vic promptly resigned. He too had been had. But as long as he believed that his boss was telling the truth, he performed masterfully for him.

Before his PR and media work, Vic was a practicing attorney during the Fifties. Where else are you going to find a man with his communications expertise and with a legal background as well?

But that's still not all. His knowledge of baseball and a few other sports is awesome. But here again, don't take the word of an admiring friend. Test him. Talk to him. Make him talk to and answer questions from the most knowledgeable baseball people you can call on.

Finally, my last and probably central point. I have been hiring people for twenty-five years, and I have picked some prizes—in both senses. After many years and a series of good and bad calls, I came to a conclusion that has never deserted me. Perhaps you have come to the same conclusion. Character comes first. Make no mistake. I'm not undervaluing professional talent, as I think my remarks above will indicate. But it all takes second place to integrity. With character, you have the discipline to work around the clock if you have to.

You have the honesty not to double-deal. Above all, you have the strength not to wilt when they turn up the pressure-cooker. (And nothing in baseball, even a strike, can match the pressure under which Vic has already performed with conspicuous grace.)

As you have guessed, I write as a good friend of Vic's (for upwards of twenty years) and no apologies. But I do want to assure you that I am writing on my own, simply because I believe your job cries out for a man of Vic's stature. He knows nothing of this letter.

I ask you only one favor. Have one of your people give Vic a preliminary check. His address is 6309 Beachway, Falls Church. Virginia 22044. His phone number is 703-998-7711. He will pass this test; I am willing to make a sizable bet against reasonable odds that you will find nobody in your search that has his qualities and talents. Class is in short supply these days, but not where Vic Gold lives.
Kindest regards,
Neil McCaffrey

P.S. One experience I've had with Vic over the years may be instructive. I am not generally lumped among the stupid, yet I've never spoken to Vic that I haven't learned from him. For all their closeness to the game, the club owners—and the players too—would have the same experience. Vic Gold would show them fresh, original ways of looking at problems they have been worrying about all their working lives.

അ

April 15, 1983

The Wanderer
201 Ohio Street
St. Paul, MN 55107

Editor:
Richard Myers objects (April 14, 1983) to a statement in the Conservative Book Club ad offering the original McGuffey Readers, the 1836-37 edition. Our ad spoke of later editions as "still excellent texts, but no longer Christian texts." If Mr. Myers had troubled to check with the Club or with the publisher of the original Readers, Mott Media, before going public with his complaint, either Mott or the Club could have supplied him with overwhelming documentation for this simple statement of fact. Indeed, he need only have consulted the definitive book on the subject, *McGuffey and His Readers: Piety, Morality, and Education in Nineteenth-Century America* by

John H. Westerhoff III. In these pages Dr. Westerhoff underscores our point in elaborate detail. E.g.:

> "McGuffey compiled the 1836-37 edition of the Reader . . . numerous significant changes were made by the various editors of the series, the most dramatic changes being found in the 1857 and the 1879 editions. While McGuffey's name continued to be carried on these radically revised editions, he neither contributed to them nor approved their content. . . . Few lessons from the 1836-37 edition are to be found in the 1879 edition. . . . The theistic view, so dominant in the 1836-37 edition, slowly disappears. God is mentioned more rarely: in one lesson in the 1879 edition of the First Reader, in two lessons of the Second Reader, in four lessons of the Third Reader, and in just ten lessons of the Fourth Reader. While each of the 1836-37 editions contains numerous stories from the Bible, the Sermon on the Mount and the Protestant version of the Lord's Prayer are the only pieces of scripture to remain in the 1879 edition.

> "None of the first edition emphasis on salvation and piety remains. In their place is a morality of industry, self-denial, sobriety, thrift, propriety, persistence, modesty, punctuality, conformity, and submission to authority. The spirit of self-reliance, individualism, and competition fill the 1879 edition. Virtue is rarely its own reward, but material and physical rewards can be expected for good acts. Likewise, wickedness will be punished. It is hard work and frugality that bring prosperity. Responsibility for success or failure lies with the individual. No matter how bad life may appear, however, persons should be satisfied with their lot and not be distressed over any present social, political, or economic arrangements. Still, the affluent should use their wealth in socially responsible ways."

In short, precisely as we describe the later editions: "still excellent texts, but no longer Christian texts." The Westerhoff book, incidentally, was first published by Abingdon in 1978, so it can't be dismissed as a puff for the original McGuffeys. When Mott Media reprinted the originals last year (the first reprint in nearly a century and a half), George Mott bought paperback reprint rights to the Westerhoff book because it explains so convincingly why Christian readers will prefer the 1836-37 edition. (It also makes interesting reading in its own right as a slice of Americana.) Mott Media distributes the Westerhoff book free to buyers of the McGuffey set, and so does the Conservative Book Club.

When George Mott told me about a year ago of his plan to bring

out the McGuffeys, I have to confess that I was surprised. Why yet another set when at least two are available? George explained that his would be the first edition. Still in the dark, I asked him why. After all, later editions of classics usually incorporate improvements, or else why do a new edition? Then George told me why the first edition was unique. He explained that the secularists, led by people like Horace Mann, were already working their changes in the public schools, and these changes were reflected in the 1857 and later editions of McGuffey. So we decided to sign up the set for the Club, with results I can only call spectacular. I think George Mott rates an award for imaginative Christian publishing.
Neil McCaffrey

ও

April 15, 1983

Dear Mr. [Al] Matt:
I'm enclosing a letter for publication [the preceding letter], in reply to the Myers attack on the Club's McGuffey ad. Beyond that, however, I must say that I think *The Wanderer* could have handled this with more consideration for the Club. Print the letter, of course. But why hold it for six weeks until we run the ad again? Or if this seemed to you the right time to run the letter, and in the most prominent spot at that, why did you not give us a chance to reply in the same issue? That would have been courteous, though of course not mandated by journalistic practice.

Yet when you run the letter without a reply in the very same issue in which we run the ad that offended Mr. Myers, it begins to look like a scene out of a Marx Brothers movie—except that a faithful advertiser got pie in his face, from the blind side. I assume that you won't be billing us for the ad.

Actually, however, I have an idea that could come closer to restoring equity. We will pay for this ad and you will reciprocate by giving us a free rerun in the same issue in which you run my letter; and, I should add, you will run my letter in the same top spot that you accorded Mr. Myers for his attack. Fair enough?
Cordially,
Neil McCaffrey

ও

February 6, 1989

New York Times Book Review
229 West 43rd Street
New York, New York 10036

Editor:
Having recently laughed my way through *The Body Politic* by Victor
Gold and Lynne Cheney, I began your review wondering what parts
Julia Johnson would find funniest. Before I was halfway into the review
the light began to dawn: I was reading a *tour de force*, of sorts. Miss
Johnson had managed to read this comic masterpiece without allowing herself one smile. It was as if one had turned to the movie page
and read: "*Duck Soup* is the only film in the Marx Brothers *oeuvre* that
deals with larger themes. Yet as a political statement it remains unre-
alized. Groucho, cast as the reformer, displays nothing of the vision
one expects of such a figure. Fredonia, scene of the struggle, manifests
none of the preconditions for revolution adumbrated by the eminent
thinker who, alas only by coincidence, bears the same surname as
the starring brothers. Margaret Dumont provides the only moments
of significance. Passive and helpless, she is the symbol of Woman as
plaything in the dark ages just now ending. Yet this bold portrait is not
enough to redeem a trivial film, even in an election year."

Next time you plan to review a book on Italian opera, keep the
Times standard flying. Take care to send the book off to a reviewer
who is tone-deaf.
Neil McCaffrey

ॐ

August 16, 1985

Dear Mr. [Michael] Koplen:
Funny, I approach your letter with something of the same feeling of
pessimism that prompted you to write. In fact, my first instinct was
not to reply. But then I reflected that, even though we disagree on the
point you raise, you are probably a person I would be glad to have as
an ally on most issues.

I dare to hope that you will be less angry and more understanding
if we trade hats for a moment. Consider the poor Christian, now for a
generation a member of the dispossessed majority. When he turns on
the tube or goes to the movies or picks up a magazine, chances are
good that he will see his moral sense and beliefs under assault (much
as you and your Orthodox Jewish friends do, I was glad to note in

your letter). It gets to us after awhile. We have feelings too. When somebody pricks our finger, we also bleed. And please don't think I'm exaggerating. Rev. Wildmon gives example after example, but he has simply tickled the surface.

How would you react to this? How would you respond if Jews were routinely portrayed unsympathetically and Jewish values routinely mocked or travestied?

And what if, at the same time, you noticed that Christians were generally portrayed with sympathy or at least with understanding, and Christian values respected? You would begin to suspect that people who exercised influence in the arts and the media were either out to get the Jews, or at least were insensitive to their concerns.

My own conviction (and I suspect I am typical) is that most of the people we are talking about, whether Jewish or Gentile, are at least insensitive to what I care deeply about, and at worst hostile. I think we are talking not about a conspiracy in the flamboyant sense but rather a generalized attitude. Nothing you say will persuade me otherwise; but I also believe, when I put it in these terms and you think about it soberly, that you will find it hard to disagree with me—especially if you number yourself among those of your friends who won't turn on the tube or go to the theater, or at least will do so only with caution. Our backgrounds and beliefs differ in ways you and I are both aware of, but they also coincide in a host of critical areas.

What is the answer? I don't know, but I suspect that the suit by the ADL that you mentioned in your letter is a gesture in the right direction. I can't imagine on what grounds the suit could be successful because anti-religious writing and entertainment are protected under the Constitution. Nevertheless, the instinct is generous and reflects a handsome concern for our bruised sensibilities. Jews are highly visible in entertainment and the media, so I think that Jews who don't share the media views should make it a point to dissociate themselves from these attitudes. My Jewish friends (none of them as far as I know Orthodox, though most of them generally conservative in their attitudes) think as I do about the media people; and I am equally sure that your Christian friends are not anti-Semites.

I am entering your resignation from the Club as you instructed, but I dare to hope that you may some day reconsider. In fact, if you will let me, I'd be glad to send you a copy of the Wildmon book with my compliments. If you look through the whole thing you will undoubtedly find passages you disagree with, but I am confident that you will wind up putting the author on the side of the angels.
Kindest regards,
Neil McCaffrey

P.S. A Jewish friend called me just the other day. He is a writer. He had thought of a clever phrase. He explained the context of what he was writing and then gave me the phrase: Immaculate Perception. "I'm calling you because I don't want to be insensitive about this. What do you think of my using that?" "Well, Vic, you know I'm not a fanatic about these things." "I know. That's why I'm asking you." "Well, whenever I run across something like that my first reaction is to gasp inwardly. Then, if I like the writer, I begin to reflect, to rationalize, to make excuses, to 'understand' what he is really saying." "Okay," he interrupted. "You've answered my question. I won't use it." I'm still not sure he shouldn't have used it. But I did appreciate his sensitivity. We need more of it.

⅓

Allen Brodsky
Bensalem, PA 19020

August 18, 1985

Dear Mr. McCaffrey:
I have been a happy member of the Conservative Book Club for three years now; you offer many valuable books that aren't always available at my local bookstores, and you offer these books at significant discounts.

However, I was disturbed by one of the main selections in the August Bulletin, namely, Donald Wildmon's *The Home Invaders*. The Bulletin contained this quote from Wildmon's book: "Buchanan was no doubt referring to the fact that Hollywood and the theater world is heavily influenced by Jewish people."

Aside from being ungrammatical, this sentence is classic anti-Semitism. The bulletin goes on to quote another paragraph in which Wildmon takes the old anti-Semitic line that there is a Jewish conspiracy, in this case to keep Christians out of "the theater world".

One gets the opinion Christians aren't allowed to gain positions of influence.

It shakes my confidence in the Conservative Book Club that your reviewers would not only recommend this book, but that you would publish an anti-Semitic passage in the Bulletin to show this book's purported virtues.

I hope you'll drop Wildmon's book from your list, and, in the future, avoid the danger of letting your agreement with part of a writer's book blind you to a reprehensible undertone in it.
Yours truly,
Allen Brodsky

And Rightly So

August 26, 1985

Dear Mr. Brodsky:

Your thoughtful letter deserves a serious reply. Maybe if we trade hats for a moment you will sympathize with the position of Christian conservatives. Imagine yourself a Christian conservative. Almost every time you turn on the tube or go to a movie or pick up a magazine, you see your moral sense and your Christian values under assault. This has been going on for a quarter of a century. Suddenly you realize that you are a member of the dispossessed majority. This is painful.

Now put aside your Christian hat and resume wearing your yarmulke. Suppose you had been noticing for a quarter of a century that the media were dominated by Christians. No problem there. But suppose you also observed that people obviously Jewish were often portrayed invidiously, and almost never with sympathy and understanding. Suppose you also noticed that Jewish values were usually depicted in caricature or openly attacked. If at the same time Christians and Christian values were portrayed sympathetically or at least with understanding for their faults and quirks, wouldn't you begin to suspect that the media were out to get the Jews?

I recommend the article by Nathan Perlmutter (an old Club author, by the way) in the September 6 *National Review*. His point is that Jews should have the right to react to anti-Semitism; and I don't know anybody who would rise to challenge him. Rev. Wildmon is making the same point for Christians, and I think if you look at it in that context you won't disagree. By the way, he says explicitly in the same passage that it would be equally wrong to treat Jews as Christians are treated on the tube.

I don't, of course, hold to a flaming conspiracy theory, and I suspect most Christians would agree with me. But I am absolutely certain that there is a generalized anti-Christian attitude on the part of most media people, whether Jewish or Gentile. Since no such anti-Jewish attitudes would be tolerated, and since Jews are highly visible in the media, you can understand why Christians feel put upon.

All that Rev. Wildmon is asking is something like the equivalent of an Anti-Defamation League for Christians: not as far as I know in any formal sense, but in the sense that the same sensitivity to Christian feelings would be manifest. In short, sauce for the goose.

Kindest regards,
Neil McCaffrey

ॐ

March 12, 1986

Dear ———:
Just a line to thank and congratulate you for the wonderful affair.
[Murray Rothbard birthday dinner]. The note of bloated solemnity
was blessedly absent, which makes it unique. When I think back on
all the similar affairs I've attended, my eyes glaze over. They are all a
blur, and I guess it's just as well. But this is one that Joan and I will
both remember, and Neil and Maureen agree. Call it a celebration of
friendship without tears.

Speaking of which, I'm sorry to report that Neil has pneumonia.
Thank the Lord, he seems to be mending. Now our problem is to
keep him from coming back to work too soon. He had a fever of
104 on Friday—and came to work on Saturday! That boy needs
watching.
Best,
Neil

ॐ

December 29, 1986

Dear Holly & David [Franke]:
Thanks so much for your nice card. I was taken with your new
address. Though I hope the Lord allows me to die in my own
home, I have always felt that if I were starting from scratch I would
live on Tory Lane in Scarsdale. But now, all things considered, I
think I would opt for Poverty Hollow Road. What a coup you have
pulled off!

Things are going nicely at CBC. Membership is now around
38,000, a record. I think we have a pretty good chance to pass
40,000 in 1987.

If you ever get down this way, pop in and fill us all in on your
doings.

All the best for the New Year.
Best,
Neil

ॐ

June 1, 1987

Rev. Harold J. Drexler
St. Luke Catholic Church
First and Chestnut
Hopkinton, IA 52237

Dear Father Drexler:
On behalf of Father Blum, I would like to thank you for your letter
of May 26. Please know that the Catholic League shares your anger
and frustration at the way in which anti-Catholic bigots use isolated
examples of homosexuality among the clergy to defame the entire
Catholic Church.

At the same time, I do not believe that Father Rueda's intention
in writing *The Homosexual Network* was to provide ammunition for
the enemies of his own church to assail the priesthood, although
the book could obviously be used for that purpose. He intended
rather to document the extent to which a small but vocal minority
of homosexuals and homosexual sympathizers have come to dictate
official policy in the Church.

It is certainly a prudential question whether or not this kind
of information should be brought out in public and Catholics of
good will may well disagree on this point. However, as far as I am
concerned, Father Rueda's sincerity and right intentions are beyond
doubt. Furthermore, apart from the standard sensational type used
to sell books, I could find nothing seriously objectionable in the
Conservative Book Club ad.

Nevertheless, I appreciate the opportunity to respond to your
letter and I am passing it along to Father Rueda and the Conserva-
tive Book Club in case they would like to speak in their own defense.
Sincerely yours,
Kevin G. Long, Ph.D.
Director of Public Affairs

CC: Father Enrique T. Rueda
       Mr. Neil McCaffrey

03

June 8, 1987

Dear Kevin:
A nice reply to that crank letter. The notion that God is served by
covering up scandals certainly dies hard, if it dies at all. And of

course, it continues to extend all the way up to the top, as witness the way they have handled the Vatican bank scandal. It is an attitude that grew up in plain defiance of the Gospels. But there is no arguing with this mentality.

That was a most perceptive review of the Bozell book. You are too young to remember Brent's serial afflatuses, but you went to the heart of his problem with rare insight.

Be sure to visit us again next time you are around.

By the way, Brent started *The Warren Revolution* in 1964 or probably earlier, but he didn't finish it until the year we published it. This would be 1967, if memory serves.
Best regards,
Neil

ଓ

July 7, 1987

Dear Art [Arthur J. Donovan, Jr.]:
I take the liberty of calling you by your first name because we almost know each other. Your father and mine were close friends, maybe best friends, when they were growing up together in Highbridge. For some reason they didn't see each other much after they married and moved out of the old neighborhood. My folks moved up to Pelham in 1930. I don't think our parents socialized much. My father and yours would run into each other at sporting events and sometimes at NYAC. Sometimes I was there, and you can bet I was in awe of your father because I was a sports fan. In truth, my own father grew a few inches taller when he told me that he and your father were good friends. But he didn't have to tell me. I remember when they met once after not having seen each other for several years. Let me tell you, it was an emotional meeting. You say in your book that your father was not an emotional man. Neither was mine. But they all but embraced—in an age when men just didn't do that. Your father called mine "Neilie", the only person I ever heard call him that. They talked long about the old days, and made great promises of getting together. Unfortunately, that didn't happen often—if at all. I'm not sure.

As you might gather, I gobbled up your book, especially when you were talking about the old days. Another funny coincidence: when we moved up to Pelham, we lived across the street from the Smiths. So I've known Howie since before I reached the use of reason. (I was born in 1925. Your publicity says you were born that year but the book says 1924. I think the book is right, from internal evidence.) Howie is still around, spry and alert for a man who must be close to 80. I'm sure he will be thrilled with your book.

Yet another coincidence: my mother's family, the Watermans, moved back to the Bronx in 1935. They found themselves with a big house in Pelham, not much money, and only two of the seven children still living at home. So they moved down to an apartment a block or so away from you, on the Concourse half a block north of St. Philip Neri, on the southwest corner. I don't recall hearing that they and your father ran into each other at Mass, but they probably did. And I think they would have known one another, because the Watermans also came from Highbridge.

I'm sorry Jack Coffey talked you out of going to Fordham after the war. We sure could have used you. I guess you helped beat us once or twice, not that it was hard. But actually, if we had dumped Danowski and kept Lombardi instead of the opposite, Fordham football after the war would have been a different story. As it is, we were pretty good in 1949 and good enough to get a bid to the Gator Bowl (8 won, 1 lost) in 1950; a bid we turned down because the Jebbies no longer had their heart in football.

I read your book in galleys, just finished devouring it. We won't be able to use it in our Club. Too much macho language for our conservative members. But I do want to urge you to do one thing. On pages 81-83, you reproduce a section from your father's diary. It bowled me over. I can't remember ever reading a finer piece of sports writing, and I'm including Red Smith. Your father was a vivid writer, a stylist, and he had something to say. After all the times I've seen films of that fight, and after all I've seen written about it, it was like reading about it for the first time. The reason, of course, apart from the fine writing, is the fact that your father saw the fight with the eyes of a pro. He saw things nobody else saw.

Anyway, what I'm getting at is this. You should take that section and get your agent to send it to a major sports magazine. You are sitting on something of real value. Better than that, you should go through the diary and put together several such articles. If enough of the diary survives, you will have a number of publishable articles, and I hope a book. Not only will this be an incomparable record of many of the greatest fights in history by the greatest referee; it also captures a whole era, and a different (and better) way of looking on life.

Your father's writing is a minor miracle. I don't suppose he ever wrote anything for publication. I don't suppose he ever thought of himself as a writer. But believe me, he was one. He could give us all lessons.

How to explain this phenomenon? It isn't just an accident of talent. People from his generation were better schooled. And it helps to be a first or second generation Irishman. That soil seems to grow people who know how to use the mother tongue.

Good luck with your book. And please, share with us more of that treasure you are sitting on.

Best regards,
Neil McCaffrey

CB

February 11, 1988

Dear Patti and Vic [Lasky]:
We were all heartsick to see what they did to you. God help anybody who has to trust himself to an American jury, especially as presently constituted.

I can only guess at what a bitter blow this is to you. I wish I had the power to repair some of the damage. The only consolation, and it isn't a small one, is that you have bounced back from some bad times before. You can do it again. You both have your health, your marbles, your friends, and especially each other. I would take bets that, after you take time to recover, you will be all right. If we can cheer you up or help you in any way, you know our number. For that matter, don't be shy (though I know you are) about asking any of your friends for whatever kind of boost they can give you. Don't forget, you do have friends, probably more than you can even remember. And good ones.

Chambers, alas, was right. We are the losing side. But any slob can be on the winning side.

Love,
Neil

CB

December 23, 1988

Dear Vic [Gold]:
I was able to work in another plug for the book on the back page of the enclosed Bulletin, in the "And Rightly So" column.

But I confess that I blush to show you this Bulletin. Can you spot the typo on the front cover? The long dash is missing before "and". I guess it bothers me more than it bothers the members. Our artist got cute and had the printer run the dash in another color, black. The printer, no master, sometimes forgets to do this. We usually catch it. Not this time, alas.

The good thing about being a perfectionist is that it holds down the mistakes. But the pain can be severe, because perfection is elusive.

And that is my message for the old year. Have a good new one.
Best,
Neil

cs

December 29, 1988

Dear Helen [Mrs. Michael Bernstein]:
You probably sent us a copy of Jonny's article (really two articles) in your role as Proud Mother. But we take it as a favor, because we really were interested in reading it. It has already routed throughout part of the family, and Joan and all three boys are as enthusiastic about it as I am. You and Mike gave a lot to both of your children, and it comes out here (as elsewhere).

Jonny did everything he had to do, and more than most reporters do on assignments like this. Like all of us, I had admired the Savimbi side from afar. Jonny gives us the feel of the movement, the texture, and now we admire them even more. Jonny is comfortable with ideas, as we would expect of a Bernstein; but not in kneejerk fashion. He captures the present ambiguity of the movement; it is really in transition right now. But more than all that, he is almost unique on our side, a superior journalist. If he were on the other side, his report would at least be considered for some kind of award.

I have to add a minor editorial carp (if I don't, I may lose my union card). I found a few spots dense, heavy going. He crowded so much information into a few paragraphs and a few over-long sentences that I had to stop and go back to get my bearings. Shorter sentences and gentler transitions would have taken care of that problem where it arose. And I realize that the trouble spots (not many, to be sure) were probably not his doing. I am well acquainted with the problems of last-minute copy fitting. It simply goes with the job. There probably isn't a writer alive who hasn't suffered from this.

Please give Jonny our congratulations, and be sure to keep us alerted to his new assignments. We mean to follow him all the way to glory.

From all of us to all of you, a very good New Year.
Best,
Neil

03

December 30, 1991
MEMO TO: Roger
FROM: Neil

[Re Bill Buckley's attempt to undermine Pat Buchanan's presidential campaign by implying in *National Review* that he was anti-Semitic.]

The only effective way to deal with Buckley is not to deal with him at all. To reply is to dignify his attack, to make it respectable and even friendly. His aim: to destroy with a smile. In his peculiar code, that is the behavior of a gentlemen.

To refuse a reply, whether public or private; to refuse in fact to take his calls or to see him—that will shake him up. It will spoil his strategy. His strategy is to pretend that his was friendly criticism. He wants, always, to have it both ways. His tactic through the years, whether he has actively destroyed somebody or allowed that person to be destroyed, has been the "civilized" stab in the back. But this requires that the victim stand still for the stabbing. Nothing will disturb that ego so much as being ignored. Remember, his latest stab in the back is going to cost him something in friends, in money, in readers. To reply is to make his knifing respectable. To decline to reply is to shake him up. Nothing is gained by replying. Nothing is lost in this case by silence.

If Pat [Buchanan] continues to do well, he will begin to sweat in earnest. There are signs that he is beginning to already.

Some might argue that it is better to make peace and make friends. But a false friend like that can continue to do damage; whereas keeping him at a distance can do no harm, since he has already done his worst. The real meaning of his attack could not be clearer: he aims to destroy what he can't control. He brooks no rivals.

But the cardinal point should never be forgotten (though it must be taken on faith among those who haven't had dealings with him): keep well out of the range of that devilish charm of his. Few are proof against it. Remember the fate of our mother Eve . . .

I look upon this as the latest chapter in the life of Dorian Gray.

03

January 22, 1992

Dear Murray:
Roger tells me that he enjoyed every minute of your talk, though he

never expected to sit through any talk of ninety minutes and want more. I hope you publish it.

The enclosed article by Tom Bethell is judicious.

Did you see where Jeff Hart is now co-chairman of the New Hampshire effort? A deft flick in the direction of his boss.

Speaking of which, I have a theory. My first thought on reading Rosenthal's attack on Buckley in yesterday's [New York] *Times* was: good for him. He got what he deserved. Now I have second thoughts. I'm all but certain that Bill solicited this. He will run it in his book. It will enable him to pose as the sovereign mediator between the two extremes. Above all, it will soften some of the wrath of our people.

Of course, it is all contrived. The man is Mr. Devious. The true mean between two extremes is not the one that happens to fall into the middle. It is the one that is right. In this case, we have one strident attack then one sneak attack by Bill. The latter poses as moderate, and as such will deceive the mindless.

Love to Joey.

Best,
Neil

○З

August 26, 1993

Dear Dr. Smant [Dept. of History, Indiana University, South Bend]:
Thanks for your interesting letter. I'll be glad to contribute some recollections of Frank Meyer. I counted him a close friend. Yet part of his genius for friendship was in making literally scores of people think that each was among his special friends. I guess I *was* among his close friends; say, his twenty-five or so closest friends. But not, I think, among his very closest, say his five or ten closest friends. I do know that we spoke by phone several times a week. We spoke so often, in fact, that our long conversations were cutting into my reading time and I had to ask him, clumsily, if perhaps we could ration our conversations. The truth is that, living in his mountain eyrie, he craved stimulation and got it over the phone. I think he lived vicariously by way of those of us who led more active lives. I first met him around 1957 when I began doing circulation promotion for NR on a freelance basis (when I was working at the Doubleday book clubs). So I knew him for fifteen years, until his death. In fact, we went up and said goodbye a couple of days before he died. He was only half conscious. I helped arrange for my old priest friend, Monsignor Eugene V. Clark, to visit him at the end and, as it turned

out, receive him into the Catholic Church.

I don't have many letters either to or from Frank. As you suggested, he much preferred to use the phone. His phone bills (paid by NR) were astronomical. Like many an old radical, he slept through the day and worked and talked and read through the night. It was no use calling him before four or five in the afternoon. When we spoke, we gossiped about what was going on among conservatives, argued about politics and religion, and in general exchanged ideas about anything and everything. Frank was always involved in ideological arguments between the (relative) hardliners and (relative) pragmatists on and off NR. Although I tended to side with Frank, I also felt that he exaggerated the differences between himself and his *bête noire*, Jim Burnham. But, old radical that he was, he tended to transmute even personal squabbles into ideological disputes.

His mind was much sharper than his heavy-handed literary style would suggest. The style went with the territory. Those old Communist thinkers carried heavy ideological baggage. But Frank's mind was as sharp and quick and pointed as his writing was labored. He also had a keen knowledge of psychology and how it could be turned against people when he analyzed them. Yes, Frank had an instinct for the jugular. In fact, I think he overindulged it. Rarely did he describe anybody, even his very closest friends, without adding a few notes of denigration. This of course made him superior to the person he was denigrating. It was not one of his nicer qualities.

But don't let me leave with negative feelings. Frank was a fascinating companion and a loyal friend. Yet one had to realize that he was always aware of one's failings; perhaps more aware of them than anyone this side of the friend's wife. He was a pitiless judge of human frailty.

He was always fascinated with the Catholic Church—and, characteristically, thought he knew more about it than he really did. But, like many an intellectual of his day, he had great respect for the Church (at a time when the Church commanded more respect than it does today). I was always at pains to tell him that he really didn't know nearly as much about the Church as he thought he did. And in fact I think I taught him as much about it as anybody. I have to add, however, that I was surprised when he elected to be received into the Church on his death bed. I never thought he would take the big step.

Have I been of any help? I hope so.

Good luck with your biography!

Kindest regards,
Neil McCaffrey

And Rightly So

☙

May 12, 1994
MEMO TO: Murray Rothbard and Company
FROM: Neil McCaffrey

May I make a suggestion? You know I'm going to anyway, so what the hell.

When Murray goes off on these long discussions of foreign policy, I urge you, solemnly, not to lead off the issue with it. This is the time to lead with Lew, who collects lively items that stir the blood; or with Joe, always graceful and usually provocative and quotable. This suggestion, I think, is especially pertinent now that you have so many new readers who were attracted by the promise of liveliness rather than learning.

When Murray does something more on our minds, like murder in the White House, then of course lead off with him. But do think like good journalists. Run the hot stories up front.

If you can uncover three of your readers who give a damn about Bosnia and Haiti, I will buy you a gourmet dinner at the nearest hamburger stand.

☙

July 20, 1994
MEMO TO: Murray
FROM: Neil

I thought your remarks on McCarthy generally sound and valuable. But Bill Buckley and Willi Schlamm get a bum rap. In truth, no group did more to keep McCarthy's name alive than NR. I know. I was there.

First, let's get our chronology right. Joe was censured in the fall of 1954. NR made its debut one year later. The second issue featured a major cover story by Joe himself (actually by Brent, of course). Subsequent issues for the next year carried frequent references to him, invariably favorable. He died exactly one and a half years after the magazine's founding, in May 1957. The issue after his death was a memorial issue. Editors and contributors contributed heavily. They managed to touch most of the bases, and it was a powerful vindication. None, incidentally, wrote more powerfully in that issue than Willi. His piece was an uncompromising defense of Joe and a savage attack on his enemies. By the way, when the news came out

326

that Joe had died, Willi was in the office. He wept. Years later he wrote for others, but as far as I know never repudiated Joe. I might add that I write this not as a buddy of his. I didn't hate him, but I found him unlovable.

As for the magazine itself, by coincidence I began doing circulation promotion the very month of Joe's death. From then until 1959 or 1960 (and Goldwater), almost all of our promotions were built around Joe. They went out by the hundreds of thousands every year (an unheard-of number in those primitive times when conservative mailing lists hardly existed). They were explicitly—and if I may say so, powerfully—pro-McCarthy. And the results proved it. The first or McCarthy wave of NR promotions raised the circulation from 17,000 to about double that. It saved the magazine (not that you would ever know it from anything anyone has ever written about NR).

As for Bill himself, his second wave of prominence after the Yale book came as Joe's most eloquent and popular apologist. I refer not only to his book but to subsequent writings and speeches, like the piece he featured in the magazine and reprinted in *Up From Liberalism* about that con man who fooled all the liberals, Paul Hughes. I remember one talk he gave in the late Fifties or early Sixties, one of his most stirring. It all led up to a blockbuster peroration: "You see, we are McCarthyites." It brought the audience to their feet, roaring.

The truth is that Bill has carried Joe's cross with him into the liberal world. I was long afraid that he would find a way to get out from under. He has resisted that temptation—and I'm sure it was a temptation. Instead, he adopted essentially the position Sam Francis asserts (long before Sam used it): Joe made his mistakes, but they are as nothing compared to the enormities visited upon him. Nothing wrong with that. In fact, it has the merit of being not only rhetorically effective, but true.

To carry the point further, I think you should make a resolution to become a slave to accuracy when you attack somebody. What good is an attack if it doesn't respect the truth? But beyond the moral dimension, when you give an opponent full marks where he deserves them (and every opponent deserves some), you make your criticisms more credible.

Finally, I can't resist descending to the ad hominem level. As the lawyers say, you "opened the door". Where were you, old man, when Joe was looking for defenders?

ⵢ

August 4, 1994

Dear Murray:

A fine reply. Between what you say and what I say, I think we have hit upon the truth. Bill has certainly not pushed McCarthy over the past three decades. I think it is partly that he is weary of it, and even more that he sees no future in it. I think he feels comfortable only as part of the right wing of the Establishment, and this has been true for a long time. At the same time, however, my point was correct. He has never stabbed McCarthy in the back.

I was delighted to read your adventures rousing the rabble. I had no idea. I don't, as you know, put anything like the conspiratorial spin on many of these events that you do. So I regard Bell, Viereck, Kempton and such as simply liberals reacting to Joe—as well they might have, since he represented a much greater threat to them than Hitler ever did. By the same token, however, people like Cohn and Schultz always tried, for the most part vainly, to accommodate liberal anti-Communists. Our crowd felt the same way, but we were never under any illusions that people like Nat Weyl went all the way with us. Joe and his followers, let us be clear, never thought of themselves as a great populist uprising. We really did consider Communism and its allies the main enemy, and were therefore more willing than you to tolerate liberal anti-Communists.

I still think that was the correct posture for the period. But now, of course, we are in an entirely new situation, and the notion of making common cause with Sidney Hook types is not far from grotesque. And this is doubly true as modern liberalism plunges ahead on its rake's progress. I now think it represents a greater danger to souls and to civilization than even Communism.

By the way, I have to laugh at these heavy liberal thinkers like Lipset. They impute to the Birch types their own levels of hatred. In reality, the Birchers are mighty sore; with good reason. But their anger is like the squabbles of children by comparison with the hatreds of the Left. And I am talking about the respectable Left.
Sincerely,
Neil

ɔ෪

On Frank Meyer
(April 3, 1972)

Frank Meyer died two days ago. In that time two problems came up. My first instinct was, "Call Frank." Then I remembered.

But there was nobody else to call, and there won't be. There will never be another Frank Meyer.

When Frank signed on with the Right about two decades ago, he found a decentralized conglomerate of Taft Republicans, Southern Democrats, fundamentalist Protestants, anti-Communist Catholics, free enterprisers, disaffected Marxists, and even a sprinkling of literary romantics. It was messy, and Frank decided it needed tidying up. So he sorted everything out, and it became the conservative movement. Though his construct may never achieve political power, it remains a *tour de force*.

Frank reminded Americans (and we need reminding) that we are heirs of the Christian West. So when he asked, a few hours before his death, to be received into the Catholic Church, it was a homecoming. The angels had been expecting him.

But now we are left without our mentor and gadfly and friend. Still, I think Frank will be even more helpful to us in the years ahead, now that he's Home.

Neil McCaffrey
President, Conservative Book Club

附

5

Music, the Good Old Days, and Life in the City

Music, the Good Old Days, and Life in the City

To The Editor   March 1955
The Pelham Sun

At first glance, the proposed town library looks like a project thoughtful citizens should support. Let's take a second glance.

Our neighbors in New Rochelle and Mount Vernon maintain excellent city libraries. Both libraries serve populations about five times as large as ours, and they receive funds correspondingly larger than a Pelham library could hope for. This, of course, means that they can buy more books. Furthermore, these libraries have been in existence since 1893 and 1896, respectively. The titles they have amassed over the years—books for the most part now out of print—give them collections that a new, smaller library could never equal.

These facts might be interesting but irrelevant—except that Pelham residents can use either of these libraries for a moderate three dollars a year. In other words, we not only have two better libraries nearby, but using them costs a mere fraction of what we would spend to build and maintain our own. All this, and economy too.

If the choice were between a town library and no library, most of us would vote for the library, and never mind the expense. A library is, after all, one of the adornments that distinguish a community from a menagerie. But fortunately, our alternatives are not so stark. We have these two neighboring libraries glad to serve us: our admittedly inadequate North Pelham library; libraries in all the local schools; and two libraries maintained by local churches. Surely, Pelham has plenty to read!

Bloated federal and state budgets are pretty much beyond our control: local expenses are something else again. In this age of swollen taxes, nothing else than harsh necessity should induce us to add this—or any—major item to our town budget.
Neil McCaffrey

ᘓ

April 1, 1955

Mr. Ed Browne
The Pelham Sun
89 Wolf's Lane
Pelham, New York

Editor:
Mr. Richard D. Mathewson states the case very well for the proposed town library.

His first point is what the philosophers might call the Argument from Civic Pride, and it is a strong one. Anything that makes us more appreciative of our local heritage is all to the good.

His second point is equally telling, reminding us that even a small library has resources far beyond what appear on the shelves. Users of the North Pelham Village Library might bear in mind that they can draw on larger libraries when their own can't fill their needs. But this, unfortunately, is no help to residents of Pelham Heights and Pelham Manor.

If Mr. Mathewson's third point is true, that a town library would cost each of us between $3.50 and $5.00 a year, then he has made a convert. Let's start building right away! But are these figures accurate? Is it possible to buy land, build a library and maintain one for a few dollars a year per family?

This appears to be the crux of the matter, and the supporters of the library would do a service to the town if they would furnish an estimate of the total cost.

Mr. Arthur John Egan takes his stand for quality over quantity. Few will dispute him, though it is possible to question whether this principle applies here. A big public library buys mediocre books when mediocre books are being published. Its book purchases can only reflect the current output. Is this any less true of a small library? Mr. Egan thinks that a small library will concentrate on quality, yet drug store libraries are the smallest of all—and the least selective.
Sincerely yours,
Neil McCaffrey

&

June 7, 1960

Dear Garry [Wills]:
Dr. Swaim, our Protestant advisor at the National Council of Churches, had this to say about your manuscript: "The author has a genuine feeling for the subject, and the chosen passages are given effective settings—they are made to shine like a jewel in a ring." Dr. Swaim is like this.

He proposed a few minor changes which seem all right. At any rate, I don't propose to show them to Stachen, who is one of our tamer authors.

With fingers crossed, I reiterate that the Baptism will be Sunday, at three. All the monsters are over their chicken pox, and it only remains to see if Susan gets it. We rather think that she won't. If she is to get them, they will hit sometime from Friday through Monday, so you may be getting a last minute call from me. But why don't you plan to come; I think it will be safe to bring the baby. We can keep him and Susan apart; at the same time we can discuss their marital arrangements. I intend to be very tough about the dowry.

Directions: stay on the Parkway a couple of exits beyond where you got off for the old house, to Sandford Boulevard—last exit before the toll. Right on Sandford to first light. Right at Wolf's Lane for about one-third of a mile. Left at Esplanade. (Note that Esplanade is a broad street divided by a large island. Each side of the road goes one way, so to go left you must go beyond the island.) Stay on Esplanade till it stops, then right on Grant for two blocks. Right at Washington. We are toward the end of the block on the left side, and our name is out front.

Why don't you plan to arrive early to allow for the catastrophes—and of course plan to stay for the evening. If Natalie decides not to risk John's health, we insist that at least she come.

Would you return these clippings Sunday?

Best,
Neil

ા

September 27, 1960

Dear Bill [Rusher],
I was delighted to learn from one of the disciples that you will be bringing the gospel into this heathen land I inhabit on October 25. My first thought was to ask you up for dinner that night, but it would be too hectic with you having a time schedule to meet. So why don't you join us for dinner at Abe Levine's, where you will be fortified with a good steak and less than ten minutes' ride from the place of your lecture.

The schedule would work out well. I could meet you at either the 4:55 or 5:15 train; we could pick up Joan and allow the children five awe-inspiring minutes with you; and be off to an early and leisurely dinner. I hope you can make it.

Sincerely,
Neil

ા

June 12, 1963

Dear Bill [Rusher]:
I just returned from the luncheon Pete O'Donnell and Larry Douglas had for about twenty of us in communications. I saw Rita [Bree] and

learned that the New York office was being closed.

This seems shortsighted to me. Granted the [Goldwater] national headquarters should be in Washington, but New York is still on the map. Not only is it the communications capital; the folks out there think of it as a kind of national capital. You're not really big time without a New York office. If they close down here, I think they will find in a matter of months that they are obliged to reopen. Indeed, a booming movement should have a psychological drive aimed at opening a few more offices. No big outfit can get by without branch offices.

Maybe you can make them see the problem in these larger terms. I do think it is important.
Best,
Neil

P.S. I mean, are they fully aware that almost any communications activity must limp if it doesn't emanate from New York?

ൡ

542 Main Street
New Rochelle, New York
June 30, 1965

The Standard Star
251 North Avenue
New Rochelle, New York

Editor:
Until recently, the railroad station was the only place I know of where a person could get a shoeshine in New Rochelle. Lately the stand at the station has been closed.

This points up an opportunity for some enterprising young man. He could get himself a shoeshine kit and make a regular tour of the stores and offices along the main thoroughfares in the city. After a few trips he would discover that he had many regular customers. He could make himself a good deal of extra money. As a matter of fact, many men do this very thing for a livelihood in New York. They make regular trips through certain office buildings and show up every three or four days. They have their regular customers, and apparently they are able to make a living from this.

We hear a great deal these days about unemployment among our youth. Is there no old-fashioned enterprise among them?
Cordially,
Neil McCaffrey

ᲝᲘ

May 12, 1967

Dear Gene:
I am sorry they made you Monsignor. It has led me to a crisis of
faith. I don't know why this should be.

But I am glad you got the office, before they abolish it.

My prayers will follow you in your awesome new responsibili-
ties.
Best,
Neil

ᲝᲘ

March 2, 1968

The Pelham Sun
89 Wolf's Lane
Pelham, New York 10803

Editor:
Four cheers for the Pelham Civic Association and its constructive
report on our schools. The air always clears when someone dares to
point out that the emperor is wearing no clothes.

The strategy of Pelham's educationist establishment has been
transparent from the start; transparent but slick. The ploy has been
to beg the question, to assume that we have to spend millions more
on schools, to move the issue from "Shall we spend it?" to "How
shall we spend it?" Now they stand exposed, and Pelham owes the
PCA its thanks. Several million dollars worth of thanks.

The PCA report points up the contrast between creative private
groups and the ritualistic, bankrupt response of the establishment.
Like their heroes in Albany and Washington, Pelham's bigtime
spenders have no answer for any problem but higher taxes. And, if
no problem exists, they'll invent one.

Could the PCA now be prevailed upon to run a rival slate for
the Board of Education? And maybe to do away with that clubby,
self-perpetuating charade laughingly known as the Citizens Nomi-
nating Committee?
Neil McCaffrey

ᲝᲘ

337

And Rightly So

April 9, 1970

National Review
150 East 35th Street
New York, New York 10016

Editor:

The main trouble with the Rolling Scum is that they gather so much dross. Take Tom McSloy. At first glance I wondered that a hobble-dehoy's rant should provoke such agonizing. Yet on second thought I'm glad your staff took the trouble to lay it on the line—once and, let's hope, for all.

My objections to rock are fourfold: moral, cultural, political, musical.

Moral: as an unapologetic traditional Catholic, I abhor a music that glories in vice and attacks the laws of God not just incidentally, but right down to its rotted core. And I think my response would be no different if I were a traditional Protestant or a traditional Jew.

Cultural and political: your staff said it all, most notably Messrs. Meyer and Rusher.

Musical: rock is square, fellas. *Square.* A bore. It has nothing fresh to say, and never did. If any of you had ventured uptown to the Apollo back around 1941, you could have heard some fourth-rate jump band like Al Cooper and His Savoy Sultans playing much the same music, only better; and they were fourth-rate. Those of us who have been swinging for 30 or 35 years don't need musical lessons from the zoo. The rock beat is to the jazz beat as a pneumatic drill is to Michelangelo's chisel. Rock chords and harmonies are to jazz what a men's-room scrawl is to a Renoir.

Ah, but doesn't rock have "soul"? Perhaps, but only in the sense that rotgut retains a little of the qualities of vintage wine. People like Big Bill Broonzy and Bessie Smith were folk artists. As such, they worked with limited materials. But they explored them in depth, with dignity and economy, with an instinctive restraint that conveyed a feeling of power held in reserve, above all without pretension. But now their bastard offspring are run to seed, and what comes out is a sub-animal caterwauling that defaces the name of music.

Neil McCaffrey

☙

June 2, 1971

Editor
New York Magazine
207 East 32nd Street
New York, New York 10016

Dear Sir:
I remember Bob Daley. He was the class cut-up in freshman year. Lots of laughs. We were sorry to lose him, when he had to do freshman year all over again.

Bob was so repressed at Fordham that I'm not surprised he recalls so little about the place. Girls, for example. They were all over campus. Except for two colleges in the university, Fordham was always coed. The graduate school, which Bob tells us he attended, was coed. I bet Bob really has sat next to a girl in class. If only the Jesuits had told him how to spot one. (Yes, they did know how.)

Bob's religion may have deserted him (before Fordham, I suspect), but his wit hasn't. He has a wonderful time at the expense of your readers. Not for him the hoary tales of Jesuits with horns. Better a tall one about Hemingway proscribed. But come to think of it, maybe Bob really thinks he was forbidden to read Hemingway. I can almost hear Father Hennessy now: "No Hemingway, Mr. Daley, till you turn in that term paper that's three weeks late!"

And all those religious exercises Bob was forced to attend. There were two: the annual Mass of the Holy Ghost to open the academic year, and the annual three-day retreat (a blessed break from classes, to those of us less studious than Bob). Bob reveals that they left grooves in his soul. I wonder.

I took the same 48 credits in philosophy and religion as Bob. That's why I went to Fordham. Why did Bob go? By the way, they came not to "almost half" the curriculum but to 48 of the 138 credits I took. Bob gives us a clue to his scholarly habits when he identifies Father Gannon, in the days of Fordham's football power, as America's best-known cleric. I think he confined his researches to the pages of the *Fordham Ram*. Elsewhere, (the then) Monsignor Sheen and Dr. Fosdick were making a bigger splash, to say nothing of Father Coughlin.

Some Bronxites will be surprised to see the neighborhood around Fordham, c. 1950, described as a Catholic ghetto. For his next assignment, I hope you send Bob to Tel Aviv. He's sure to come back calling it priest-ridden.

For all my quibbling, I have to agree with Bob's main thrust: he

does belong on the Fordham campus today. Catholics don't. In fact, Bob would be more at home there than at his present job as PR man for the New York cops, who don't need this extra burden.
Neil McCaffrey (Fordham, 1950)

ᘉ

June 11, 1971

Dear Bill:
I always knew that Starr owned rock stations. Apart from finding all such stations unappetizing, I confess I never really focused on the matter until the article in *New York*. The article (a brilliant job, by the way) left me feeling sick, and angry, and unclean.

I'm juggling a lot of hats as I write this letter. I'm writing as a friend, as a fellow Catholic, as an ally in the struggle to salvage something of a good country and a great civilization, as a not insignificant stockholder, as the chief executive officer of the most profitable segment of your business (or the second most profitable, if you count the television station and if it surpasses us; I don't know). No matter what hat I wear, I find myself saying the same thing. And I can't find any soft, comforting words to describe corrupting the young. For anyone to do it is wicked, morally despicable. For you—for *us*—it is doubly evil. I only hope that you were less aware of what went out over the airwaves than—well, than you should have been. Fortunately, I think there is one way to rescue this ugly situation. But first I would like to explore other possibilities that I am afraid you might have recourse to.

Joan and I spent a long time thinking and talking about this last night. Our worried guess is that your first instinct will be to fire back, to try to make this another debate. This would be the worst possible response. Souls and lives would continue to be wrecked, and evildoers would chortle, pleased to have such a prestigious spokesman. It won't do, either, to chide the people responsible and tell them to tone things down. These are people who have shown they can't be trusted. The first time, you might have been innocent; I hope so. But now the thing is out in the open, and the only proper moral response is to clean house. "Fool me once, your fault. Fool me twice, my fault." Toning things down isn't enough, now. If a toned-down station does only half as much damage, that is still a terrible burden to take to the Communion rail, or to the grave.

Financially it might be rewarding to sell off these stations, but I think we must be prepared to forego that route. It would be dirty money, and the poison would still pour out, though from different dispensers.

I think you do have one recourse, though it won't be easy. I think you should announce that the offending stations will change their policies immediately, and clean house. Not only that, but I think you can prove your concern by calling on fellow broadcasters to do the same, by mounting a campaign to stir up public opinion against the corrupters, by pouring on the heat in every way you can. This would be the decent thing to do, the noble thing. It would restore your moral authority.

I am aware that this could cost you—*us*—money, at least for a time; though I'm not even sure of that. After all, we accounted for half of Starr's earnings for the first nine months. If you divide the other $160,000 or so among some eight radio stations, we aren't talking about imposing amounts. But no matter. We are talking about something much more important: Harry and his little needle, Charlie and his Molotov cocktail, Sally and her dose. The decision has already been handed down for us: "He that shall scandalize one of these little ones that believe in me, it were better for him that a millstone should be hanged about his neck, and that he should be drowned in the depth of the sea."

Of course there are other considerations, not unimportant, except by comparison. There is your position, everything you have come to stand for. Please, Bill, don't imagine you can brazen this one out. It is too serious in itself, and too damaging in the terms set forth so devastatingly in the article. It is as if Comstock had been found out owning a brothel. Two of our people came into my office yesterday to tell me about the article before I had read it. Independently, they both said essentially this: it will ruin him on the Right, with the *non*-kooks. I have since talked about this with seven other people, some of whom work here and some of whom don't. People of various ages and backgrounds. One was of two minds; the other six think that you must act to correct the situation.

I do hope you realize that this *cannot* be transmuted into a conservative cause. I don't say that all your legions would desert, only most of them. As for the loyalists, they and their standards would never be the same again, because they would be in the impossible position of having to defend drugs and revolution.

Bill, this is a nasty business. But not so nasty that it can't be turned around. If you can set a good example here, rally broadcasters and listeners, and stick to the campaign, it will be recorded as grace seized, your finest hour.

But I don't pretend it will be easy. I'm having a Mass offered for you.
Best,
Neil

P. S. Another point made by three people and implied above but not made explicit: "Oh, the *good* he could do with those stations!"

☙

To Bootleg or Not to Bootleg
[*Libertarian Review,* September, 1975]

I am sitting here breaking the law, sort of. I'm listening to a bootleg recording of Benny Goodman playing in the Manhattan Room of New York's old Hotel Pennsylvania on October 30, 1937. How come I don't feel guilty?

As the record business boomed in the sixties, record piracy boomed right along with it. It's no great trick to pirate a record, and even easier when you pirate it on tape or cassette. So free enterprise flourished—*really free* enterprise, since the pirates paid nobody.

They were taking advantage of a loophole in the outdated copyright law of 1909, which gave no protection to recordings. The record companies, with their enormous royalties and selling costs and overhead, found themselves undersold by parasites who simply copied every hit record. Artists and composers got no royalties. Correcting a manifest injustice, Congress made record bootlegging a criminal offense in 1972.

But, perhaps because of inhibitions about *ex post facto* justice, Congress applied no sanction to copiers of pre-1972 records. Subsequent legal decisions seem to open the door to prosecution of the latter, but the situation is fluid at the moment. Up until now, it hasn't deterred the pre-1972 pirates.

While pop and rock hits were attracting pirates who peddled albums and tapes in the hundreds of thousands, the same *methods* were available to, and used by, aficionados of opera, and classical, jazz, and show music. Though the profit motive was hardly absent from their reckoning (despite the pretensions of a few who are always prepared to nominate themselves as Altruists of the Month), devotion to a favorite kind of music figured prominently in their motivations. More to the point, their bootlegging filled a need. Why not, they reasoned, turn a profit for providing a service—and, not so incidentally, for taking some risks, financial and otherwise?

So another brand of record bootlegging has emerged over the past decade, and it poses tricky legal and ethical questions. Since I'll be dealing with jazz records in this column, many of them bootleg, it might be interesting to *LR* readers to explore why the bootleggers now dominate jazz issues of the twenties through the fifties—in my judgment, the golden age.

A bit of history will help explain what gave the bootleggers their opportunity. Record companies mushroomed after World War I. Then the Depression and the rise of radio staggered the industry. Only three companies survived the shakeout: RCA, Columbia, and Brunswick, the last two merging in the mid-1930s. Decca, launched in 1934 and now absorbed by MCA, soon established itself as one of the Big Three. Thus, three labels took care of virtually all recording from the early thirties until the mid-forties—essentially, the classic period of jazz and dance music.

Note that this was also the era when you heard the big bands on late-night radio over all four networks—every night, as regular as the 11 o'clock news today. At the same time, home recording appeared: not tape, but discs on which you could cut radio broadcasts, or even family arguments. This, in fact, was the source of Benny Goodman's famous Carnegie Hall concert album. The results were usually listenable but sometimes atrocious; I have more than a few on which an eloquent sax solo gets interrupted by a blast of static. Two selections from the Goodman concert recorded so badly that they had to be left out of the Columbia album.

RCA, Columbia, and Decca thus own most of the popular recordings from the golden age. Individuals own the airchecks they laboriously recorded on their primitive home equipment. All but a handful of the recordings have long since vanished from the catalogs of the Big Three, victims of changing tastes and the "latest-hits" plague. Are these records to be lost forever, save to the dwindling band who collect old 78s? The thought offends: we are talking about the golden era of the most creative popular music the world has ever known (unless, perhaps, you count opera in its creative years as popular music).

So thank the bootleggers, and their customers. It still isn't a big business. It's a crew of entrepreneurs with offices in their basements. As the business grows, *if* it grows much more, it may become big enough to attract lawsuits calculated to discourage all but the manically litigious.

Are we talking about a nonissue, a few intrepid Robin Hoods ripping off big bad General Motors? Not quite. First of all, I can't buy the notion that big bad General Motors, or RCA, is fair game. Moreover, the musicians and composers may also be getting shortchanged. The composers are easily disposed of. Most of the best are organized as the American Society of Composers, Authors and Publishers (ASCAP), the rest as Broadcast Music, Inc. (BMI). These groups negotiate performance fees with broadcasters, record companies, and such for the use of compositions by their members. Some bootleggers pay these fees. Those who don't, should. The matter of bandleaders and sidemen is more complicated. Where leaders were paid a flat fee for a record, there's no problem. They sold all rights to the record company. Where they had a royalty deal, surely the bootleggers have an obligation to honor it.

The sidemen are no problem as regards record dates. They were paid for them, But what about the rash of aircheck LPs? These were originally broadcasts, for which the musicians were paid. Nobody dreamed they would one day be issued as records.

The nabobs at the musicians' union have no doubts on this issue. They say that every musician must be paid union scale for these airchecks, just as if the sidemen had gathered in a recording studio last week. Not only that, but they want the boys paid at today's scale. The rate for a three-hour session, once $30, is now up around $100. The union allows four tunes per session. For a typical album of 12 songs, that's $300 per man: for a big band, $4,000 to $5,000.

Can you picture some little guy who bootlegs a pressing of maybe 500, even 5,000 records contemplating artists' fees of that size? They are formidable enough to discourage even the industry giants from issuing airchecks of anyone more obscure than Glenn Miller. A classic case of union greed killing the goose that lays the golden egg. Union rates make it all but impossible for the visible companies, those vulnerable to union reprisal, to issue aircheck albums. Result: the albums are bootlegged, and musicians get—zilch.

The plot thickens. We now come to the cultural dimension. Should the Big Three be allowed to sit on perhaps 99 percent of the material they recorded during the golden years? They are not interested in reissuing most of it (or find it unprofitable, which comes to the same thing). Ah, you say, why don't they *license* the little guys to do these reissues? Why indeed. I've tried to get licensed. Friends of mine have tried. You're lucky if they talk to you long enough to say no. (I have a theory about why this happens, and it may be worth a footnote in *The Organization Man*. The big boys make little or nothing on jazz reissues, what with their big overhead and all. They are budgeted for blockbusters. But if they license the humble 500-10,000 sellers, and a little guy does modestly well with them, somebody upstairs is sure to ask why the hell they are "giving" away the company product. So they don't "give" it away. In a perverse way, the frightened organization men probably *prefer* bootlegging to licensing. Bootlegging spares them the anguish of Making Decisions.)

Is this, then, a classic confrontation between property rights— those of the Big Three—and what might be called, ever so loosely, the cultural rights of society? So it seems, at first. But I think the union and the Big Three have boxed themselves into a false dilemma.

The union, quite simply, shouldn't be so greedy. It should accept a simple royalty payment for the musicians on aircheck albums, a modest cost that the entrepreneur can figure into his price and work off *as he sells his albums*. In other words, the *consumer* would pay. And should.

The record companies might adopt the rights provisions that are conventional in book publishing. When an author signs over book rights to a publisher, the contract provides that the author may recover his rights if his book goes out of print for longer than, typically, six months or a year. Surely this is fair all around. If a publisher (record company) wants to retain rights to a book (record), he owes it to the author (artist) to keep it in print. Why should RCA retain rights to thousands of recordings they haven't made available for thirty or forty or fifty years? Does an entrepreneur have the right to suppress a significant part of a cultural heritage?

Whatever the answer, there is no prospect for a solution that makes any effort to reconcile the several interests. The music business, never a haven for the ethically sensitive, is reverting to the jungle; and to pursue the metaphor, I would cast the musicians' union as the wild boars. All of which leads to a log-jam of snarling selfishness—which, predictably, the free market rushes in to break. People want this music, and if they can't buy it from legitimate companies they'll buy from bootleggers.

Every now and then, however, one of the giants bestirs itself. RCA did, about five years ago, with its splendid Vintage series. It ran about a year, yielded maybe fifty albums, then dried up. Now RCA has started another reissue program.

Remember the old Bluebird label? Launched by RCA in 1933 to compete with the cheap dimestore labels then flourishing, it was the home of most of the better Artie Shaw and Glenn Miller records, not to mention hundreds of pop, jazz, hillbilly, and blues artists of every sort. Now it's back, the vehicle of the most ambitious reissue program ever undertaken by any label. *Item:* They're promising the complete 1935-39 Benny Goodman corpus—the "King of Swing" years. *Item:* They're promising Glenn Miller from 1939 through 1942—complete except for a score of early records that are more curiosities than musical achievements. *Item:* They're even doing dance music. *George Hall and His Taft Hotel Orchestra* 1933-1937 is already out, a pleasant, unpretentious period piece featuring then-famous vocalist Dolly Dawn and her little-known, more interesting predecessor Loretta Lee.

Producer Frank Driggs has made other wise decisions as well.

Every album is a double and sells for a tempting $7.98. Every album comes with a full battery of discographical and personnel data and informed liner notes. Every selection is programmed in chronological order—valuable for tracing an artist's development.

The new line debuted with a blockbuster, *Willy Bryant and Jimmie Lunceford and Their Orchestras 1930-1936*. Why combine the two bands? It was an imaginative response to a numerical problem. Bryant recorded 22 songs for RCA, Lunceford 10. It works out just right for two LPs.

Willie Bryant's band is all but forgotten today, but it provides an example of a generalization I'm willing to defend across the board: even the minor Harlem bands of the thirties swing. They are, in fact, a revelation, especially when compared to what came after. They almost never took themselves seriously. They were low-key. Whether playing jazz or pops (and no decade yielded more and better pop tunes than the '30s), they played for dancers or for one another, not for the galleries.

Something else. These records were all issued as 78s. That is, the artists were limited to not much more than three minutes per song. This made for economy, and I suggest that economy and discipline are hallmarks of superior art. The arrangers had to fashion a three-minute cameo. The soloists had to say it all in 8, 16, at most 32 bars. Contrast the self-indulgence of the typical LP: the solos go on and on, till the soloist is exhausted. (The listener has usually arrived at that point long since.)

The Bryant sides are a fair cross-section of what a second-rank band recorded in these years—a band that had to settle for mostly second-rank songs. There are jazz originals and standards, pop tunes, novelties. Especially the latter. Bryant was mainly an entertainer.

But whatever the genre, bright arrangements and convincing jazz solos abound. Teddy Wilson, just before he joined the Benny Goodman Trio, is featured on piano on six tracks, as tasty then as now. Famed tenor saxophonist Ben Webster blows five of his earliest solos, not ponderously as in his later work. Most of the soloists, however, are little known - and the more interesting for bringing us the delights of discovery. Note especially trumpeters Richard Clark and Otis Johnson, tenor saxist Johnny Russell, trombonists R.H. Horton and Johnny Haughton, alto saxist Stan Paque.

If the Bryant tracks are good, some of Lunceford's are classics. "This band was the bridge," observed the band's arranger-trumpeter Sy Oliver recently: the bridge that brought Negro bands to the attention of white audiences. So it was. Sure, whites were aware of Cab Calloway—for his novelty songs—and Duke Ellington—for his pop songs. The Lunceford band captivated white and black alike.

It deserved to. These records, among the rarest he ever recorded, capture the band when it was just finding the style that made it the most influential big band in history (save perhaps for Fletcher Henderson, Benny Goodman, and/or Count Basie). How to describe the style? Its main feature was a unique approach to the four-to-the-bar jazz beat. It was twobeat, but *not* Dixieland twobeat. It was much lighter, more subtle, *easier, looser* than the Dixie beat, Credit arranger-pianist Ed Wilcox, arranger Oliver, bassist Moses Allen, above all drummer Jimmy Crawford.

Another Lunceford trademark was its careful treatment of pops. Other bands played pops perfunctorily. Never Lunceford. Two obscure tunes here are small miracles of song and performance. May this album rescue from undeserved obscurity "Leaving Me" (by Fats Waller and Andy Razaf) and "Remember When" (by Will Hudson and Eddie Delange—remember the old Hudson-Delange band?). The typical dance band arrangement of 1934 sounds quaint today. These date not a bit; and in their day they opened up new possibilities for dance music. Trombonist Henry Wells renders the lyrics with warmth, understatement, and musicianly phrasing. (My one beef, incidentally, is that Driggs reissued take 1 of "Remember When." It has two clinkers, which he could have avoided simply by reissuing take 2.) "Breakfast Ball" shows how the band could tear into a rhythm tune, this one by Harold Arlen and Ted Koehler from *Cotton Club Parade* of 1934. Alto saxist Willie Smith, most famous soloist in the band, shines here on vocal and alto. And don't overlook Eddie Tompkins. Here and through the thirties he plays most of the jazz trumpet with the band. I can think of no defensible reason why he was never given his due.

The first thing that strikes you about the band is its brilliant section work. The brass could roar and soar, but they kept it light and buoyant (at least until the forties). None of your Kentonesque walls of sound. The reeds, led by Smith and anchored by baritone saxist Earl Carruthers, were voiced wide and contrived to sound at once light and gutsy, and always swinging. A consensus of informed opinion would probably call this the greatest sax section of them all.

Did you think I had forgotten Lunceford's flag wavers, "White Heat" and "Jazznocracy"? They're both here. A white band, Glen Gray and the Casa Loma Orchestra, pioneered breakneck tempos. It remained for Lunceford to marry speed and power. These pieces may not bowl you over in the post-Kenton, post-Herman Herd era; in 1934 they were awesome. Not the band at its musical best, they became two of its most popular jazz efforts. Ironically for those Crow

Jim critics who reflexively assign white jazzmen the role of copycat, both are the work of composer-arranger Will Hudson. (Reality tends to disappoint ideologues.)

To sum up, the Bryant sides are good, and may introduce you to an abiding pleasure in the jazz experience, the minor Negro bands of the thirties. As for the Lunceford tracks, most are indispensable. And if you need another reason for buying the album, your purchase will encourage RCA to liberate more treasures from the vaults.

∞

December 1, 1975

Dear Murray:

Thanks for the nice review. I'm so glad you enjoyed the set. It makes a song buff drool, doesn't it?

I also enjoyed Curmudgeon. I like the way you act as the conscience of the movement, as with your strictures on libertarian rip-off artists. But I'm surprised that you're surprised at libertarians falling for these con-artists. Most libertarians, like most people, aren't ruled by reason. Man is made for God, and when he rejects Him, he sets up false gods. Nowadays they take the form of ideologies or gurus, if ever man rises above one-track-mind sensuality. Hell, some of them even try to make you a guru, but you are missing two essential qualities: mendacity and hubris. Honesty keeps breaking through, so you will never do for them. But the growing popularity of libertarianism is more psychological than intellectual. They are looking for an excuse to do as they please.

Back to music. I have been over the years mostly a band/musician buff. But over the last decade or so, I've also become something of a song buff, like you. Which gives me an idea. How would you and Joey like an evening of excellent to great songs that you've never heard? Come as you are. Come to dinner. But we won't set a table. We'll just usher you into the record room. I will go through the collection and find rare gems. I will avoid the warhorses. I will not descend below the excellent level, so none of the songs will be merely very good. I will try to stick to great songs, but I don't think I have quite that many obscure ones to get us through an evening. But I won't descend below excellent ones.

If you like the idea, also let me know a dozen or so of your favorites that you haven't heard for a while. I might not have all of them, but chances are good that I have most of them.

But if you don't like the idea, don't be shy. Tell me. After all, if I am playing songs that you haven't heard before, they might be a

little harder to enjoy. After all, you have no previous associations to fall back on. You have to learn the songs right then and there. So in a way it is a little harder than just playing the warhorses. Harder, but I think more rewarding for a buff. I can promise you some gems.
Best regards,
Neil

ꜩ

January 5, 1977

Dear Gene:
Mary Lou [Williams] belongs in the jazz pantheon. Not among the twenty or so who form the first rank; but comfortably with the few dozen in the second rank.

Yet she and Cecil Taylor (a hopeless modernist) will have no easy time filling Carnegie, notwithstanding the fact that she spans half a century and can play any style. She was always admired and still is, but she is no big draw at the box office.

I do sympathize with her, trying to impart a feeling for jazz to young barbarians who have thrown away their heritage. But that is the American story. Meanwhile, keep her the hell out of the sanctuary. Jazz isn't that kind of music. But that's another story.
Best,
Neil

ꜩ

January 24, 1979

"Best Bets"
New York Magazine
755 Second Avenue
New York, N. Y.

Dear Ms. [Ellen] Stern:
I think I have the Best music/food/ambience Bet in town for you. Have you been up to the Red Blazer Too at 1576 Third Avenue, between 88th and 89th? (The "Too" is correct. There is another Red Blazer, and I guess somebody got cute with the name of the second place.) Food?

Quite good, and the prices are more like 1969 than 1979. Ambience? I'm sure it was a neighborhood bar before Prohibition, and it still has that feel; but the crowd is cosmopolitan.

As for the music, it is the best spot in town for traditional jazz, of various schools. They feature a different band or combo every night. I much prefer Tuesday night when the regular feature is Vince Giordano and his New Orleans Nighthawks. This band is a phenomenon. It is a revival band, but unlike most revival bands, it does *not* recreate the music of the swing era. Instead, it plays nothing but the music of the late 20s through 1934; i.e., the music of the *pre*-swing era, both jazz and dance music.

Does it sound like the band and the audience are populated by graybeards? Guess again. Leader Vince Giordano is in his middle 20s. So is vocalist Vince Fitzpatrick (who sounds amazingly like one of the better singers from the very dawn of radio, around 1930). But Giordano also includes, and gets the respect of an impressive array of stalwarts from the Big Band Era: 70-year-old Clarence Hutchenrider, star clarinet with the Glen Gray band; Jimmy Maxwell, from the 1939-1942 Goodman band; Bernie Privin, veteran of the Shaw, Miller, Goodman and Barnet bands; and others only a shade less well-known. So Giordano really does bridge the generation gap, and the audience, ranging from teenagers to geriatrics, responds in kind.

I have introduced a few dozen people to the place, and I have yet to find anyone who is less than enthusiastic. And I have run the gamut from my eighteen-year-old daughter to Ruth Ellington (Duke's sister), I guess in her early seventies. In fact, when I brought my twenty-one-year-old daughter, a girl who has never shared my passion for the music of the Golden Age of Popular Music, she stunned me by asking if we could have Vince Giordano play for her June wedding. (P.S. He is.)

If you go, I bet you like it.

Incidentally, I'm not handling PR for the band or the joint. I just like to see class get noticed.
Kindest regards,
Neil McCaffrey

ભ

CHRIS & EILEEN
June 9, 1979

We are privileged today to play host to what may be a unique band. I think you'll enjoy the band even more if you know something about it.

Though the Nighthawks are an abiding enthusiasm of Joan and me and perhaps twenty of you who have joined us on a Tuesday night at the Red Blazer Too, we must credit Eileen with the inspired idea that brings the band here today. (She always did know how to get around her old man.) Left to myself, I'm afraid I'd have felt it was indecent to enjoy the music so much at my own daughter's wedding.

I had hoped that the band's first album would be ready for this great event. But the album hasn't yet worked its way onto the production line at the little factory in eastern Siberia where it's scheduled to run. Never mind, I've heard a tape, and it's worth waiting for.

Till then, however, I'll take the lazy way out and simply reprint below the first part of the liner notes I did for the album. But the personnel will be a bit different. Dennis Drury will probably be on trombone, having reclaimed his original chair. Dave Boeddinghaus will be striding across the keyboard. And the first trumpet chair will be occupied by Bill Moriarity, a refugee from the St. Louis Symphony who is so good that I suspect even the great Jimmy Maxwell couldn't win his old job back. If you enjoy the band half as much as you should, please remember to a) go back for seconds some Tuesday at the Red Blazer Too, and b) thank Eileen.

P.S. As noted below, the band plays nothing beyond 1934—one reason it's unique.

TUESDAY NIGHT AT THE RED BLAZER TOO
or, *The Untouchables Revisited*

You make your way up to Yorkville, one of Manhattan's last surviving ethnic neighborhoods. Dominating Third Avenue between 88th and 89th is the Red Blazer Too. But something doesn't look quite right. Oh, that's it—where's the El?

(By the way, for the literary purist, Red Blazer *Too* is not a typographical error. It seems that Dennis Carey, the Godfather of the establishment, owns another oasis called the Red Blazer. So this one is the Red Blazer Also.)

An awning, no less, guides you in. You expect a door with a peephole. You're ready to say that Jimmy sent you. (Jimmy Walker, naturally.) But no, this spot is wide open. And inviting. It's a tennis court and a half long, no more than 25 feet wide. A bar runs the length of the outer room. But the action is in the back room. Of course.

There's music. *Real* music. Music the like of which ushered in Repeal, and made Prohibition endurable. On a bandstand that could comfortably accommodate the Boswell Sisters sit not three but, somehow, ten musicians, complete with horns and tuxedos. They're playing makes-you-wanna-Charleston-down-to-Charleston music. All that's missing is Frank Nitti. (He'll be in later.)

Your favorite stars crowd the walls: Gary, Cary, Mae, Bing, even

351

promising starlets like Judy and Lana (though Judy and Lana were still picking daisies when they launched this music). The crowd—and it *is* crowded—is all of one generation: the 18-to-88 set.

High atop the bandstand, his shock of light brown hair brushing the rafter, the string bass/tuba/bass sax player is calling the tunes—to men old enough to address him as grandson. Can it be that a fellow born only yesterday, in 1952, is leading *this* band? It can't; but it is.

The man is Vince Giordano, and he presides over not so much an orchestra as a phenomenon. The New Orleans Nighthawks are a *revival* band with a difference. The Glenn Miller band is a Miller revival band. Even Mercer Ellington leads a revival band. Bless 'em all but why revive only the Swing Era? After all, the New York Philharmonic is mostly a revival band. No need to apologize for Vince and the Nighthawks.

No need at all. The music covers the decade just before the Swing Era changed our lives in 1935, and is considerably more than quaint. It was the decade when dance music emerged from behind the potted palms . . . when jazzmen found their solo voices . . . when pioneer arrangers like Don Redman and Fletcher Henderson, Bill Challis and Duke Ellington, Joe Haymes and Benny Carter discovered they could make whole sections and big bands swing . . . when Bing Crosby and Mildred Bailey and Ethel Waters taught their fellow vocalists how to leave off declaiming and start singing.

It was a decade in music when simplicity lived comfortably with sophistication. (Come to think of it, the Thirties was the last decade that could make that statement.) The Nighthawks also remind us that the Golden Age of Jazz was the Golden Age of Dancing. This was no coincidence. In fact, it is a truism among the *au courant* that when jazz wanders far from the dance floor, it first struts a bit before the hoi polloi, then pauses to contemplate its navel, and finally settles into therapy. Jazz is an art, all right; but deliver us from the Jazz Artist.

No such pretentiousness finds its way onto the Nighthawk bandstand. Greybeards mingle in easy camaraderie with players who look like they're still learning to shave. Professionals all, they kid one another—and respect one another.

The respect is well founded. As this album demonstrates, many of the charts are demanding—the more so when Vince hands them out for a first reading right there on the bandstand, as he does several times a night. The old pros, and their young heirs, glance over them for at most a minute; Giordano counts off the tempo; and away they go, *sightreading* a new arrangement with, usually, a mere three or four fluffs. When a first run-through or a second goes especially well, the men punctuate the coda with laughs of honest pleasure. Mind, there's no showboating. The laughs are like the spontaneous outburst of a golfer who has just sunk the impossible putt. They'd laugh the same if they were rehearsing out in the garage.

If Tuesday night at the Red Blazer Too were just an evening of timeless music, decent food, honest drinks and 1969 prices, Nitti himself would manage a smile. But it's more. There on the bandstand are survivors from the Heroic Age—and more than survivors. When Clarence Hutchenrider or Moe Dale picks up his horn to solo, it isn't merely Old-timers' Day. The decades melt away, and you realize with warm surprise that they still play in the big leagues.

But what about the day after tomorrow? Will we then really be reduced to the phonograph? Vince Giordano and the Nighthawks say No, and this album should make you a believer. Here the torch is passed on to the Second Generation, players like Dick Wellstood and Bobby Pring; and above all to the Third Generation, embryo stars like Vince Giordano and Mike Peters.

If the 18-to-88 crowd at the Red Blazer Too is any index, we might be witnessing the birth of a cult—and more than a cult. "Impossible," whines a chorus of Moog synthesizers. Well, maybe. But it wouldn't be the first Renaissance in the history of Western civilization.

THE PLAYERS

The Nighthawks average perhaps two dates a week, so the personnel will sometimes change if any regulars are committed to a longer engagement with another band. Fortunately, Vince Giordano knows most of the compatible musicians in the New York area, so substitutes present no insuperable problem. Since the band assumed its present identity late in 1977 (it experienced two earlier incarnations under Rich Conaty and Dick Sudhalter), other skilled bands besides those featured here have toiled in the vineyard. Among them: trumpeters Bill Moriarity, Warren Vache, Pee Wee Erwin, Chris Griffin, Randy Reinhardt and Ed Polcer; trombonist Dennis Drury; saxists Adrian Tei and Sal Pace; pianists Dave Boeddinghaus, Johnny Varro and Bill Jones; banjoists Carmen Mastren, Art Ryerson, Jack Hotop, Alan Cary and Bill Dern; drummers John Gill and—Vince Giordano. (The same. He probably also doubles on clavichord and harp.) Featured here:

VINCE GIORDANO—*leader, tuba, bass sax, string bass, vocals, arranger, band manager, publicity manager, band boy, chauffeur, therapist.* Vince learned arranging under pioneering Goldkette-Whiteman chartsman Bill Challis, and studied tuba under Joe Tarto of Five Pennies fame. He played his first professional date at 14. Since then Vince has toured with Clyde McCoy's dixieland group, appeared in Broadway's short-lived *Doctor Jazz*, and made it to Carnegie Hall via the New York Jazz Repertory Orchestra and the New Paul Whiteman Orchestra (fittingly, since he boasts a nearly complete collection of Whiteman records).

Which isn't all he collects. The band owes its astonishing repertoire to Vince's collection of some 4,000 arrangements, largely stocks, from the pre-1935 era. (Yes, Virginia, once upon a time a band could buy orchestrations for 75 cents each—stock arrangements by famous arrangers. That was in the Dark Ages, when instead of supporting a dozen big bands, America had to make do with three thousand or so.)

BERNIE PRIVIN—*trumpet.* When Bernie climbed into the vacant trumpet chair on the bandstand of the Hotel Lincoln's Blue Room late in 1938, Artie Shaw was the hottest name in music. Nothing daunted, the Brooklyn 19-year-old was soon dispatching about three-quarters of the trumpet solos, inventively. Later, Staff Sergeant Privin and Bobby Nichols split the jazz trumpet book with the Glenn Miller Army Air Force band. Bernie also saw service with the wild (in both senses) Charlie Barnet crew before the Army, and with Benny Goodman just after it. Then he settled into the lush life of a New York studio musician, pausing along the way to become the Squire of Lower Westchester. If you ever get to hear the Nighthawks in person, pick a seat near Bernie, and listen hard for his droll *sotto voce* remarks about music and the passing scene.

ARTIE BAKER—*lead alto sax, clarinet.* In many a Forties band, Artie was one of those anonymous workhorses. You may have caught him with Raymond Scott or Charlie Spivak (isn't that Artie's clarinet on Spivak's hit, *Brother Bill?*) or, in another setting, with Toscanini, no less. And when Artie Shaw stepped down from the swollen bandstand that carried his swing-and-string ensemble in late 1941 and early 1942, it was Artie Baker who rose from the sax section to front in the maestro's absence. Now, with the Nighthawks, the ebullient Mr. Baker finally gets to stretch.

CLARENCE HUTCHENRIDER—*alto sax, clarinet.* Nothing you hear from the Nighthawks is really new to Hutch. He was playing these same arrangements with territory bands in the mid-Twenties. He rose to eminence as the principal jazz soloist with the Casa Loma orchestra during its years at or near the top, 1931-1943. Who can forget his clarinet soaring through the band's theme, the haunting *Smoke Rings?* Hutch is an original, and may be the most underrated clarinetist in jazz history.

MOE DALE—*tenor sax, clarinet.* If one player in the band can be singled out as underappreciated, Moe's the man. His first notable job was with Tal Henry, who led one of the better Southern bands of the Twenties and Thirties. He did time with Ted Lewis in the mid-Thirties, escaped without harm, and landed with one of the later Paul Whiteman orchestras. His long, rolling lines recall nameless swinging saxists from bands like that of Gene Kardos, and his solos fit the Nighthawk charts to perfection.

MIKE PETERS—*banjo.* Mike, like Vince Giordano, is another amazing young musician who in his mid-twenties has already absorbed the whole mainstream jazz tradition. Mike put in two years on guitar with Joe Venuti (who knew a bit about good guitarists), and even served as executor of the estate of the jazz giant, though he's young enough to be Joe's great-grandson. With violinist Charles Wizen, Mike is co-leader of Jazz a Cordes, a group that hearkens back to Django, Stephane, and the Quintet of the Hot Club of France.

EDDY DAVIS—*drums.* Eddy is the most powerful, the most influential man in the band. All the other bandsmen must show up in black tie and tux; Eddy gets to play in a sleeveless sweater. Rumors abound as to the source of his power. Is it something sinister? Or could it be because he keeps good time?

VINCE FITZPATRICK—*vocals.* Vince joined the band in October 1978, and promptly made himself indispensable. What, after all, is a late Twenties-early Thirties dance band without a crooner who sings into a megaphone? As if that weren't enough, Vince looks like the fellow in the John Held sketch, the one in the tux who is doing a snappy two-step with the girl who looks like Lorelei Lee. Vince already owns two distinctions that make him unique in American music: 1) he is the first singer since 1931 (at the latest) to hitch his wagon to Scrappy Lambert's star, and 2) he will soon be the first band vocalist to earn his Master's in philosophy (at Fordham). He is now being urged to do his doctoral dissertation on *The Esthetics of Aristotle as Realized in the Music of the New Orleans Nighthawks.*

Thus, eleven good men and true. If you were raised on the bands that covered the Paramount stage with an acre of brass, ten pieces may strike you as skimpy. Not to worry. They do everything they have to. As it happens, the Nighthawk instrumentation—three brass, three reeds, four rhythm—was the usual lineup of a dance band of the late Twenties and early Thirties. It sounds just fine. And doesn't make your ears ache.

Cʒ

June 18, 1980

Dear Kathleen and Dan [Mahoney]:
Joan tells me that you are wondering what to do with Neil's [Kathleen's brother] books and records. As far as I know, there is no great secondhand market for classical albums. There is a small and presumably profitable secondhand market for Catholic books, especially those from the Dark Ages before the early Sixties. However, it would be foolish to try to build a mailing list unless you are planning to go into the business and use it regularly.

Therefore, I think you will get by far the most value from the books and records if you donate them to a Catholic college, of traditional bent. I can give you the addresses of a few poor, young colleges that would really appreciate the books. Moreover, they would be going to just the right audience, and I think Neil would approve of that.

If the collection is sizable, it might pay you for tax purposes to make some sort of listing. Then you must get the library to acknowledge receipt. If you have the list, you can provide the library with a copy.

I think you could probably take something like retail value on the albums. As for the books, nobody knows. But I can provide you with secondhand lists of Catholic books, and you may be surprised to see the prices they command. All this will be useful for tax purposes. If the collection is sizable, your deductions could run well into the thousands of dollars.

Another point, and I can't help thinking a vital one. Dan, Joan got this idea during Mass, so we must assume either divine inspiration or venial sin. I opt for the former (though I must own that I have yet to be delegated a judge in these matters).

You've been reading that Europe is not taking Reagan seriously. You've been reading correctly. We hear it from European sources. What Reagan should do is to meet Brutus Coste and take him along with him to Europe. He should not, in fact, go anywhere in Europe without him. There is nobody on our side who knows half as much. He is lucid, utterly trustworthy, tough, better informed than anybody, and realistic—about the past as well as the present. It is a national disgrace that he has not been consulted regularly since 1945, and on the highest level. Perhaps, just perhaps, it is not too late to repair some of the disgrace. So this is your assignment. You have, believe me, never had a more important one.

I enclose his resume. But please don't just pass it along in the mail. This is worth a call to Reagan himself. If you need further priming, I am sure you can call Brutus himself and get him to visit you. If you want, I'll arrange a dinner. But really, that won't be necessary. If you talk to him for an hour, you will come away a believer.
Best,
Neil

P.S. Just this minute I read that Reagan is not going to Europe. But he should be still using Brutus—preferably every day.

അ

July 11, 1984

Dear Bill:
I don't read contemporary poets; in fact, I read hardly any poetry, sad to say. But when they announced the new Poet Laureate a month or so ago, I recognized the name of Philip Larkin with pleasure. Frank sent me his jazz book around 1970 for a brief. By happy chance I came upon the review over the weekend, and I enclose a copy for its curiosity value [see Neil's letter to Murray Rothbard in Section 3]. *NR* readers had advance notice of his splendid esthetic.
Best,
Neil

അ

1/2/85

Dear Vic,
The word from Dale is that you are threatening to buy dinner next week—again. This will strip me of what remains of my manhood. I owe you so many I've lost count. You are generous, but also quixotic. Why not exploit my outrageous expense account?

My therapist concurs. Ever since I heard this, she has found me regressing, and fears a major setback. To forestall this, can't I pick up the check? Please.

Happy New Year!
Best,
Neil

P.S. You remind me a little of my grandfather, who had to buy a round for everybody, every time he walked into a bar. "Nobody ever bought a drink for Joe Waterman," my father once remarked. He is the same grandfather who, when I'd ask him why he played the horses, always replied solemnly, "Because it's the sport of kings."

☙

April 1, 1985

Dear Mr. Daly:
Saturday night we had an appalling experience at the Rainbow Room. In all our evenings there over the years, this was the first time anything like this has ever happened. Since your spot stands for something, I think you will want to know about it.

Good friends were up from Washington. We wanted the evening to be something special, so, as we often do, we chose the Rainbow Room. Since we were going first to a matinee, we made an early reservation for 5:30. We made the reservation a couple of weeks in advance because we know that you get a good crowd on Saturday. Then a few days ago we confirmed the reservation.

We arrived on time and settled in for what we thought would be another delightful evening. After a spell the ladies (there were six of us in all) went over to the north window to look out at the Park. They chose a spot where there was an unoccupied table and stood there a few minutes, admiring the view. The captain came over and told them they were annoying people and made them move. Of course, they weren't annoying anybody. And, as you know, people often go over to look out the window because that is one of the attractions of the Rainbow Room.

Then, about 6:30, the maitre d' and the captain came over (their names were Gregory and, I think, Albert) and asked us if we would like to order dinner because we would have to leave at eight o'clock. I was stunned. I told them that we were planning to spend the evening. They replied that they had two sittings and that we were scheduled to leave at eight. I pointed out that this was never done at the Rainbow Room; that we had been there many times, sometimes early, but had never been told this; that we had made a reservation and confirmed the reservation, but neither time were told anything like this. I guess I was expected to come up with a handsome tip for the privilege of staying.

At this point, my guest took charge. He is a prominent writer, and I don't exaggerate at all when I describe him as a legendary figure among Washington media people, for one notable reason: he takes no nonsense from anybody. True to form, he announced that we were leaving. Nobody in our party objected, after the treatment we had received. The only reason, incidentally, why I don't give you this man's name is that he is the speechwriter for a leading government official, and I don't know whether he would want me to give his name. But your staff picked on the wrong man to hustle. Don't be surprised if the incident becomes immortalized in one of his articles.

But of course, it shouldn't matter whether your patrons are prominent or not. If we all had hay growing out of our ears, we would still have been entitled to the traditional Rainbow Room treatment as long as we were behaving ourselves, as we assuredly were. Instead, we were treated as though we had wandered into a tourist trap.

I write this letter sadly. My wife and I have been coming to the Rainbow Room ever since you brought back good bands. We have been among your most enthusiastic cheerleaders. I guess we've brought twenty people as guests over the past several years. I know that some of them have become fans and in turn brought their own guests. One of our guests, the chairman of the New York Conservative Party, liked the place so much that he took it over one evening on one of your off nights about a year ago.

Nor has my own cheering been confined to word of mouth. I guess I've written at least half a dozen times in praise of the Rainbow Room. Only a month or so ago my latest plug appeared in a brochure I wrote about the Ray Noble band for the Franklin Mint Record Society. Now I'm afraid I can no longer praise you either in print or by word of mouth. I would be misleading the public.

But above all, the whole unpleasant experience leaves us sad. We have lost one of our favorite dining and dancing spots. Even sadder, this wonderful spot seems to have forgotten its own splendid tradition. We can't afford to lose traditions like yours.
Cordially,
Neil McCaffrey

ⳍ

November 25, 1986

Dear Murray:
Many thanks for your note. The good news is that the Blazer will open in January—I hope in time for you to go at least once before you leave. The story is that Vince is forming another band and will play there again. Meanwhile, practically all the members of the old band have formed a co-op called the Bluebird Society Orchestra. They are playing party dates and have a gig in Nyack every Sunday night. We haven't gone yet because of schedule problems but we'll

go eventually, if the band continues there. So things are looking up.

When you come home for the holidays I hope you will reserve a Friday night when you expect to have a car. It would be fun to play records again. I have a bunch of albums that I think you will want to tape, all by somebody you probably don't know, Ben Selvin. They are fine dance records from 1930-33. The songs are good and many of them are probably not familiar to you. Moreover, if you check your Rust, you will discover that they feature famous musicians in their youth, most of them playing very well, especially Benny, who played in those years better, I think, than he ever did afterward.

I was interested in your letter to *Policy Review*. My, but you have certainly gone into this question. I confess I never have because esoterica seldom fascinates me. It is all based on an absurdly literal reading of portions of Scripture that are *meant* to be obscure, unclear and mysterious. The common note of *all* utopian movements is that they brush aside human nature as irrelevant. But human nature takes her revenge. The movements then either fall apart when they rub up against reality or they become totalitarian—necessarily.

I met Chris Weber briefly when he was up to talk to young Neil. Nice guy, as you've said.

Love to Joey.
Best,
Neil McCaffrey

଼

June 3, 1987

Dear Mr. O'Shaughnessy [Station WRTN]:
Somebody has taken to programming a lot of rock on a previously blameless station. Please put a stop to it. Rock will not attract a single listener. Rock people have a hundred stations to wallow in. Those of us who loathe rock have few refuges. Rock will only make us reach for the dial. I already have, several times.
Kindest regards,
Neil McCaffrey

଼

Jobs go begging
[June 9, 1988]

Editor [*New Rochelle Standard Star*]:
Concerning your May 16 story observing the 25th anniversary of Youth Employment Services in Mamaroneck, the YES people

deserve all the praise you heap upon them. But your story does point up a problem that might be worth a stray comment: there are more jobs than students to fill them.

We are always eager to hire people recommended by YES, both for our warehouse and for clerical duties. I'm sorry to say that the applicants are few and usually lacking in even the basic qualifications. Yet we always offer more than the minimum wage and we also offer young people a chance to try the lower rungs of the publishing ladder. And publishing, remember, has always been regarded as a glamour industry. What's wrong?

Your story suggests part of the answer. Young people today are affluent and over-indulged. But that is only part of the answer.

Not all students are affluent. Many can use the money they could earn after school or over the summer. Students are encouraged to think—by the schools, media and perhaps sometimes by parents—that the world will be theirs for the asking. It doesn't work that way, and why should it? Young people still have to start modestly, and when the bigger jobs come they go to the people who have proven themselves in the smaller jobs. Why is such an obvious fact a carefully guarded secret? Back in ancient times, when I was breaking into publishing, a summer entry-level job of any sort would draw a line of applicants that would stretch around the block. Alas, no more.
Neil McCaffrey
Harrison

ଓ

Miracle on 43rd Street
[60th birthday celebration for Msgr. Gene Clark,
hosted by Bill Buckley, 1985]

Monsignor Clark agreed to be interviewed for this profile, then proved impossible to track down. I will therefore focus on some points in his many-faceted career that were scanted by earlier biographers.

Jimmy Walker's election as mayor, followed a few weeks later by the birth of Eugene Vincent Clark, ushered in New York's penultimate Golden Age, an afflatus the city would not experience again until the Age of Dinkins. When we contemplate a man of Monsignor Clark's vigor, it comes as a shock to realize that he is old enough to remember when organ grinders, trolley cars and virgins could still be found on the streets of his beloved East Bronx.

After Stalin and Hitler shook hands over the prostrate body of Poland, young Eugene, sensing the vanity of human wishes,

361

enrolled in the prep school division of the archdiocesan minor seminary, Cathedral College. There, it must be admitted, he fell in with a fast crowd. One member was caught dealing jazz, and Eugene was exposed to this. Fortunately, it didn't take, though he would sometimes make arcane references to black and white styles long after such distinctions had become unfashionable.

One other influence, however, endures to this day in Monsignor's apostolate. Fast crowd, fast cars. One classmate named Jud had use of the family Buick. No school rules governed this circumstance, simply because it had never arisen before. Gene and Jud were drawn to each other, whether out of mutual regard or mutual need. Services were exchanged: homework for brash rides up the West Side Highway. The arrangement worked until exam time. Then the gap between Jud's homework and his blue books became manifest even to the faculty, and he was urged to work out his salvation in the lay apostolate. But the seed planted on West End Avenue would burgeon across two continents. Come to think of it, with St. Christopher consigned to legend and the car business looking like downtown Detroit, Monsignor Clark may yet be destined for patron sainthood.

Eugene's graduation from Cathedral was darkened by the passing of his idol, Franklin Roosevelt. He emerged from the ordeal more determined than ever to renounce all worldly ambition and proceed to the major seminary at Dunwoodie. There he played a major role in the founding of a new religious order, the Outlates of the Highway. Like most such ventures, it met with early opposition from stodgy superiors. The Outlate ethos had to await the post-conciliar Church before it would prevail.

To advance the work of the Outlates, Eugene and two classmates, Roger Pryor and Ed Hauck, resolved to adapt contemporary methods to the timeless mission of the Church. Boldly breaking with seminary regulations, they risked all and invested in a car. Though cars were hard to come by in the late Forties, they had found a gem. It was a green Packard no older than the new owners; a family car complete with a drain on the floor in front of the back seat; what our parents called, with the optimism of their generation, a touring car. Who knows what price it would command on the vintage car marts today. Surely enough to retire the debt in one or another of Monsignor Clark's parishes. Alas, it was not to be. The Green Monster (for so the envious spoke of it) was burdened with one fatal flaw. It was unable to execute a turn sharper than twelve degrees. How did the Monster meet its end? Monsignors Clark and Pryor get a faraway look in their eyes when asked, and profess not to know. Perhaps Father Hauck took the secret with him to his grave; or maybe the matter is still in litigation.

As soon as he discovered that Eugene was about to be ordained, Douglas MacArthur hurried home from Korea to celebrate the event with a march up Fifth Avenue past the Cathedral. As readers will recall, Father Clark's biographers commonly speak of the first period of his priesthood as The Ascent to Mount Kisco. Then, after several years of parish work, scholarship beckoned. Father Clark embarked on his doctorate at Notre Dame under the great scholar of the English Reformation, Philip Hughes. Father, however, wrote his thesis on Newman. Though the dissertation is now a collector's item, one high Vatican official has acknowledged (not for attribution) that the campaign for Newman's canonization picked up momentum only after the Clark researches.

Around this time Father Clark caught the eye of Cardinal Spellman and became his aide. But earning his doctorate was not enough to bank Father's passion for research. Between quiet sessions where Spellman and Clark plotted the future of the Church in New York, Father became intrigued by rumors of an early marriage attempted by our first post-Catholic President. Father's investigations took him north and south and even into deepest Greenwich Village. He emerged with a new respect for the royal family, who had anticipated his every move. Failure? A grateful prince of the Church thought otherwise, and Father Clark accepted the purple.

What next for Monsignor Clark, after the conversion of the Helmsleys? Perhaps chaplain to the Mario Cuomo Center for Unborn Children? Or delegate of the American bishops to the African National Congress? The fields are ready for the harvest.
Neil McCaffrey

C೩

THE GOOD OLD DAYS . . .[5]

. . . will be a column devoted to nostalgic trivia. Nothing solemn. If anything resembling a Deep Thought ever finds its way into the column, suspect the worst. It will be your signal that some impostor has done away with me and taken over.

I recently studied the entire roster of one big newspaper syndi-

---

5 Neil McCaffrey sent around, to a variety of outlets, samples of a proposed syndicated nostalgia column to be entitled "The Good Old Days." It seems that no one picked up the idea and that none of these was ever published. They make for interesting reading nevertheless, and it is a kind of poetic justice that they can be included in this volume.

cate. *Not a single feature was geared to the over-40 generation.* Which prompts me to offer four radical theses:

1. The over-40 generation reads the papers.

2. But sometimes, what with TV competition and squeezed budgets, they quit taking the papers.

3. The over-40s *buy.* (The ad agency boys, in their commendable zeal to nab young consumers while their buying habits are still being formed, sometimes give the impression that you have to be under 35 before they'll let you into a store.)

4. THE GOOD OLD DAYS will give one syndicate the only column in town for the over-40s.

Not that the readership will all be over 40. I preside over the Nostalgia Book Club (see below). We did a member survey that left me amazed. The average age of our members turned out to be a mere 40, the median age 41. And we are constantly getting letters from members in their teens. I guess the old movies on TV get to them too.

THE GOOD OLD DAYS will generate mail. When it gets going, part of most columns (a section called TOWN MEETING) will enable readers to buy/sell/trade nostalgic items, exchange correspondence and memories, get their trivia questions answered, etc. Items like these seed themselves. My experience with a similar exchange in the Nostalgia Book Club Bulletin tells me that I'll soon be getting more material than I can handle. This is a sample of what this part of THE GOOD OLD DAYS will read like:

TOWN MEETING

Victor Gold, 6309 Beachway, Falls Church, Va. 22044 is looking for Alabama football memorabilia, old fight films on 8mm. . . .Sally Southern, 18 Market, San Pedro, Cal. 96111 claims to be the youngest reader of this column ("I just turned twelve"), nevertheless loves King Clark Gable and wants to correspond with other fans her own age. . . .Got any old beer bottles down in the cellar? Vito Vitale has 8,000—and wants more. If you have bottles (empties, of course) from Midwest regional brewers dating back before 1950, write Vito at 11 Fifth St., Dayton, Ohio 11111 or call him at 111-222-3333. Yes—he'll pay you for them. . . .Ron Jackson, 41 W. 41 St., Brooklyn, N.Y. 11112 has over 100 old Sinatra 78s, will trade for old Bing Crosby platters. . . .Jack Ripper, 160 Main, Kalamazoo, Mich. 11122 grew up in Terre Haute, would enjoy hearing from anyone who went to Easton High from 1935-1940 and hung out at Kay's Kampus Koffee Korner.

You can see the possibilities. This sort of thing can be addictive, especially since I'll take care to mix the hobbies and addresses so that readers will always feel there *might* be something for them in tonight's column.

So, a nostalgia column has possibilities. But why me?

I'm not aware of anyone who has earned a Ph.D. in Nostalgia. Not yet, anyway. But I do bring some expertise to the subject. I started the Nostalgia Book Club early in 1968 and still serve as president. I dog old movies on TV, take loving care of my 7,000 vintage pop and jazz records (most from 1925-1950), edit and publish nostalgia books, and generally keep in touch.

I was born in 1925. I remember the Thirties vividly, the Twenties a little. Mention the Thirties, and the horror stories start flowing like beer in Milwaukee. Nonsense. Sure, millions went hungry in the Thirties—but *most* of us didn't. Most of us have *good* memories of the time, and later.

THE GOOD OLD DAYS will keep the good memories green.

Ω

THE GOOD OLD DAYS
(Column #1)

Why nostalgia?

The fashion is becoming epidemic. *Item*: Films no longer have to be good. As clinkers like *The Great Gatsby* and *Class of '44* prove, they just have to be nostalgic. *Item*: A friend of mine has for years been taking a ribbing from his kids every time he sneaks a few of his old Glenn Miller and Tommy Dorsey records onto the phonograph. But just the other day he discovered his son and daughter taping Pop's records. They were going to take the tapes back to college for their "touch dancing" campus hops. *Item*: 1974 saw four new books on—Babe Ruth!

But let's be clear about one point. The Savage Sixties and the Sagging Seventies didn't invent nostalgia. My father was always nostalgic—about World War I and earlier. My grandfather was always nostalgic. For him the good old days were the Gay Nineties. For that matter, I guess I started feeling nostalgic around the age of thirteen.

The difference today, the reason why nostalgia is becoming an institution, is technology. In the past, people could reminisce about the old days, or read books about them. Today we can actually live them again—see them, hear them.

The movies we grew up with are still around, looking better than ever. And now we can watch them right here in the living room.

The songs we used to sing and whistle and dance to—have you visited your friendly record store lately? The big record companies are beginning to get the message: not everybody is rock-happy. So Columbia and RCA and Decca are reaching back into their vaults to reissue Bing and Benny and Billie [Holiday]. Old Blue Eyes can never make too many comebacks. And Lawrence Welk goes on forever.

To be sure, the record companies reissue only a tiny fraction of the records you found on the Sweet Shoppe juke box back in 1941 A.D. Suppose you want to hear some of the others, and you can't find them up in the attic? Don't lose hope. We'll tell you in future columns how to find almost any old favorite—usually at prices way below what you might expect.

"Ah," you say, "but what about old radio? Gone forever! If only I could recapture the thrill of curling up next to the old Atwater Kent."

You can. They didn't have tape recorders back before the war (that's *the* war, Mac), but radio stations and a few hobbyists had home recorders. If you owned one of these rigs, you literally *cut* your own record on a turntable. Thanks to home recordings, thousands of old radio shows are still available. They've long since been transferred to tape, and now the tapes circulate widely among old radio buffs. They're even beginning to find their way back on radio, mostly on small FM stations.

So now, yesterday is forever. As some wise man once said, "The past is all we truly possess." This little column will try to help. Meanwhile, let's have two rousing choruses of "My Little Bimbo Down on the Bamboo Isle."

&

THE GOOD OLD DAYS
(Column #2)

By 1928, vaudeville had seen much better days. Silent films played at movie palaces all over town, and talkies were just around the corner. People were staying home listening to the new radio networks on their Stromberg-Carlson consoles.

So vaudevillians feared for the future. But meanwhile, they were keeping pretty busy. There were still over one thousand vaudeville houses in the U.S. and Canada, and they drew over two million customers a day.

Three Sunday punches in 1929 and 1930 finally kayoed the old two-a-day circuit. Talkies became widespread, radio became more widespread, and the Depression became super-widespread.

How many names of W.C. Fields' movie roles can you remember? Answers below.

Even if you're a dumb Dora, you remember Zeppelins. Curling irons. "Wanna buy a duck?" That daring novel, *Anthony Adverse*. Technocracy. G-men cards. The days when, if you made an out-of-town call, it meant somebody was dying.

New Rochelle is a small city in Westchester, one of the nicest suburban counties surrounding New York City. It was even nicer back in the Thirties and Forties, but it still has some lovely sections. So I was interested the other day when my wife was telling me about the house her folks rented there back in 1940.

It was on the northern end of Webster Avenue, one of the prettiest parts of town. It had ten rooms. Rent: $85.

Three years later, the family decided to move to Pelham, then and now one of Westchester's loveliest small towns. They found a place on beautiful Highbrook Avenue. But by 1943, inflation was soaring. Their rent shot up to $90. Still, this time they got eleven rooms.

But they soon tired of paying this ridiculous rent. So they bought the place, for $10,000. The house changed hands a couple of times. When it was sold around 1970, we heard that it went for $69,000. Which means $85,000 or more at today's prices.

Among the deathless characters portrayed by W.C. Fields, you remember Otis Criblecoblis, Chester Snavely, Mahatma Kane Jeeves, Charles Bogle, Dr. Peppittone, Cuthbert J. Twillie, Prettiwillie, Eustace McGargle and Larson E. Whipsnade.

ଓଃ

THE GOOD OLD DAYS
(Column #3)

Sinatra?

I remember Frankeee. Before he was Frankeee, Harry James hired an unknown vocalist for his swinging 1939 band, his first male singer. Frank was a slim little guy with a thin little voice. Everybody yawned. I'd like to be able to say that I saw the greatness that was to come, but the fact is that I yawned too.

Meanwhile, back at Tommy Dorsey's, the Sentimental Gentleman wasn't getting along with star vocalist Jack Leonard. After four years with the band and hits like "Marie," Jack in 1939 was the most popular male band vocalist around. Bob Eberly, with Jimmy Dorsey, was a year away from stardom. Brother Ray Eberle (he kept the family spelling of the name) was just emerging with Glenn Miller. Kenny Sargent, popular through most of the Thirties with Glen Gray, was nevertheless no longer a serious rival to Leonard. When Jack quit

Tommy that November, everyone wondered how TD would ever replace him.

Tommy first tried with a journeyman singer named Allan DeWitt, who lasted a couple of months (but soon caught on with another good band. Do you remember which one? Answer below). Dorsey had better luck with his second choice. Frank joined early in 1940 and stayed two and a half years. Maintaining my record as a seer without peer, I assured my friends that Tommy's band would never be the same with this skinny kid trying to step into Jack's shoes.

Though Frank became one of the top band singers with Tommy, nobody guessed what was going to happen when he quit Dorsey in September 1942 to try it as a single. Anyway, I didn't.

It is now December 30, 1942. The Paramount, brightest jewel on Times Square when Times Square was Times Square, is about to usher in the New Year with a show that is, even by the Paramount's standards, fairly sensational. The picture is *Star Spangled Rhythm*, one of those wartime musicals with a hundred and umpteen big names. The band is Benny Goodman—no longer Number One, but among us aficionados still the King. Oh yes—second billing goes to that former Dorsey vocalist.

The day is raw with sleet. My hip friends and I arrive early, about 9:30 a.m. The crowd is already winding around toward Eighth Avenue. We finally get in and sit through the movie. Then, the great moment. The band climbs onto the stage (which is down in the pit during the movie. The stage moves up like an elevator for the in-person show). Benny gives the downbeat. The Paramount swells with the swinging sound of the Goodman theme, "Let's Dance." The stage rises. The lights go up. Three thousand voices become one roar.

I want to tell you about Benny and Frankeee and that stage show—and, not to forget, about the band that Allan DeWitt joined after Dorsey. But time is running out. Tune in next column to find out what happens to Frankeee.

෬

THE GOOD OLD DAYS
(Column #4)

We were talking about Frank Sinatra and his debut at the Paramount as a single that stormy day before New Year's Eve 1942. Recently a vocalist with Tommy Dorsey, Frank was happy enough to get second billing after Swing King Benny Goodman.

My friends and I stood out in the sleet for Benny, not Frankeee. Didn't everyone? What a surprise we were in for.

Meanwhile, here's Benny. I quickly scanned the sections and noticed a host of changes. There were four trumpets, not three—among them stars Yank Lawson and Lee Castle. There were three trombones, not two—and they included the legendary Miff Mole, a giant two decades before with the Original Memphis Five and later with Red Nichols. Pianist Jess Stacy was back, now that the war had scattered Bob Crosby's Bobcats. Young Lou Bellson was on drums, reminding you of Krupa. Dave Barbour, later Mr. Peggy Lee, strummed his guitar.

Benny opened with "Bugle Call Rag," a galvanizing arrangement based on the old one but half new. He followed with a rollicking version of a novelty of the day, "Rosie the Riveter"—which Benny himself sang! Benny was in good spirits, and the band sounded brilliant. (Did any hall ever show off a band's sound like the Paramount?)

Then, a collective gasp from three thousand oglers. Peggy Lee! Trim and young and blonde, beauteous in something white, Peggy had just made her breakthrough with two BG hits, "Why Don't You Do Right?" and "Somebody Else Is Taking My Place." She sang these along with something torchy which I forget. Then Benny came on with the Quintet for "Lady Be Good," followed by a dance act.

Then, Frankeee.

With my habit of underestimating Frank and his fans, I was dumbstruck at the ovation that welcomed him. But I should have expected something. There were more girls than usual in the audience. Indeed, they surrounded us. "Is that bad?" you may ask. In this case, yes. The girls chattered while Benny was playing. Clearly, they were there for something else—and now, here he is.

Frank sang four songs, all in the bedroom style he favored at the time. Songs like "There Are Such Things" and "She's Funny That Way." Of course, there was an encore. There were *four* encores—as far as I know, unprecedented at the Paramount.

Benny looked less than ecstatic. We felt the same. In fact, we got even with the girls, making irreverent remarks to interrupt their transports. I've since learned to enjoy a good ballad. But in those days, swing was mostly for guys, ballads were for girls.

Something happened that morning, but I was too dim to see it. There was none of the squealing or phony swooning over Frankeee. That came later, around fall 1943, as I recall. But that morning at the Paramount heralded the beginning of the end for the Big Band Era. The singers were about to take over.

Last column I sprang a teaser on you: do you remember the band Allan DeWitt sang with after he left Tommy Dorsey? It was Jan Savitt and His Top Hatters. He replaced Bon Bon. You remember Bon Bon (real name: George Tunnell). He was a great vocalist, one of the first Negroes to sing with a white band. He made hits out of attractive tunes like "720 in the Books" and "It's a Wonderful World."

And, at least in 1939 and 1940, Bon Bon was singing better than Frank. If you doubt me, go back and play the old records. Can't find them? In a future column, I'll report on where they can be found.

ೞ

Glossary

Contributed by Joan (Mrs. Neil) McCaffrey in the interests of clarity.

A

Abend, Dr. Martin—Professor at Jersey City University who became a popular conservative news commentator on Channel 5 in New York City.

Adler, Polly—Well known in her day as a New York madam.

Alt, Bruce—Starr Broadcasting employee.

Antonelli, Cardinal Ferdinando—Secretary for the Post-Consiliar appointed by Pope Paul VI.

B

Band, Richard—Editor at Arlington House Publishers, then a financial newsletter writer.

Barth, Marcus—Protestant theologian and son of theologian Karl Barth, he was a professor of Scripture and commentator on the Bible.

Bauman, Bob—Congressman from Maryland, a founder of Young Americans for Freedom, rising young star of the conservative movement until he was charged with soliciting a male minor.

"Bix" Beiderbecke—Jazz cornetist and composer of the 20s, most influential for his solos. He played with the Goldkette and Paul Whiteman bands and died very young. A big favorite of Neil's.

Bell, Jeff—Republican activist, candidate, speechwriter, and one of the younger Nixon campaign aides who later worked for Ronald Reagan as well.

Bellarmine, Cardinal—Brilliant Jesuit saint of the Counter-Reformation who defended the papacy but did not exaggerate its prerogatives.

Bernstein, Mike—Republican counsel for the Senate Labor and

Education Committee, very close to Senator Robert Taft and then to Senator Barry Goldwater before and during the Goldwater presidential campaign. He orchestrated Neil's successful recruitment of a number of important Washington names as sponsors for the Conservative Book Club.

Berrigan, Rev. Daniel, SJ—Catholic priest who protested the Vietnam war along with his brother, Phillip, a Josephite priest. They used marches, draft card burnings, sit-ins and other means of civil disobedience.

Blanshard, Paul—Left-wing journalist and author of *American Freedom and Catholic Power*, bitterly anti-Catholic. Head of an organization, Protestants and Others United for Separation of Church and State.

Bouscaren, Anthony—Vocal anti-communist professor of political science at Marquette University who was forced to resign from that post. He then taught many years at LeMoyne University and wrote a number of books on foreign policy and for *National Review* and other journals.

Bozell, Brent—Bill Buckley's roommate at Yale and then his brother-in-law, as husband of Bill's sister Patricia (Trish). One of the original editors of *National Review*, an exceptional speaker and debater, thought by many to be better than Bill. He was the real author of Barry Goldwater's "Conscience of a Conservative" and often wrote speeches for Barry. He went on to found *Triumph*, a Catholic magazine of quixotic bent.

Bradley, Father Robert, SJ—Jesuit priest of the Oregon province who was upset by the liberal turn of his order. He joined with fellow priests to try to change that direction.

Bree, Rita—Assistant to Cliff White during the Goldwater for President days, most efficient and knowledgeable. She knew where all the bodies were buried.

Bressler, Martin—Attorney at the time for Conservative Book Club and Arlington House. He was also the attorney for the Ben Shahn estate (the 20th century left-wing painter) some of whose works had been purchased for the Vatican Museum under the aegis of Pope Paul VI.

Brogan, Colm—Scottish journalist and author, contributor to *National Review.*

Buckley, Priscilla ("Pitts")—Sister of Bill and managing editor of *National Review*, loved and admired by all.

Burnham, Jim—One of the founders of *National Review*, former Trotskyite, political philosopher and analyst, author of *The Managerial Revolution* and other books and one of the early giants of conservatism.

Burton, Natalie—An editor at Doubleday, British convert to Catholicism.

C

Catchpole, Terry—Writer for *National Review* and *Human Events*, the Washington conservative weekly, author of books on politics.

Cenet, Jean—French homosexual writer.

Chambers, Whittaker—Former Soviet spy, author of the best selling book on his life in the communist party, *Witness.* Accuser of key Roosevelt-Truman administration State Department figure Alger Hiss at his trial. An editor at *National Review* in the early days, Neil met him at an editorial meeting and liked him immensely.

Clancy, William—At the time an editor at *Commonweal*, the liberal Catholic journal. He and Bill Buckley were in the midst of several public debates, liberal vs. conservative Catholic. He later became an Oratorian priest.

Clark, Father Eugene—later Monsignor, secretary to Cardinal Spellman and Cardinal Cooke. Like Father Donald "Roger" Pryor, a friend since freshman year at Cathedral College Prep, New York's minor seminary. Very much a "man-about-town" and full of charm, he had friends in "high places."

Cogley, John—Religion editor for the *NY Times*, more liberal than Catholic, active in liberal causes and at the end of his life was at odds with the Church over its stands on birth control and marital issues.

Cohalan, Father Florence D.—Later Monsignor, professor of history at Cathedral College Prep, longtime mentor of Neil, Fr. Gene and Fr. Roger, extremely knowledgeable about prewar NY politics where his father, Judge Daniel Cohalan, had been active in the Democrat party yet a foe of Franklin Roosevelt.

Cooley, Jack—Graduate manager of athletics at Fordham University, presided over the Golden Age of Fordham football.

Coughlin, Father John—First priest to use radio as a forum, speaking on "social justice," not religion. He had a large following, originally supporting the "New Deal" but later souring on Roosevelt. He was accused of anti-semitism and was silenced, his newspaper *Social Justice* forbidden by Church authorities to be sent through the mail.

Cousins, Archbishop—Liberal archbishop of Milwaukee.

Cowles, Robert—President of Publishers Hall Syndicate which provided columns to newspapers, mostly left wing.

Croce, Arlene—Dance critic of *National Review*, and later of the *New Yorker* for many years.

Cronin, Father John F.—He worked at the beginning with Nixon on anti-Communist measures and was a sometimes speechwriter for him. He had been an economics professor and a functionary of the bishops' Social Action Department. He became more liberal and active in the civil rights movement.

D

Davies, Michael—British Catholic writer, ardent defender of Archbishop LeFebvre and the Tridentine Mass. Neil published his books defending the Tridentine Mass and was eulogized by Davies upon his death in 1994.

Davis, Thurston, SJ—Editor of the liberal Jesuit magazine, *America*, which tried to read Bill Buckley out of the Church.

De Chardin, Tielhard—Jesuit scientist and paleontologist of the 20th century who had unorthodox ideas incorporating science and theology. He was lightly sanctioned by the Vatican.

Dirksen, Everett—Senator from Illinois, supported Senator Robert Taft in 1952 against Gen. Eisenhower at the Republican convention. Not always reliable as a conservative.

E

Econe—The seminary founded in 1970 by Archbishop LeFebvre in Switzerland for the Society of St Pius X.

Evans, Stan—Conservative journalist and author, an editor at *National Review* and *Human Events*, influential because of his intellect and wit.

F

FEE—The Foundation for Economic Education, a free market think tank.

Fenton, Father Joseph—Professor of theology at the Catholic University of America and advisor to Cardinal Ottaviani, opposed to John Courtney Murray's formulation of religious liberty which changed the centuries old position of the Church and which carried the day at Vatican II.

Fitzpatrick, Jim—Public high school teacher of Social Studies, conservative and a fine writer. Neil published him. He was planning a book *How to Survive in a Public School.*

Fraser, Hamish—Scottish Catholic, editor of *Approaches*, a convert to the Catholic Church after being an ardent Marxist, and a staunch defender of the Faith.

G

Galvin, Bob—Motorola CEO, contributor to conservative causes.

Giroux, Bob—Well-known editor, later partner as well, of the NY publishing company, Farrar, Straus.

Gold, Victor—Political consultant and writer, top aide to Barry Goldwater during his presidential campaign, later press secretary for Vice President Agnew and for Vice President George Bush. Known for his wit, loyalty, intelligence, and sometimes volatile nature.

Gracian, Baltasar—Spanish Jesuit, 17th C. author of *The Art of Worldly Wisdom*, a book of maxims with commentary, e.g., "Show not thy wounded finger."

H

Hartnett, Vincent—Anti-communist, author of *Red Channels* which identified communists and "fellow travelers" in the broadcast/entertainment industry. He was sued by John Henry Faulk and lost, spent the rest of his life paying the judgement, was hounded out of his career, and ended up teaching high school.

Heath, Aloise Buckley (Mrs. Ben)—Oldest sister of Bill, writer for *National Review*, usually about family life (she had a large family), often very amusing.

Herberg, Will—Former communist, Jewish intellectual, author of *Catholic, Protestant, Jew*. He was religion editor of *National Review* and professor at Drew University. He was purported to have become a Catholic at the end.

Herblock—Herbert Block, Leftist cartoonist.

Herr, Dan—President of the liberal *National Catholic Reporter* in 1968, later started the *The Critic* and Thomas More Association and publishing company.

Higgins, Msgr. George—Known as the "Labor Priest," a liberal activist and writer.

Hook, Sidney—Former communist, a philosopher who became an anti-communist social democrat, sometimes allied with conservatives.

K

Kandalintsvez, Anatoli—Neil got a form letter from him from the Russian Embassy about publishing a book.

Kempton, Murray—Liberal journalist and columnist, friendly with Garry Wills and Bill Buckley.

Kendall, Wilmoore—Professor of political science at Yale, taught Bill Buckley and Brent Bozell there, paid off to leave Yale and he then went to teach at the University of Dallas.

Kephart, Bob—Publisher and one of the owners of *Human Events*, later a very successful publisher of financial newsletters with free-market/Libertarian leanings.

Kilpatrick, Jack, "Kilpo"—Editor of the *Richmond News-Leader* where Garry Wills was working as an editorial writer.

Kingsley, Charles—"Broad church" Protestant clergyman, fierce opponent of John Henry Newman and anti-Catholic.

Kirk, Russell—Popularizer of American conservative ideas and author of *The Conservative Mind*, which had a great influence on the rising conservative movement, and other titles. Virtually a co-founder of *National Review* and *Modern Age* and a movement godfather.

Knox Translation—Monsignor Ronald Knox, British convert, prolific writer and speaker, was asked by the hierarchy of Britain to undertake a translation of the Bible into modern English. It was completed and published about 1944.

Koether, George—Libertarian economist and writer, a corporation PR executive.

Kubek, Anthony—Historian of American foreign policy, especially the Far East, chairman of the Department of History and Political Science at the University of Dallas, contributor to *National Review*.

Kuehnelt-Leddihn, Eric—Austrian conservative Catholic, multi-linguist, author of several books, including novels, sometime columnist for *National Review*. An admirer of Neil, and vice versa.

L

Laetare Medal—An award given by Notre Dame University to a Catholic or Catholic organization for outstanding service to the Church and society, usually given to a liberal in recent years.

Larkin, Philip—British 20th century poet who was an admirer of jazz and wrote disparagingly of rock, although he couched his criticism of the latter in euphemisms because he was paid to write a modern music column.

Larkin Sr. Rose M., OSB—St. Scholastica Priory, Duluth, Minnesota.

Lasky, Patti and Victor—Victor was an anti-communist newspaperman and author, one of Nixon's few close friends in the press, especially well-known for his *JFK, The Man and The Myth* which became a bestseller for a few months but was taken off the market when JFK was assassinated in 1963. Neil had brought the book to Macmillan Publishing Company when he was the advertising director there. After a wrangle with some editors and a member of the board of directors, a friend of the Kennedys, the book was supported by the then president of the company, Jerry Kaplan, and made history. This letter refers to a libel lawsuit by Victor against someone for false accusations made at a public lecture. He lost and was severely hurt financially.

Lawrence, Mike—Young fundraiser on the Right, on the staff of *Triumph* at the time.

Lehrman, Lew—Businessman of notable distinction and Republican/Conservative candidate for governor of New York in 1982.

LeMay, Curtis—Army general who ran as the vice-presidential candidate on the George Wallace ticket in 1968.

Leo, John—Started out as a liberal, an associate editor of *Commonweal*, the liberal Catholic magazine, and columnist for the *National Catholic Reporter*, *The New York Times*, and *Time* among others. He became more conservative in recent years.

Liebman, Marvin—Conservative promoter and PR executive. He specialized in "The Big Rally" with zillions of balloons at the right moment and he organized right-leaning committees for the cause of the moment. He was close to Charles Edison, son of the inventor and a former governor of New Jersey, who financed a number of Marvin's projects.

Linen, James III—Publisher of *Time* magazine. His son, the IV, was an active conservative who died tragically young in an accident. The IV's uncle was William Scranton, former Republican governor of Pennsylvania and sometime presidential candidate.

Lipset, Seymour—Sociologist who moved from socialism to neo-conservatism.

Lit, Ted—Writer for Fulton Lewis, Jr., his radio program and newsletter, later an editor at Arlington House.

Loisy, Father Alfred—French priest late 19th early 20th century who was a modernist leader of the "higher criticism" of the Bible. He was condemned by the Vatican and later excommunicated.

Lyons, Gene—Senior editor of *Reader's Digest* and contributor to *National Review* and anti-communist publications, journalist and former fellow traveler who hadn't joined the Communist Party in the 1930s because the Party found him more useful outside. He broke after experiencing life in the Soviet Union as a United Press correspondent and seeing first hand the constant lies and horrors of the regime and Party.

M

Mahoney, J. Daniel—Co-founder of the Conservative Party of New York with his brother-in-law Kieran O'Doherty. For a while that party pulled New York a bit to the right, actually electing a Conservative Senator, Jim Buckley, brother of Bill, in 1970. Later Dan was attorney for Bill Buckley. He became a judge of the Federal Second Circuit Court of Appeals, nominated by President Reagan. When he died he was replaced by Sonia Sotomayor.

Mahoney, Jim—Bishop in the NY archdiocese, vicar of Westchester County, a friend and classmate of Neil's from their days at Cathedral College.

Manhattan Twelve—A group of conservatives leaders, including Neil, who met in 1971 in Bill's home in NY to discuss how to counter Nixon's liberal turn.

Manion, Dean Clarence—Dean of the University of Notre Dame Law School and founder of the Manion Forum, a widely syndicated weekly conservative radio commentary on hundreds of stations.

Manning, Cardinal Henry Edward—19th entury British convert from Anglicanism who was concerned with the education of the poor and conditions of the working man.

Marra, Bill—Longtime professor of philosophy at Fordham University, founder of The Roman Forum lecture series at Fordham University, radio program host for Catholic Media Apostolate.

Marshner, Bill—A Catholic convert, editor at *Triumph* and a founding professor of theology at Christendom College.

Martin, Malachi—A priest who had been dispensed from his vows as a Jesuit, best-selling novelist and briefly religion editor of *National Review*. He was distressed by the results of Vatican II.

Martinez, Mary Ball—American expatriate journalist, conservative and Catholic, sometimes not careful enough for Neil. Her brother, William Ball, was an attorney prominent in Right-to-Life causes.

Mason, Michael and Scharper, Phillip—Editors at Sheed and Ward, Catholic publisher in London and New York.

Matt, Al—Editor of *The Wanderer*, an independent Catholic newspaper published in Minnesota.

Maurras, Charles—French pre-war 20th century monarchist, nationalist, and anti-semite, head of the "Action Française" movement which was condemned by the Church, an atheist until the end of his life when he returned to the Church.

Maye, Mickey—President of the New York Firefighters Association, a very big man and former boxer, who threw out a group of homosexuals who tried to make trouble at a dinner he was attending.

McClane, Don—Old friend of Neil's from the early fifties. He was originally an engineer but changed his career path to work in the Church in various capacities, head of religious education in one diocese, publisher of *Triumph*, and president of Catholics United for the Faith among other positions.

McFadden, Jim—After Neil's success as promotion director at *National Review*, they needed someone "in house" to handle the follow up. That person was Jim. Neil quarterbacked him.

McKissick, Floyd—Black lawyer and leader of the Congress of Racial Equality (CORE).

Meany, George—Longtime head of the AFL-CIO union, strong anti-communist.

Meyer, Frank—Former Communist organizer and one of the founding editors of *National Review*. He championed a fusionist political philosophy of conservatism and libertarianism. He was one of the most important intellectuals of the conservative movement.

Miller, Tom—Conservative top-level CBS executive who advised Neil and Bill Buckley, and any others who needed help, on the vagaries of the TV world.

Moley, Raymond—One of President Roosevelt's original "Brain Trust" who broke with him and became a conservative. He wrote a weekly column on politics for *Newsweek* and was a professor at Columbia University for many years. He was close to Nixon.

Molnar, Thomas—Hungarian intellectual, political philosopher, writer and professor. He spent part of World War II imprisoned by the Germans in Belgium and emigrated to the U.S.

Morriss, Robert—Former chief counsel for the Senate Internal Security Subcommittee, lost in the New Jersey Republican primary to Senator Clifford Case. He then went to Dallas, Texas to head the University of Dallas.

Moynihan, Senator Patrick—Democrat Senator from New York, sometimes let reality influence his writings and positions, before giving himself over to the Left. Wrote a famed report on poverty and racial problems for President Nixon.

Muggeridge, Malcolm—British intellectual, journalist and TV host who started out on the left but became conservative after he witnessed life in the Soviet Union. He eventually became a Catholic.

Mulloy, John—Catholic teacher and intellectual, close to Christopher Dawson, the Catholic historian, an ardent defender of the Faith, who became a writer at *The Wanderer*.

N

Neumayr, Dr. John—One of the founders of Thomas Aquinas College and a professor there.

P

Pearson, Drew—Political columnist, known for sensational accusations, whether true or not, including many against anti-communists.

Pegler, Westbrook—Journalist, a popular columnist noted for his caustic opposition to the New Deal and criticism of Mrs. Roosevelt.

Peikoff, Leonard—Philosopher and author, follower and expert on Ayn Rand's Objectivism.

Pflock, Karl—Editor at Arlington House.

Podhoretz, Norman—Neo-Conservative editor at the time of *Commentary*, the magazine of the American Jewish Committee.

Pryor, Father Donald (Roger)—Later Monsignor and Superintendent of Schools of the Archdiocese of NY, classmate and good friend of Neil's in high school years at Cathedral College Prep, the minor seminary. Called "Roger" after a band leader of the era, Roger Pryor.

R

Rabinowitz, Dorothy—Astute culture critic on the *Wall Street Journal* and TV panelist, and conservative.

Rausch, Bishop James—Liberal bishop of Phoenix, active in "Call to Action" after Vatican II which produced resolutions for a married priesthood and the ordination of women.

Read, Leonard—Libertarian founder of the Foundation for Economic Education, contributor to *National Review*.

Red Blazer Too—Restaurant in NY city that hosted jazz bands. On Tuesday evenings Vince Giordano and the Nighthawks played the music of the late 20s and early 30s, favorites of Neil.

Rickenbacker, Bill—Author of *Wooden Nickels*, and other financial books published by Neil, and contributor to *National Review*, son of Eddie Rickenbacker, the World War I flying hero (later president and founder of Eastern Airlines).

Rorty, Richard—Liberal Professor of Philosophy and Humanities at several prestigious universities.

Rosenthal, Dan—An editor at Arlington House, libertarian. He later had a newsletter, "The Gold and Silver Report."

Rothbard, Murray—Libertarian economist, professor of economics at the University of Nevada, Las Vegas, great fan of the old jazz, which he had in common with Neil.

Rousselot, John—Congressman from California, rousing speaker, ignoring his physical handicaps, he was a tenacious anti-communist fighter and member of the John Birch Society.

Rusher, Bill—Longtime Publisher of *National Review*, former counsel on the Senate Internal Security Subcommittee. He had a shrewd political sense and was behind the scenes in the Draft Goldwater movement, also behind the Reagan nomination, the New York Conservative Party, Congressman John Ashbrook's run for the Republican nomination for President.

Rust, Brian—British jazz historian and expert. Neil published (and edited) one of his jazz discographies.

Rynne, Xavier—Father Francis X. Murphy, a Redemptorist priest, used this pseudonym as he wrote articles for *The New Yorker* about Vatican Council II 1962-1965, describing the clash of liberals and conservatives.

Ryskind, Allan—One of the owners and an editor of *Human Events*, son of Morrie Ryskind, a celebrated screenwriter in Hollywood who was anti-communist.

S

Salazar—Prime Minister of Portugal 1938-1968, he opposed communism, nazism and fascism and kept Portugal neutral in World War II. He was vilified by the left, but his rule brought his nation peace and prosperity.

Schlamm, Willi—Austrian Jewish refugee journalist who was an editor at *National Review* in the early days. He was separated from NR after criticizing Pat Buckley, Bill's wife.

Selig, Bud—Commissioner of Major League Baseball.

Shuster, George—Liberal Catholic president of Hunter College, NY.

Smant, Dr Kevin—Department of History, Indiana University, South Bend.

Sudhalter, Dick—Intellectual jazz musician, friend of Neil's, *NY Times* reporter, critic and author of jazz books which Neil published.

T

Templeton, Ken—Officer of the William Volker Fund, a libertarian think tank largely financed by owners of the Eli Lilly company.

Tonsor, Stephen—Conservative intellectual historian, longtime professor of history at the University of Michigan, one of the earliest contributors to *National Review* and *Modern Age*.

V

Veuillet, Louis—French ultramontanist of the late 19th century.

Vierech, Peter—American early self-styled conservative professor who preferred to be not a conservative.

Von Mises, Ludwig—Founder of the Austrian school of economics, author of *Human Action*, a hugely influential book on the basis of free market economics, rejuvenated by Neil at Arlington House along with other Mises titles.

Von Hildebrand, Alice (Lily)—Belgian born wife of Dietrich, and professor of philosophy at Hunter College in New York, an author and a formidable presence in the Catholic world.

Von Hildebrand, Dietrich—German refugee, anti-Nazi, prolific author and philosophy professor at Fordham who expressed reservations about much of Vatican II and the proscribing of the Tridentine Mass. He had the respect and prestige to have his voice heard.

Von Hindenburg, Paul—German general and statesman, became president of the Weimar Republic. He was prevailed upon to name Hitler Chancellor of Germany in 1933 as his party had a plurality of voters.

Glossary

Von Papen, Franz—German Catholic nobleman and diplomat and anti-communist, Chancellor for a short time in 1932. He persuaded Von Hindenburg in 1933 to appoint Hitler Chancellor and himself as Vice-Chancellor, saying that he would control Hitler.

W

Wallace, George—Governor of Alabama who ran on a third party ticket in 1968. He was a segregationist, but raised other issues of concern to a constituency that crossed party lines. Conservative leaders, including Bill Buckley, hastened to condemn him, and when Neil pointed out that he was addressing issues that conservatives should be addressing, there were those who said Neil supported his run for the presidency.

Wallace, Lois—A prominent literary agent in NY who was Bill Buckley's agent.

Wanderer, The—Conservative Catholic midwest newspaper which was loathe to criticize the bishops or Pope or Vatican pronouncements.

Ward, Maisie—Wife of Frank Sheed, Catholic apologist, speaker and writer. She was the daughter of Wilfred Ward, British convert and writer. With her husband she founded the publishing company Sheed and Ward, referred to in the letter from Garry Wills. The book in question was his biography of G. K. Chesterton.

Ward, William "Ideal"—The latter name came from his work *The Ideal of the Christian Church*, written as a Tractarian. He soon after entered the Catholic Church and was a strong defender of papal authority.

Warren, Earl—Chief Justice of the Supreme Court, appointed by Eisenhower, responsible for many liberal rulings on the Constitution that changed the course of America.

Waugh, Auberon—Son of the British novelist Catholic convert Evelyn Waugh, and a novelist as well.

Waugh, Evelyn—British Catholic novelist, critic, biographer, reviewed Garry Wills book on Chesterton for *National Review*. He was not impressed, referring to it as a PhD thesis. Bill felt bad about publishing the review, but it was a great coup to have Waugh write for the magazine.

Weiss, George—Protestant editor of the "Know Your Bible" program at Doubleday.

Welch, Robert—Head of the John Birch Society, given to extreme accusations about who was a communist. Many of the members were not in sync with him.

Weyl, Nathaniel—Former communist, writer and economist, he had been a member of the Washington communist cell, the Ware group, which Alger Hiss once attended. Neil published a book by him.

White, Cliff—Organizing force behind the Goldwater for President movement, without whom it would not have succeeded in the GOP primaries.

Whitehead, Kenneth—President of Catholics United for the Faith, a group of orthodox Catholics alarmed by the liberal lurch of the Church after Vatican II but unsupportive of the Traditional Latin Mass.

Wilhelmsen, Fritz—Catholic philosopher, political thinker and writer, contributor to *National Review* and a founder with Brent Bozell of *Triumph*. In his last decade, a professor at the University of Dallas.

Williams, Mary Lou—Black jazz pianist, composer and arranger, she had become a Catholic.

Wills, Garry—Early writer for *National Review*, and close friend of Neil's but by 1968 his views turned left and continued steadily in that direction. Their friendship and his friendship with Bill did not survive that turning. He later won a Pulitzer Prize, continues to write books, and taught for years at Northwestern University.

Winter, Tom—Co-owner and editor of *Human Events*.

Wisner, John—One of the original editors of *Triumph*.

Dr. Peter Kwasniewski, Thomistic theologian, liturgical scholar, and choral composer, is a graduate of Thomas Aquinas College and The Catholic University of America. He has taught at the International Theological Institute in Austria, the Franciscan University of Steubenville's Austria Program, and Wyoming Catholic College, which he helped establish in 2006. He writes regularly for *The New Liturgical Movement*, *OnePeterFive*, *Rorate Caeli*, and *LifeSite News*, and has published eight books, including three on traditional Catholicism: *Resurgent in the Midst of Crisis* (Angelico, 2014), *Noble Beauty, Transcendent Holiness* (Angelico, 2017), and *Tradition and Sanity* (Angelico, 2018).